P9-DNB-984

DATE DUE

APR 27 '98	

BRODART, CO.   Cat. No. 23-221-003

DISCARD
BETHANY COLLEGE LIBRARY

Reprints of Economic Classics

HISTORY OF POLITICAL ECONOMY
In Europe

HISTORY

OF

POLITICAL ECONOMY

IN EUROPE

BY

JEROME ADOLPHE BLANQUI

[1880]

REPRINTS OF ECONOMIC CLASSICS

AUGUSTUS M. KELLEY · PUBLISHERS
NEW YORK 1968

First American Translation 1880

(London & New York: G. P. Putnam's Sons,
The Knickerbocker Press, 1880)

Reprinted 1968 by
AUGUSTUS M. KELLEY · PUBLISHERS
New York New York 10010

Library of Congress Catalogue Card Number

67-29494

Printed in the United States of America
by Sentry Press, New York, N. Y. 10019

HISTORY

OF

POLITICAL ECONOMY

IN EUROPE

BY

JÉRÔME-ADOLPHE BLANQUI

SUCCESSOR TO J. B. SAY IN THE CHAIR OF POLITICAL ECONOMY IN THE CONSERVATORY OF
ARTS AND TRADES (COLLEGE DE FRANCE) ; MEMBER OF THE ACADEMY OF MORAL
AND POLITICAL SCIENCES (INSTITUTE DE FRANCE) ; PROFESSOR OF
HISTORY AND INDUSTRIAL ECONOMY AND DIRECTOR
OF THE SCHOOL OF COMMERCE AT PARIS.

TRANSLATED FROM THE FOURTH FRENCH EDITION

BY

EMILY J. LEONARD

WITH PREFACE BY

DAVID A. WELLS

APPENDIX AND INDEX BY TRANSLATOR

———

NEW YORK & LONDON

G. P. PUTNAM'S SONS

The Knickerbocker Press

330.94
B611 2YL4

/02176

1041p

INTRODUCTION.

The plan of the accompanying translation, from the French, and reprint for the first time into English, of Blanqui's *Histoire de L'Economie Politique en Europe*, received from the outset the very cordial approval of the writer and was recommended by him to the publishers.

However much authorities may differ among themselves as to the exact definition of what is called "Political Economy," and even disagree as to whether the name itself can be properly regarded as designating a science, all will nevertheless probably agree that under this general name is embraced—in the form of historical record, or of principles deduced from the philosophical study of such record—the results of the general experience of mankind in endeavoring to improve their material condition; and if their material condition, then also their social, intellectual and moral condition. For it is to be remembered, if to any the last part of this statement may seem more broad than is fully warranted, that the material needs of man must first and always be fairly satisfied before morality, certainly in any high degree, is likely to exist among the masses; and furthermore, that something of material abundance or wealth must be earned and saved before leisure for study can be obtained or the scholar can exist.

Man became an *economist* at the moment when, through foresight and the exercise of labor and frugality, he began to anticipate and make provision for his future material needs and contingencies; and he undoubtedly at the same time began to appreciate the fact that the acquirement and use of capital—in the first instance undoubtedly a rude implement or contrivance for facilitating the obtaining of food and clothing, or a domesticated animal —by rendering him superior to his physical surroundings, elevated him at once in the scale of being. He became a *political economist* at the moment, when in association with his fellow men, he began to exchange the products of his labor, and to provide for increased abundance and better and more varied products, through the division of labor, the protection of life and property, and the invention of tools and machinery for the facilitating of both production and exchange. Political economy thus first established, developed and became complex as civilization advanced, as wealth and the forms of wealth multiplied, and as the facilities for social and commercial intercourse and the interchange of products became greater. According to this view, it is a mistake (as M. Blanqui has pointed out) to refer the origin of political economy to a very recent period; so recent in fact, as many suppose, as the latter half of the eighteenth century. It is indeed true that at the period referred to, the record of the experience of mankind in the work of bettering their material condition was for the first time carefully and philosophically studied, and the principles deducible from such experience elaborately formulated by Turgot, Quesnay, Adam Smith and others. But as already shown, the experience itself dates back to the very dawn of civilization, and in its lessons and applications has ever since constituted the foundation and framework of every structure of progressive human society, irrespective of locality upon the earth's surface or race differences in its individual constituency.

To attempt a narration of these experiences in Europe from the earliest period—their successes and their failures—was the task that M. Blanqui proposed to himself in writing the history under consideration. The result of his labors has been of necessity imperfect, because the material for constructing a complete record does not exist; and because the restriction of the discussion of such material as is available, which the author at the outset seems to have prescribed to himself, namely, two small 12mo volumes (in the French edition), did not admit of the entering at any great length into details, or the accomplishment of much other than the presentation of the more important economic transactions in the history of Europe, and the extent of their influences in promoting or retarding the world's material progress and development. Nevertheless the book as it exists to-day, with its record terminating in 1842, is in the highest degree instructive, and in a popular sense, exceedingly attractive. It is moreover, one of the comparatively few books published during the last half century which has attained a world-wide reputation, and its translation and present re-publication fills a place, which so far as the observation of the writer extends, is not supplied by any other work in the English language.

Important, moreover, as was the original publication,

considered as an instrumentality for the diffusion of a branch of knowledge most useful among men, its reproduction and circulation in the United States at the present time would seem also to be most opportune. For there is no one truth or series of truths concerned with our material progress as a nation, which the people of this country need more to have continually demonstrated, and in season and out of season impressed upon them, than that labor exercised conjointly with skill and frugality, is the only path for the permanent attainment of great material abundance ; and that all attempts to increase the production and equalize the distribution of wealth by establishing through legislation, *fiat* money or *fiat* property, (credits, titles, interest in property created without labor), by interfering with and restricting exchanges , by arbitrarily regulating the price of money or other commodities or services, and by instituting inquisitorial, vexatious, and unnecessarily multiple taxes, invariably tend to encourage the spirit of speculation rather than of production, to undermine and weaken popular morality, and to impair rather than further a healthy national development. The authors of such attempts at the present time, as well as in former days, have undoubtedly in many instances a sincere belief, that they have discovered something new in the domains of economic truth, and that the circumstances in respect to which they propose to legislate are peculiar, untried, and not to be judged by the results of any former experience. An examination of the records of the past would, however, soon satisfy them that all such schemes, in place of having anything of originality, are but repetitions of old imbecilities ; and that their authors are simply following in the footsteps of many predecessors, who have thought to bring reputation to themselves, and prosperity to the masses by making warfare upon natural laws, with the result, in every instance, of failure and disaster. And in presenting evidence in support of these propositions, derived from unquestionable historic precedents and experiences, and in such a manner as admits of ready comprehension, the history of Political Economy by M Blanqui is calculated to perform a service the value of which cannot well be over-estimated.

DAVID A. WELLS.

January, 1880.

BIOGRAPHICAL SKETCH OF M. BLANQUI.

Jérôme-Adolphe Blanqui, the economist, was born at Nice, in November, 1798. His father, Jean Dominique Blanqui, a magistrate, had been one of the deputies to the National Convention, where he represented the department of the Maritime Alps; and he was among those who, in 1793, signed the protest against the Jacobin measures of May 31st and the following days, and was one of the seventy-three whose arrest was decreed; he was subsequently member of the Council of the Five-hundred; was afterwards sub-prefect of Puget-Theniers, until 1814; sub-prefect of Marmonde during the hundred days; a resident of Paris from 1815; and the author of many interesting reports on moneys, weights and measures, canals and highways, as also of a pamphlet entitled "My Ten Months' Agony," which contains many curious facts in regard to contemporary history.

Of the mother of Jérôme-Adolphe, we find no mention in any biographical notice of him.

Under the direction of his father, Jérôme-Adolphe Blanqui pursued an excellent course of study at the Lyceum of his native city, which he subsequently continued at Paris (where he went in 1814), and completed with much distinction.

He early began his career as an instructor, giving his time to chemistry and other sciences allied to medicine, and acting as assistant professor of the humanities in a famous school— *L'Institution Massin.* This brought him into connection with the eminent economist, J. B. Say, who wished him for a disciple. The benevolence and the counsels of M. Say inspired in his young friend a love for economic studies, which he consequently pursued with much ardor ; and the patronage of this most renowned professor, by procuring for the young Blanqui the chair of History and Industrial Economy at the School of Commerce, opened to him a career to which he was to devote his labors and his life. Blanqui applied himself to his work with indefatigable zeal, and had the rare merit of combining remarkable talents with practical good sense. In 1830, he rose to the position of director of this important school, and in 1833, he succeeded J. B. Say in the professor's chair in the Conservatory of Arts and Trades. It was during these professorships that he wrote this History of Political Economy, the first edition of which was published in 1837. A course of lectures which he delivered in the latter year, on " The History of Industrial Civilization among European Nations," was largely attended. Other courses, both at the School of Commerce, where he delivered several remarkable lectures, and at the Conservatory of Arts and Trades, in connection with his professorship there, all had for their aim the promotion of manufactures and commerce. Among the lectures were his report on the economic and moral condition of Corsica, in 1838, read at the Academy of Moral and Political Sciences, to which he had been elected in June of the same year ; the report on the economic condition of French possessions in Algeria, the first writing giving a true account of affairs in that country (whither he had been sent by the Academy to examine and report), read at the Academy in 1839, and his report on the Life and Labors of J. B. Say, also read at the Academy. In all these we find clear indications of his zeal for manufactures and commerce. He made several journeys for the same object, during which he traveled over nearly all Europe and a part of Asia and Africa. These travels served to increase his knowledge and give maturity to his judgment. He was one of the founders of the *Journal des Economistes*, and one of the editors of the Dictionary of Manufacturing, Commercial and Agricultural Industry. Spirited articles from his pen were constantly contributed to papers and magazines where matters on political economy and questions of public policy found access, from the *Producteur*, which raised the standard of St. Simon. to *Figaro*, the *Courrier Français*, and the *Dictionnaire des Mer-*

chandises. Few writers or professors have had so great ardor and activity, or been distinguished by labors so facile or so fecund.

From 1846 to 1848, Blanqui was member from Bordeaux of the Chamber of Deputies, where he was noted for his enlightened views and his labors on commissions. In 1851, the Institute (Academy of Moral and Political Sciences), which highly valued his abilities, sent him to London to make a report of the World's Fair, and also to furnish a complete account of London in its financial and other aspects, a task which he performed to the satisfaction of the savants who employed him. He also contributed a series of articles to the journal *La Presse*, in 1851, on the London Exhibition.

By order of the Academy, he had undertaken the great and important work of investigating the condition of the Rural Population of France, and had devoted three years to the study of the subject and was preparing to give the public the result, when death terminated his labors, Jan. 28, 1854.

Blanqui stood in the foremost rank among contemporary economists. He belonged to that school (now embracing nearly every economist of reputation) which advocates the principles of commercial freedom. His addresses at the Free Trade Congress held in Brussels in 1847, attracted much attention.

Blanqui was ever a vigorous defender of industrial education. At one of the sessions of the Academy, he startled the Academicians by asking where a man could be found who could give the history of a table-spread, from the wool of the sheep to the hall of the Institute. And then he added : " Do you even know by what process the goose-quills are prepared, by the aid of which so many men of genius write ? " The Academicians, it is said, smiled, taking the compliment to themselves.

Besides a great number of journalistic articles, M. Blanqui published : Travels in England and Scotland (1824) ; Journey to Madrid (1826) ; Résumé of the History of Commerce and Manufactures (1826) ; Elements of Political Economy (1826); A Series of Reports on the Products of French Industry in 1827 (1827); The English Minister Huskisson, and his **Eco-**

nomic Reform ; History of Political Economy in Europe from the Ancients to our day (1837 and 1842); Report on the Economic and Moral Condition of Corsica (1838); Report on the Economic Condition of the French Possessions in Algeria (1840); Travels in Bulgaria (1841); Considerations on the Social Condition of European Turkey (1841); The Working Classes in France (1848); Report on the World's Fair in London (1850); and the Life and Labors of Jean Baptiste Say.

A Series of interesting letters between Blanqui and M. Emile de Girardin, in which free trade and protection were discussed, appeared in 1846 and 1847.

Blanqui was generally alluded to by his French contemporaries as Blanqui *ainé* (the elder), to distinguish him from a younger brother, Louis Auguste (born in 1805, at Nice), who took a somewhat prominent part in the civil troubles of France from July, 1830, to the *attentat* of May 15, 1848, and was consequently imprisoned. In 1879, while still in prison, Louis Auguste Blanqui was elected to the Chambers. He has since been pardoned.

As a writer, Jérôme-Adolphe Blanqui was noted for research, lucidity, occasional sallies of wit, frequent passages of great brilliancy, and at times a sustained eloquence of diction.

His History of Political Economy in Europe is the most famous of his works.

(Consult *Nouvelle Biographie Générale*, Didot frères, Paris, 1862 : *Dictionnaire de la Conversation et de la Lecture*, Didot frères, fils et Cie., 1873 : *Catalogue général de la librairie française*, etc.).

TRANSLATOR'S PREFACE.

The principal considerations which have led to this translation are the following:

Blanqui's history is the only existing work combining records of the more important economic experiments in the different parts of Europe from the early days of Greece and Rome down to the time when it was written. Some of these records have been obtained from rare documents, and most of them are from sources inaccessible to the average student. The reputation of the author, too, in consequence of the important services he rendered France through his professorship, his writings, and the investigations and reports he made under the direction of the Institute, give additional value to his production, and have created a desire that it be brought within reach of all English-speaking readers who are interested in economic questions.

The translator has, for the most part, followed the phraseology and the construction of the original, so far as the differences of idiom between the two languages permit, hoping that the reader may thereby be brought into closer contact with the author and be led to a fuller appreciation of his thought. The few deviations from this method consist principally in the simplification of some technical terms that would not be generally understood. If the method has been faithfully followed, the translation will discover both the merits and defects of the original, except in so far as it is impossible to adequately convey shades of meaning from one language to another. Whether there has been a measurable degree of success, must be left to the decision of those who appreciate the work of a translator.

An explanation is perhaps due in reference to the employment of the terms " exploit " and " exploitation." These words, though not common in our language, are in occasional use among our best writers, and have been retained because no other good English words combine the meanings of the French verb " *exploiter* " (to work, use, manage, make capital out of, speculate upon, take advantage of, make a tool of, etc.), and its corresponding noun. So long as people continue to be " exploited " for political and other ends, we think our readers will not object to the use of a well-derived word to express the act, and especially to one already accepted and employed by good authorities.

The quotations from the speeches of Mr. Huskisson and Lord John Russell, as also those from the writings of Adam Smith, Malthus, Godwin, and Dr. Ure, have been verified, and stand as in their published works.

So many of the old world experiments have been repeated with similar results in the new, that the temptation has often been great to forget that this is the history of political economy in *Europe*, and to append facts on production, trade and finance, drawn from the experience of the United States. This has been particularly the case in matters relating to tariffs, on which the various writings and carefully collected statistics of Hon. David A. Wells, and the lectures by Prof. Sumner on the history of protection in the United States, afford such a rich mine of information.

The translator entertains a hope that some one may be induced by the publication of this work, to prepare a similar one embodying the principal economic experiments of the United States and Canada, with their results. Such a work would be an important addition to economic literature.

A still greater production will be that which shall trace the development of economic principles in the world, and complete the work whose scope Blanqui partially apprehended, and which it belongs to the Economic Philosophy of the future to carry to a successful termination.

E. J. L.

Meriden, Ct., March 4th, 1880.

TABLE OF CONTENTS.

CHAPTER XXI.

CHAPTER XXII.

CHAPTER XXIII.

CHAPTER XXIV.

CHAPTER XXV.

CHAPER XXVI.

CHAPTER XXVII.

CHAPTER XLI.

CHAPTER XLII.

CHAPTER XLIII.

CHAPTER XLIV.

CHAPTER XLV.

CHAPTER XLVI.

AUTHOR'S INTRODUCTION.

It may perhaps be well to state here the motive which induced me to undertake this work. When called, about twelve years ago,* to the chair of History and Political Economy which I occupy to-day in the school of commerce, I was not long in perceiving that there existed between these two sciences relations so intimate that a person could not study the one without the other, nor thoroughly understand them separately. They lend each other constant support ; the first furnishes the facts ; the second explains their causes and deduces the consequences from them. As I advanced in the exposition of doctrines, examples were wanting ; and the study of events was in its turn incomplete, until political economy cast its light upon them. Gradually, while combining the labors of my two courses and strengthening them by each other, I came upon a multitude of prejudices which passed for truths, even among the the best instructed and most advanced men. Thus, the authors of all the treatises on political economy, without exception, traced its origin no farther back than the first attempts of Quesnay and Turgot ; as if never, before the works of these celebrated men, had any systematic writing called the attention of savants and statesmen to the phenomena of the production of wealth.

---

* The first edition was published in 1837.

From this time, I devoted myself earnestly to researches among the historians of all ages for the facts of most interest in the study of economic and social questions. I had soon found paupers at Rome and at Athens, as there are at Paris and at London; and I must confess that privileges, taxes, and fiscal vexations were no more rare among the ancients than in our day. Then, as now, the least ray of peace and liberty was followed by a shower of riches and prosperity; the same causes, in short, produced the same effects, notwithstanding the difference of customs and institutions. The distress of the people may always be recognized by the inequality of the burdens, the vicious distribution of the profits of labor, and the prevailing tendency of a few designing classes to place abuses under the protection of law.

But the world did not always remain indifferent, in the presence of these social calamities; and more than once, in the course of the centuries, magnanimous protests were made in favor of the disregarded rights of humanity. A few noble sovereigns aided in these efforts, which were sometimes perseveringly followed up, at others interrupted by the misfortunes of the times. There was, then, a political economy among the ancients, as there is among the moderns; not a systematic and formulated political economy, but one arising from facts, and practiced before being written. Such has been, moreover, the course of all sciences since the origin of society. The first comers conceive, act, execute; the later ones reason, and improve and complete the work of their predecessors. To well appreciate the labors of modern economists, we must then become acquainted with the principal phases of the social movement which has been going on since the ancients, by means of revolutions, and which presents in its progress so many sudden and glorious enthusiasms and so many dramatic catastrophes.

It is this movement which I have attempted to trace in the work I offer to the public. The great states of

antiquity and those of the middle ages did not fail without a cause ; so great wealth was neither created nor destroyed without its creation or its annihilation being connected with causes susceptible of analysis and worthy of meditation. It is impossible not to recognize the finger of Providence in these successive transformations of the social principle, which takes refuge now in one institution, now in another, without distinction either of time or place, as if to hold itself continually at the disposition and service of humanity. Here, it is a great man who preserves the sacred fire ; in another place a slave rekindles it; Sokrates at Athens, Spartacus at Rome. From the very depths of barbarism issue the first rays of labor and of order; Charlemagne conquered the wave which had born him along; the Hanse towns arose from the depths of marshes which served as a retreat for piracy.

The feudal system, so fatal to the laborers, who were enslaved to the land, is full of instruction valuable to the political economist. It was the extreme division of sovereignty, as we to-day behold the extreme division of property. The Roman Empire, momentarily reconstructed by Charlemagne, had seen centralization carried to its last degree : the feudal system shows us that great political power reduced to atoms. On the one hand, we see gigantic syntheses ; on the other, almost microscopic analyses. What a difference must there not be between the political economy of the chief of forty millions of subjects and that of a country squire looking down upon the country from the height of his castle keep ! But, from hatred of this castle, the bourgeois begin to settle down in cities, to organize themselves into brotherhoods, to make themselves respected by their numbers. Their money is no longer taken from them, it is borrowed from them ; and this apparently insignificant fact affords to the economist an explanation of an entirely new social order.

I have followed these great events step by step, and it has seemed to me that the political economy of the an-

cients had no other pretensions than that of the moderns. In all the revolutions, there have been but two parties confronting each other ; that of the people who wish to live by their own labor, and that of those who would live by the labor of others. These two classes dispute with each other the powers and the honors only in order to repose in that beatific region where the conquering party never lets the conquered sleep in tranquillity. *Patricians and plebeians, slaves and freemen, guelphs and ghibellines, red roses and white roses, cavaliers and round heads, liberals and serviles,* are only varieties of the same species. The question that divides them is always that of their well-being, each one wishing, if I may be permitted a common expression, to draw the coverlid over himself at the risk of uncovering his neighbor. So, in one country, the fruit of his labor is taken from the workman by taxes, under pretence of the *welfare of the state ;* in another, by privileges, declaring labor a royal concession, and making one pay dearly for the right to devote himself to it. The same abuse is reproduced under forms more indirect, but not less oppressive, when, by means of custom-duties, the state shares with the privileged industries the benefits of the taxes imposed on non-privileged classes.

See the Romans in their conquered countries and the Spanish in their American colonies : more than a thousand years apart, you find the same contempt for human life, the same abominable paradoxes on the necessity of some being worked for the profit of others. This is more distressing than what happens among animals, where the devouring species live on the devoured without at least erecting their voracity into a system, and because they cannot do otherwise. All these horrible social iniquities have been propagated for ages, under various forms, sometimes tempered by the progress of human reason, but always alive at the bottom, and everywhere sustained, sometimes with audacity, sometimes with hypocrisy. At one time, it is the clergy who seize all the

property and deign to give alms to the dispossessed human race, threatening with anathema whoever dare trouble the repose of the house of God. Farther on, the tithe belongs to the lords, because they are lords, and because there are no lords without tithes. Peasants are still sold in Russia,* like agricultural implements, and the English aristocracy haggle with the poor Irish about a few blades of straw and the scanty supply of potatoes which they share with the cattle.

It is not, then, so far as one may think from the Greek and Roman political economy, cruel, insatiable, inexorable, to the political economy of more than one country in Europe. In our beautiful France, so rich in vines and harvests, several millions of men eat no bread, and drink only water. Salt abounds under their feet, but the tax weighs on their heads, and the *gabelleur*, the odious tax-gatherer of the middle ages, has only changed his name and dress. If one discovers a new plant, tobacco, for example, the law will forbid its cultivation. We may well exclaim with Rousseau: " Everything is good when it comes from the hand of the Creator: everything degenerates in the hand of man." Those poor girls of Lyons whose fairy fingers weave satin and poplin, have no chemises; the *canuts* who decorate with their magnificent tapestry our palaces and our temples, are often without sabots.

No, this is not the final word of Providence, for of those who formerly would have been bound, struggling for breath, to the soil, not a few live to-day in the bosom of opulence, and this number is constantly increasing. There is not an important event of history which does not concur in this great result. After the crusades, land begins to be divided ; maritime commerce opens new sources of profit ; the arts and manufactures emancipate thousands of vassals. Listen to to the sad complaints of the people: what do they ask, when they raise their

---

* All this is now fortunately changed, though the spirit of tyranny still lingers, as recent events (May, 1879) testify. Ireland, too, breathes a freer air than when Blanqui wrote.

voices? Reductions of the taxes. What wished those wild peasants of the *Jacquerie*,* weary of seeing themselves decimated by famine, by leprosy, and by despair? A more equitable distribution of the profits of labor. They were still more modest; they asked people who did not work, to at least let them live from the humblest part of the fruit of their toil. The first who had that audacity perished under torture, as might have happened at Rome if any slave had dared to ask the least right of his master.

Thus appear to the economist all the struggles whose sanguinary details fill the pages of history. It would be a great error to suppose that the truly religious thought of the general welfare passed unperceived through these two thousand years of wars and continued efforts for its triumph. We shall see in the course of this work, that more than once the cloud which hid it from the eyes of people, was dispelled for the best governments, charged with the destinies of civilization. Most of these were obliged to act in an empirical manner, and without proclaiming their projects, for fear of causing them to fail: others obeyed, without suspecting it, the law of progress, which led them on in spite of themselves: but never has there been a complete dearth of courageous men to accelerate this great work; and I have been more than once surprised, in taking a survey of history, at the boldness and clearness of their views.

The Capitularies of Charlemagne, the Institutions of Saint Louis, the maxims of the commercial government of the Italian republics, are all full of clear and definite provisions, having for their aim the development of public wealth, according to the intelligence and the prejudices of the times, to be sure, but with the most generous and lofty intentions. In private and public assemblies which discussed affairs, remarkable opinions were often

* An insurrection of the peasantry, which broke out in 1358, when the French king was prisoner in England and the country was in a state of anarchy. The peasants burned castles, murdered noblemen and committed other outrages, doing, they said, as had been done to them.— *Trans.*

enunciated; I have had occasion to quote very curious fragments of these scientific opinions.   If these productions are no longer known, it is because, down to our time, readers have preferred the narration of facts to a strict analysis of the causes which brought them about. Besides, these writings, examined separately, do not seem of great importance; it is only when compared with each other and studied methodically, that they truly represent the links of a chain of economic doctrines adopted by governments at each memorable epoch, as a rule of conduct.

Sometimes, when after long discords, the two principles of exploitation and of liberty seem near succumbing before each other, and make, so to speak, a final summation, the social problem appears in all its simplicity, just as our fathers laid it down on the famous night of August 4, 1789; as the insurgent communes of Spain had already submitted it to Charles V by Padilla; * as, in short, it tends to become formulated before the Commons of England since the reform of 1832.   All the theories of political economy, then, may be reduced to short maxims which clearly sum it up in the view of the people : freedom to work: freedom to have the profits of one's labor. The protestant reformation, the insurrection in the Netherlands against Philip II, the independence of the colonies of North and South America, the civil wars and the foreign wars, are only symptoms of this irresistible movement which bears humanity along.   I have thought it better to point out carefully its principal economic phases, than to neglect entirely European history and make a science as ancient as society commence almost with our century.

Such a course would have been prescribed me by a simple feeling of justice, even if the nature of my subject had not made it a duty.   It is an error to believe that, even if we take no account of the systems attempted by governments, political economy dates simply from the

---

* See Chap. xxi.

second half of the 18th century. More than two hundred years before, Italy had very remarkable treatises on a multitude of special subjects which depend upon it. The republics of Venice, Genoa, and Florence, knew too well how riches are multiplied, not to have left good ex. amples to follow and good books to consult. Several accounts rendered by their doges and their podestats might be placed on a par with the most complete messages of American presidents. I have quoted* a discourse of the doge Moncenigo marked by the most judicious economic maxims, and a budget of Florence, more clear and more circumstantial in its brevity than are ours with their indecipherable columns. And the system of Law, which our authors affect to reject in the heroic times of political economy, what was it, pray, if not the uncertain dawn of public and private credit as developed in our day? What! Should the fine financial reforms of Sully, the bold attempts of Colbert, the famous Navigation Act of the English, as well as the revolution effected by the crusades, the vast operations of the Jews, and the monetary convulsion which followed the discovery of the New-World, pass unheeded!

If the study of the causes which have retarded or developed the progress of public wealth were nothing but a simple affair of arithmetic, it would not perhaps be necessary to go back so far; I could have counted for nothing the advent of Christianity and have limited myself to a simple recital of the fine dissertations of the economists on *value* and *utility*. But because I think I have seen in political economy a science truly social, rather than a theory of finance, I have wished to show, as far as the vison of man can extend, the providential thread which guides nations in the accomplishment of their destiny. I firmly believe that some day there will be no more pariahs at the banquet of life, and I find the source of that hope in the study of history, which shows

---

* Chap. xx.

us the generations marching from conquest to conquest in the career of civilization. By the progress that has been made, I judge of that yet to be; and when I see labor, extricated from the Roman galleys, take refuge in feudal servitude, then organize into corporations and fly across the seas on the wings of commerce, to rest at length in the shadow of political liberty, I feel that there is in economic science something besides a question of words, and I trust I shall be pardoned for having sketched in bold outlines the history of its progress through nations and ages.*

The first volume contains such an exposition from the time of the ancients to the ministry of Colbert. More than once, in tracing it, I have experienced regret for having circumscribed my subject within the limits which I had imposed upon myself. The materials which I had at hand were immense in quantity, for the most part unpublished, though extracted from works well-known. A simple list of them arranged in order would alone form an economic monograph extremely curious; and more than one well-informed reader would be very much astonished to find, in these too long-neglected documents, an inexhaustible mine for study and meditation. Such facts are not what we ordinarily look for among historians, and most of the latter have at all times so well understood the indifference of the public to facts of this kind, that they have been very quiet about them, and feared so much to burden their annals with them, that we are obliged to obtain them mostly by induction. Armies and courts occupy the foreground; the *human* species, that which neither kills nor pillages, hardly figures even in the background, and that at a distance so obscure that one scarcely knows what became of it for thirty centuries.

The writers on political economy must be excused for having shared in that respect the general indifference, or, if one prefers, the general ingratitude. They almost all

* In the French editions, the work is divided into two volumes.—*Trans.*

date from the eighteenth century, because it was then, for the first time, that humanity really asked for its accounts and laid out in clear terms the programme of the future. But, in truth, that science did not spring fully armed from the brain of the economists during that century. In proof, I should wish but their gropings, their disputes, and their unfortunate attempts. It was reserved for their successors of the English school to lay the true foundations of the economic edifice and to prepare the way for the reform which is to be accomplished in our day. The history of that period, so rich in productions forever celebrated in the annals of science, forms the second part of my book. It will be perceived what efforts I have had to make to keep from exceeding the limits necessary to the unity of my recital. I use this word intentionally, to justify myself in advance from a reproach which I fear to have incurred from some exacting minds. I had two routes to take : I could follow the beaten track, develop the preliminary discourses of J. B. Say, M. de Sismondi, and Mr. McCulloch on the course of political economy since Quesnay, adding a few words of politeness for the preceding centuries, or I could go further back, and connect political economy with general history, noting their reciprocal influence from the ancients to our day.

The reader will judge whether this latter course, which I have taken, was the better. By placing myself at this point of view, I avoided entering into discussions of doctrines, controversies, and in consequence, interminable tedious passages. I ran over history at one breath, pausing simply at epochs of great influence on wealth and civilization. I showed labor always finding a refuge, in one country or another, and preparing wealth everywhere as an aid to liberty. I attempted, in short, to connect the present with the past, in place of treating the science as a hybrid hatched in the breath of the eighteenth century, *prolem sine matre creatam.* I wished ancestors for this fine science, which concerns the welfare of the human race and holds in trust the means of procuring for it the remedy compatible with the infirmities of our nature and the exigencies of our social condition. On seeing how slowly reforms come about, and estimating at their just value the obstacles they have encountered, the most ardent reformers of our epoch will learn to moderate their impatience and to demand of the times in which we live only their concurrent part in the movement which bears us along. On this subject, I have told all that our past conquests permit us to expect in the near future. I have created no system; I frankly acknowledge that I have not in manuscript any plan of universal regeneration and prosperity. I have recounted what our ancestors have done and what our predecessors have proposed, to realize the part that can be realized of that generous utopia. Some day, doubtless, I shall increase my book, if I obtain for this first attempt the sole success of which I am ambitious, that of popularizing economic science by showing that its elements are found in the history of nations as well as in the writings of economists.

I have terminated my work by a critical bibliography of the most important works on political economy which have been published, in all the European languages. This catalogue is certainly far from being complete; but it is the most extended which has appeared up to this time, and it may serve as a basis for a quite important special library.* I have read and made notes on most of the writings whose titles I have given and whose subject matter I have analyzed, so that the friends of the science may know the spirit of an author, before undertaking to read his works. It will readily be perceived that this part of my work was not the least difficult; but I hope thereby to have reinstated more than one economist who has been ignored, and to have made our fellow citizens ac-

---

* The bibliography was completed by the editor up to 1859 inclusively in the 4th edition from which this is translated. — *Trans.*

quainted with a fruitful source of investigation and information. This simple catalogue will alone suffice to prove that the science is more ancient than is supposed, and that it had already attained its majority when people supposed it still in the cradle. I hesitated a moment as to whether I should include in my list of names living writers, and especially whether I could characterize their works with impartiality; but their absence would have had greater disadvantages than the risk my judgment makes me incur, and I determined to speak of these contemporaries as if they were dead, while earnestly praying that they may yet live a long time.

One important motive especially influenced my decision. The living economists, with a few exceptions, form a new school, as far from the utopias of Quesnay as from the severity of Malthus; and I see with a philosophic and patriotic satisfaction that this school originated in France and is composed almost entirely of Frenchmen. This school it is which will mark out the course of political economy during the nineteenth century. It will consider production no longer as an abstraction independent of the fate of the workers: it is not sufficient for it that wealth be created, but it must be equitably distributed. In its view, men are *really* equal before the law as before the Eternal. The poor are not a text for declamations, but a portion of the great family, worthy of the deepest solicitude. It takes the world as it is, and knows how to stop at the limits of the possible; but its mission is to increase daily the circle of guests at the legitimate enjoyments of life. I say that this school is eminently French, and I am proud of my country that it is so.

May I be permitted, in closing, to render it an homage which will be contested by no one, since it comes from the simple display of its titles. See the books for which we are indebted to it for the past twenty years; the *Nouveaux Principes d' Economie Politique*, by M. Sismondi ; the *Traité* of M. Destutt de Tracy, that courageous man preëminent for good sense and probity ; the excellent book of Duchâtel on *La Charité ;* the *Nouveau Traité d' Economie Sociale*, by M. Dunoyer, so deeply marked by judgment and philanthropy ; the *Traité de Législation*, by M. Ch. Comte, which gave the last blow to colonial slavery ; *L' Economie Politique Chrétienne*, by the viscount of Villeneuve-Bargemont, which has described in so new and so remarkable a manner the. pest of *pauperism* in Europe ; *L' Economie Politique* of M. Droz, which has made the science an auxiliary to morals, and *L' Essai sur l' Esprit d' Association*, by M. Delaborde, to which we are fortunate to have recourse to-day, in the general disorder of unlimited competition. These works have already powerfully modified the rigid theories of Malthus and the algebraic formulæ of Ricardo. Independent in form and often in the choice of subject, they nevertheless are connected by a common thought, which is the general welfare of men, without distinction of nationality.

Nor have I been unmindful of the services rendered to science and to humanity by the Saint-Simonian school, at the time when the good spirit of its founders knew how to keep it from the invasion of mysticism and utopias. This school has scattered in Europe the germs of a reform which is manifesting itself on every side : it has recognized the rights of the working class, and defended them with a talent and a strength of conviction which must have made an impression on even its fiercest adversaries. The Saint-Simonians often made mistakes, like the Economists of the eighteenth century, with whom they have more than one point of resemblance ; but whatever may be said of their intentions and their morality, they were, above all, men of heart and of probity. England herself, who railed at them, imitates them : and the new works on political economy published in that country, are all impregnated with their reformatory ideas. It is the Saint-Simonian school which has de-scribed most forcibly the sufferings of the laboring classes, and if the great problem of the relief of these multitudes is not yet solved, it remains at least in the order of the day among all civilized peoples.

It is upon this ground that all questions of political economy must henceforth be decided. The true aim of the science from this time forward is to call the greatest possible number of men to a share in the benefits of civ-ilization. The terms *division of labor, capital, banks, asso-ciation, free trade,* have no other signification. Such is, at least, the tendency of the modern school, to which I have the honor to belong, and under the inspiration of which appears the work which I to-day offer the public. If some conscientious minds should wonder that I could embrace in two volumes the history of a science as im-portant and as vast as political economy, I would reply to them with one of its most illustrious founders :* "The history of a science does not resemble a narration of events. It can be only a statement of the more or less fortunate attempts that have been made at different times and in different places, to ascertain and solidly establish the truths of which it is composed. It becomes more and more brief as the science grows more nearly perfect."

* J. B. Say, *Cours Complet d' Economie Politique,* Vol. ii.

HISTORY OF POLITICAL ECONOMY.

CHAPTER I.

Political Economy more ancient than supposed.—The Greeks and Romans had theirs.—Its resemblance to that of our time.—The differences between them.—Successive modifications of the science.—General view of the subject.

A NOBLE spectacle and one well worthy of meditation, is that of the attempts made in the different ages of the world, to ameliorate the physical and moral condition of man. Each century brings its tribute of fanaticism to this grand cause, which counts nations and kings among its martyrs. Never does humanity rest: one experiment immediately succeeds another, and we advance through revolutions toward unknown destinies.

If we carefully study the history of the past, we perceive that this movement is of remote origin, that it has impelled our fathers and that it is bearing us and our children along with it. Sometimes nations appear to obey it blindly, as when Europe was invaded by the barbarians; more frequently they yield to it with a confused sense of the eternal laws which direct it. This accounts for the innumerable experiments of governments, which experiments, however, seem constantly to gravitate around a few immutable principles, such as personal security and respect for property.

The history of political economy can, then, be only a summary of the experiments which have been made among civilized nations to improve the lot of mankind. The ancients were not so much inferior to the moderns in that respect as many writers suppose; and it is quite wrong to attribute to economic science, as people generally do, an origin as recent as the second half of the eighteenth century. Who does not know of the institutions of Sparta and of Athens, and the magnificent works of Roman administration? We could hardly pass over in silence the economy of those times, especially since there we find the origin of almost all the institutions which govern us and of the systems which divide us. There was certainly in the laws of Lykurgus more Saint-Simonism than people think, and the quarrels of patricians and plebeians were no more fierce in Paris in the period of terror, than they were at Rome during the proscriptions of Sylla. The resemblance is still more striking between the insurrection of the workmen of Lyons and the withdrawal of the Roman people to the Sacred Hill.* How many times since Menenius Agrippa, has there been occasion to relate to a mutinous populace the famous apologue of the stomach and the members!

By excluding from the history of political economy everything connected with the ancients, modern economists have voluntarily deprived themselves of a fruitful source of observations and comparisons. They have rejected two thousand years of experiments tried with the greatest boldness, on a vast scale, by the most ingenious and most civilized people of antiquity; they have failed to comprehend history, which has carefully gathered up the least traces of these very experiments which we are to-day again making, too often with less ability and less

---

* The author alludes to the insurrection at Lyons in November, 1831, which originated simply in a question of wages. The workmen were masters of the city for two days; but their taking arms differed from the withdrawal of the Roman people to the Sacred Hill, in not causing any change of their condition, as none could be brought about.—Fr. Ed.

necessity than the Greeks and Romans. This bias of the economists is due to the fact that the ancients left no special work summing up their views on economic science; but if these views were not stated in a book, they are found in their institutions, in their monuments, in their jurisprudence. The relays of horses, established from Rome to York, the especial pains taken by the Romans for the maintenance of highways and aqueducts, strongly attest their comprehension of the principal necessities of civilization. The legislation of the Greek colonies was better than that of the Spanish colonies of South America.

Sparta, Athens, and Rome, had their political economy, as France and England have theirs. Usury, excessive imposts, tariffs, exorbitant charges for collecting the revenues, insufficient wages, and pauperism, afflicted the old communities as well as the new, and our ancestors made no fewer efforts than we to get rid of these scourges. One would be strangely mistaken to suppose that they never reflected on the difficulties in accomplishing the reforms of which they felt the need. Every page of their history presents us proof to the contrary, and we doubt not that the great insurrection of slaves under Spartacus made the economists of the time pass very bad nights. If historians have not acquainted us with their anxiety, it is because at Rome no one dared speak of that secret pest which was undermining the republic and which made the blush mount to the face of its greatest citizens. Later, when the emperors decided to distribute food to the inhabitants of the eternal city, were they not practicing political economy as the monks do in Spain at the doors of their monasteries? Is there much difference between the maxims of the Athenians who prohibited the exportation of figs and those of the French who lately prohibited that of silk and rags? All that one can say is, that the Greeks did not find, as we do, authors to support these absurdities by sophisms·

but that does not give us the right to despise them. When we study attentively the financial legislation of the Greeks and Romans, we can but recognize that the most weighty questions of political economy had at all times the attention of these nations. It suffices to see with what solicitude they guarded their international relations, the civil status of foreigners, the nature and effects of taxes, the encouragements to be given to agriculture, and the direction of navigation. I shall have occasion in the course of this work to cite irrefutable proofs of their perfect apprehension of these matters. There was nothing, even to the most complicated phenomena of the division of labor, which escaped their investigation ; and we find in the second book of the *Republic* of Plato an analysis which would do honor to the most learned disciple of Adam Smith. Xenophon's *Economics*, hitherto insufficiently studied, contain observations of great clearness : and we know no better definition of money than that which Aristotle has given us in the first book of his *Politics*.*

One would, however, be mistaken if he considered the attempts made by governments, or extolled by the writers of Greece and Rome, as the result of an economic system conceived according to truly scientific premises, or inspired by a deep philosophy. The Greeks and Romans despised labor and stigmatized the industries as beneath the dignity of a free man. Slavery appears on every page of their history, to give the lie to the writings of their philosophers and the theories of their economists. But do we not find in our history contradictions as shocking? By studying them among the ancients, where we can judge them with more impartiality, we can easily recognize among ourselves the danger or the inutility of a great number of experiments which, though appearing new, are nevertheless revived from the Greeks and Romans.

The ancients tried everything; and we resemble them

---

* See chapters vi and vii of Aristotle's Politics, Book i.

in too many respects, to neglect their political economy. Sparta had her helots, as the middle ages had their serfs, and our colonies their slaves. A few modern states have still their disgraced castes, like the Jews in Switzerland, Prussia and Poland; but what principally distinguishes the political economy of the moderns from that of the ancients, is freedom of labor and the employment of credit. Everything around us has changed since the inventions of printing, the mariner's compass, and gunpowder. We know and employ in immense quantities, raw materials unknown to our ancestors. Cotton, iron, wines, mineral coal and steam, have become for us inexhaustible sources of wealth. Three or four plants, the potato, beet, sugar-cane and tea, furnish nourishment to millions of men, and cargoes to thousands of vessels. The ancients lived by conquest, that is, by the labor of others; we live by industries and commerce, that is, by our own labor.

The distinctive characteristic of Greek and Roman political economy, is slavery; the irresistible tendency of ours, is liberty. We shall see how the influence of Christianity contributed to give it this direction, interrupted, however, sometimes by barbaric invasion, sometimes by religious fanaticism; but no serious obstacle has been able to arrest its progress. The feudal glebe had its counterpoise in the corporations. These were somewhat of an advance, since they developed the spirit of association. Corporations in their turn have disappeared before the emancipation of industrial labor. Every step has freed man from some bondage and conferred upon him some useful product; so that we may say that liberty has never come without bringing with it some benefit. The Greeks and Romans who oppressed humanity under deceptive appearances, were without underlinen and had no windows to their houses; we ourselves have only just begun to enjoy a little comfort in material life since the acquisition of liberty.

To justly appreciate these radical differences, and also the resemblances between the political economy of the ancients and our own, we must study at the same time their institutions and their writings, that is to say, the facts and the doctrines of their times. I have chosen for that study in Greece, the time of the greatest prosperity of Athens, and in Rome, the first centuries of the empire. Athens, in fact, best represents Greek civilization, and imperial Rome, Roman civilization. The institutions and writings of these memorable epochs exercised on the contemporary world an immense influence which has extended even to the generation which we represent. The Roman laws still decide, in many respects, the most grave questions of our civil state, direct our marriages, regulate inheritance, and govern our property. Custom-duties existed at Rome before the reign of Nero, and the Athenians were acquainted with public loans. They knew very well the wealth to be gained by commerce: they made bottomry loans[1], and they at all times gave much attention to the exploitation of their mines. In reading their history, we might think we were reading ours, so much resemblance is there in the facts, and so true is it that humanity moves ever in a sphere of like passions and desires!

At the fall of the Roman world, a profound revolution is effected in the course of political economy. Slavery takes a new form, continually modified by the influence of Christianity; ideas of equality begin to be diffused. To an affected contempt for riches succeed the first elements of the art of acquiring them. A few great sovereigns set the example of order and economy: Charlemagne has the eggs of his chickens, and the vegetables from his gardens, sold in market. The conquerors become conservators, and it is easy to find in the *Capitularies* * the germ of the new ideas which are to take the place of the old Roman policy. The crusades later ex-

* See the Capitulary *De Villis*, art. 30. edit. of Baluze.

ercise their share of influence, by making the fortune of the maritime cities of Italy, which become the refuge of civilization from the barbarism of the middle ages. The ownership of lands, hitherto concentrated in the hands of the lords, is divided by coming into the hands of the *bourgeois*, who purchase them from the crusaders. Contact with the Orient inspires new tastes, and gives rise to desires for luxury which the industry of the Italian republics hastens to satisfy. There is nothing even in the errors of the time, which does not coöperate in the continual work of progress, and the persecuted Jews create the science of credit and exchange. Saint Louis appears and organizes industry. The trades are divided into brotherhoods and put under the protection of the saints against the tyranny of the barons. The commune is formed, and the middle classes (*bourgeoisie*), from which the clergy are recruited, begin that long struggle against the aristocracy which hardly ends in the remarkable days of 1789.

Three great events, almost contemporary, the invention of gunpowder, of printing, and the discovery of the new world, change, in their turn, the face of Europe and the conditions of public wealth. The precious metals, previously so rare, become abundant; unknown products, as well as ideas, circulate more rapidly; brute force is dethroned by gunpowder. I cannot comprehend how, in the face of these marvellous elements of social regeneration, any one could persist in dating political economy only from the last years of the eighteenth century. It was, however, at that time, that pauperism began again with the concentration of fortunes; then, too, the great schism of protestantism, by overturning the convents, struck with slow but sure death the principle of tithes and the religious exploitation of man, which had itself succeeded his military exploitation. Who would dare affirm that these great revolutions modified in no manner the economic institutions of European nations?

Many like events were, without doubt, necessary, to
determine statesmen and savants to trace them to their
first causes, the study of which to-day constitutes economic science.   Our fathers were for a long time practicing political economy, without knowing its principles,
as most men live without being initiated into the
physiological phenomena of life.   Colbert alone appears
to have had a system, as later Law was to have his,
and as the economists of the eighteenth century proclaimed theirs.   But these lofty intellects cannot be considered as the primitive source from which the science
came ready made.   When we have set forth the ideas of
Plato, Aristotle and Xenophon, on the questions so admirably stated by Adam Smith, and so vigorously con-
troverted in our day, one can but recognize that these
geniuses of antiquity had a glimpse of their importance
and prepared the way for their solution.

The common error comes especially from the writers
of the eighteenth century, who thought they had found
the secret of social science, because they had analyzed
with a penetration until then unknown, some essential
phenomena of production.   They had opened the way
for research, in a new and bold manner; and they passed
for having created the science, because they had a glimpse
of it in a prism with many illusions.   The services of
agriculture had been too little understood; the school of
Quesnay restored it to the place which it should occupy
among the agents of production.   After him, Adam
Smith reinstated labor and unveiled the true causes of
the wealth of nations.   Malthus uttered a cry of alarm
at population, which, according to him, had become too
numerous; J. B. Say extolled freedom of trade and the
advantages of unlimited competition, of which Sismondi
soon, in an eloquent and paradoxical manifesto, showed
the fatal consequences.   Ricardo laid boldly the foundations of the modern monetary edifice, which, in his view,
has been raised only in America, and that for but a moment.

Such are the principal causes of the indifference which savants have always manifested toward the study of the economic facts of antiquity and of later times remote from us. I have thought it would be useful to fill that gap, and set forth succinctly and clearly the efforts of our predecessors. I shall confine myself to the most characteristic facts and doctrines of the different periods which pass in succession before us. Athens, Rome, the Barbarians, Christianity, the Crusades, the Renaissance, and the Reformation, will present us epochs full of bold experiments and memorable instruction. Everything is connected, all forms one chain in the general history of man. In view of the strong opposition of intelligent people, now manifested in the United States,* to the gradual emancipation of the blacks, it is impossible not to recall the odious maxims of the ancients on slavery, and not to recognize, under different names, the same prejudices.

---

* Written in 1837.

CHAPTER II.

Political Economy among the Greeks.—Their ideas on slavery.—Administration of their finances.—They live from the labor of their slaves and the tributes of their allies.—What the *theorikon* was.—The Kleruchiæ.—Every citizen considers himself a fund-holder of the State.—What a family needed in order to live.—Public property.—Mines.—Money.—Temple at Delphi a true bank of deposit.—Interest of money in Greece.—Importance attached to the finances.—Habits of the Athenians.

WE read in the first book of the *Politics* of Aristotle *
these remarkable words : " The science of the master reduces itself to knowing how to make use of his slave.
He is the master, not because he is the owner of the man,
but because he makes use of his property. * * * The
slave constitutes part of the wealth of the family." Xenophon † proposes, as a means of revenue to the republic,
to appropriate the slaves and let them out to the highest
bidder, after having branded them on the forehead lest
they should escape. All the philanthropy of the ancients
is found in this, and also a good part of their political
economy. It is evident that when their philosophers
speak of the people, they mean simply a domiciliated
middling class, for whom the masses work, subject to the
most intolerable bondage. Their susceptibility is extreme whenever there is any talk of according to a man
the title of citizen, that is to say, of making him pass
from the state of exploitation (*i. e.*, of being worked for
the advantage of others —*Trans.*) to that of independence. There was no one, even to the most humble pri-

---

* Chap. iv.

† Means of increasing the revenues of Attika. Chapter xi.

vate citizen, who did not possess one slave to care for his house. Heads of families of moderate fortune employed several in grinding corn, baking bread, cooking and making clothes. Several thousands were employed in the workshops for which Athens was renowned ; but generally they were subjected to the severest labors. They were sent to the river to drink with the horses.

The institutions of Greece were, then, made for a small number of privileged individuals. The Athenians showed no more sympathy for the sufferings of their slaves than our manufacturers feel for the wheels of their machinery. But when we place ourselves at the exclusive point of view of this cruel social state, we cannot help recognizing in several of its adaptations much ability and penetration. The administration of the finances was directed with remarkable order and exactitude. All the regular imposts were farmed out to contractors who paid the amount into the public treasury, under the surveillance of comptrollers. A wise distinction had been established between the public domain properly so called, and the especial property of the communities. The avails of the fines adjudged by the tribunals, the revenues of the temples and of the customs, were turned over into the hands of responsible receivers, who took note of the sums received and prosecuted the delinquents. A superintendent of the public revenues, a virtual minister of finance, had direction of all the funds, ordered the payments, and balanced the expenditures with the receipts. Especial departments were charged with the making of the roads, the construction of vessels, and the public edifices. All these departments had their accounts and consequently their scribes, the latter being most frequently chosen from the slaves, as these could be put to torture to obtain confessions. Popular distrust was even carried so far that no person accountable could go away, or make a will, until he had rendered his accounts to the public officers appointed to receive them.

Everything which pertained to the finances was subject to public scrutiny. The accounts rendered were engraved on stone so that every one could know and criticise them. Time has spared us several such inscriptions almost intact and even a few stones on which may be found the conditions of certain contracts, such as the leasing of the salt-works, the fisheries and the woods. The devastator of Athens, Lord Elgin, brought away one of these stones, which is deposited in the British Museum. The people, besides, were merciless toward those who betrayed their trust or were delinquent in their payments. Nothing was more dangerous than to become a public debtor. Ten days after a judgment rendered to that effect, arrest for debt was ordered : the condemned was forever excluded from public affairs; his children and grand-children became responsible for his misfortunes or his faults. No one could demand abatement, unless the favor of speaking on that subject was accorded him by an unanimous decree of six thousand voices. This extreme susceptibility in financial matters will not surprise those who are acquainted with the social organization of Greek republics.

At Athens especially, the public treasury was a sort of common purse, not only for the collective necessities of the population, but also for the expenses of each private citizen. Every citizen was a fundholder in the state after the establishment of the *theorikon* [2] under Perikles, which was a veritable *jeton de présence* [3] accorded to patriotic and garrulous idleness, and which soon degenerated into a poor-tax. From that time, the Athenian people wished to be fed and entertained at the expense of the public treasury. There were periodic banquets, ruinous festivals, the originators of which sought popularity at the expense of the real prosperity of the country. Hence that passion for confiscations and fines which was nearly always manifest in the popular assemblies, and by which Sokrates, Miltiades, Themistokles, Aristeides, Thrasybulus, Kimon and the great Perikles himself were in turn overtaken or

menaced.   These fines and confiscations were inflicted for
the greatest crimes as well as the smallest offences.

The people were mischief-making because they were
avaricious.   They banished honorable citizens on the
slightest pretext, who then conspired to return to their
native country, and who more than once desolated it because it had not known how to be just.

The allies were only tributaries on whom taxes were
levied in consideration of an altogether arbitrary contingent of soldiers.*   Karia, Thrace, the shores of the Helles-

---

* Recent labors have vindicated the Athenian democracy from a great
part of the reproaches of historians.   Mr. Grote, notably, has positively refuted the calumnious accusations of which the ancient writers on the aristocratic side were so lavish toward the free institutions of Athens.   The confederation of maritime cities which was formed under the auspices of Athens,
two years after the combat at Mykale, arose spontaneously from the circumstances, and we cannot to-day contest its utility to all Greece and the allied
cities themselves.   The contribution to which the confederated cities had
pledged themselves, consisted for each in a sum of money and a certain
number of ships of war ; and according to the acknowledgment of those interested, it had been regulated in a perfectly equitable manner by Aristeides,
at the time of the establishment of the confederation.   If, thirty years later,
Athens the president became Athens the despot, to use Mr. Grote's expression, it was greatly through the fault of the allies themselves, who preferred
to convert their payments in men and vessels into pecuniary payments, and
who proposed to transfer to Athens the treasury of the confederation previously lodged at Delos.   The total contribution had been fixed by Aristeides,
in 476 B.C. at 460 talents (less than $500,000) ; at the commencement of
the Peloponnesian war, it was still only about 600 talents (about $630,000),
and that increase certainly did not arise from the increase of the proportional share imposed on each confederate, but from the admission of
$630,000), and that increase certainly did not arise from the increase of the
proportional share imposed on each confederate, but from the admission of
a great number of new allies and from the conversion of payments in kind
to payments in money.   (Grote, Hist. of Greece, vol. v.)

At the time when the Peloponnesian war began, the total revenue of
Athens amounted to about 1,000 talents, 400 of which arose from the receipts
proper of the city itself and the rest from the contributions of the allies.
Now, in time of peace, the funds arising from that contribution were not
expended, but were turned over to the treasury formed by Perikles, and
amounted at one time to 9,700 talents.   " This system of public economy,"
says Grote, " constantly laying by a considerable sum year after year—in
which Athens stood alone, since none of the Peloponnesian states had any
public reserve whatever,—goes far of itself to vindicate Perikles from the
charge of having wasted the public money in mischievous distributions for
the purpose of obtaining popularity ; and also to exonerate the Athenian
Demos from that reproach of a greedy appetite for living by the public
purse, which it is common to ascribe to them."   Grote, vol. vi, p. 10.

It would, moreover, be unjust to consider as unproductive expenses the
magnificent edifices which Perikles caused to be constructed at Athens, the
works of art with which he adorned the temples, the considerable sums which
he consecrated to festivals and theatrical entertainments.   May we be permitted again to invoke the authority of Grote on this point : " The schemes

pont, Ephesus, and the isle of Rhodes, became thus virtu-ally Greek fiefs. Aristophanes counted more than a thou-sand cities subject to the Hellenic yoke, and he jestingly proposed to put twenty Athenian citizens in each of them on a pension. Sometimes metropolitan despotism went farther, and the Athenians seized, on the slightest pretext, a portion of the territory of their allies. The lands thus conquered bore the name of Kleruchiæ. The conquerors made them virtual colonies, of which the resident Athe-nians composed the aristocracy, always dependent on the central government. The father of Plato was a klerouch. The citizens whom the state sent to these colo-nies usually received arms and money, and they soon became odious to the native population there, who more than once rose to recover their independence. Every-thing was then consistent in the social system of the Athenians : they levied contributions at home, they levied contributions abroad ; here by confiscations and fines, there by war taxes or monopolies. No one dreamed of the resources that could be found in labor. The pas-sion for the *theorikon* caused new expedients to be daily invented to provide for the living of those exacting talkers who were eternally deliberating without ever accomplishing anything.

However, if an exaggerated idea of their superiority

of Perikles were at the same time eminently Pan-Hellenic. In strengthen-ing and ornamenting Athens, in developing the full activity of her citizens, in providing temples, religious offerings, works of art, solemn festivals, all of surpassing attraction—he intended to exalt her into something greater than an imperial city with numerous dependent allies. He wished to make her the centre of Grecian feeling, the stimulus of Grecian intellect, and the type of strong democratic patriotism combined with full liberty of in-dividual taste and aspiration. He wished not merely to retain the adherence of the subject states, but to attract the admiration and spontaneous deference of independent neighbors, so as to procure for Athens a moral ascendency much beyond the range of her direct power. And he succeeded in elevating the city to a visible grandeur, which made her appear even much stronger than she really was, and which had the farther effect of softening to the minds of the subjects the humiliating sense of obedience, while it served as a normal school, open to strangers from all quarters, of energetic action even under full licence of criticism, of elegant pursuits economically followed, and of a love of knowledge without enervation of character." (Vol. vi, p. 24.) —*Note of French editor.*

had not turned the Athenians from the regular ways of
production, they would perhaps have resolved the great
problem of the most general distribution of the profits
of labor.   All their institutions aimed to make the citizens participate in the benefits of association; but they
excluded from them the slaves, who formed nearly three-
fourths of the population.   The state maintained public
physicians, (Hippokrates was at Athens), professors, and
artists charged with beautifying the monuments of
which each citizen considered himself co-proprietor; the
offices of notary and of procurator, which have become
among us sources of exactions so onerous to families,
were salaried by the state.   Instruction was free.   The
children of deceased soldiers received their education at
the expense of the public treasury, and all orphans found
in the care of the magistrates a truly paternal protection.
The reputation of Demosthenes as an orator commenced
with a suit against his tutors; and against them he won
his first case.

The Athenians had a general principle that no citizen
should be in want, and they granted help to those whom
bodily infirmities rendered incapable of providing for
their own subsistence.   But that liberality which they exercised toward themselves, soon brought on its natural
consequences, by multiplying beyond measure the number
of the idle and improvident; and when the misfortunes of
the Peloponnesian war had exhausted the sources of taxation, poverty appeared in all its horror.   An actual poor-tax
had to be levied, the uncertain amount of which has been
discussed by Professor Boeckh with his accustomed clearness in his excellent work on "The Political Economy of
the Athenians." *   At the same time, the spirit of association aided them in struggling against the distress of
the treasury.   Several private individuals formed a society called *Eranos*, with the condition of paying an assessment, which was distributed according to the neces-

---

* Book II., chap. xvii.

sities of the members. This society bore the name of
Community of *Eranists*, and its head was called an *Eran-
arch.*

It was to these anti-economic habits of living almost always at the expense of the public treasury, that the
Greeks owed the loss of their freedom and the small development of their industrial power. The public distribution having assumed a periodic character, all the ambitious who were desirous of popularity purchased the
favor of the multitude by bounties, which exhausted the
state without enriching those to whom the gifts were
made. Plato justly remarks that this fatal system had
rendered the Athenians idle, covetous, intriguing and
fickle. Perikles, who was the author of it, was by no
means under an illusion in respect to its disadvantages,
but he needed it to maintain his power, and so persisted
in it. Hence arose the perpetual intrigues of the orators,
whose interest it was to flatter this sovereign with twenty
thousand heads, called the people, whose avidity could be
satisfied only by enormous taxes on the rich or by confiscations. Demagogues had come to the point of declaring in their harangues that if such or such a citizen were
not condemned, it would be impossible to make up the
amount of the payments to the people. Those of the
rich who were threatened, sometimes sacrificed themselves to conjure the storm ; then an extraordinary distribution was made and all the malcontents were called
to the quarry.[4] Thus arose the *theorika,*[2] and Demades
ventured boldly to declare that the distributions of money
were the cement of the democracy. Do we not find,
after a lapse of more than two thousand years, this
very system of the Greeks revived in the payment of
forty sous a day, accorded in 1793 to the sectionists[5] of
Paris?

Everything was calculated among the Greeks to secure
pay to every class of citizens. The orators had themselves paid for speaking, and the people for hearing ; the

judges, true *jurés*,* had not allowed themselves to be forgotten either. Whether from policy, or as is more likely,
to secure positions for popular notabilities, two, three, and
even ten ambassadors were accredited to each power at
the same time. Certain public criers, and certain copyists
of the decrees of the people, were supplied with food at
the Prytaneum, in which doubtless the state also furnished
them lodgings. There were physicians and poets maintained at public expense; in short, the multitude of salaried persons was so great, that it was necessary to establish severe rules against plurality of offices, that leprosy
of our modern finances.

It is easy to form an idea of the enormity of the taxes
which the payment of all these salaries required, when we
know that the poorest family † could not live on a less income than 400 francs (less than $80) in our money, unless
they contented themselves with simply bread and water.
Considerably more was therefore needed to live becom-
ingly: besides, the piety of the Greeks toward the dead
made them often incur great expense for funerals and for
tombs; they also invested much in furniture, clothing and
jewels. Most of the good houses contained not only the
articles necessary for the ordinary purposes of life, but
also the implements indispensable for the practice of
several trades, such as weaving and baking, which were
done at home by the slaves.

Vanity had led to the luxury of **costly vessels** of gold
and silver; and they increased in number so much, that
in order to supply those who could pay but little, some
had to be made of a thickness not exceeding that of the
skin. Now, if we consider that there were about ten
thousand houses at Athens, independently of the constructions of the ports, the small towns and villages, and
about 360,000 slaves, we can form an idea of the accumu-

---

* The *jurés*, or wardens of trade corporations, were famous for their exactions of fees from the workmen who aimed at promotion to the position of
master-workman.

† Of four persons, according to Bœckh.

lated wealth in that republic, and by analogy, of the relative power of the other Greek republics.

One however demands with surprise how the Athenians
succeeded in paying these universal emoluments, distributed to the various classes of citizens. At the beginning,
the temples and priests were supported by means of the
sacred lands, tithes, and sacrifices.* The magistrates of
the judiciary order received fees. Later, when Solon had
divided the people into four classes according to the extent of their fortune, each class was taxed according the
taxable capital which it was supposed to enjoy, but, however, so that the wealthiest class paid a larger proportion
of its income than the poorer ones : this mode of taxation
appears to have had all the characteristics of a quota tax.
To establish it on an equitable basis, there existed a register of property which was revised every four years.
This register did not, however, secure the object of our
records of mortgages. The lender who wished to take
security, contented himself with putting a tablet on which
he inscribed his name, before the field of his debtor.
Besides the quota tax, which alone brought considerable
sums, and the tributes of the allies, which were a sort of
war-fine rigorously paid in time of peace, the Athenians
had the revenues of their mines, the fines, and the avails
of the confiscations of which we have already spoken, and
the custom-duties. The state and the communities possessed property whose rent brought in a considerable
amount. This property ordinarily consisted of pasturage,
forests, houses and salt-works. These were let temporarily or permanently to a farmer-general, who pledged
himself to pay the revenues regularly into the public
treasury.

The Greeks, and principally the Athenians, early manifested their aversion to anything resembling a personal

---

* At certain religious festivals, there were sometimes sacrificed at Athens
as many as three hundred cattle, whose flesh and skin were distributed to
the people.

tax, and especially a land-tax. There was not among them any door- and window-tax. Their usual revenue came from the public domains and the property of the communities. They liked especially to lay taxes on foreigners; and they had free recourse, even under ordinary circumstances, to indirect taxes, imposed, however, with great moderation. But they attached especial importance to the products of their mines. Those of Attika and Laurion appear to have furnished from the earliest times considerable treasure, since it was to success in working them that Themistokles owed the means of carrying to its greatest height the maritime power of the state. These mines, however, were not long in becoming exhausted, and at the time of Strabo there was hardly enough taken from them to cover the expenses of exploitation. It is probable too, that the imperfect acquaintance of the ancients with chemistry prevented their getting the full advantage of them. The work of mining was performed by bands of slaves naturally ill-instructed, quite badly disciplined, and whose condition bore a close resemblance to that of those unhappy Indians with whom the Spaniards worked their mines in Mexico and Peru at the commencement of the conquest. Nothing, therefore, could equal the despair of the Athenians when these resources suddenly failed them, and they saw themselves, like the Spaniards of our day, reduced to seek in labor, of which they had lost the habit, a refuge against poverty and ruin. That change must have been the more distressing to them, as the mines had been divided up among a greater number of proprietors or farmers, hitherto very rich and ranked with the most opulent agriculturists and merchants.

Everything leads us to believe that the ancients shared the modern prejudices in regard to the precious metals. We shall see in the account of the *Economics* of Xenophon that they considered gold and silver as preëminently riches, and that it was always an aim in their policy to make these metals flow into the national territory by all possible means.   Consequently they levied on foreign merchandise a tax of a fiftieth, which was a custom-duty. This impost was to be paid at the time of unlading the merchandise, in money and not in commodities, an easy operation if one considers that almost all the trade of Greece was by sea.   There was likewise to be at the gates of certain cities a veritable *octroi*,[6] a source of fraud like ours ; for authors report several extremely curious cases of smuggling, among others that of a peasant who introduced casks of honey into sacks of barley, and who was discovered by the officers for collecting town-dues, who had come to the aid of his fallen donkey.

Money of gold and silver was quite rare among the Greeks before their expeditions to the East.   The conquest of a part of Asia by Cyrus caused an immense mass of money to flow to the West ; and without doubt the fabulous stories of the riches of Krœsus and of the Paktolus with its sands of gold, owe their origin to facts which the imagination of the Greeks had exaggerated.   The great variety of kinds of money imported gave rise to the business of money-changers, who speculated, like those of our day, in the exchange of different moneys.

The Athenians, moreover, practiced a strict surveillance over the coinage of money, and theirs was of so good quality that it was favorably regarded in all markets. Although Pliny the naturalist, Strabo, and Diodorus of Sicily, have left us valuable documents on the metallic wealth of the ancients, we can but regret the loss of the special work that Theophrastus appears to have written on the metallurgic art three hundred years before our era, and of which there remain a few scattered fragments in the works of subsequent writers.   That was the source of all the documents relating to the money of ancient times.

Philip of Macedon maintained war against the Greeks as much with gold as with iron.*   Alexander, his son,

---

* *i. e.,* the sword.

obtained millions from his expedition into India, and distributed with extraordinary liberality among his soldiers. The Ptolemies, his successors, are supposed to have collected more than a milliard of francs (about $193,000,000) in specie. Silver was, besides, rarer than to-day relatively to gold. In the nineteenth century, the price of gold is fifteen * times higher than that of silver, while in the times of the Greeks it was only ten times greater. A *billon* money, a combination of iron and copper, served for the usual intercourse in small transactions, but had no currency beyond the frontiers.

The extreme importance attached to gold and silver, gave rise among the Greeks to financial institutions which were not without analogy to ours. The temple at Delphi received annually, under the protection of Apollo, deposits of considerable sums belonging to private individuals and even to cities. The priests, interested in seeing gold amassed at the foot of their altars, encouraged this disposition, and the temple at Delphi became a bank of deposit respected throughout Greece. Meanwhile, as no interest was obtained for sums deposited there, several competitive institutions became established, and it was not long before the occupation of banker became quite lucrative. The lowest rate of interest appears to have been ten per cent and the highest thirty-six. Usury took wide limits, on account of the profit that could be derived from capital by the aid of slaves, and especially because of the little security of the lenders. The same phenomenon is reproduced in our time in slave-holding countries, as likewise is seen in our colonies, where, besides, the formalities of getting possession are so slow, that a dishonest debtor can make his creditor die of the trouble. Also, lenders were in the habit of taking out in advance the full amount of the interest, which they loaned anew

---

* The relative value of gold is now (1879) considerably higher. Whether the present relation will continue depends upon causes (production, legislation, distribution, commerce, etc.), that cannot be predicted.—Trans.

on rigorous conditions, braving the public contumely
mingled with deference and flattery, which was bestowed upon monied men then as in our day. Usury
appeared again, not less hideous, at Rome and
throughout all Europe, in the middle ages—a fatal
symptom of ignorance of the true laws of production,
and of contempt of the most simple demands of morals. One may judge from these facts what must have
been the rents and farming charges, the rates of which
were always more or less governed by that of interest for
money. Professor Boeckh estimates the amount of the
house-rents at eight and a half per cent on the capital;
the rents of lands were a little lower. People built for
speculation a sort of inn, the apartments of which were
let to the various strangers whom politics or commerce
attracted to Athens and who had no right of citizenship
there.

It is easy to conceive, from these data, upon what
onerous terms the public loans must have been effected.
The lack of security and the perpetual tendency of these
people to juridical spoliations, permit a doubt whether a
single loan of this kind was consented to freely. They
preferred to have recourse either to augmentations or
creations of taxes, even on real property, when the necessities of the state became too pressing. The temple at
Delphi and that of Delos more than once lent a part of
the sums which had been entrusted to them. From time
to time, anticipations of the taxes were decreed, veritable
forced loans pretty nearly like those of our day, which were
to be borne by the rich. At last, they went so far as to
create a fictitious money of iron, which was considered as
real, by means of which they filled the place of the gold and
silver exported by foreign commerce, until the iron money
was bought up and annulled, like our assignats. Then
came more shameful and deplorable alterations of the
money, combinations of silver and lead, and of silver and
copper, the ordinary expedients of governments at bay;

but these departures were always of short duration, and if one excepts Sparta, where the money, for reasons inherent in the constitution of that utopian republic, long consisted of heavy and coarse bars of iron, Greece kept faithfully the reputation of her monetary system.

The statesmen of this country always attached great importance to matters of finance. It was a difficult science at a time when no public debt permitted loading the future with the burdens of the present. The extraordinary expenses weighing heavily upon the tax-payer, it was necessary to engineer in a thousand ways so as not to reach capital, and consequently affect production at its source. Unfortunately, popular intervention, often little enlightened, occasioned serious damage ; monuments of art arose in great numbers to satisfy the national vanity; the habit of living at the expense of the allies turned the citizens from the regular paths of labor. The existence of the state depended then on the outside provinces, and became consequently very insecure. This is what impressed Xenophon when he wrote his treatise on the *Revenues of Attika,* of which we shall soon have occasion to speak.

Such a system must necessarily have exercised a great influence on the morals and customs of the inhabitants of Greece. The Athenians were inclined to games and ease. They were often seen sitting before the porticos of their public edifices, arguing on political affairs, discussing the news of the day, then, cane in hand, visiting the shops, the markets and the public baths. Sometimes they had a slave follow them carrying a folding chair which they opened to sit upon when they were fatigued. Their repasts were generally sumptuous, and the bread that was sold, even to the most humble workman, was of excellent taste and dazzling whiteness. Their markets were furnished with game, fish, vegetables and fruits of every kind. At Sparta, it was quite the contrary ; and yet the results of the Lacedæmonian system differ little from those of the habits at Athens. The Spartans never rose to the height of a civilized nation, because they sought to stifle every desire; and the Athenians quickly descended from that height, because they were willing at whatever cost, to satisfy their desires, and to create also new ones every day.

" If we take a general survey of the whole public economy of the Athenians, which the financial systems of the other Greeks who enjoyed liberty, Sparta excepted, more or less resembled, we recognize that many of its parts were judiciously *calculated*. The Greeks were neither poor nor indifferent to wealth; but the quantity of the precious metals in circulation was not as considerable as in the states of modern Europe, and consequently many things were done with little money. As property gave pretty large returns, private citizens could bear high taxes. Athens nobly expended large sums for the worship of the gods and to perpetuate generous thoughts and great deeds by monuments which manifested an exquisite taste in the fine arts. But the gratuities and the salaries engendered love of ease, the people persuaded themselves that the state ought to support them, and that their only concern was to direct the general administration. It was a problem for the public men, to find out how they could enrich the people, not by labor and manufactures, but by sacrificing to them the revenues of the state; for the commonwealth was regarded as a common property, the proceeds of which should be divided among the individual citizens." *

* Boeckh, Public Economy of the Athenians, Book iv., Chap. 22.

CHAPTER III.

WE do not think that any country has ever ventured
upon a system of public economy as extraordinary as the
laws of Lykurgus at Sparta. The strictest regulations of
a community, the most radical forms decreed by the National Convention, the harmonic utopias of the Owenists,
and, in these later times, the adventurous preaching of
Saint-Simonism, have nothing which can be compared with
those laws, in point of boldness and originality. They
seem the dream of a contemplator rather than the result
of the meditations of a statesman, and yet they had quite
a long existence, and penetrated deeply enough into the
morals of a celebrated people, to occupy a place in the
history of the science. The principal characteristic which
distinguishes them, is their having been, so to speak, improvised and applied at once in the government of a
people who had until then laws very different. In reading them, one seems to be looking over the rules of a college rather than the code of a nation. Everything there
is so singular, that the existence even of their author has
been doubted by many savants, who are persuaded that
there was more than one Lykurgus, as it was long thought
there was more than one Homer.

Still, whatever may have been the origin of the laws of
Lykurgus there is abundant evidence that they directed
for many centuries, more or less intact, the destinies of

the Spartans. They pass for having realized the utopia
of a general division of property, and of a common education for all citizens. They embrace at the same time
a complete system of political economy, a catechism of
beliefs, and a universal manual for the industrial arts.
They regulated the order of succession to the throne, and
that of dishes at repasts. What could be stranger than
the division of the territory of Sparta into nine thousand
portions, and the rest of the country into thirty thousand
other parts, assigned to so many fathers of families, on
condition of distributing their products to their wives
and children? How could that temporary equality of
fortunes last? I acknowledge that I can hardly comprehend a society in which it is forbidden to buy or sell any
portion of land, or to bequeath it by will. How can that
prohibition be reconciled with the right of primogeniture
which existed at Sparta, unless we suppose that the eldest
of each family was obliged to maintain his brothers, and
then what became of equality, that imaginary aim of the
laws of Lykurgus?

It was not permitted to settle a dowry upon girls; but
men probably wedded them without any uneasiness in
regard to the future, since the state assumed the burden
of bringing up and providing for the children they brought
into the world. Happy country! where each citizen had
only to seat himself at table, sure of finding there a
repast, provided he brought his contingent of barley or
vegetables! Most wonderful of all, there were neither
imposts nor a public treasury: and yet, if we credit Aristotle, this philosophical people sometimes found means of
lending money. Aristotle assures us that when the deputies of Samos applied to their treasury, the general assembly ordered a universal fast of twenty-four hours,
men and animals included, to obtain a little saving to bestow upon the allies. But since it was forbidden to buy
or sell, of what use was money at Sparta? Notwithstanding our respect for antiquity, I greatly fear that

these and many other stories of loans are mere fabrica-
tions. What is certain, however, is that there was a time
in Sparta when the sense of property seemed to have become extinct, and to have given place to a patriotic unconcern founded on an entire absence of personal wants;
for the legislation of Lykurgus was perfectly consistent.
By destroying the foundations of property, it made persistent war on the desire for acquisition, and consequently
on all the tastes which inflame it.

This was, in fact, what the legislator had in view. All
the children, withdrawn from maternal influence at the
tenderest age, ceased to belong to their families and became the property of the state. Whatever their parent-
age, they were brought up in common, according to invariable principles, under the surveillance of the magistrates, and almost on the public place. The whip was
decreed preëminently *the* institution. Children were despoiled of their hair in the interest of neatness; they
walked barefooted at all seasons; they lay down to rest
on a litter of dried leaves. They were taught to steal
fruit for their repasts, and whipped when they allowed
themselves to be detected. When they reached adoles-
cence, a new apprenticeship began for them, that of war,
and they practiced its exercises with such boldness, that
blood flowed in those disgusting arenas, where, half-naked,
they tore each other under the eyes of their mothers.
"You bite me, like a woman," said one. "No, but like
a lion," replied the other; and the spectators applauded
these furious youths making free use of their nails and
their teeth. What detestable people! and what name
should we give to such virtues!

The education of the women presented anomalies no
less shocking, and our reason refuses to admit the pretended moral efficacy of the system adopted in regard to
them. An intelligent critic has justly said that they were
considered at Sparta rather as females than as companions of man. They were esteemed only according to the

strength of their bodies and the vigor of their constitution. They were early put to practice in handling the javelin and running almost nude in the arena, in the presence of all the citizens and even of young men of their own age. Shall I speak of the infamous custom of substituting paramours for husbands, in a multitude of circumstances legally provided for? Must we recall the incestuous unions and the breeding combinations which led these gross people to promiscuity of the sexes, under pretext of improving the race and strengthening the offspring? I am not surprised that time destroyed the monuments of Sparta, if ever Sparta had monuments. We read in Plutarch that the houses of the Lacedæmonians were very small and constructed without art. The doors were wrought with no other tool than the saw, and the floors with only the axe; trunks of trees scarcely stripped of their bark served for beams;—habitations quite worthy of such a people, and which seem to belong rather to nomad tribes than to a civilized nation. Had they not a horror of fine language, of the sciences, which they called vices, and of everything which constitutes the glory or the charm of life? Even in their theatres, they preferred boxers to poets : that tells all.

It is not surprising that the industrial arts have little place in their history. What art was necessary for people who lived on black broth, who used badly-hewn blocks of wood for seats, who generally walked with head and feet bare! The few artisans that were seen in Sparta, pursued, as in Egypt, the trade of their fathers, and most of the inhabitants followed none. These men, so different from the Athenians in everything else, resembled them completely in their horror of manual labor. Labor was to them a symbol of slavery,—a deplorable error which ruined ancient civilization, and which to-day keeps in a state bordering on decay, our young republics of South America. Woe to the nations that commit to slaves the care of providing for their needs, and to such hands en-

trust national production! Between the helots of Sparta
and the negroes of the European colonies, where is the
difference? and what difference, moreover, is there between the Spartans driving out the helots and the
Spaniards driving away the Indians! The end of each of
these dominations was the same, for brute force can
indeed conquer, but it belongs only to true liberty to
conserve and to civilize.

Still, the institutions of Sparta have excited to the
highest degree the admiration of the ancients and the
moderns. Aristotle, Plato, and Xenophon have left us
vivid and animated pictures of them. But ought not
these representations to be considered as works of imagination, rather than as serious scientific treatises? Should
we not see in them a philosophical thesis, instead of economic doctrine? I cannot quite bring myself to that
opinion. The institutions of Greece did not spring from
chance; most of them were the result of the study of
many celebrated men, who prosecuted their development
with a quite systematic inflexibility of logic. One might
say that they wished to see the end of their experiments,
as with us the executive power insists on the enforcement
of the laws which its initiative has caused to be enacted.
When Plato wrote the dialogues which compose his *Treatise on the Republic,* he proved quite clearly that political
economy, such as we understand it to-day, was not foreign
to his most enlightened contemporaries. He pointed out
the advantages of division of labor with a lucidity so perfect that it seems to us to take from Adam Smith the
merit of that discovery, if not the priority of the demonstration. We will quote just here the most curious passages of that dialogue, so natural, so true, and so admirable for precision and simplicity.*

"What gives rise to society, is our powerlessness to
provide for our own needs, and the desires we have for a
great number of things. Thus, necessity having led one

* Republic of Plato, Book II.

man to unite with another, society is formed to the end of
mutual assistance."—" Yes ; but one gives another what
he has, to receive what he has not, only because he thinks
it for his advantage to do so."—" Certainly."—" Let us.
then build a city in thought. Our necessities will form
it. Is not the first and greatest of all, food ? "—" Yes."
—" The second need is shelter, the third, clothing."—
" Undoubtedly."—" How will our city meet these wants?
Will it not be necessary to that end, that one be a farmer,.
another, an architect, another a weaver ? Shall we add a
shoemaker or some similar workman ? "—" Certainly "—
" Every city is then composed of many persons ; but is it
necessary that each one of the inhabitants labor for all
the others ; that the farmer, for example, raise food for
four and take four times as much time and trouble, or
would it not be better that, without concerning himself
with the others, he should employ the fourth part of the
time in preparing his own food, and the three other parts
in building himself a house, making his clothes and his
shoes ? "—" It seems to me that the first way would be
more convenient for him. In fact, we are not all born
with the same talents, and every one manifests particular
inclinations. Things would then go better, if every man
confined himself to one trade, because the task is better
and more easily accomplished when it is adapted to the
tastes of the individual and he is free from every other
care."

Surely the advantages of division of labor have never
been more clearly defined than in this remarkable passage. We shall soon see how ingeniously the author
will be led to a definition of money. " Just see," re-
sumes one of the interlocutors of Plato, " the carpenters,
the blacksmiths and the other workmen, who are going
to enter our little city to increase it. It will be almost impossible, henceforth, to find a place from which
it can draw everything necessary to its subsistence."—
" The city will need people to go out in the vicinity to

seek for what it lacks."—" But these persons will return without having received anything, if they do not carry to the neighbors something to satisfy their wants."— " Assuredly, and people must be found who will take upon themselves the charge of importing and exporting commodities. These are called traders."—" Yes, and besides, if the trade is carried on by sea, another set of people will be needed for navigation purposes."—" But, in the city, how will our citizens distribute the results of their labor?"—" It is evident that it will be by sale and purchase."—" Then we need a market, too, and a money, symbol of the contract."

Might not one think, in reading these lines so simple and so terse, that he was looking over one of our best treatises on political economy? It would, in fact, be difficult to explain more clearly the natural progress of industrial development in a city at its commencement. In proportion as that imaginary city increases in wealth, its situation becomes complicated: the distribution of its riches takes place unequally, and often raises many questions not easy to resolve. " What ruins artisans?" says Adimantus. And Sokrates replies: " Opulence and poverty."—" How is that?"—" In this way. Will the potter who has become rich trouble himself much about his trade?"—" No."—" He will daily become more idle and negligent?"—" Doubtless."—" And consequently a worse potter?"—" Yes."—" On the other hand, if poverty takes from him the means of providing himself with tools and with everything necessary to his art, his labor will suffer from it; his children and the workmen whom he is training will be less skilful on that account."— " That is true."—" Thus wealth and poverty are equally injurious to the arts and to those who practice them."— " So it appears."—" Then there are two things to which our magistrates will be careful not to give admission into our city, opulence and poverty: opulence, because it engenders effeminacy and idleness; poverty, because it pro-

duces baseness and envy : both because they lead a state
to revolution."

We can but recognize here the perfect competency
of the ancients to examine the most serious questions of political economy. After more than two thousand years, we have not yet obtained the realization
of the utopia of Plato, of that just economic middle
securing to each an equal share of the profits of labor.
We have still rich potters who neglect their art, and poor
workmen to whom the tools must be furnished which
they are not in a condition to procure for themselves.
People have then long been thinking on these terrible
problems of the social state, which revolutions continually touch upon without ever resolving ! Dictatorship,
slavery, liberty, pillage, association, aristocracy, democracy, everything has been exhausted in the attempt : the
enigma remains still inexplicable. Happy our generation, if science some day gives it the key !

After having so ingeniously defined the city and analyzed the division of labor, Plato stops all at once and
advises a common possession of the women and children.
" I propose," he says, " that the wives of our warriors be
common to all ; that no one of them live solely with any
particular one ; that the children be common, and that the
latter should not know their parents, nor the parents their
children." * I quote literally this astonishing passage, to
give an idea of the degree of boldness to which the spirit
of system could lead one of the finest geniuses of antiquity. Community of property, another chimera, was also
considered by Plato as a sovereign remedy for the most
inveterate diseases of society. There would no longer be
troubles, nor disorders, nor insolence, nor servility. Usury
would disappear with avarice and the vices that an immod-
erate love of wealth multiplies among men. No more
lawsuits, hence no more chicanery ; we should all live as
brothers. " We cannot, however," adds Plato, " hope to

---

* *Republic*, Book V.

realize the plan of this perfect republic. As skilful painters delineate in bold outlines models of an ideal beauty,
impossible to find in individuals, so we only attempt to
present a finished type. The more the legislators approach this model, the more suitable will their constitution be to lead men to happiness." Such was the opinion that Plato himself had of his doctrines, a remarkable
mingling of observations full of correctness and of utopias unworthy of attention. One can hardly reconcile,
in fact, the dreams of equality which agitate this philosopher, with his profound contempt for the laboring classes.
" Nature," according to him, " made neither shoemakers
nor blacksmiths; such occupations degrade the people
who engage in them, base mercenaries, nameless wretches,
who are excluded, by their very condition, from political
rights. As to tradesmen, accustomed to lie and deceive,
they will be suffered in the city only as a necessary evil.
The citizen who shall degrade himself by shop-keeping,
will be prosecuted for this offence. If convicted, he will
be condemned to a year's imprisonment. The punishment will be doubled at each repetition of the offence.
This sort of traffic will only be permitted to those among
foreigners who shall be found least corrupt. The magistrate will keep an exact register of their bills of goods and
of their sales. They will be allowed to make only a very
small profit." * Xenophon is not less explicit. He thinks
" the manual arts are infamous and unworthy of a citizen. Most of them deform the body. They oblige one
to sit down under shelter or near the fire. They leave
time neither for the republic nor for one's friends."

It is this doctrine of *men of leisure*, resurrected among
us, which sums up all the political economy of the ancients. M. de Sismondi very sensibly observes † that
they at least always recognized that wealth had no value
save as it contributed to the general happiness, and

---

* Plato. *Treatise on the Laws.* Book XI.
† *Nouveaux Principes d'Economie Politique.* Book I, chap. ii.

that it was on account of not having considered it ab-
stractly that they often had on that subject ideas more
just than ours.   The political economy of the Greeks was
eminently governmental and reglementary.   Their writers
desire the law to concern itself with everything and leave
almost nothing to the individual freedom of the citizens.
The city is to them only a vast association, where every
inhabitant plays an allotted part, or rather a grand machine of which he represents one of the parts.   They
concern themselves exclusively with the masses and neglect the individual—a dangerous abuse, in comparison
with which there is nothing more dangerous except the
contrary abuse, into which in our day the great nations
civilized by industry appear to fall.   And yet we must
not forget that when they speak of the masses at Athens,
they are only talking of that small number of free men who
are supported by hosts of slaves.   In this sense, Mr. Dunoyer was right to say * that the slavery of the useful occupations had been the economic régime of every newly-
established society.   Rousseau claimed that this régime
was indispensable, " because there are unfortunate positions where one can keep his liberty only at the expense
of that of another, and where the citizen cannot be perfectly free unless the slave is entirely a slave. " † This singular doctrine proves how far the finest geniuses will go
astray in blind admiration for the institutions of antiquity :
but we to-day should not err with them.   A more philosophical study of ancient history shows us the Greeks a
prey to civil dissensions, to foreign war, and to the intrigues of public life, in consequence of the lack of employment in which the labor of slaves permitted them to
live.   They excelled in driving chariots in the race-course,
quibbling over grammatical subtilties, and making bad
music ; and, having become rhetoricians after having been
pillagers, they succumbed for lack of courage to defend

* *Nouveau Traité d' Economie Sociale.*   Vol. I, p. 234.
† *Contrat Social.*   Book III.

themselves and lack of money for mercenaries to defend them.

The political economy of Xenophon rests on no different bases from that of Plato. Whenever there is any
attempt to analyze the operations of labor, to go back
to the source of revenue, and to determine the utility of
things, the clearness of that writer is remarkable; but as
soon as there is a question of division of profits, Greek
prejudices resume their sway, and the author falls back
into the politics of Plato and of Aristotle, those faithful
interpreters of contemporary oligarchy. What a pity that
these men, so clever in explaining the essential phenomena of production, did not more judiciously deduce the
consequences of them. Listen to Xenophon in his definitions : " We must understand by wealth only that which
can be useful to us. The lands we cultivate are no longer
wealth, when we lose by their cultivation. Money even
is not wealth, if no use is made of it." J. B. Say has not
given a better definition of productive and unproductive
capital. The Greek author elsewhere utters these remarkable words: *" One has very long arms, when he has
those of an entire people."* He proposes to grant gratuities
to those of the merchants' tribunal who should most
speedily and with most justice terminate cases; but he
seems to us less fortunate when he maintains that a great
abundance of money will not make it lower in value. Besides, the writings of Xenophon, though abounding in
intelligent advice to agriculturists and in considerations
very important to philosophers, cannot give us a complete
idea of the true economic views of the ancients. The
author has confined himself to recommending temperance,
activity and a good distribution of labor. He has carefully traced the spheres of man and woman under the influence of marriage, the advantages of order, of emulation and of rewards. Finally, he has energetically manifested the profound contempt which manual labors inspire
in him. " The people who devote themselves to them,"

he says, " are never elevated to responsible positions, and
it is rightly thus. Most of them being obliged to sit all
day, and some even to experience the continual heat of a
fire, they cannot fail of having the body injured, and it
could hardly be otherwise than that the mind should feel
the effects of it.   Besides, the labor consumes all the
time ; one can do nothing either for his friends or for the
state."

Such is the forced conclusion of all the economic theories of the ancients.   One cannot conceive, while reading
these vehement philippics against the working class, that
the great authors of them deigned to write such fine things
as they did in favor of these very workers whom they
overwhelm at every opportunity with their sarcasms and
contempt.   Agriculture alone, in the eyes of the ancients,
passed for a respectable branch of industry ; for it alone
they reserved their care and their admiration.   Xenophon
consecrates to it the most important part of his *Economics*.
He there treats of the means of forming good farmers, of
becoming acquainted with the properties of the soil, of
the times favorable for work, of seeds, planting, clearing
lands, and of trade in grain ; but so briefly, and in a manner so sentimental, that his book, notwithstanding the excellent data it gives, more resembles an elementary book
of morals than a scientific treatise.   However, one finds
there with interest the usual prejudices of the ancients on
certain important questions of science, notably, in favor
of the precious metals.   " Silver," says Xenophon, " does
not resemble the other productions of the earth.   Let
iron or copper become common, to such a point that works
of these materials sell too cheap, and the workmen are
completely ruined.   The same is true of agriculturists, in
years when wheat, wine, or fruits are very abundant.
With silver, it is quite the contrary.   The more mines
are found and the more they are worked, the more we see
citizens eager to possess them.   *   *   *   In case of war,
silver is also necessary to support the troops and to pay

the allies. It will perhaps be objected that gold is at least as useful as silver. I shall not maintain the contrary. I will simply remark that if gold should become more common than silver, the latter would rise in value, and gold would itself fall." *

Thus, in these governments of Greece, so often quoted as models of patriotism, war was made only with silver, and defenders and allies were found only for such pay. And how could it have been otherwise? The rich class was alone invested with the privilege of the city; they were incessantly occupied with political intrigues and were obliged to confide to mercenaries the honor of protecting the national independence. A day came when the laws of Lyk·irgus and those of Solon had a common destiny. The portions that these legislators thought they had secured to each citizen in the property of the territory, were finally absorbed by a few ambitious men; and, when external dangers suddenly burst upon them, no one would defend a country which had become the property of a few families.

This fatal crisis appears still more inevitable if we read the economic treatises of Aristotle. In truth, these writings belong much more to politics than to political economy; but they explain the economic doctrines of the Greeks so clearly and systematically that they should be considered the most valuable monument of their history. The *Politics* of Aristotle is divided into eight books. In these he examines in succession the elements of the formation of societies, the qualities which distinguish a good citizen, the various forms of government, the causes of revolutions, and the bases on which all good legislation should rest. Nothing is more singular than the reasoning by which this ingenious publicist has sought to justify slavery as an institution of natural law. "It is Nature herself," he says,† "who has created slavery. Animals are

---

* *Means of Increasing the Revenues of Attika*, chap, ix.
† *Politics.* Book iii, chap. i.

divided into males and females. The male is more perfect; he commands. The female is less complete; she
obeys. Now, there are in the human race individuals
as inferior to others as the body is to the soul, or as the
beast is to man; these are beings suitable for labors of
the body alone, and incapable of doing anything more perfect. These individuals are destined by nature to slavery,
because there is nothing better for them than to obey.
* * * Does there then exist, after all, so great a difference between the slave and the beast? Their services
resemble each other; it is by the body alone that they
are useful to us. Let us then conclude from these *principles* that nature creates some men for liberty and others
for slavery; that it is useful and just that the slave should
obey."

After having proclaimed the strange principles on which
the whole structure of his politics rests, Aristotle examines under the name of *speculation* the theory of wealth,
of which he would make a science by itself, and proposes
to call it *chrematistics*. M. de Sismondi has appeared to
attach much importance to the adoption of that exclusive
name, which would tend to nothing less than to limit political economy to the simple elements of the production
of wealth. But the efforts of the learned professor of
Geneva have not succeeded in imposing on modern economists that subtilty of the philosopher of Stageira.
There is something for us besides the study of material
production in the science whose history I undertake to
write; all the world agrees in finding in it the means of
ameliorating the fate of the human race; and the book
of Aristotle presents incontestable proof of it. Why
should he have joined to his bold attempts at social organization everything that concerns the science of wealth
if he did not consider these great questions inseparable?
And would that he had been as happy in the former as
he showed himself enlightened in the latter!

Scarcely has he explained wherein consists the wealth

that he calls natural, when he devotes himself to that which he calls artificial. " Every article of property," he says,* " has two uses, both inherent in the article. One is the natural use, the other the artificial use. Thus the natural use of covering for the feet is for aid in walking; its industrial use is to be an object of exchange." Might not one think he was reading the definition of value in use and value in exchange, popularized by Adam Smith, and become in our day the basis of all the treatises on political economy?

Aristotle has set forth not less truly and clearly the advantages of money. After having cast a glance over the different kinds of trade, he explains very well how necessity gave rise to the invention of money. " People agreed," he adds, " to give and receive in transactions a useful material of easy circulation. They adopted for this use iron, silver and other metals. This first symbol of exchange was valued at the beginning only according to its volume and weight; afterwards it was stamped with a mark which denoted the value, in order to dispense with any other verification. After the necessary adoption of money for exchanges, a revolution took place in the manner of speculating; traffic appeared. Its beginning was perhaps quite simple. Soon it found out more clever combinations, in order to derive the greatest possible benefit from the exchanges. Hence it happened that people became accustomed to restrict the art of speculation to money alone; they thought the only function of the speculator was to amass the precious metals, because the definite result of his operations was to procure gold and riches. Nevertheless, is not money an imaginary wealth? Its value is wholly in the law. Where is that which it has from nature? If the opinion which admits it into circulation changes, where is its real value? What necessity of life could it relieve? By the side of a heap of gold, one might lack the most indispensable food. What

---

* *Politics.* Book i, chap. vi.

folly to call riches an abundance in the midst of which one dies of hunger!"

It is impossible to characterize more justly the true properties of money. Elsewhere Aristotle has estimated with the same accuracy the consequences of usury and of a spirit of monopoly. "A Sicilian," he says, "had a sum of money in store. He bought with it all the iron there was at the forges. Soon merchants arrived from different countries, and found iron only with him. He had not raised the price too high; however he doubled his investment, which was fifty talents."

Several modern economists have with some reason been reproached for having included in their estimates of the contributors to public wealth only the material producers, as if the magistrate who dispenses justice or directs the administration did not render to society as many services as the artisans or the agriculturists. Plato himself fell into that error, which is earnestly refuted by Aristotle: "Ah! indeed! Is the city only established for physical wants? Will farmers and shoemakers supply every want? What is the part of man which constitutes his essence? It is the soul rather than the body. Why then should the occupations which provide only for the prime necessities compose a city, rather than the occupation of impartial arbiter of rights, or that of a senator deliberating for the good of the state? Are not these occupations the very soul of the city?" * Thus had Aristotle, long before J. B. Say, reinstated these creators of immaterial products, the classing of whom has passed for a discovery of our time. He had also indicated with admirable precision the causes of the old struggle which has existed between wealth and poverty, from the earliest ages of the world. "Every political society," he said, "is divided into three classes, the rich, the poor, and the comfortable citizens who form the intermediate class. The first are insolent and untrustworthy in great affairs; the second

---

* *Politics.* Book iv. Chap. iv.

become intriguing and knavish in small matters ; hence a thousand injustices, the necessary result of deceit and insolence, which render them equally out of place in a council or in a tribe, and very dangerous in a city. The rich imbibe independence with their mother's milk ; raised in the lap of all enjoyments, they commence at school to despise the voice of authority. The poor, on the con- trary, beset by distress, lose every feeling of dignity. In- capable of commanding, they obey like slaves ; while the rich, who do not know how to obey, command like des- pots. The city is then only an aggregation of masters and slaves ; there are no free men. Jealousy on the one side, contempt on the other ; where shall we find friend- ship and that mutual benevolence which is the soul of society? What a life, with companions regarded as ene- mies ! "

" The middle class, therefore," continues Aristotle, " is the surest basis of a good social organization ; and the city will necessarily have a good government, if this class has the preponderance over the two others combined, or at least over each of them separately. This is the class which, by ranging itself on one side, will keep the balance even and prevent either extreme from ruling. If the government is in the hands of those who have too much or too little, it will be either a fierce demagogy, or, on the other hand, a despotic oligarchy. Now, whichever be the dominant party, the passions of the democracy and the haughtiness of an oligarchy lead straight to tyranny. The middle class is much less exposed to all these excesses. It alone never rises in rebellion : wherever it is in the majority, this restlessness and these violent reactions which agitate governments, are unknown. Great states are less ex- posed to popular uprisings. Why? Because the mid- dle class is numerous in them. But the small cities are often divided into two camps. Again why? Because we find there only poor and rich, that is, *extremes* and *no means.*"

It seems as if these lines were written but yesterday
and thrown out to the readers by one of the thousand
voices of our times.   I have quoted them at some length,
because they give an exact idea of the economic views of
the greatest writers of antiquity.   In pleading with so
much warmth the cause of the middle classes, they did
not allow themselves to wander off in pursuit of a vain
utopia ; they knew what takes place in civil struggles
where social questions are agitated between rich and poor.
" The party which gains the victory, does not remain the
master without opposition.   It takes good care not to
establish a constitution on principles of equal rights.
The conqueror regards the government as the prize of
victory : he gives it the livery of his party." *

The more one reads Aristotle, the more one recognizes that this great writer summed up in all things the
most advanced ideas of the civilization of his time.   For
there were in Greece and at Rome, as in the rest of Europe since the Christian era, epochs and men that
merited better than others the privilege of representing
the character and the thought of several generations.
Thus can we account for the powerful influence of the
great men and great writers of Greece, notwithstanding
the diversity of interests of all the republics which occupied that little territory.   In spite of the numerous changes
which the institutions of these republics experienced in
the various ages of Greece, they rested on principles
nearly alike, but of which slavery always formed the basis.
All that was not Greek was considered as barbarian ;
the priests, the legislative philosophers, the warriors, and
the orators, in turn took their place in power without
shaking the old foundations of Greek civilization, horror
of industrial labor, contempt for trade, and indifference
to everything foreign or servile.   In vain did the great
expeditions of Alexander and the development of their
maritime power facilitate among the various Greek nations

---

* *Politics.*   Book iv. chap. xi.

the establishment of a great oriental empire ; their intestine divisions and the abuse of servitude made them
lose that glorious opportunity, and Greek federalism disappeared before Roman unity, as soon as the latter was
manifested.

CHAPTER IV.

The Greek colonies and their relations with the metropolis.—They contributed to extend over a great part of Europe the ideas whose centre was at Athens and Sparta.—They were founded like ours, by emigrations, but they enjoyed a greater independence.

THE history of ancient Greece presents, like that of modern Europe, the remarkable phenomenon of a confederation of small states keeping in submission immense countries, by the simple ascendency of moral superiority. The map of the Greek colonies resembles a world, when one compares it with that of the Peloponnesus and other metropolitan dependencies of the main-land. The Greeks had in fact colonies in Asia Minor, on the borders of the Black Sea, in Cyprus, Krete, Sicily, Gaul, Spain and Africa. They counted their cities in these places by hundreds, and we cannot doubt that most of these cities enjoyed the greatest opulence, in the sense even that we to-day attach to this word. Originally, they were the result of conquest ; their inhabitants were seized as slaves, and their lands as public property. Later, the conquered nations were received on capitulation ; the Greeks sent to them the excess of their famishing and turbulent population, and a genuine union was formed between the natives and the immigrants. So long as the metropolis could keep them obedient by means of its fleets, the dependence was real : but any interruption in the communications was sufficient to bring its supremacy again into question. Thus the defeat at Ægospotami made Athens lose all her *kleruchiæ*.

We cannot, however, doubt that the colonial government of the ancients was, in general, more independent of metropolitan influence than ours. The Greeks had not at their disposal the immense fleets of modern nations, nor the artillery force which acts at a distance, without necessitating disembarkations. Whenever one of their colonies rebelled, they were obliged to transport troops thither at great expense, and these troops had to be very numerous to resist the attack of the enemy. So most of the Greek settlements ended in becoming entirely free from external influence. Work was honored in them, commerce flourishing, and a competency much more general than in the great metropolitan cities. Ephesus, Smyrna, Phocæa and Miletus, rose to an unprecedented degree of prosperity. Miletus alone had four ports and a fleet of more than a hundred vessels. The marvels of Rhodes, the riches of Smyrna, and the boldness of the Phocæan navigators, the founders of Marseilles, are well known. The Asiatic Greeks early brought to a high degree of perfection the dyeing of wools, the exploitation of mines, and the smelting of metals. Their wise men all contributed to the progress of the sciences: philosophy and astronomy are indebted to them for brilliant discoveries; the fine arts, for magnificent monuments. They had also their own constitutions, and they became sufficiently powerful to make conquests. The isle of Krete long maintained its independence by commerce, and only succumbed before Roman domination.

A great part of present Europe, as Southern Italy, Gaul, and Spain, long existed in the condition of Greek colonies. Sicily alone was a veritable empire, and the settlements located in the portion of the present kingdom of Naples*, which is bounded by the two Calabrias, attained such a degree of splendor that they surpassed the glory of the mother country and merited the name of *Magna Grœcia*. All these states traded freely with each other,

---

* Written in 1837. *Trans.*

and with the parent states. But the very wealth which they derived from commerce contributed to their decline, by weakening their warlike tendency and creating in the heart of their cities an unbridled democracy enervated by pleasures, and equally unfitted to maintain a government and to substitute another in its place. See Korinth: what a magnificent situation for commerce! She was seated upon two seas: she opened and closed the Peloponnesus. She had a port to receive the merchandise of Asia; she had another to receive that of Italy; and Italy was the Europe of that time. How many stores! how many vessels! how many monuments! but soon she began to build temples to Venus and to maintain in them thousands of courtesans—a deplorable abuse of civilization and wealth, which made wealth and civilization flee from those fine places! Thus perished all the Greek colonies when they had become nations. They consecrated to luxury and pleasure treasures which they might have employed to consolidate their independence, and to-day we find only under the turf the traces of their former splendor. They did nothing for misfortune and for poverty—no asylums, no help for the ill-favored classes; none of those economies which create capital. They lived from hand to mouth, consuming their capital as well as their income, until the moment, when, drawn into the orbit of the Roman world, they lost their independence and their fortune.

CHAPTER V.

Political economy among the Romans, in the different ages. They are essentially warriors and plunderers under the Republic.—Engineers and administrators under the Empire.—Their contempt for labor.—Immense devastations committed by them.—Fall of Carthage.—First attempt at organization under the emperors.

We distinguish three great epochs, perfectly character-ized, in the history of the eleven centuries which separate the foundation of Rome from the accession of Constan-tine. The first, almost savage, ends at the beginning of the Punic war; the second, wholly warlike, terminates with the battle of Actium; the third comprises the reign of the emperors: it is that of despotism and of adminis-tration. The true political economy of the Romans dates only from the century of Augustus; until then, they were but husbandmen or conquerors; under the empire, they begin finally to become civilized. Then alone the government exercises a universal influence and they become really masters of the world. Notwith-standing these successive modifications in their consti-tution and in their internal policy, the Romans pre-serve, from the first days of their history to the fall of the Empire, an appearance always the same, and tendencies nearly uniform. Placed, at the outset, in the midst of independent states, such as the Æqui, the Volsci, the Sabines, and the Samnites, they become con-querors so as not to be conquered. As conquerors, they preserve their military habits, the principal characteristic of which is contempt for labor. Labor, in their eyes and from the earliest times, is an affair of prisoners and slaves. So one of their historians can justly say that at this time their only trade is to crush grain and men. Their religion is on a level with their morals, and they raise temples to Jupiter the Plunderer, *Jovi prædatori.* The fine arts, manufactures, and commerce, are still unknown to them. At the time of the first Punic war, they know not what to do with the fine paintings which they find in the city of Tarentum. At Korinth, their soldiers play dice on the most magnificent pictures of the greatest masters, and one of their generals ventures seriously to say to the captain of a ship charged with transporting to Rome the master-pieces of Greece: " If you lose any, you shall replace them."

At this period, their language even did not exist. It was just what the execrable language of notaries, advo-cates and bailiffs is to ours. The change of years was marked by a nail solemnly planted every year in the wall of the temple of Jupiter, at the beginning of the month of September. There were only three divisions of the day ; a money of coarse copper sufficed for all wants ; and every industrial occupation, as in the Greek repub-lics, was in the hands of slaves. Their first poets be-longed to that despised caste : Ennius, Plautus, Terence, and many other great writers were from it. The Romans of that time had a special horror of navigation, and their ignorance of that art caused them disastrous mistakes. They therefore made the destruction of the vessels the first condition of their treaties with the conquered ; at Carthage they burned more than five hundred. This aversion to a marine degenerated with them into a real monomania, and when they became masters of the sea, it was not by their vessels, but by the absence of enemy's vessels. Had it not been for the pirates, who defied them with impunity in the Mediterranean, even to blockading their ports and taking away their public functionaries, they would have gladly renounced navigation, which was in fact only maintained by the aid of foreign crews, Greek, Egyptian or Sicilian. Augustus himself, who gained the naval battle of Actium, had a distressing fear of the water.

It is at the time of their first struggles with Carthage that the edicts proscribing commerce appear. "The commercial nations must work for us," say they; "our business is to conquer them and levy contributions on them. Let us then continue war, which has rendered us their masters, rather than give ourselves to commerce, which has made them our slaves." Cicero himself, notwithstanding the great superiority of his mind, shared, at a most advanced period of the republic, the aristocratic prejudices of his fellow citizens. "What worthy of honor can come from a shop?" he naïvely exclaimed: "commerce is a sordid affair, when it is of little consequence, for the small traders cannot gain without lying; it is a business only tolerable at best, when carried on on a large scale and in order to supply the country with provisions." * With such doctrines on commerce, it is not astonishing that the Romans sought, in conquest and pillage, resources which they thought it unworthy of them to seek through labor. Their first riches began with plunder, and their history for several centuries resembles that of a nation of freebooters. We find in their writers only recitals of robberies and devastations: now, it is the sacking of Syracuse, then that of Tarentum, of Syria, of the cities of Numidia, then at length the triumph of Paulus Æmilius, whose triumphal car is followed by one hundred and fifty wagons full of gold and silver. Manlius strips Asia Minor; Sempronius, Lusitania; Flaccus, Spain. Seventy cities of Epirus are sacked and destroyed, a hundred and fifty thousand inhabitants are reduced to slavery: the ruin of Carthage alone produces 500,000,000 in our francs, (nearly $100,000,000). It was a fine day for Rome when she despoiled that rival, whose temples were lined with

---

* Cicero, *Treatise on Obligations*, Book i, Sec. 42.

sheets of gold, the product of the mines of Spain and of the immense trade of the Mediterranean!

It has been often asked what would have become of civilization, if Carthage had triumphed over Rome and if the commercial spirit of the great African city had won the day over the warlike policy of her implacable enemy. Suffice it to say that Carthage was at the same time an industrial and a commercial city, and that she supplied all the ports of the Mediterranean with her merchandise and her raw materials. Navigation was there carried to a high degree of perfection, if we may judge by the *Periplus of Hanno*, which is one of the finest monuments of that science in ancient times. We must, then, forever regret that a power which contained all the germs of a peaceful civilization should have fallen before a people exclusively warlike. The immense capital destroyed in that catastrophe would have supported works of great benefit to humanity, and it went to Rome to become lost in the coffers of patricians and give birth there to the most infamous excesses of usury which have sullied the history of any nation. Rome seems from that time to have become a prey to a fever of speculation and agiotage ; we hear only of citizens prosecuted for debts, of the building of castles, of unfortunate ones dispossessed of their property. Brutus and Cassius, Antony, Sylla, and even the great Pompey become lenders of money on short time at exorbitant rates, and do not blush to take off beforehand forty-eight and even seventy per cent. interest. Verres succeeds in exhausting Sicily ; and Sallust constructs fabulous gardens with the fruits of his plunder in Numidia. Cicero, governor of Cilicia, believes himself a benefactor of the province, for having lowered the interest to twelve per cent and a commission in case of a delay or renewal. Finally, Juvenal can exclaim, later: " *We are devouring the people to the very bones*," after Sallust had said that his contemporaries " troubled money " in every way.*

---

* " Pecuniam omnibus modis vexant."

These are the men whom we admire and this the civilization given us for a model, from our most tender infancy! Behold the political economy of the Roman people, until the first years of the empire! *

---

* The economic history of ancient Italy presents a most remarkable fact, which has only been brought into full relief by recent writers, notably by Dureau de la Malle, in his *Économie Politique des Romains*. It is the depopulation of Italy caused by the disappearance of small estates and the concentration of the lands in the hands of a small number of families, who finally possessed all the peninsula. Before the Punic wars, Italy was covered with a close population of hard working peasants who themselves cultivated their little capital in land, and from whom those Roman armies were recruited which conquered the West. In the time of the Gracchi, this vigorous population had sensibly diminished, and the end to which above all the reformers of the democratic party tended, was to reëstablish it by a division of the lands of the state. But this end was not attained. On the débris of small proprietorship were formed immense domains (latifundia) : cultivation on a small scale was superseded by exploitation on a large scale by means of slaves ; the fields of grain were converted into pasturage , the same land which had supported from 100 to 150 families of free peasants, was cultivated by about fifty slaves for whom there existed no marriage and consequently no posterity. Under these circumstances, the depopulation was necessarily rapid, and it was easy to comprehend the causes. Pliny said : *Latifundia perdidere Italiam.* But what was more difficult to understand, was the economic reason of that absorption of small proprietorships by great ones, of that impoverishment of the cultivator in the midst of the increasing wealth of the country.—*Fr. Ed.*

On this subject, see Mommsen's *Römische Geschichte*, 2d edit., Berlin, 1856, vol. i. p. 814 et seq.

Mommsen attributes this state of things in part to the bad habits and disinclination to labor which nearly always follow long wars, but chiefly to the bad policy of Rome in monopolizing the trade in grain of her dependencies, thus making it impossible for the Italian peasants to deliver grain in market at the prices that ruled at Rome. So their lands were by degrees sacrificed to the wealthier land owners.—*Trans.*

CHAPTER VI.

The political economy of the Romans from the beginning of the Empire. —Abuses of the conquests.—Contempt for commerce.—Condition of the laboring classes.—Insolent aristocracy.—Famished populace.—People take refuge in celibacy.—Public and private self-interest.—Absence of manufactures.—Utility sacrificed to grandeur.

IN the midst of the chaos of wars and conquests by which Rome was agitated until the early days of the empire, one discerns some attempts at social renovation, and sees production become established on regular bases. The pacificatory genius of Augustus undertook that great task, which was never completely abandoned by his successors. A general census of the population and of the resources of the empire, a veritable *domesday book*, which unfortunately has not come down to us, furnished him the essential elements of the reforms he contemplated. Statistics came in, in aid of administration. People could know the number of landed proprietors, that of the soldiers, the slaves, and the freedmen.

The imposts were levied with more order, discernment, and impartiality. The right of succession was fixed at the twentieth; a general tax of one per cent on consumption reached all commodities. Custom duties, that poison so mild and at the same time so fatal to modern industry, were established on a most rigorous footing, not for the sake of protection, but as means of revenue; raw products were subject to them as well as merchandise. The duties were paid back in case of reëxportation for lack of sale; but the custom-house officers, it must be confessed, were no more tolerant than ours. They were authorized to open packages and even to unseal letters, as Terence expressly affirms. The omission of the affidavit within proper time led to confiscation,* or, if it was recognized as involuntary, the payment of double duty. Nero wished at one time to suppress that impost in order to render himself popular; but the senate represented to him that if that were yielded, the people would soon attack all the others; and the emperor surrendered to this gloomy consideration. History has preserved for us one of these tariffs, and the knowledge that I have obtained of it permits no doubt that in point of absurdity our custom-houses are not much worse than those of the ancients.†

Later, when the empire was divided, under Diocletian, into four great prefectures, which embraced several kingdoms, a remarkable unity was established in all the branches of Roman administration. The laws were the same from the Tiber to the Danube, from Spain to the Black Sea. Thirty legions, forming an effective force of about 400,000 men, kept to their duty a great number of people, differing in language, habits, and interests. Magnificent roads connected these vast camps, which were situated on river banks, at mountain passes, or on the borders of countries still unconquered. Post-relays, kept up with extreme care, took the orders of the central government to all parts of the empire. Immense aqueducts supplied with water opulent cities, the number of which seems to us to-day fabulous. Notwithstanding the prodigies of which our century has been witness, this Roman grandeur still astonishes and overwhelms us; the greatest monarchies of modern Europe pale before the hundred millions of subjects of the emperor Claudius. But people have until now contented themselves with admir-

---

* " Quod quid professus non est, perdat."

† Pepper, cinnamon, myrrh, ginger, some perfumes, skins of animals, ivory, diamonds and other articles of luxury, figure in this document; but our tariffs have spared nothing, not even matches.

ing the imposing height of the imperial colossus, without measuring it, without tracing out the prime causes of its elevation, and without seeking the explanation of that astonishing existence. By what means could supplies be obtained for the consumption of those myriads of men? From what budget were the necessary resources drawn to feed and clothe that world so different from ours? Were there any paupers? Did people work at great enterprises, in workshops, or as during the republic, around the domestic hearth? What was the lot of the agriculturist and of the mechanic? How was trade carried on? Political economy awaits the solution of these grave questions, whose importance the Roman writers seem not to have suspected.

The slave appears always as a social element in the constitution of the state. It is no longer Greek slavery, nor even that of the middle period of the republic, which had the character of a simple domesticity; the empire has become so great that the enormous amount of labor indispensable for the maintenance of so considerable a population can no longer be demanded of the slaves alone. The people must themselves put their hands to the work; and in fact, Rome was full of manufactories * where paid workmen shared with slaves consigned to the rudest tasks, the fatigues, though not the profits, of manufacture. The most opulent senators carried on these works by means of capital and slaves, the latter of which they possessed by thousands. New products, unknown fruits and useful plants, such as flax and lucerne, were daily naturalized.

But how many lands there were abandoned and fallen to waste! How many magnificent domains transformed into sterile parks, while husbandmen were dying of hunger! Pliny the Elder deplored this abuse, which we

---

* We must not understand this word in the acceptation generally given it to-day. The Romans had, in fact, no manufactories like those of our day, but vast establishments where they made their slaves work under the direction of free overseers.

find again described with the same energy in the writings of Columella. People by degrees deserted the industrial occupations to devote themselves to callings which were becoming fashionable, and there was a time when dramatic performers, gladiators, astrologers and cooks were the men most in request. The people soon adopted the habits of the great; they must have perfumes like the patricians; and the Emperor Adrian, on a day of public entertainment, had them openly distributed to all the citizens. Ivory, amber and incense became articles of prime necessity, and it was necessary to import them at the cost of an enormous sum of money, for the Roman people had no products to give in exchange.

Here the principal cause of the fall of the empire, and one of the deepest plague-spots of its political economy, begins to manifest itself. The Romans were especially inclined to consume without producing, and that error brought about the permanent exportation of the greater part of the money that they had taken from conquered nations. The monumental constructions with which they covered Europe, absorbed also notable quantities of it ; and these immense amounts of capital passed through their hands without leaving either trace or profits. They thought themselves the pensioners of the whole world, and it never occurred to them that this revenue so easy to be consumed would finally no longer be reproduced. They used to take a siesta after their repast, in galleries adorned with flowers, where their clients were in the habit of coming early in the morning (*officia antelucana*) to pay their respects, after being announced by slave *nomenclators* who were the ushers of these almost royal dwellings. The patrician families became organized by degrees into a powerful aristocracy whose members had themselves addressed as "Your Sincerity," "Your Gravity," "Your Excellency," and "Your Highness," which has become with us, "Your Most Serene Highness." Their chariots, profusely ornamented with decorations of chased silver, went through the streets with horses at full speed, followed by a horde of slaves burning perfumes. The people, in their turn, desired their share in the perpetual gayeties to which the lords of the time abandoned themselves; distributions were therefore made to them of bread, wine, oil, and even baths. The theatres were entered at day-break; the most eager sometimes passed the night in them.

In this general disorder of manners and customs, which extended back to the latter days of the republic, there arose at Rome and throughout the whole empire, a virtual conspiracy against marriage. Everybody took refuge in celibacy as an asylum inaccessible to the cares and burdens of a family; and more than one emperor, after the time of Augustus, saw himself obliged to proceed by edicts against that mania, which in the times in which we live is reappearing from other causes. A censor seriously invited the citizens to marriage as to a patriotic obligation, and the state seized upon inheritances falling to recalcitrant celibates. All the Romans were attacked by an invincible repugnance to the spirit of order and enterprise, in regard to everything pertaining to forethought and economy. The proletary' workmen found in the slave workmen a competition the more formidable as these slaves were supported at the expense of their masters, and consequently in a condition to injure wage-paid workmen. Besides, the number of indigent was considerable; they lived heaped together in narrow and fetid dwellings, a prey to the most shocking excesses, and to the most cruel privations. Their clothing, generally of some woolen material, and rarely renewed, would have soon propagated among them deadly epidemics, if the use of the baths,* universal at Rome, had not prevented any such attack. Public beneficence, unknown in those times of despotism and slavery, had not yet organized asylums for poverty and disease, and Voltaire has truly said:

---

* One took a bath for two farthings : "*quadrante lavari*," a poet has said.

"When a poor devil fell sick at Rome without having the means to be taken care of, what became of him? He died."

So in the midst of the magnificence of the Roman power, we perceive only a confused mass of proletaries, enslaved, free, domestic and artisan, who work to furnish supplies for the unproductive consumption of the great owners of capital and of lands. The liberal arts, so glorious and so noble, are abandoned to servile hands; medicine even is practiced only by slaves. Commerce remains in infancy, unless we call the baneful operation of changing the gold of the conquered countries for the merchandise brought from them, commerce. No Roman city is mentioned as celebrated for any especial manufacture, like our great industrial cities, Birmingham, Lyons or Manchester. No port of the empire can be compared with that of Marseilles, Liverpool or New York.* And yet the great cities are numerous all over the surface of the Roman world, and there is something in their incredible opulence which always overwhelms us; but this opulence does not at all resemble that of our contemporary states, where the most modest private citizens have at their disposal more enjoyments than the privileged individuals under the empire. All Roman grandeur was external and theatrical; monuments were multiplied through ostentation, rarely with a view to utility. By the side of these magnificent monuments, the people inhabited dwellings unworthy of the nation's splendor, and whose badly lighted apartments were nevertheless exposed to the inclemency of the seasons. We should judge very erroneously of the alimentary regimen of the masses, if we only considered the elegance of the utensils which they commonly employed for domestic purposes. The graceful forms of these excite our admiration, and seem to have been suitable only for a rich or artistic people: but these

* Cicero said: "Nolo eundem populum imperatorem esse terrarum et portitorem."

articles were very far from answering all the purposes
of similar utensils in modern times.   The Romans knew
of neither paper nor pens; they wrote in capital letters
on leaves of papyrus or on parchment, with styles of
iron or wood.   Their seats were elegant, but very hard ;
and their chariots, placed on the axles, without springs
or braces, were scarcely more comfortable than our carts.
The only things which we can unreservedly admire
among the productions of their genius are the aqueducts and the great public roads ; and besides there is
reason for astonishment that constructions so gigantic
should have been established only in a purely military
interest and for the embellishment of a few cities.

CHAPTER VII.

Importance of means of communication among the Romans.—Services their great roads might have rendered to civilization and commerce.—Sketch of the principal Roman laws in matters of public economy.—General view of their commerce.

THE great roads of the Roman empire surpassed in grandeur and solidity the most magnificent constructions of this kind that have been executed from time immemorial; their ruins, which we still admire under the grass which covers them, do not permit us to question the importance that was attached to perfecting these mighty elements of power and civilization. And yet these great roads do not seem to have rendered to civilization all the services which it derives from them to-day: they did not become to Rome the source of great commercial prosperity: they rarely prevented poverty and its consequent evils. The Romans saw in them only the means of transporting their armies rapidly from the centre to the frontier,—in a word, only an instrument of conquest and not of industry. Never in any country in the world were more treasures consecrated to that important work, and never did any people gather less profit from such great sacrifices.*

The reason of this fact is very simple. The only occupation of the Romans was agriculture, the products of which were generally consumed on the spot, or within a very narrow circle from the centres of production. The great supplies of the capital city usually came by sea,

---

* " *Opera magna potiùs quàm necessaria,*" said Suetonius.

which was the only way by which the grain of Sicily and of Egypt, those two granaries of the empire, arrived. We can then explain the magnificence of the Roman ways only as a necessary consequence of the military system of this anti-industrial and anti-commercial people. They made their soldiers, their administrators, and their subjects, contribute to them with equal zeal. The supervision of the roads was an imposing magistracy with which the greatest citizens appear to have been honored. No tax seemed too high when the maintenance of the roads was in question; and the severity of the government was so great in that regard, that more than once legions revolted in consequence of the excessive labors to which they were condemned in the care of them. Whatever were the vicissitudes of the empire, the maintenance of the roads was never abandoned: the worst rulers watched over them with the same solicitude as the most just: Nero and Caligula constructed almost as many as Trajan and Adrian.* The labor on them was either by corvées or by contributions, each person working or contributing according to the importance of his property bordering on the road, estimated by referees and taxed accordingly. The communications were divided into two great classes, the royal or military roads, and the roads for the accommodation of a parish or community.† The former were maintained by the state, and the latter by the market towns or villages.

The popular sympathies were always with the rulers, the magistrates, and even the private citizens, who devoted themselves to this difficult task. Crowns, medals, and triumphal arches were lavished upon them. History is therefore full of the extraordinary efforts made to merit

---

* See Bergier, *Histoire des grands chemins de l' Empire Romain*, Book i, Chap. 16.

† Viarum omnium non est una et eadem conditio. Nam sunt viæ publicæ regales, quæ publice muniuntur: sunt et vicinales viæ quæ de publicis divertunt in agros; hæ muniuntur per pagos.—Siculus Flaccus, *De Conditionibus Agrorum.*

these distinguished proofs of gratitude from the Roman people. In the time of Tiberius, one could travel over all Italy, Gaul, and a part of Spain, with unheard of rapidity, and Pliny relates that this ruler made, on a journey to Holland, more than a hundred leagues in twenty-four hours. The nature of this work forbids us to give here the well-known details of the mode of construction of the imperial roads; but we must acknowledge that in this kind of labor we are much inferior to the ancients; and although their roads did not have great influence over the destinies of commerce, we can but wonder at their lasting more than a thousand years, while ours, more necessary, will with difficulty keep for a few years intact. Nothing was forgotten there; the pedestrians had their foot-paths, and the horsemen their resting stones for mounting and alighting. The monuments to the dead usually arose in their vicinity, as if to obtain the regard of the living. The Appian way is the most admirable master-piece of this kind which has ever come from the hand of man.

It would seem, then, as if the Romans ought to have derived immense advantages from the fine system of roads with which they had covered the empire as with a vast network. But these roads more frequently saw the chariots of warriors roll over them than the peaceful conveyances of commerce and the industrial arts; they contributed in no manner to the rise or fall of profits and wages, because free labor did not yet exist, and everything was established, as we have said, for grandeur rather than for utility. The great roads of the empire had no other end than to facilitate the transportation of soldiers and of tributes.* The movement of specie which continually took place from all parts of Gaul towards the city of Lyons on the account of the public treasury was immense, but there was no commercial circulation in the sense that we attach to the phrase. Strange to say, the

---

* " *Ut omnia tributa velociter et tuto transmitterentur,*" said Procope.

invention of bills of exchange has furnished us a substi‚
tute for the principal use of the great roads of the
Romans; and the especial service for which they seem to
have been made is exactly that which can best be dis-
pensed with to-day. Thus the magnificent works of
Roman administration exercised no influence over general production, because they participated in the exclusively military character of the nation and the general
spirit of its institutions.

All the Roman legislation, from the great days of the
republic to the fall of the empire, is only the faithful reproduction of the incurable prejudices of the people
against labor and the industrial arts. A rapid glance will
suffice to give an idea of it. In the beginning of their
power, they brought forward a multitude of agrarian
laws,* all inspired by a vain desire for division of the
lands and equality of fortunes. The *Terentian* Law provided that five bushels of grain a month should be distributed to every needy citizen; the *Sempronian* law
created a *maximum* for the price of the grain which the
state should sell them; the *Claudian* law decreed a gratuitous distribution of it. Another law fixed the expense
of the meals; the *Caninian* law forbade any one to free
more than a certain number of slaves. At the same time
that they were thus increasing the number of the indigent
by inconsiderate largesses, veritable premiums were accorded to fecundity; every man who was the father of
three children, enjoyed a multitude of privileges, of which
the principal consisted in a triple gratuity of wheat. In
other circumstances, the law authorized debtors to become free by paying simply a quarter of their debts.

While the spirit of independence and enterprise was
paralyzed by this legislation, which protected idleness, all
classes of citizens were kept in the strictest subordination,
commencing at the domestic hearth, where the father of

---

* Leges Cassia, Licinia, Flaminia, Sempronia, Cornelia, Servilia, Flavia,
Julia, etc.

the family reigned as absolute master, armed with the right of life and death over his children. The wife, degraded to tutelage, was only the servant of her husband. Outside of the family, every freed man recognized a patron, every soldier a superior. Military organization rested upon the whole city, like an iron yoke from which no one dared to obtain release. No citizen could leave his caste, even to go below it, and industrial occupations were forbidden as a low and sordid thing, to those who had not been condemned to them by birth. Augustus pronounced the penalty of death against the senator Ovinius for having stooped to direct a manufactory; and this decree, to us so extraordinary, seemed to the Romans perfectly natural. Who cannot see that from that time every industrial occupation was impossible at Rome, since intelligence was excluded and only machines tolerated? And what machines were these unhappy slaves, brutalized by blows, by the debauchery of their masters, and especially by the absence of any kind of wages! In the country, the consequences were the same: no farmers, no instructed cultivators. The agriculture resembled that of our slave colonies, with this difference, that the soil of the tropics compensates by its fertility for a deficiency in the labor of man, while the Roman fields offered no such compensation. Competition and personal interest, those great motives, did not act upon minds preoccupied with ideas of war and pleasures. There might constantly be seen hurrying to Rome myriads of adventurers, intriguers, and vagrants, attracted by the distribution of food and by the spectacles of every kind which the emperors lavished on the populace in order to obtain from them a few plaudits.* The outskirts of Rome became cities, and the government had not a few difficulties to conquer to supply food to this innumerable crowd of unproductive consumers.

Notwithstanding the infinite precautions taken to avoid

---

* Mengotti, *Del commercio de' Romani.*

it, famine at times made sad ravages in the capital and
the provinces.   In vain the fleet, loaded with provisions,
bore the name of the *sacred fleet* ; a gale of wind sometimes prevented its arrival and put in peril the imperial
security.   The art of governing was soon no longer anything but providing for the daily needs of an idle and
fickle populace ; and the least occasion gave rise to num-
berless abuses, which, by frequent repetition, grew into the
force of law.   The death of a mistress of the ruler, the
birth of a successor, a bloody war, an innocent triumph,
equally necessitated copious distributions.   The Roman
emperors kept their crowns at this price, and maintained
their authority only by paying scrupulously the poor-tax
to their hungry subjects.   " These dogs," said one of the
Cæsars, "cease to bark only when they have a full stomach."   We can reckon by the number of famines that of
the improvements brought about in the affairs of commerce
and navigation.   A first famine under Augustus is followed by the establishment of a fleet and of public storehouses
for the sale of grain ; a second famine under Tiberius gives
rise to the system of bounties on the importation of
grain.   A third under Claudius decides the ruler to
have the port at Ostia repaired ; a fourth under Nero procures for the grain merchants medals and an exemption
from duties ; another under Antoninus Pius causes the
port of Terracina and the light-house of the jetty-head at
Gaëta to be repaired.   During the reign of Marcus Aure-
lius there is another famine, followed by laying in a seven
years' supply of provisions ; finally, during the administration of Commodus, catastrophes of the same kind become fatal to the grain merchants, who are prosecuted
and punished as monopolists.   This is all they knew how
to do at Rome for commerce—I might almost say for the
only commerce in good repute, that for means of subsistence.   Nowhere do we find a single trace of regular measures ; people live from hand to mouth, without dreaming
of the resources that might easily have been developed in

the heart of the empire, and they give scarcely any attention to the other branches of production.

Thus, wool,—almost the only raw material of all the
cloths used at Rome, from the clothing of the senators to
that of the lowest soldiers—wool, from which they made
sheets, curtains, carpets, furniture of every kind, was
never the object of any system of encouragement on the
part of the emperors.   Never did a Roman statesman
descend to industrial details which would lead us to suppose that he comprehended the importance of these great
questions.   Every country furnished its tribute : Arabia
its perfumes ; Africa its cereals ; Spain wax and honey ;
Gaul its wines, oils and metals ; Greece artistic and fancy
articles ; and the shores of the Black Sea, leather and
skins. Rome consumed, and paid with the gold from the
imposts. When the latter did not correspond to the previsions of the imperial budget, a new tax was levied on
manufactures.   Alexander Severus did this several times.
In proportion as the emperors surrounded themselves
with lawyers and jurists, their disposition toward the laboring classes became daily more threatening. Compilers
of laws suggested to them shameful expedients which
they justified by sophisms ; it was a public prosecutor
who taught them how to debase the coin.   Constantine,
their most worthy pupil, likened salesmen in shops to
women of the town, and pursued with his dreadful anathemas the men who had the honor to earn their living by
the sweat of their brows.

The manner in which imposts were levied testifies no
less to the strictness of the Romans in matters of finance.
Clouds of publicans were posted at the entrances to the
ports, at the mouths of rivers, at the exits from the valleys, and there they mercilessly taxed the merchandise.
They also often had, in addition to their fees as collectors, the profits of the monopoly of certain articles of consumption.   There was no legal limit to the sum total of
the taxes, which had become so elastic in the hands of

these functionaries, that the cultivator could never know exactly upon what part of his products he had the right to count. Nero himself had more than once a feeble desire to repress these abuses which caused the fortune of his favorites, but he encountered difficulties before which his absolute power was obliged to recoil. It is well known how far the exactions of the proconsuls extended even as early as the time of Cicero, and the financial operations of Verres fully equalled those of the Turkish pachas.

One single branch of commerce appears to have long withstood the restrictions of every kind which the cupidity of the government and its agents placed upon relations with foreigners, namely, the trade in perfumes and spices from India, the consumption of which at Rome surpassed anything we can imagine. Extravagant sums were lavished by mere private citizens on the purchase of these ruinous and useless articles, which kept almost as many ships employed as were engaged in provisioning the capital. Besides the real dangers braved in going to the most distant coasts in search of them, imaginary perils, such as winged dragons and ferocious beasts that it was necessary to conquer to reach the country of pepper and cinnamon, were taken into account. In the apartments of the Romans, one everywhere breathed the fragrance of the most exquisite perfumes: their hair and clothing were permeated with them. The halls of the baths and the places of public assembly offered no less luxury, in this respect, than the residences of the most opulent citizens. One fine day, the emperor Adrian inundated the vestibule of the theatres with a wave of the sweetest oils. The soldiers used to rub their bodies with them, and these were a kind of rations whose distribution the emperors could not with impunity neglect. Diamonds and precious stones, other useless articles, shared with the perfumes the frenzy of the Roman people: in the Augustan age, people made immense collections of them, and Mæcenas prepared a catalogue of his, which has been substantially preserved for us in the writings of Pliny the Naturalist. The use of rings became so general, that the Romans wore them on all the joints of the hand and changed them every day in the week. In such things was sunk an immense amount of capital, a better employment of which would have sufficed to keep the empire from the misfortunes which it afterwards had to undergo. Even Tiberius was alarmed, for in a letter to the senate* he deplored the exportation of money, occasioned by the excesses of luxury and vanity. One of his edicts prohibited the employment of gold in plate for the table, and the use of silk for garments. Notwithstanding all these prohibitions, the Romans became daily more and more habituated to the use of the most showy and expensive articles of foreign manufacture. Persian carpets, India muslins, ivory, ebony, tortoise shell, and plumes of rare birds, had finally become to them articles of prime necessity. How much wealth they must have consumed unproductively in the purchase of these articles for display, in exchange for which they had only gold to give! †

One can hardly comprehend, in view of this system of lavish expenditure, luxury, and idleness, how the Romans could have covered the world with the monuments of their architecture and with the magnificent works of their engineers; but we must consider that these astonishing works cost them very little. Only the invention of them was wholly theirs; their execution was the work of conquered peoples. The greater part of these edifices were constructed by means of *corvées*8 and special contributions which were in addition to the ordinary imposts. Captives or slaves formed the working class of their time, and proceeded to their work like flocks of sheep, without murmur or complaint. We shall find this

---

* Tacitus, *Annales*, Book 3. Chap. 53.

† Minima computatione millies centena millia sestertium annis omnibus India et Seres, peninsulaque illa, Arabia, imperio nostro adimunt; tanti nobis deliciae et feminae constant!—Pliny, *Hist. Nat.*, Book 12. Chap. 18.

system again in the *corvée* of the feudal times, when Christian Europe in its turn became covered with monuments inspired by other beliefs, but executed by the same means.

Moreover, the Romans never lacked resources whenever it was necessary to tax themselves to make up for the inadequacy of the treasures furnished by conquest and pillage.* There were three sorts of taxes, the *portorium* or custom duties (a fortieth of the value), which were paid on imports and exports, the collectors of which took the name of *portitores* or collectors of customs; the tithes, *decumae*, including the tenth part of the grain and the fifth of other agricultural produce, was the land-tax; lastly, the tax known under the name of *scriptura*, a sort of octroi on such property of communities as pasturage and public woods. There was for a long time a tax on salt, but it was suppressed at a time which authors have neglected to state. The collecting of all these taxes was publicly let out by the censors to contractors who gave security and who shared with their respondents the chances of loss or gain. A great number of other taxes, of a temporary nature, were established under the emperors; thus, Augustus decreed the impost of a twentieth on inheritances, which still exists among us; Caligula levied on articles of food a tax the collection of which excited the most bitter complaints †; Vespasian invented the urinal tax. A duty of five per cent on all merchandise brought also considerable sums. This was only paid on effects exposed for sale in the public place, and at fairs and markets, or sold at auction; but we can only approxi-

---

* In the year of Rome 586, the annual tributes of the people were remitted, the treasury having been filled by the immense sums which Paulus Æmilius deposited there, after the defeat of Perseus.

† Vectigalia nova atque inaudita, primum per publicanos, deinde, quia lucrum exuberabat, per centuriones, tribunosque prætorianos exercuit nullo rerum aut hominum genere misso, cui non tributi aliquid imponeret.— Suetonius, in Calig. Cap. 40.

mately estimate the importance of these revenues, because of the loss of the famous *Rationarium Imperii*, that valuable collection of statistics of the empire, prepared under Augustus and destroyed under his successors.   M. Guizot,* however, estimates the amount of the taxes at the sum of nine hundred and sixty millions of francs a year.

---

* Notes on his translation of Gibbon.   Vol I. p. 377.

CHAPTER VIII.

Rapid decline of the empire.—Its principal causes.—First appearance of Christianity.—Influence of Asiatic manners at Constantinople.—Modification of civil, religious, industrial, and commercial ideas.

IN the midst of that apparent prosperity, the Roman world contained active germs of decay and dissolution. The great number of foreign peoples which conquest had successively united to the 'empire, by insensibly modifying its habits, was weakening its power. These peoples were not all unresistingly merged into the great unity, and several kept faithfully in memory their former independence. The numerous privileges which the inhabitants of Rome enjoyed were an object of ambition to all men of importance in the conquered provinces, so that people no longer wished to be considered of the empire, but of the city   A radical transformation was thus taking place by degrees, favored by the accession to the throne of that long series of Italian, Spanish, Gallic, or Batavian candidates, thrust into power by murder, intrigue, or military seditions. Then comes the turn of the Barbarians. After the Antonines, we see only Thracians, Pannonians, Dalmatians and Illyrians dispute with each other the empire ; sixty of them perished by violent death in a century and a half. The one who opens that fatal series, Maximin, chosen for his form and his colossal strength, coarse, speaking with difficulty the language of the people he rules, excels in drawing a wagon, splitting trees, reducing

stones to powder, and training wild horses; he fills several cups with his sweat. Thus the reign of intelligence
ends to make way for brute force.

Political economy does not undertake to explain the
long saturnalia of the empire during this period of in-
famy and decrepitude. Who could form a correct idea of
such a movement of decomposition, complicated by
slavery, by invasion, by the mixture of races, of languages, of customs, and of vices—a sort of social chaos
in which science is arrested and imagination goes astray?
What political organization could have resisted the extravagances of monsters like Commodus, Caracalla, and
Heliogabalus? When such beings appear on the earth,
they can figure on it only as elements of dissolution, and
some new light will not be long in coming forth from the
darkness they have made. That light, which shines in
the later horizons of the empire, is Christianity: let us
attempt to study it at its dawn and to explain its great
influence, destined to change the face of the world.
When it began to appear, one could scarcely have foreseen the brilliant career which it was to run, and yet all
things were already concurring to prepare its triumph.
Philosophy was attacking the pagan deities; Greek scep-
ticism, having arrived from the country of Plato, was already making war on the old Roman beliefs, and henceforth augurs could no longer look at one another without
laughing. In vain had each trade taken a god for protector: the sailors, Neptune; the blacksmiths, Vulcan;
the farmers, Ceres; the vinedressers, Bacchus; and the
merchants, Mercury: the gods were already having difficulty in protecting themselves, and were making ready
to give place to other patrons more powerful.

Legions, encamped on the frontiers, and composed of
soldiers levied in the conquered countries, were returning
toward the centre, and auxiliaries were becoming enemies.
Meantime, orators were declaiming in the cities; slaves,
trained by their masters to voluptuousness and excessive

refinement, were becoming weary of the yoke; Lucian, the Voltaire of the time, was ridiculing social distinctions of superiority; stoics, epicureans and academicians were preaching bold doctrines; and all the old edifice of the Romans was falling away. A violent reaction had already warned them, under Mithridates, to mistrust fortune, the day when he caused sixty thousand to be slaughtered; and at another time, Spartacus, that great chief of the slaves, had beaten four of their generals. Who then would henceforth be willing to shed his blood for the old national cause? There was no longer a nation properly so called, but rather a confused assemblage of nations. The empire was composed of cities separated by deserts, forests, or impenetrable swamps; the inhabitants of the villages, *rustica proles*, had by degrees become infiltrated into the cities, where the public spectacles, the distributions, and enjoyments of every kind attracted them continually and enervated them.

It was at the time of this universal decadence that Christianity began to appear in some parts of the empire. The first official information received of it is found in a letter from Pliny the younger, governor of Bithynia.* Immediately the new doctrine spread like lightning, timidly at first, but without any one having time to take note of it. Scarcely had one finished reading what the governors of the provinces were saying, when Tertullian was already boldly crying out: "We are only of yesterday, and we are filling your cities, your colonies, the army, the palace, the senate, the forum; we leave you only your temples." In vain bloody persecutions attempt to stifle the new religion at its source; Constantine gives it temples, and its destinies become accomplished.

* The following is a passage from that letter: "The thing has appeared to me worthy of consultation, principally because of the number of the accused; for many persons of every age, both sexes, and of every condition, are put in peril. This superstition has infected not only the cities, but the market towns and the country. * * * They are accustomed to assemble a certain day before sunrise and repeat together, in two choruses, a canticle in honor of Christ as a god."

The historians of that grand epoch have sufficiently re-traced all the circumstances which prepared the way for it; our part is to study the humanitarian results, and to find out by what happy transition Greek and Roman slavery was obliged to give way to respect for labor, to the régime of liberty and equality.

The division of the empire into two vast fragments singularly favored that unprecedented revolution. Constantinople was more suitable than Rome to receive the God of the Christians; a city entirely new, it was marvellously appropriate for a new worship. It was from ingratitude that this worship adopted, in later times, Rome for its cradle; the true cradle of Christianity was at Constantinople. There it was that the Christian religion, having become a state religion, began to be organized on regular bases; there it established itself, radiant, on coming forth from the catacombs of Rome and from the obscure asylums of persecution. By degrees all the high intellects, weary of Roman polytheism, rallied about it, and the priests everywhere took the place of the *curiales*, who were the municipal officers of the time. The laws began to give them privileges which the confidence of the people ratified, and which they everywhere endeavored to justify by their knowledge and ability. There is no study more curious than the transition by means of which that revolution was brought about. Constantine published in the same year two edicts, one of which recommended the observance of Sunday, and the other gave directions for consulting the augurs. At the same time, the first distinctions were made between the spiritual power and the temporal power. On another side, the lawyers invaded the empire with law-texts, substituting thus the influence of the laws for that of the sword, and becoming, perhaps without suspecting it, the most powerful auxiliaries of religion. Dying Rome perished shrouded with monuments; rising Constantinople arose upon heaps of books. Lawyers and priests succeeded

architects and warriors. The Pandects, the Institutes,
the Gospel, henceforth shared the respect of the people
and were of universal influence. An incessant hum of
counsellors' pleas succeeded the shout of battles, and the
single prefect of the prætorium employed seven hundred
and fifty barristers. The patriarchate was no longer
anything but a life dignity ; heredity had been taken
from it. The empire, divided into several *dioceses*, as
large as kingdoms, and governed by *vicars*, saw completed
the work of decentralization which was to favor at the
same time the attacks of the Barbarians and abuses
in the administration of justice and in the processes of
law. The world was going to be a prey to lawyers, who
are threatening it still more seriously at the time when I
am writing. Their fortunes were so rapid, and their exactions so scandalous, that the Theodosian code was
obliged to threaten them with the penalty of death.*
Details on this subject may be found in Ammianus Mar-
cellinus† which might lead one to singular comparisons
with the abuses of our days.

The division of the seat of the empire also brought
about notable changes in the system of assessment. Constantine and his successors preferred a simple and direct
tax to the more complicated system of Roman origin, of
collecting tributes. The collection of that tax was effected by the cities, and formed one of the heaviest burdens
of the *decurions*, members of their municipal senate.
These administrators were responsible to the amount of
their personal property for the return of the tax, and
they were even compelled to take on their own account
lands abandoned by possessors who could not satisfy
the agents of the treasury. On them alone devolved the
disagreeable duties of assessors, which exposed them to
the dissatisfaction and often to the violence of the people.

---

* " Cessent rapaces jam nunc officialium manus ; cessent, inquam ; si
moniti non cessaverint, gladiis præcidentur."   Lib. i. vii, Law i.

† Lib. xxx.

All the lands of the state, the patrimony of the emperor not excepted, were subject to the tax, and every new proprietor had to pay the debts of the previous one. An exact register, revised every fifteen years, allowed the boundaries to be determined with sufficient impartiality, since care was taken to mark on the registers the particular nature of every piece of property, whose value was estimated by the average income for five years. The tax was generally paid in gold money; but a considerable part of it was required in provisions, of every kind—wheat, wines, oils, wood, and forage—which were to be transported at the expense of the tax-payers to the store-houses of the emperor, and which gave rise to fearful contentions. Complaints having become general, the emperors had recourse to other expedients, among which may be classed the invention of licenses, which were required for the carrying on of every industrial art and of commerce. People were even obliged to pay the public functionaries in kind; and Lampridius * tells us that independently of a salary of about 4,000 francs in our money in specie, the governors of the provinces received six jugs of wine, two mules and two horses, two official robes, one simple robe, a bath, a cook, a muleteer, and finally, when they were not married, a concubine: *quod sine his esse non possent,* says the author. When they gave up their office, they were always obliged to return the mules, the horses, the muleteer and the cook. If the emperor was satisfied with their administration, they kept the rest; if not, they were obliged to return fourfold. We see in other writings that the governors of two great provinces received oil for supplying four lamps.

Some Asiatic custom was daily introduced into the financial government and into the practices of the empire. Eunuchs, spies, and officers of domestic service, were multiplied beyond measure, and with them meanness, accusations and favoritism. It was at this time that the Bar-

* Chap. xlii.

barians about the shores of the Black Sea, at the mouths
of the Danube and on several other frontiers, began to recognize the vulnerable parts of the empire and to prepare
for the great invasion which was to change the face of the
world, after they had themselves been changed by Christianity.   Let us then examine the influence of Christianity
on social development in Europe, and learn what modifications its definite establishment brought about in the
political economy of the ancients.

CHAPTER IX.

Changes in the social economy of Europe through the influence of Christianity.—Its vigorous and able organization.—The monasteries create community life.—The religious principle gives rise to hospitals and asylums.— The priest to-day unequal to his task.—Opinion on this subject.

THE sensation was great in Europe, when Christianity, hitherto proscribed and humiliated, suddenly rose to the rank of the dominant religion and in its turn persecuted its persecutors. What a revolution! Everything changes almost at once ; everything becomes reorganized on new bases as if by enchantment. Political power, hitherto maintained only by physical force, seeks auxiliaries in reason and in creeds; it surrounds and fortifies itself with the prestige of religious authority, which has taken deep root in the hearts of the people. It is marvellous to see the readiness with which the world, still pagan in worship, hastens to deduce conclusions from the gospel word, and the admirable instinct with which each oppressed one divines that the hour of freedom is about to strike for him. Although the Christian church appeared all organized, with its noble and austere hierarchy, every one had soon comprehended the principle of equality which it bore in its bosom. It pleased the great by its dogmas of subordination and obedience, and the humble by its doctrines of independence and of equality before God. It raised the slave without lowering the master, and presented to the human race bowed under the yoke, a refuge from the tyranny of this world in the hopes of the other. Paganism had rarely mingled with politics; but the first Christian priests took part in affairs, and they were already governing before any one had a suspicion of their power. The heresies even which troubled Christianity at its beginning, were not useless to the cause of social progress; they opened in Europe the right of discussion.

The majesty of this fine structure excites astonishment and commands respect even in those who are not very rigid Christians. We cannot, without lively admiration, see that vigorous and stately organization form, complete in all its parts, with its magnificent dependencies, and spread over the world, everywhere consistent with itself, like a great wave over the surface of the strand. The first bishops, so imperious and at the same time so gentle, so intolerant to doubt and so indulgent toward weakness, so proud with the great and so humble with the poor, seem to be tribunes of the people, come to protest in the name of the imprescriptible rights of humanity. Everything there recalls the old maxims of the Roman republic; as, for example, the public election, and the preaching renewed from the *forum*, the general assemblies, and the admission to the highest dignities without distinction of fortune or of birth. Nothing was remaining of the ancient prerogatives of the citizen except a barren and confused remembrance; the Christian religion has regenerated everything, restored everything to honor. Only a few years after the reign of Constantine, the affranchisement of slaves is permitted on the simple attestation of a bishop; concubinage is proscribed; the property of minors and of women is exempt from confiscation, the prisons are visited, the poor succored, *beneficence is discovered*. We shall reason about it later; meanwhile, they practice it.

Political economy is also under many other obligations to the influence of Christianity, which made that narrow and egoistic sentiment of nationality disappear, the source of the long quarrels of Athens and Sparta, of Carthage and Rome, those deplorable arenas where so many social resources were exhausted which another principle might have made fruitful! The single creation of councils was one of the most happy conceptions of the genius of Christian civilization, even considering them only as congresses where all intelligent minds were convoked for the discussion of an idea. How much time was necessary for these noble inspirations to triumph over a war-like and barbarous prejudice! It is but a few years since J. B. Say finished demonstrating, in his fine theory of markets, the doctrine of the commercial solidarity of nations; and in our day it has not been without difficulty that the solution of differences between nations has been remitted to diplomacy rather than to the sword. What prepared these results, if not Christianity? And what to-day is civil, religious and commercial freedom, but the development of the fundamental Christian thought? Without the new principle of equality before God, Greek and Roman slavery would still infest the world, weakness would be always at the mercy of physical power, and wealth would be still produced by some to be consumed without compensation by others.

Viewing it in respect to the distribution of power, there is no human institution which can be compared with the truly admirable organization of the church since the official appearance of Christianity. A Pope sits at Rome and holds under his power the high dignitaries of the clergy, who themselves assign to the members of lower rank their respective duties. All these are subjected, to the same rules and the same garb, from Paris to Japan and from China to Rome. The same service is celebrated in the same language throughout the world; the names of the saints of Christianity figure at the head of our registers of births, and we distinguish the days of the year only by the nomenclature of its apostles and martyrs. The Sunday of the Christians has become a day of universal repose ; everywhere, when the church opens its temples, labor closes its workshops. There is not a single important circumstance of life which escapes the influence of religion or which takes place without its intervention. The Christian priest awaits at the baptismal font the newly-born babe and bestows upon him a name ; later he blesses his marriage ; finally, when the end of life has come, he accompanies him with prayers to the tomb. How many powerful motives of action Christianity has since discovered, to take hold of the entire existence of man ! Everywhere we see the priest become the instructor, and direct childhood by his counsels. The catechism assures him that conquest without effort ; a first sacrament, the communion, creates an additional bond, strengthened by the mysterious and awful communications of the confessional. Then, as if these first successes were not enough, the bishop appears in all the majesty of his ecclesiastical authority and administers the confirmation, grants dispensations, pronounces censures, binds and unbinds as supreme arbiter and vicar of God. Thus, neither childhood, nor mature life, nor old age, nor death, can withdraw one from the influence of the priest, the most complete and the most inevitable which ever existed in the world.

This is not all ; and we can scarcely more than indicate the unlimited prerogatives of the religious power. Who is to-day the magistrate that has at his disposal in the smallest village a vast place to assemble the people, prompt and sure means of convoking them, and a tribune for harangues to move or convince them ? It is the priest. He alone is master of the temple, the pulpit, and the bells ; he assembles his flock at his pleasure, and without the permission of the civil authorities ; he orders and people obey. In the eyes even of the most unbelieving, Easter, Christmas, Whitsuntide, All-Saints day, and all the Christian feasts, are still holidays, and the fasts are days of privation. Our streets and our cities bear names of saints; the arts and the trades take saints for patrons. Despairing mariners vow orisons to Our Guardian Lady. People mow on St. John's day; they gather their vintage on St. Michael's. Now and then the irritated priest gives stern warnings; now he covers our brow with ashes to teach us the vanity of human things; again he refuses aid to the petitions of the heirs of a man who has died impenitent. He mounts the scaffold to guide penitent criminals to the bosom of divine mercy, and he frightens the timid young girl in regard to the consequences of some simple act confessed. He describes hell, and people tremble; he gives a glimpse of paradise, and they hope. When at times a bold unprincipled wretch steals his consecrated vessels, every one is aroused and grows indignant; the guilty one is called an impious fellow and the crime a sacrilege for which expiation is due. In olden times, one would see the faithful prostrate themselves and fervently kiss the pavement of the temples, beseeching with tears, prayers, and fasting, pardon for these great crimes.

This power of religion, so peculiar and so sudden, and the profound changes it caused in the social order, are especially manifest in the establishment of the monasteries, which have raised and resolved so many questions among men. In the East, the monasteries aimed at solitude and contemplation, to satisfy the desire to isolate one's self, to escape from pleasures and from human relations; in the West, on the contrary, they began in community life and the need of combining to render mutual aid. While society, a prey to general demoralization, no longer offered any centre of national, provincial, or municipal activity to elevated minds, the monasteries opened asylums for those who wished to live, think and discuss in common; and they soon became the most ardent centres of the intellectual movement. It was here that originated those bold theological and philosophical opinions maintained with resources so ingenious, and those trials of severe mortifications which gave new life to souls deadened by the régime of pagan civilization. An active correspondence and often keen contests arose between these various solitudes, already peopled like cities by the influx of all men whom liberty of thought and regularity in material life attracted to them. This was soon the way of those ambitious of attaining honors, and the sanctuary of literature, exiled from a world exclusively occupied with pleasures and sensualities. The inhabitants of these fortunate oases were not long in perfecting in all ways the occupations necessary to maintain their independence and their preservation. The industrial arts, which, under the republic and in the first days of the empire, had been pursued at home by slaves for the profit of their masters, became to the religious communities a learned study; they did not long live on dry fruits or vegetables; they needed trades, and these trades were exercised with the same superiority which distinguished the newly constituted society in other matters. I do not doubt that this was the true source of the industrial corporations, whose organization has been attributed to St. Louis. St. Louis disciplined the societies of arts, but he did not create them. Their origin is involved with that of convents. It was from these that the industrial arts came forth free, to become established afterwards in the heart of the cities of the middle ages under the protection of the principle of association.

Another creation of Christianity completes the distinction between it and all that social régime which is falling away, and that is, the precept of mutual benevolence put into practice and converted into a sacred obligation for all citizens. If there is anything which surprises us in Roman polytheism, it is that profound indifference to the sufferings of the poor and the grievances of the oppressed. There was in the old Roman society an impassable line of demarcation between rich and poor, between patrician and plebeian; one might say that the latter was *fated* to be the prey of the former, as in the animal kingdom certain species are predestined to be the food of others. Christianity brought these together by prescribing public and private charity, of which the Emperor Julian himself, that philosopher styled the Apostate, felt the imperious necessity. "Ought we not to blush for shame," said he,* " that the Galileans, those impious people, after having given food to their poor, take care also of ours, who were in absolute destitution!" There the creation of hospitals, of asylums, of alms-giving, is indicated very definitely by the most formidable enemy of Christianity.

What a step has political economy taken! and if, since, that great mission of Christianity has not been more completely accomplished, if it has been given to other causes to arrest in its course the development of the sublime thought which invited all humanity to the banquet of life, without distinction of fortune and of caste, we have confidence that they will some day take their place there, and that *the will of God will be done.*

Thus ancient civilization, wholly founded on slavery, was transformed, under the auspices of the Christian religion, into a new civilization resting upon freedom. A part of that honor, however, belongs to the great geniuses of antiquity, Sokrates, Cicero, and those noble philosophers whose writings have survived the fall of Greece and Rome, and who had glimpses of the better destinies toward which we are progressing. Everything was still pagan in Rome and in the empire, when the Christian revolution was flagrant; Lucian was turning the gods to ridicule at the very time when Christ was overthrowing their altars. A few capable slaves were emancipating industry by force of talent, when religion came to extend to them her hand; they were already compelling their

---

* Nam turpe profecto est, cum impii Galilæi non suos modo, sed nostros quoque alunt, et nostri auxilio, quod a nobis ferri ipsis debeat, destituti videantur. *Juliani Epist.* 49.

masters to have consideration, before the doctrine of beneficence and of equality before God had made it their duty to do so. So the transition from the old régime to the new is difficult to apprehend; the most celebrated writers are lost in conjectures in treating of it, and one of the finest works which have been devoted to investigation in the laws, for the causes of that transfiguration,* leaves much to be desired.

When one recalls the glorious memories of the early days of Christianity and the grand details of that organization so simple and so intelligent, he cannot refrain from a feeling of profound sadness, at seeing that religion to-day threatened with a serious decline. Unquestionably the structure, though undermined on every side, still stands and projects over the present the great shadow of the past : the services are solemnized, the temples are open, the hierarchy is the same ; but what a change in the fervor of the beliefs! and how the parts have changed ! The priest no longer gives the impulse, he no longer knows even how to receive it ; he employs, in vain struggles against social progress, forces weakened by intolerance and by the shock of revolutions. He occupies the pulpits, but the pulpits are mute : their voice no longer thrills the heart of the people, as formerly when it led them in masses to the conquest of the Holy Places. The religion still exists, but it no longer has ministers who rise to the height of its needs and of ours. And, nevertheless, in spite of our numerous attempts at political regeneration, no human constitution is yet like that of the church, no central power can make itself obeyed like that : the misfortune is that there is no one who knows how to command worthily in its name. There are questions of political economy which will remain unsolved until religion shall put her hand to them. Public instruction, the equitable division of the profits of labor, prison reform, the advancement of agriculture, and many other

---

* *History of Roman Law in the Middle Ages*, by M. de Savigny.

problems besides, will receive no complete solution except by her intervention, and that is justice; she alone
can, in fact, resolve the questions well, which she has
well stated.

Shall we be permitted to behold this so earnestly desired consummation? We think not, although the religious reaction which is everywhere manifest, appears to
give hope of it. It is in effect a fine homage rendered
by Europe to the sublime influence which formerly gave
us the principle of all liberties; but that homage the
priests have taken for a simple return to the old ideas,
for a disavowal of progress rather than for progress itself!
—a fatal error, which is arresting the world in its course!
Strange blindness of a caste who persist in living outside
of humanity, and drag themselves along after it instead
of marching at its head! Ah! if the priest knew to-day
of what an admirable metamorphosis he could be the
instrument, and what a prodigious influence it depended
on him to exercise over human destinies! Hospitals,
prisons, schools, workshops, public and private relations
of nations and of individuals, agriculture, communications, employers and workmen, everything would be
within his province, all would willingly take as arbiter
and guide a priest who was a civilizer after the fashion
of the nineteenth century, a priest tolerant, enlightened,
speaking a little less of the terrors of the other world than
of the needs of this, and refusing to politics no longer the
coöperation of his zeal and his devotion. People would
soon remember that priests were a long time the first
missionaries of civilization, and we should hear in the
temples something else than declamations against the
corruption of the age, and against luxury and wealth.
The singular struggle which we witness, the pacific
tendency of the world under a warlike attitude, would
have already given place to the universal harmony toward which we are progressing, if the fine organization
of Christianity had been represented by men in a con-

dition to comprehend it and to preserve it. But I do not fear to say that the Christian religion to-day is as far from that influence, as the Roman polytheism was from its ancient power at the moment when Christianity gave it the last blow. What has she done for Spain, for Portugal, and for South America, her most magnificent domains? What, in her hands, has unhappy Ireland become?

CHAPTER X.

Economic consequences of the invasion of the Barbarians and of the dismemberment of the Roman empire.—New elements introduced into the social organization.

As the last rays of Roman power became extinct in that wave of corruption, cowardice, and weakness which finally engulfed the empire, the Barbarians appeared in the horizon to have a share in the wreck. In fact, they had for a long time kept up secret communication with persons in the heart of that immense empire, the governors of which had committed the folly of entrusting to them its protection. There were more Barbarians than Romans in the legions which guarded the frontiers ; and when they began their march to conquer the empire, rations were all that was needed to conduct them over its territory, exposed on every side. However, before reaching the goal of their conquest, they had a long journey to make : this journey lasted more than a hundred years. The fathers had set out ; the sons alone arrived. What were these men? Whence came they? What impulse were they obeying, when they untiringly advanced over the ruins of the Roman world in such a cohort that we cannot clearly distinguish their true names and their mysterious native land? What appears certain is that they came from a region where slavery was unknown * and liberty indomitable ; for they made their

---

* The illustrious author of the *Etudes Historiques sur la Chute de l'Empire Romain*, Chateaubriand, (vol iii, p. 146), thinks that the Barbarians were acquainted with slavery. If he says this because by virtue of the right

chiefs pass through rough ordeals, and were not greatly unlike those Arabs of the Atlas, in Africa, with whom we have recently been made acquainted.

When they presented themselves on the frontiers, al-most all on horseback, followed by their beasts and their tents, there was among them only one law, force ; only one passion, the desire to use it. They found the empire occupied with philosophical, theological and political dis-cussions, and they had not much difficulty in making those legions of doctors who reasoned instead of fighting, flee before their frameas⁹ (javelins of the ancient Franks.— *Trans.*) instead of fighting. Their singularity even, their strange costume, their odd and horrible weapons, all contributed to spread terror on their path ; and the Romans of the decline were not less frightened at their approach than the inhabitants of Mexico were a thousand years later at the sight of the soldiers of Fernando Cortes. They were a new race in all the force of the term ; robust, intrepid, lofty, who returned with usury the contempt with which the Romans had constantly treated them. One should read in contemporary histories the de-scriptions they have left us of the character of these people ; by the frightened air with which they speak of them, it is easy to see what an effect of profound stupe-faction their appearance had just produced. Tacitus seems to have been seized with a prophetic presentiment, when he related the massacre of the legions of Varus.

It was written, however, that civilization should pass through these wild hands, to get rid of the impure var-nish with which it had been covered during the decline of the empire. From the very moment when barbarism advanced to the encounter with the ancient world, one sees the metamorphosis commence : slavery grows weak,

---

of war, they imposed it temporarily upon the conquered, no one questions it ; but they had not, like the Romans, markets for human beings. Their slavery did not at all resemble that ; more than this, it was not slavery, in the true acceptation of the word, otherwise liberty could not have sprung from it.

because people no longer come from the country of slaves. They are more costly; people treat them as a rare thing, or perhaps employ them as a defence. In proportion as the power was lost of renewing them by conquest, and their numbers could only be increased by their own fecundity, they became members of the Roman family; they lived in a condition nearly like that of our domestics, and their masters insensibly lost the habits of despotism which attach to the idea of property. Thus was brought about the transition from slavery to serfdom, two régimes very different, since the former enfeoffed man to man, and the second simply bound him to the soil. Everything on the contrary seemed favorable to liberty in the codes of the Barbarians; the division of property between children of the same father, was made in equal portions, and if any preference was permitted, it was in favor of the youngest, that is to say, the weakest. They especially protected the person from damage, for their penal laws seem rather for the protection of man than of property. The horse alone, the companion and the instrument of their independence, participated somewhat in the protection accorded to man; there were heavy fines for simply mounting him without permission. The chase was subject to laws, and the forests were placed under the safeguard of all, as the common asylum and the bulwark of liberty.

There were fines for wounds made through violence or by carelessness; so much for four teeth broken, so much for an eye put out, so much for the thumb-nail or for the membrane of the nose. The penalty of death was rare, and these men, so harsh, were more sober than we. Nothing is more surprising among them than the uniformity of rules, or, if one may say so, of *principles*, notwithstanding the diversity of their origin; for some came from the north, others from the south and east: one might say that in giving themselves a common rendezvous, they had made an exchange of habits and had prepared a pass-word. "I had a passion for effacing the Roman name from the earth," said Ataulf, the successor of Alaric, at the time when the vanity of the Romans treated their conquerors as *generals in the service of the empire*. Rome was disappearing before that civilization come from the woods, and she thought herself still reigning, even when she was ceasing to exist. The little regard that her conquerors kept for her was accorded to a power which conspired with them for her ruin, and which aided them to achieve it. This power was the Christian Church. The Christian Church met the Barbarians on the route to the conquest of the pagan world, and offered itself to them as an auxiliary: it was accepted. It had an organization already made, an established hierarchy, sympathies already old in the hearts of the people, and it appeared as an intelligent arbiter in the midst of those confused cohorts who knew how to proceed only by fire and sword. Disorder had indeed succeeded in reconciling itself with invasion; it would never have been able to subsist with a regular establishment. The Church had already taken possession of the municipalities; the Roman commune had been transformed into a parish of which the church-wardens might be considered as the administrators. Such were the first rallying points of the new system, and we have the evidence of it when Alaric, after having obtained possession of Rome, caused the sacred vessels of the Christians to be placed in safety, escorted by a double row of Romans and Goths, with sabres in their hands and chanting hymns in praise of the Anointed ! *

There were, in fact, numerous points of contact, notwithstanding their dissimilarity, between the doctrines of the Christian church and the habits of the barbaric régime. Everything was elective among the first Christians as among the Germans: the assemblies of the faithful, either in the temple or in council, deliberated

---

* Orosius : Hist. Book vii, chap. xxxix.

on the affairs of religion, as the Barbarians deliberated in those assemblies at once parliamentary and military, which were transformed later into periodic May assemblies. A little after, the priests took the guidance of those men of imagination who needed at the same time to be incited and to be directed. It was the hand of religion alone which arrested those arms so indefatigable that a full third of Europe had succumbed to their strokes. Pestilence, famine, fire, served them as attendants; cities fell by thousands, as if overthrown by earthquakes. " If the ocean had inundated the Gauls," said a poet, " it would have caused no more terrible ravages than that invasion. In the East, the neighborhood of Constantinople had not less to suffer from that frightful cataclysm ; the sun soon disappeared under the brambles, and the animals even seemed to have quitted the woods." To whatever part of the old Roman dominion one turns his eyes, the same spectacle is presented before him; Sicily, Spain, Africa, Great Britain, are invaded. Torrents of Barbarians roll their devastating waves over these fine countries, and cause not only their monuments, but all the resources of industry and all the traditions of the ancient arts, to disappear.

From this chaos the new civilization was to rise. All the Roman world was obliged to pass through this test before experiencing a complete renovation, as those old cities which rise again more beautiful after a fire. At the first moments of the awakening, the change was already visible. There were no longer any pagan temples, and everywhere arose Christian churches, flanked by monasteries where pious cenobites gathered in silence what was left of the sciences and the arts. The solitudes were peopled with unfortunates who fled from the spectacle of public desolation, and who imposed on themselves privations worse than those of the world they had just left. They thus grew in public esteem, and around them flocked a crowd of admirers who ardently propagated the doctrine of the separation of spiritual from temporal power.

The church thus laid in the presence of the sword the foundation for independence of thought ; happy if, after having founded this independence against barbarism, it had not one day endeavored to stifle it in the interest of despotism ! The Barbarians had indeed a remarkable in‐ clination to exercise this independence. We have noth‐ ing in modern times, unless perhaps the character of the North American tribes, to be compared with the habits of these new men, for whom the open air, a wandering life, the absence of restraint, even at the price of a thousand dangers, seemed an inexpressible felicity ; and yet we have inherited from them many virtues and many vices which have by degrees penetrated our society without our being able clearly to trace them to their source.

Let us render thanks, however, to that Barbarian influ‐ ence, in virtue of which, personal dignity, I might almost say the generous susceptibility of man, resumed its sway, after coming forth from the long oppression in which it had languished under the oriental yoke of the Roman emperors. If a hierarchy and subordination are fine ele‐ ments in the social order, individual liberty is an element not less worthy of respect ; and although it has come to us closely following the Barbarians, we must nevertheless recognize the immense service they rendered us in bring‐ ing it. They thus prepared the emancipation of the la‐ borers and an end of the exploitation of human beings, by favoring the mingling of castes previously irreconcil‐ able, and by subjecting them for the time to a common oppression. We cannot comprehend how enlightened minds could see in these facts so simple and so evi‐ dent, the justification of a theory condemned in advance by observation and experience. What, for example, shall we think of those who have divided European nations into two castes, one of which includes the posterity of the conquerors and the other that of the conquered ?

And who to-day could seriously maintain that the church should be forever the mistress of the world, because it temporarily ruled its masters? Twelve centuries have passed over the mingled dust of those generations so different in origin, and if reconciliation is not yet complete between the children of so many dead, it is every day being brought about more and more on the altar of civil equality and at the hearth of association of labor.

The contrast was striking between the social habits of the Barbarians and the Roman civilization with which they were coming to mingle. They were nearly all encamped in villages, leading a pastoral and agricultural life, when they set out for the conquest of the Roman world, which they found almost entirely established in cities. Great as was the decline of the Roman power, its organization still subsisted and the wheels of administration still performed their functions, notwithstanding the general enfeebling of politics. There was in all the cities a local hierarchy still respected, when the first wave of the Barbarians reached their walls. Who can say what were the sensations of these irregular hordes, at the sight of the regular and methodical order of the great Roman cities which were frightened at their aspect? The Cossacks entering Paris in 1814 on their horses covered with skins of beasts, could not have been more astonished at the spectacle of our civilization. By degrees, as the invasion extended, these conquerors became proprietors ; they seized a multitude of rural domains, and either from sympathy for their former rural habits, or from disdain for a city residence, they established themselves in preference in the country, which they were not long in covering with villages. From this position, they kept the cities in awe ; and they thus laid the foundation for the supremacy of landed property. The Gallic, Batavian, Italian and Spanish peasants that they found scattered about, fell under their immediate yoke, cultivated the fields for them, and were their colonists before being their serfs ;

then, the need of defending themselves against each other, perhaps also against the sedition of the cities, transformed the cottage into a castle-keep and the village into a fortified camp, *avant-couriers*, as it were, of the feudal system.

Thus these purely military chieftains, after having taken as their share of the booty vast portions of land, the sources of great revenues, became accustomed to wealth, and forced their subordinates to labor and tribute. Their contact with Roman customs contributed daily to modify the prejudices they had brought with them from the depths of their forests ; they forgot their own manners, or they modified them under the influence of the people of the cities. They were no longer pure Barbarians, since they had made a halt in the midst of a world which was assimilating them to itself on every side. If the fusion had taken place suddenly and without other shock than the arrival of the conquerors, the change would not have cost humanity so much blood and so many tears ; but Heaven willed that, having no more enemies to conquer or people to subjugate, they should rend each other. It was not the first invasion that was the most fatal ; it was the second, it was the third, it was the fourth : it was that series of new tribes which pressed upon each other and disputed with each other the lost and silent wreck of the Roman world. The Franks, the Visigoths, the Burgundians, who occupied vast portions of our territory, did not penetrate it all together, and they established themselves in it on very different bases. Opinions were often quite opposite at the court of Toulouse, that of Lyons, and that of Soissons, if it is allowable to give the name of *courts* to those general quarters of conquest ; but one general idea dominated in them all, namely, that leisure was a sovereign right, and that labor was the exclusive lot of the conquered and of men without property. It must be acknowledged that the Romans had singularly prepared the way for that transition, by the manner in which they had continually treated the subject nations. When the Barbarians came, they had only to take the place; it was all ready for them, and was yielded to them without resistance.

What, during all this time, became of manufactures, and the arts, and the Roman institutions, the system of taxation, the commercial habits of the world and its great markets, Africa, Spain, Asia-Minor, Sicily and all Italy? A profound revolution suddenly was manifest in them, and destroyed at once the great centres of intelligence and rational progress. All of Greek and Roman philosophy which Christianity had turned aside to its advantage, all those schools which it had recast and animated with its spirit, disappeared before the exigencies of conquest, until the new religion had conquered in its turn all the conquerors, and had made them serve for the triumph of its destinies. In material order, there was also effected a great and sudden change; the fine arts, if not proscribed, were at least abandoned as superfluities. The gigantic constructions, the bold enterprises which inflamed the enthusiasm of the Romans, even at the time of their greatest decline, almost suddenly ceased. Of what use henceforth were those graceful forms in furniture and domestic utensils, those statues, those elegant fabrics, to half-savage consumers who could not appreciate their use, and would not be willing to pay for the workmanship? The abandonment became such, that most of the industrial secrets were lost, and several have never been rediscovered. A few artisans preserved in their workshops the transmission of the most indispensable trades: but between Roman art and Christian art there is nothing. No sensible transition binds the temples of paganism to the piles of the new worship, and one cannot recognize an intermediary character in those heavy and shapeless rudiments of the purely barbaric period, which have no name in any language. To find

again something grand, something truly noble and majestic, we must wait until the Christian people have succeeded the Roman people by stripping off the Vandal
bark.

One cannot, however, deny that the barbaric invasion
brought notable changes in the social constitution of Europe. It simplified Roman legislation, which was encumbered with texts and had become inextricable by reason
of subtilties. It even permitted the conquered peoples
to adopt or reject the new régime, on condition of profiting by the advantages which it presented to them, or of
being deprived of them, according to the resolution which
they should adopt. Thus the Salic law decreed that the
life of a Roman was less valuable than that of a Barbarian—a cruel insult of the conqueror, of which we only
find the corrective in the ripuary * law, which placed
the members of the clergy above the dominators themselves. Insensibly this influence of the church manifests itself so efficaciously that the Barbarians consent
to abandon their titles, and to substitute for them the
Latin names of dukes, counts and prefects. For the
exact and circumstantial evidence required by Roman
jurisprudence, they substitute the religious tests by fire
and water, and soon after, single combats, which latter
bad practice we have kept. What testimony to their
victory and their sovereignty could be stronger! Since
God directs the issue of national wars and gives the palm
to the most just side, why should we not consult him
by appeal to arms in private affairs? That is what
they said, convinced that, in their private quarrels, the
Romans would not attempt, as individuals, a struggle in
which they had so badly succeeded as a nation. Thus
that fatal innovation introduced into human disputes a
deplorable element of which future generations were long
to suffer the consequences.

The portion of the conquered lands which the Barba-

---

* Book vii, chap. xi, law 36.

rians had adjudged to themselves gave rise to vexations of every kind, and continued, under new forms, the system of usurpation which the Romans had pursued wherever their armies had advanced. Artisans were no longer free to work for themselves; they were adjudged by the right of war to the chiefs of their conquerors; and the latter, surrounded by blacksmiths, carpenters, shoemakers, tailors, dyers, and goldsmiths, added to the revenues of their lands the profits of the labor of these workmen. It was still Roman servitude, with this difference, that formerly the Romans worked others for their own advantage, and now they were worked for the advantage of others. Civilization must have lost by this change, if later a powerful hand had not organized the scattered elements of the new social order, by associating Roman intelligence with Vandal force, and bending the somewhat savage independence of that force to the régime of constraint and to respect for law. This great reformer was Charlemagne.

The essential and characteristic fact of the invasion of the tribes designated under the name of Barbarians, was their passage from a wandering and conquering state to the condition of proprietors. The manner in which they distributed among themselves a portion of the conquered territory, each tribe according to its native habits, brought about serious modifications in the system of property, without notable amelioration in the fate of the cultivators. We find, in the laws of the Visigoths and the Burgundians, that these two tribes had two-thirds of the lands: * the Franks did not follow the same plan, but took what they wished. However, they did not take all; and the Burgundians had not even exercised their right of conquest over the whole of the disposable lands, since it was stipulated in a supplement to their law † that not

---

* Montesquieu, *Esprit des Lois*.   Book xxx, chap. 8.

† Ut non amplius a Burgundionibus qui infra venerunt requiratur quam in praesens necessitas (fuerit,) medietas terræ (art. xi.).

more than a half should be given to those who should
afterwards come into the country. For a long time, each
Barbarian established himself as a boarder upon a Roman,
as the Athenians formerly did among their conquered
peoples, and as the Romans, in their turn, had done
among the nations of which they had become masters.
Thus property changed hands, but the Greek and Roman
system of living at the expense of another, still continued, and in this respect there was no change, except
that barbarism took its revenge at the expense of its
former oppressors, henceforth the oppressed. From
whatever point of view one looks at that rude transition,
he does not yet perceive the germ of a decisive economic
revolution. The new territorial aristocracy is distinguished from the old proprietors of *latifundia* only by less elegant and less polished manners ; but at the bottom, the
cruelty is equal in the two classes :—the new beat their
servants themselves ; the old, better reared, had them
beaten by others : that is the difference.

The Roman world was so strongly impregnated with
these ideas of servitude and of despotic hierarchy, that
the Barbarians had, so to speak, only to substitute their
titles for those of the imperial administration. The persons employed were almost all the same ; the power flowed
in the same channels. The Roman middle class had given
place to the *état major* of the Barbarians ; and, save the
consequences which ensued from that substitution, the
revolution which took place might have passed for a
simple change of public functionaries. But soon the
conquering chiefs accorded exemptions from taxes,
granted domains and life-benefices, which the successive
encroachments of their subordinates at last made hereditary. Distinctions penetrated civil society to the vitals ;
there were lands free from taxes, *Salic* and *allodial*;
whose proprietors gradually arrogated to themselves
rights over the neighboring inhabitants, and became,
under the title of *seniores* or lords, veritable tyrants.

The chase, of which they were passionately fond, was considered by them as a right interdicted to peasants. It was more dangerous to kill a stag or a boar than to make away with a man. Nevertheless, not all these vexatious acts were legalized, and never was there, to speak correctly, any edict for general confiscation. When that abuse of power was inscribed in the laws, it had a long time figured among accomplished facts. The clergy every day mitigated its rigors by their influence over the depositaries of force; entirely composed of natives, men able and shrewd, they neglected no occasion to make the lofty head of the dominators bend under the religious yoke; they taught them Latin, corrupting it doubtless; but in the end it facilitated their means of entering into more intimate communication with laws and customs which were, in the long run, to have influence over them.

One circumstance, justly noted by historians as very important, contributed much also to prevent the German invasion from taking entirely the place of the preceding régime. The Barbarians had the habit of assembling in their woods and swamps around the persons of their chiefs, who took counsel of the general assembly, and deliberated with it before acting. When they were scattered and located upon the conquered territories, they presented themselves with less punctuality at the assemblies, and the authority of the chiefs no longer extended beyond a limited radius. More than one Barbarian entered the sacred orders and carried there his intemperate habits; questions of doctrine were often decided by force. In Spain, the Visigoths, under the influence of the councils, caused several codes of laws to be drawn up, which were a compound of Roman principles and religious prejudices. In England, the irruption of the Saxons found the inhabitants abandoned to themselves, and their establishment there became decisive only after a struggle of more than a hundred years.

For a long time that famous island seemed effaced from the map, and was regarded as a mysterious land, of which all sorts of prodigies were related. When it was discovered for the second time, everything there had changed; seven independent kingdoms had been formed, and although constantly agitated by discord, they had made even the last vestiges of Roman supremacy almost entirely disappear. A new political order had just arisen. Gaul and Spain had been divided between the two powerful monarchies of the Franks and Visigoths; Africa was a prey to the Vandals strictly so called and the Moors. Italy was subject to foreigners; traces were no longer to be seen of Roman majesty, save in the Eastern Empire, which extended still from the banks of the Danube to the borders of the Nile and the Tigris. Outside of that, a multitude of new nationalities had been formed; we shall soon witness the development of their social state.

CHAPTER XI.

Last rays of civilization at Constantinople under Justinian.—That emperor makes a summary of all the legislation of the Romans.—Character of his *Code.*—The *Pandects.*—The *Institutes.*—The laws of Justinian are the archives of the past ; the *Capitularies* of Charlemagne, the programme of the future.

BETWEEN the new order of things emanating from the barbaric invasion, and the expiring civilization of Rome, there is an intermediary epoch worthy of interest to the economist, though not characterized by any of those profound changes which overthrow the social system of an entire people. This epoch is the reign of the Eastern emperor Justinian ; a memorable reign, which had no dawn and will have no twilight ; a veritable communication thrown between two worlds, the one of which is ending and the other beginning. It seems, in studying it, as if the genius of ancient civilization had wished to make its testament and had enveloped itself, like the chrysalis, in a tomb of silk and gold, before undergoing a last transformation. Everything is summed up and collected, laws, arts, manufactures, agricultural processes. For the first time a raw product, silk, becomes the subject of imperial solicitude and weighs in the political balance, like cotton, sugar, and tea, in our times. Monopolies are established for the benefit of the public treasury ; moneys are debased, offices are sold. We do not admire this, but we take note of it as the first indication of a systematic political economy. In the sciences even, bold experiments testify **of** the movement which is taking place; burning glasses, explosive powders, pumps for irrigation, are tried. Medicine abandons its old vagaries and architecture raises its first dome in the air.* Palaces and temples arise on every side; aqueducts, bridges, *hospitals*, are erected in nearly all the cities; there seems to be haste in multiplying the monuments of the arts, lest barbarism come too soon and interrupt their completion, and in the hope that they will survive it. From Belgrave to the Euxine, and from the confluence of the Save to the mouth of the Danube, a chain of more than eighty fortresses rises to protect the banks of the great river; one would say that Rome was laying down her final boundaries, and, weary of conquests, was at length establishing herself in an entrenched camp. But while Rome is thus providing herself with battlements in the East, where letters and arts will soon take refuge, the rest of Europe is submitting to the law of the conqueror, and Latin institutions are everywhere supplanted by barbaric customs. The German graft applied to the old Roman trunk is beginning to bear fruit, in which there still remains somewhat of the savor of the first tree. To that cohort of devastating chiefs, whom frightened Christianity dreads and baptizes, succeeds at length a great man, the true representative of the new social order, who shows as much solicitude in restoring civilization as his coarse predecessors manifested in destroying it. I mean Charlemagne, the first prince of the race of vandal conquerors, whose reign sums up the thought of those four or five centuries of invasions.

The contrast of that thought with that of the Roman emperors nowhere appears in a more striking manner than in the double enterprise of Justinian and Charlemagne. In fact, these two princes each left a monument more lasting than the memory of their victories, viz., the *Pandects* and the *Capitularies*. I know no subject for study more fruitful or more vast than these two great codes of

---

* The Church of St. Sophia, at Constantinople.

two great sovereigns, one of whom so well represents the setting and the other the rising sun. It is there that political economy must seek the condition of the people at the two extremities of Europe, when Roman civiliza- tion withdrew to Constantinople to give place to the almost universal rule of him who put on his head the crown of Germany, of France and of Italy. Thus has Napoleon's code survived his victories, and it will some day do more honor to his memory than the most mag- nificent monuments of his reign. There, will be found the most important social facts of his epoch, as we find in the laws of Justinian the clearest traces of the col- lective wisdom of the Romans.

All these laws were brought together as a whole for the first time under the reign of this prince, into three distinct books, the Code, the Pandects, and the Institutes. When he ascended the throne, the jurisprudence was en- cumbered with a confused multitude of texts, the simple nomenclature of which would have been beyond human power. Fate gave him as an auxiliary the famous Tri- bonian, who introduced order and light into this chaos and who finished in less than fifteen months the revision of the ordinances of his predecessors. This first work was called the Justinian Code and promulgated through- out the empire with unwonted ceremony. Seventeen jurisconsults, under the direction of the same learned man, afterwards prepared in three years the *Pandects*, a colossal compendium of two or three millions of sen- tences, and which had been preceded by the publication of the *Institutes*. Thus the elements of Roman law were followed by the explanation of its jurisprudence, and justice could at length consult the *eternal oracles*,* with- out fearing to lose herself in a labyrinth of laws. Un- fortunately the oracles were liars, as almost all are ; for in collecting the laws, care was taken to adapt them to contemporary customs. Tribonian became an accomplice

---

* This is the name that Justinian gave to his Codes.

in the alterations which were to bring the code of a republic into harmony with the despotism of an absolute
monarchy. At the same time, in order to prevent the
code thus amended in the interest of despotism, from
suffering in future any change which might be to the
advantage of freedom, the emperor forbade, under the
penalty due to forgery, the least commentary on the new
text. A few years later, he caused another edition of it
to be made, augmented by the *novellæ* (recent enact-
ments), which complete the imposing structure of his
jurisprudence.

One finds in the collections of Justinian very valuable
details on the condition of persons at Constantinople
towards the middle of the sixth century. Although the
citizens were, nominally at least, equal before the law,
there were no longer any rights connected with this title
formerly so honorable and so eagerly sought after. Freed
slaves obtained it without transition, and that facility contributed not a little to the abolition of domestic servitude.
The authority of masters over slaves was also considerably
restricted. The right of life and death accorded to fathers
over their sons, was abolished, and the latter could acquire
some kinds of property, which ceased from that time to
belong to the authors of their being. The abandonment
of children, long tolerated as excusable, was punished as
a crime when the death of the victims followed ; some
restrictions were put upon liberty of divorce, which had
degraded marriage to the vilest concubinage ; * and the
influence of the church was already plainly manifest in
the list of causes, which, on the part of man or woman,
could give rise to a separation. Religion had already
penetrated jurisprudence. One principally notes its intervention in the care with which the rights of orphans and
of minors were protected.

---

* Saint Jerome saw at Rome a husband who was burying his twenty-first
wife. The latter had buried twenty-two of his predecessors, less robust than
he. Seneca said of the women of his time : "*non consulum numero, sed
maritorum annos suos computant.*" *De Beneficiis*, iii, 16.

So much for persons; but property was not forgotten. The *Institutes contain* on this subject a multitude of remarkable provisions. They admit the principle of inheritance of property, in its freest extent. There is no prerogative of primogeniture ; no distinction as to rights of succession, between boys and girls. On the extinction of the direct line, the property passed to the collateral branches. Wisely composed prescriptions conciliated all interests and left little occasion for law-suits. The lengthy details occupy twelve books of the *Pandects*. Books 17, 18, 19, and 20 of the same collection contain also very remarkable provisions in regard to loans, contracts for leasing property, and the nature and conditions of leases for a term of five years. The rate of interest was fixed at 4 per cent for persons of illustrious rank and at 6 per cent for all others : this was the ordinary and legal rate. Nevertheless, 8 per cent interest was permitted to manufacturers and traders and 12 per cent for maritime insurance. The clergy, more strict or less enlightened, always condemned loans at interest, which Saint John Chrysostom and the fathers of the Church assailed with their feeble arguments, and which Shakspeare, later, called, in his vivid language, *the posterity of a sterile metal.*

Meanwhile, notwithstanding these improvements in the revision of the laws, compared with what they were previously, the people derived less advantage from them than might be supposed. Although the laws had been reduced to forms more simple and terms more precise, there still remained enough that was vague and contradictory to support hosts of advocates and legists. The residence of litigants in remote provinces involved tedious delays, uncertainties, and considerable expense, whenever there was an appeal to the highest judicial authority. Roman law became again a mysterious science which the industry of the practitioners, worthy masters of those of our day, exploited with unparalleled audacity. The rich mercilessly crushed the poor, and the costs of the suits uniformly consumed the amount in controversy. Nevertheless these forms and these delays, although very expensive, protected person and property against the caprices of tyranny and the arbitrariness of the judge, and that was some progress. How many reforms adapted to the present time and bearing deeply its impress, that single revision of the Roman laws contained! Who could have told that after more than twelve hundred years, these laws would still, in most of their provisions, direct the administration of a society so different? But, in this long passage through the centuries, they were to become penetrated with the spirit of many new institutions and to furnish to a great man the elements of a legislation which shared his glory if it did not his originality.

CHAPTER XII

The reign of Charlemagne forms the transition between barbarism and feudalism. He reëstablishes unity of power and of territory, alike broken by that host of petty sovereigns and petty states which fill all the period since the first invasion. The kingdoms of Metz, Orléans, Soissons, Paris, Aquitaine and Burgundy become absorbed in the great imperial monarchy; and all these miserable despotisms, unfitted to conceive great ideas, are swallowed up in a single one capable of carrying them into execution. For the first time since Cæsar, the conqueror and organizer, a man appears, worthy of leaving his name to his age. What especially characterizes this remarkable man, is that he was a true Frank of France, the least commingled with Roman blood that had yet ascended the throne. Almost all his predecessors, Barbarians or not, had *received* the Roman and Christian impetus; he felt himself strong enough to *give* it. The others had reigned : Charlemagne determined to govern. He might perhaps have prevented the advent of the feudal system, by powerfully restraining the aristocratic tendency of his time, if his weak successors had not let his work perish, and surrendered to chance the destinies of humanity.

His fifty-three expeditions were directed by a political

idea that seemed lost since the Romans. What he determined, first and foremost, was to reëstablish in Europe a great power, strong enough to restrain all ambitions and to subject them to a common domination. He made war on threatening independencies and hostile beliefs, and only stopped when he had attained his principal aim, which was to make an empire. In the North and the South he encountered two great opposing powers, the Saxons and the Arabs : he conquered them both. Unfortunately, his victories left him scarcely sufficient leisure to organize, and he encountered fewer difficulties in war than in peace ; but, although his great works did not survive him, the impulse that he had given to Europe had been too strong for the movement to be arrested. Europe did not again become, after his death, such as it had been before his reign : he had given it an idea to be revealed in the acts of his successors, in the politics of the states formed from the dismemberment of his monarchy, in the wars even that they make upon each other or maintain against their enemies.

It suffices to recall the pains with which he endeavored to reëstablish a strict administrative hierarchy, watched over by ambulant inspectors, *missi dominici,* sent by the master, charged with rendering to him an account of the state of the provinces, of the reform of abuses and the execution of his orders. He was thus present everywhere, and he could extend his hand even to the extremities of his empire with decisive rapidity in those times of tedious delays and over that immense surface almost entirely destitute of roads. The thirty-five general assemblies held under his reign, although they resemble scarcely at all our modern parliamentary sessions, nevertheless contributed important aid to the ameliorations which he effected. It appears that the deputies had only an advisory voice in them : the emperor made his decisions in spite of their opposition ; but in these sessions he received valuable communications on the condition of his country, its needs and its sufferings. Archbishop Hincmar has left us curious revelations of the manner in which these general assemblies were conducted and the origin of the *Capitularies* which sum up their labors. " It was," he says, " a custom of that time to hold every year two assemblies, in which, by order of the king, the articles of the law, called *capitula*, which the king himself had prepared by the inspiration of God, were submitted to the nobles."

There was, then, a preliminary examination, a discussion in State Council, for we can recognize no other character in these pacific assemblies whose debates were directed by the sovereign, *in virtue of the wisdom which he had received from God*, to use the expression of his historian. Charlemagne should then have only the more merit in our eyes, since the dominant thought in all the improvements of his reign belongs exclusively to him. And certainly, never was activity more extraordinary than his; although his numerous wars forced him to transport himself many times from one end of Europe to the other, he constantly published reform edicts on a multitude of subjects, sometimes so minute in detail, that we can hardly comprehend how the majesty of his power could descend to them. It is then in his *Capitularies* that we must look to ascertain what his political economy was, and whether it is true that this science owes to him anything essential. And first let us call attention to the fact that people have erroneously attributed to Charlemagne alone the collection of aphorisms, opinions, prescriptions and laws which bear his name. Nearly half belong to his predecessors, and a great number to his successors. The title of the work (*Capitula regum francorum*) is alone sufficient to indicate the true signification and exact nature of its contents. The best edition that we possess* is only an undigested collection, without order, without critical notes, and

---

* That of Baluze, in two folio volumes. Paris, 1677.

whose text, written in the bad Latin of the decline, dis-
courages the most intrepid students; but it is an inexhaustible mine of valuable documents, and we would
that there existed similar ones for every period of our
history.

Among the sixty-five *Capitularies* of Charlemagne, the
one which most concerns the history of economic science, is, in spite of the incoherence of its details, the
famous capitulary *De Villis*, in which this great man attempted to sum up his views on the finances and upon
the administration of his domains. It is composed of
seventy paragraphs without any relation between them,
and which considerably resemble the instructions of a rich
landed proprietor to his steward. The prince demands,
first, that he be served with probity, and that his people
be well cared for, so as to be protected from poverty.*
He will not have corvées imposed upon them, or any
fatiguing labors: if they work in the night, an account
shall be kept of it. They, on their side, must take good
care of the wine from the vintage and bottle it so that it
may not be injured. If they deviate from the course
imposed upon them, they may be punished by flogging,
or according to the good pleasure of the king and queen.
Care must be taken of the bees and of the geese, and
watch kept over the maintenance and increase of the fish-
ponds. Cows, breeding mares, and sheep must be multiplied. "We wish," adds the master, "our forests to be
intelligently managed, not to be cleared, and that sparrow-
hawks and falcons be kept in them. There must always
be at our disposal fat geese and chickens likewise ; the
eggs not needed for consumption on the farms shall be
sold. Each of our estates shall be provided with good
feather beds, mattresses, coverlids, copper vessels, lead,
iron, wood, chains, pot-hooks, hatchets and augers, so that
nothing will have to be borrowed of any one. Charlemagne wished also to have an account of his vegetables,

---

* " Ut familia nostra bene conservata sit, et a nemine in paupertatem missa."

his butter, cheese, honey, oil and vinegar; yes, even of his turnips and *other minutiae*, as says the text of the *Capitu-laries*. One cannot help asking what time he would have had to verify such accounts, if they had been furnished him.

We find also in the same capitulary a curious enumera-tion of the various occupations which he judged necessary to have on each of his great estates. There were to be blacksmiths, goldsmiths, cutters, turners, carpenters, bird-catchers, makers of nets, and men to take charge of mak-ing the cider and perry. Every slave who wished to speak to the sovereign on account of his master was to have access to his person; this favor could be refused him under no pretext. Charlemagne had fixed upon the Christmas season for the general rendering of accounts, and the good old Harpagon[10] was not more exacting than this great man in this difficult matter. The sixty-second article of the capitulary *De Villis* presents the clearest evidence of it: "It is important," it says, "that we know how much all these things yield us;" and he enumerates the cattle, mills, woods, ships, vineyards, vegetables, wool, flax, hemp, fruits, bees, fish, skins, wax and honey, old and new wines, and the rest. Everything which has not been consumed in the service of the prince must be immediately sold. The august economist in-genuously adds: "We hope that all this will not appear to you too hard, because you can exact it in your turn, each being master on his farm." His royal solicitude went still farther when the transportation of wine and flour destined for his personal use was concerned. "You will take care to have the wine carried in casks duly hooped with iron, and never in leathern bottles; as to the flour, it must be placed in carts lined and covered with leather, so as to be able to cross the rivers, if necessary, without running the risk of damage. I wish also a good account to be rendered me of the horns of my bucks and my goats, as well as of the skins of my wolves taken in

the course of each year. In the month of May, let terrible war be made without fail, on the wolves' whelps."
Finally, the last paragraph of that strange document contains perhaps the rarest nomenclature which exists of
plants of every kind and fruit trees, known in the ninth
century, of which the great regulator of the royal domains
did not wish the cultivation to be neglected in any of his
gardens.

Such is, in substance, this celebrated capitulary *De
Villis*, which sums up much better the domestic economy
of Charlemagne than his political economy. One meets in
the other capitularies of the new Cæsar exact provisions
on economic questions, notably the following passage, in
which is found, as Mr. Guizot has justly said, a veritable
attempt at a *maximum:* " The very pious lord our king
has decided that no man, whether ecclesiastic or layman,
shall, *either in time of abundance, or in time of scarcity,*
sell provisions higher than the price recently fixed per
bushel, namely, etc." There is found besides, the creation of a poor tax, with the object of suppressing mendicancy. " As to the beggars which overrun the country,
we wish that each one of our faithful should support his
poor, either on his benefice or in his house, and not allow
them to go elsewhere to beg. And if one finds such
mendicants, and they do not work with their hands, let
no one take upon himself to give them anything." Sometimes the injunctions of the legislator were formulated
under the appearance of a simple interrogation : " Ask
the bishops and abbots to declare to us truly what these
words mean which they often use, *to renounce the world* ;
and by what signs one can distinguish those who renounce
the world from those who do not renounce it ? Is it simply by this, that they do not bear arms and they are not
publicly married ? Ask again if that one has renounced the
world, who works every day, *no matter by what means,* to
increase his possessions, now promising the beatitude of
the kingdom of heaven, now threatening the eternal tor

ments of hell; or perhaps, under the name of God or of some saint, plunders some man either rich or poor, of simple mind and little on the guard?"

The language of Charlemagne was not less significant, as one sees, in his insinuations than in his prescriptions. The corruption and domination of the priests must have already in his reign acquired a very serious character, for him to resolve to address to them such severe reprimands. Besides,* he recommends to them not to swear, not to get intoxicated, not to frequent bad places, not to keep women, and not to sell the sacraments too dearly. Usury was then an abuse as habitual to the clergy as to the rest of the inhabitants; the capitularies revert to it in more than twenty instances, and constantly stigmatize it in every manner. These pious provisions, however, do not prevent the emperor from himself fixing the rate at which the people shall take *his* money, good or bad, or from condemning to heavy fines men bold enough to contest its excellence. But these tyrannical prescriptions are often compensated by measures favorable to the slaves, the peasants, and the poor, whom it is ordered shall be helped, gathered into asylums, and cared for when they are ill. The ecclesiastical rules occupy a considerable place in the capitularies. One cannot doubt, from their extent, the great importance that was attached to the clergy and the monks, who were almost masters of the administration in consequence of their superior intelligence, and were consulted by Charlemagne in the smallest details. They were exempt from military service, a painful duty then imposed upon all, *without pay*, and for an almost unlimited time. Any lack of consideration for them or any injury to their person was punished with double severity.

We find in the capitularies of Charlemagne few traces of any system of imposts. The revenue of the state appears to have consisted principally in the fines, which

---

* Capitula Episcoporum.

were numerous and high, and the farm rents of the domains of the emperor.   The minute care with which
Charlemagne had regulated everything pertaining to this
subject, does not permit us to doubt that the rent of his
lands was the most essential chapter of his budget.   A
few toll-houses situated on the high-ways, at the approach
to certain bridges, furnished supplementary resources,
and were managed in common with the great proprietors,
and became, under the feudal system, the source of the
most frightful exactions.   Moreover, to the reign of
Charlemagne must be attributed the restoration of the
Roman laws which forbade the export of grain in times
of scarcity, under penalty of confiscation, and we have
seen that he did not recoil before attempts at fixing
maximum prices, which resulted in aggravating the evils
they were intended to remedy.   Nevertheless, Charlemagne may be considered, in those half barbaric times,
as the prince who best comprehended the true interests
of commerce.   His capitularies contain a multitude of
provisions more liberal than any of those of the Roman
emperors.   He had established on the frontiers, officers
charged with protecting the relations with foreigners,
and it was he who placed the first *guard-bo.its* at the
mouths of the rivers, either for the intimidation of pirates,
or in the interest of navigation.   He had undertaken to
excavate a navigable canal joining the Rhine to the Danube.   He ordered the establishment of a regular system
of weights and measures throughout the empire, prosecuted with severe penalties the making of counterfeit
money, and forbade monopolies.   His edicts were not
less opposed to the purchase of standing crops, as a system of shameful speculation which aimed to take advantage of the poverty of the cultivators and to make provisions dear.   At the same time, he impressed the property of the churches with perpetual immobility, by opposing its ever having any other destination, and he took care
to increase it by prescribing donations in lands and tithes,

which were paid by his own domains. We are forced to acknowledge that the slaves of his time were treated with more philanthropy and decency than the unfortunate negroes of our colonies. The husband could not be separated from the wife, and the article of the capitulary which contained that provision, rests on the words of the gospel: " Whom God hath joined together, let no man put asunder." It was forbidden to buy or sell a slave other than in the presence of the deputies of the emperor. Every secret sale was annulled and punished.

That solicitude for slaves at a time and under a reign when slavery was every day extending, is easily explained. The donations of lands which the emperor was constantly making to the nobles and to the churches, daily diminished the number of cultivators who could live upon their incomes, and their condition became so unhappy that they preferred slavery, or rather, servitude. By degrees, almost all the free men disappeared, and their little inheritances were added to those immense domains granted by imperial munificence to the military and the ecclesiastical aristocracy. Thus were confounded the ideas of political sovereignty and of landed property which were to become the basis of feudal anarchy, as soon as the hand of the supreme chief ceased to keep the respect of ambitious and powerful vassals. He himself prepared the way for this great event by dividing the empire between his children and weakening his own work : here his reputation is especially vulnerable ; and it is on account of the ephemeral character of his works that many historians have felt authorized to judge him severely. It is, however, just to recognize that Charlemagne has nothing in common with most of his predecessors or of his successors. All that we know of his intelligent interest in the sciences and the generous efforts he made to promote them, of those bold attempts at centralization at a time of universal dismemberment, of that marvellous creation of a great empire in less than forty

years, can be the work only of a superior genius, and
makes us comprehend very well how Charlemagne was
honored with the name of Great during his life and
canonized after his death. He had doubtless many of
the vices of his time, and his personal morals seem too
often in contradiction with the rigidity of his capitularies ; but his thought will not be sterile, and his labors
are a grand spectacle, especially when compared with
the lamentable *gestes* of the do-nothing kings. This
prince dreamed of the reëstablishment of Roman grandeur with German elements.   A Barbarian, and the
descendant of a Barbarian, he succeeded in mastering
the tide which brought him along and he would have
had complete success, if he had not endeavored to
unite elements too dissimilar, that is to say, people
already classed by the difference of their languages,
the opposition of their interests, and their geograph-
ical situation.   " Charlemagne," says Mr. Raynouard,*
" thought he had for subjects only warriors and ecclesiastics, he was great, but by himself alone and for
himself alone.   No illustrious name appears besides
his, even beneath it ; he absorbed all the glory of
his reign. Swaved by the exigencies of the moment, by
chance necessities, he often published laws to counte-
nance the action of his government, while repressing
rising abuses ; but his legislation had no unity and was
rarely marked by any solicitude for the future." There
only remained from him the hereditary transmission of
benefices from which the feudal system was to arise with
its miseries and its germs of renovation.   It was a fearful
principle ; but in the absence of monarchical unity, this
principle was better than anarchy. We are now about to
study its consequences.

* History of Municipal Law in France, vol. 2, p. 385.

CHAPTER XIII.

The establishment of the Feudal System and its economic consequences.—
The monarchy of Charlemagne dismembered by the influence of the heredity of fiefs.—General extension of serfdom.

THE capitularies of Charlemagne especially sanction
the power of the Church, which alone is henceforward
to intervene as a mediator between humanity and its
oppressors; and its intervention is worthy of note, since
the Capitularies constituted the law in France until the
reign of Philippe le Bel. The Church alone will balance
the power of the barons, and will give it a fatal blow by
taking the side of the people, as it ended the Roman
empire by allying itself with the Barbarians. In fact,
less than half a century after the death of Charlemagne,
his empire had already been divided into seven kingdoms, and the counts and dukes, imitating the style of
this great man and taking advantage of the times, had
sought to create for themselves independent positions.
The fiefs tended to become more and more hereditary,
and the sovereigns readily consented to it. We read in
a capitulary of Charles the Bold, in 877, the following
provisions, which are decisive in that respect: " If, after
our death, any of our faithful subjects, moved by love of
God and of our person, wishes to renounce the world,
and if he has a son or other relative capable of public
service, let him be free to transmit to him his fief as he
shall please."* Another article confirmed this and com-

---

* Capitularies, edit. of Baluze, vol. 2, p. 266.

pleted the reduction of the empire; for before the end
of the ninth century, there were twenty-nine great fiefs,
more or less independent, and more than fifty, at the
end of the tenth, in France alone.*

This new aspect of social dismemberment has been
graphically described by the historians: " The kingdom
formerly so well united," says one,† " is now divided:
there is no longer any one who can be considered as
emperor; instead of a king, one sees petty princes: instead of a kingdom, fragments of a kingdom." In reality,
all the grand organization of Charlemagne had disappeared to give place to turbulent and weak confedera-
tions which would certainly have had to yield, if any
powerful aggressor had attacked them. From that time,
the history of France is no longer anything but a com-
pilation of provincial annals, burdened with purely local
details, in which one can scarcely follow the course of
civilization. The most able and conscientious writers
have been obliged to have recourse to hypotheses to
explain that unexampled disintegration, which was
brought about almost instantaneously. M. Augustin
Thierry attributes it to the difference of races, and M.
Guizot to the loss of administrative traditions and of
great thoughts on general policy. We believe these
two causes have acted in different proportions. As the
cohesion became weaker, the spirit of race or rather of
locality was developed, probably according to circumstances which it is impossible for us to appreciate: and
the Europe of those times must have resembled certain
portions of Asia at present, where a few bold pachas, a
few independent chiefs, levy contributions upon the
people who are subject to them, without having even
among themselves any federal relations.

There is consequently no reason for surprise that new
hordes of invaders made an irruption into our territory,

---

* Guizot, Cours d'Histoire Moderne, vol. ii, p. 435.
† Recueil des Historiens des Gaules et de la France, vol. ii, p. 302.

and that the descent of the Saracens at the south and of the Normans at the north caused a deluge of woes to pour down upon our unhappy ancestors. There was no longer a bond anywhere, and no more obedience; civil wars and devastations soon produced an abandonment of agriculture, and famine added its rigors to all these scourges. A handful of pirates seized Marseilles in 848, and the Normans burned Bordeaux some time after. Their barques ascended the Seine and plundered Paris, in 856. The inhabitants ran into the temples instead of fighting, and the kings consented to ignominious treaties, in virtue of which these very Normans, having no longer anything to plunder in a ravaged country, caused it to be adjudged to themselves on condition of defending it. Thus Normandy received its name from the invaders, and the capital of Charlemagne, the city of Aix-la-Cha-pelle, was profaned by a band of foreigners whom this great sovereign had always treated as pirates. How times had changed ! The edict of Piste * threw barely a gleam of good order into that darkness of anarchy and troubles ; the fortifications of the feudal barons were not yet altogether thrown down, so that they were again raised, no more to disappear until they fell before the power of Louis XI, Richelieu, and Louis XIV. A new contract was formed between the usurper of the soil and the cultivator. The great land-holding abbots, the dukes, the counts, and the lords, sought the homage and support of their vassals almost as much as their wealth. They estimated the value of the land much more by the popu-lation than by the revenue it could furnish. The donjon, menacing as it was to neighbors and to strangers, was to the vassal a protector. The younger sons of noblemen,

---

* This edict is in the *Collection des Capitulaires*, p. 174, vol. ii, edit. of Baluze. It is composed of thirty-seven articles and of three supplementary paragraphs. Its aim, among others, was the general recoinage of the money, the making of which was accorded to only ten cities ; it fixed the relation between gold and silver at twelve pounds of silver for one of gold ; it com-prehended besides various rules concerning bakeries, the regulation of the markets, and the verification of weights and measures.

the free men, and the bourgeois, were permitted, on con‧
dition of a promise of subordination, to take their share
in the profits of the land, and could marry without detriment to the interest of their masters. The latter, fight‧
ing on horseback in virtue of their privilege, allowed
them to bear arms and to fight on foot; thus were established in the tent relations of good will, and those of different ranks were brought nearer together, and the way prepared, though indirectly, for the reign of equality. Every
village soon formed a community bound together by interests, passions, and almost by kinship. Who can tell
how much this wholly municipal political system, from
which was one day to come the emancipation of the communes with the industrial corporations, contributed to the
progress of civilization and political economy! We do
not know; but the transition was long and painful, and
the donjon was not long in turning against the villages.
Discord appeared among the myriads of lords, who wash-
ed away their offences in the blood of their subjects; and
for more than three centuries Europe presented the aspect of a vast arena where the stronger pitilessly took
advantage of the weaker. There was no longer capital
to give enterprise, nor great cities to receive it, but only
convents and castles, separated by rivers without bridges,
marshes without causeways, and forests without roads.
Justice was seated in the recesses of obscure manors,
more often the victim than the companion of force; people came to plead at the feet of all-powerful lords. Commerce, reduced to simple peddling from door to door,
avoided the observation which to-day it seeks; and besides, what attractions could it have for men barded with
steel and served in even their lightest caprice, by numerous artisans? The number of these workmen, however,
diminished daily, because of the ruin of the cities devastated now by a foreign enemy, and anon by civil war;
and soon there were no other manufactures than those
devoted to the production of the most indispensable

articles. The spirit of liberty, then, became extinct with
the great cities; no more franchises, no more of those
energetic and noisy rivalries which aroused the imagination and which we shall find again in the midst of the
Italian republics of the middle ages; but a general isolation of all minds and of all localities; a confused dust of
peoples and kings. The witnesses of that epoch of dissolution were so alarmed by it that they thought the end
of the world at hand, and they prepared for it as for an
inevitable event. There have come down to us a multitude of testaments or deeds of gift which were prompted
by the supposed near approach of that fatal catastrophe.
Most of them commence with these words: *Adventante
mundi vespero, i. e., the end of the world being at hand.*
But happily it did not come, and it caused no other ravages than the consequences of the fear which it had inspired. In many places labor had ceased; slaves had
been restored to liberty, old hatreds had been appeased,
and wicked people had been converted. What a triumph
for the church! what recrudescence of fervor for the
faith! But at the same time what stupidity there was
among the people and what hope could be conceived for
them when reduced to such a degree of brutalization!

This, too, was a time marvellously suited to all audacious attempts and tyrannous encroachments. We hear
no longer of political wars, but of expeditions of brigands
and incursions of pirates. The lords, who were authorized to coin money, to administer justice, to pronounce
as sovereigns over the lands within their jurisdiction,
broke the last bonds of all national unity, and alarmed
Europe with the bloody spectacle of their discords. The
castles constructed on every side, seemed to nourish that
fever for battles, by offering secure retreats to all disturbers of the public peace. History, if its thread can be
recognized in that long series of atrocities, is no longer
anything but a confused mass of events without connection and without bearing, much more characteristic of
savage hordes than of inhabitants of a civilized country.

However, we discover in it quite a clear trace of the principal elements of the social condition of the laborers. Almost all had retired into the country, and they were there divided into three classes ; the serfs, the villeins, and the free men. The first, bound to the soil, *adscriptae glebae*, were considered as *the thing* of their masters, as veritable fixtures by destination. Notwithstanding the prescriptions of the capitularies, which had become obsolete, their masters had resumed the power over them of life and death. They shaved their hair, inflicted tortures upon them, interdicted marriage and refused them the right of testifying in court against free men. They were distinguished from the latter by a particular dress, and could not even dispose by will of the rags which but illy covered their nakedness. No authority could intervene between the master and the serf, whose condition must have been inferior, during that sacrilegious period, to that of the beast of burden. The villeins (*villani*, inhabitants of country houses) differed from the serfs in being allowed to pay their masters certain rent-dues, in consequence of which the surplus of the products of cultivation belonged to themselves. There were, however, numerous exceptions to this rule, and generally the villeins were subject to the *taille* or villein-tax and to corvées without thanks or pity. A very small number of free men still preserved a shadow of independence, under the names of *conditionales tributarii*, and *arimanni*, which prove that at the same time this independence did not belong to them unconditionally. These were probably small proprietors who paid also their share of rent to the lords, either in money or services, and whose condition was so precarious and wretched that they were in the habit of renouncing their freedom, often made more onerous to them than servitude. This renunciation of the functions of a freeman was called *obnoxiatio*, and millions of unfortunates resigned themselves to it to enjoy a protection which certain lords and certain monasteries assured to their enfeoffed vassals. Their cry of despair resounded throughout all Europe, and authors note it at the same time in France, England and Germany. Are there not still several thousands of serfs in Russia * to-day, and are not lands sold there with the peasants who dwell on them ? †

Political economy cannot throw much light on the situation of real property at that deplorable epoch. All that is known is that some real estate was possessed under a perpetual title, and some other under a beneficiary title. Insensibly most of the freeholders transformed themselves into feudatories, in order to secure protectors, as in the inferior ranks many free men had reduced themselves from the same motive to the condition of serfs. Property in land became thus the symbol of power, and by successive usurpations, there became attached to it an immense number of privileges, most of which still remain and form not the least part of the economic complications of our time. Who does not easily recognize the old predominance of feudal property in the delays in expropriations for public purposes, or for judicial reasons, in the vicious system of mortgages, in the assessment of taxes favoring altogether real estate, and in the electoral privilege which guarantees all the others? See the institutions of England and of Germany ; travel over Spain and Italy ; feudalism is still alive in them, and it is even found in France, notwithstanding the revolutionary laws which reduced real property to atoms. " The manufacturer and the trader are still, in the eyes of many people, the sons of the freedman and of the slave ; on the other hand, there is always a presumption in favor of the landed proprietor. The latter is protected, not as an agriculturist and worker, but rather by reason of his abstract qual-

---

* More than 20,000,000 were emancipated by Alexander II, in 1861, and all have been entirely free in their persons since March, 1863, and they have also the perpetual usufruct of their cottages and gardens.— *Trans.*

† See, on the condition of the peasants in the middle ages, *L' Histoire des classes agricoles en France*, by Dareste de la Chavanne, 1858.

ity of proprietor, possessor of the soil, and legatee of the patricians or of the feudal baron." * This explains how some gleams of civilization have arisen from that feudal darkness which seems to have enveloped the world for several centuries. If great political ideas disappeared, great individualities began to be conspicuous and became sufficiently penetrated with their own importance, to merit a passing glance from history. Knightly armor and the privilege of fighting on horseback strengthened among the lords the feeling of their independence and of their rights, and preserved to human dignity an asylum free from servitude. The feudal barons, true republican noblemen, less enlightened than those of Rome and Athens, created for themselves a common law, founded on loyalty to promises and respect for their pledged faith. They sought in the sacredness of the oath a guarantee against the violence of their passions which a powerful central government no longer could restrain. They put women for the first time under the protection of French gallantry, and prepared, perhaps unconsciously, the way for the more serious changes that occurred in the subsequent centuries. We shall see them, combined with the clergy, fanning the sacred flame of the crusades which civilized the world by commerce, while waiting until their dis-cords regenerate it by freedom.

---

* Letters of Michel Chevalier on North America. Vol. ii, p. 268.

CHAPTER XIV.

The Crusades and their influence on the course of political economy in Europe.—Saladin tithe.—Revolution in habits.—Progress of navigation, the industrial arts and commerce.

IN the midst of the feudal anarchy of Europe, the half-chivalric, half-religious enterprise of the crusades was a happy idea. The first suggestion of it came from the clergy ; its execution belongs wholly to the nobility, whom that generous fever was to cost so dearly ; but the people received lasting benefits from it, the first of which was, becoming rid of a multitude of oppressors. How many decisive events, in effect, grew out of these famous crusades ! The emancipation of the communes, the modification of serfdom, the appearance of the bourgeoisie, the revival of industries, the creation of commerce and navigation, and the fortune of that pleiad, so brilliant and so poetic, of the Italian republics. This was not the work of a day ; but the work, once commenced, has not ceased to go forward with a regular step towards its full accomplishment. No time has elapsed without some generation bringing its tribute of intelligence and enthusiasm ; so much did the world, weary of feudal chaos, long for repose in a contemplation of a glorious future !

It is extremely interesting to follow the progress of that revolution in the confused history of the eleventh century ; and everything from the usurpation of Hugh Capet, to the wanderings of the troubadours, coöperates in it as if by enchantment. One might have thought

that all Europe was going to continue in the East the invasion scarcely established in the West, so many travelers
presented themselves for these adventurous expeditions.

They were composed not alone of warriors; following
the soldiers was an immense multitude of artisans, traders,
lookers-on, paupers, rich people, monks, women, and even
infants from the cradle!* It was this turbulent mass
which so many times compromised the safety of the army
by their disturbances and by the wretchedness they left
along their path. Famine committed more ravages among
them than the sword of the enemy; and we cannot to-
day conceive of such excessive distress as that of which
historians have handed down to us the lamentable details.
A chronicler who had witnessed them, exclaimed, "Would
to Heaven the Pope had not permitted the weak to take
the cross; that he had given the strong a sword instead
of the pouch, a bow instead of a staff!" One fatal habit
which we shall be pardoned for alluding to, because it
has since penetrated, unfortunately, European morals,
originated at that time among the crusaders; it was the
passion for gaming. This thirst for sudden wealth made
such progress that everybody played, from the chieftains
to the lower soldiers. After the conquest of Constantinople, the knights gambled with dice for the cities and
provinces of the Greek empire. The companions of Saint
Louis, during their stay at Damietta, staked even their
horses and their arms.

What human motive could have induced so great a
crowd of men to abandon their country to incur such
risks! Religious enthusiasm had much to do with it;
but poverty, serfdom, and the hope of bettering their
condition, had still more influence. A crusader's law
granted land, a house, a city even, to him who should
be the first to raise a flag there. The first crusaders were
exempt from the villein-tax, and the payment of their

---

* Michelet, *Histoire des Croisades*, vol. vi, p. 43.

debts was stayed.* Their possessions were put under the protection of the church, and by a favor entirely contrary to the customs of the feudal system, they could pledge their fiefs and sell them, either to the laity or to the ecclesiastics, without the permission of their lords. The crusaders were henceforth amenable only to ecclesiastical tribunals. There was such a fever that artisans, traders and farmers abandoned their work and their business; barons and lords hastened to dispose of their domains. Lands and castles were sold for moderate sums ; and this circumstance, by bringing about serious modifications in the system of land ownership, contributed not a little to the gradual and definitive affranchisement of the communes. The settled bourgeoisie grew rich by degrees from the domains sold by the wandering nobility, and the power passed thus with the lands into the hands of the new possessors. There came a time when the estates no longer found buyers. The crusaders spurned everything which they could not take with them ; the products of the soil were sold at a low price, and abundance suddenly reappeared in the midst of scarcity.

When we attentively study the details of this great movement, it is impossible not to be struck with its resemblance to the invasion of the Barbarians. There were the same dreams of enjoyments and of riches ; and, just as Europe had appeared to the latter an abode preferable to their forests and their swamps, so the East seemed to the crusaders an Eldorado unequalled in the world, a ver-

---

* The following are provisions relating to that privilege : " The warriors who shall have taken the cross, shall have, in which to pay their debts, to Jews as well as to Christians, the space of two years, reckoning from the first feast of All-Saints. Interest shall not accrue to any one from the day of taking the cross. If any warrior or clerk engages for a fixed number of years, his property or his revenues, to any bourgeois crusader, or to a warrior or clerk not a crusader, the tenant shall collect that year the fruits of the land or of the revenues, and the creditor, at the end of the years for which he was to hold the engagement or the farm, shall retain them one year longer, in consideration of the year he has lost. No crusader can be summoned by law for the execution of his promises, from the day of his departure to that of his return, unless for obligations incurred before he assumed the cross."

itable *vestibule of Paradise*, as one of them naively said.* The love of adventure and of freedom, the certainty of escaping from bondage to the soil with their wives and children, attracted thousands of men. Monks, tired of the discipline of their convents, could escape from it by a pilgrimage to the holy land ; malefactors even, absolved from their crimes by indulgences, hastened in crowds to the banners of the cross, and took the road to Jerusalem. Those who had the good sense to resist the general impulse realized considerable profit from the acquisition of land and property of every kind, and from the sale of horses and arms, the demand for which increased in an unheard of degree. We know the terrible checks which decimated that stupid and coarse crowd in its first campaign towards the East, where few of the travelers arrived safe and sound. At the time of the second crusade, some little order was required in the enrollments, and some few conditions were imposed on those whose departure was authorized. The third gave rise to the *Saladin Tithe*,† a species of forced contribution the receipts from which were destined to provide for the wants of the crusaders, and from which none were exempt except those who paid with their person. The feudal system had so penetrated the morals and the laws, that the principal grievance against the recalcitrant tax-payers came from their refusing to Jesus Christ, as suzerain, the homage which every good vassal was supposed to owe his lord. When, notwithstanding these numerous expedients, the

---

* Others were more specific. In his letter to the Count of Flanders, Alexis named, among his motives, "*amor auri et argenti et pulcherrimarum fœminarum voluptas.*"

† The text of that curious document has been preserved by Rigord, the chronographer of Philip Augustus, who compiled in bad Latin a journal of the reign of that prince. This is the beginning : "All those who are not crusaders shall give this year at least a tenth of all their movable property and of all their revenues. The warrior not a crusader shall give the crusader lord whose liege man he is, the tenth of his own personal property and of the fief he holds from him. All the laity shall give their tithes under oath and the penalty of the anathema, and the clerks under that of excommunication."

managers of the crusades lacked money, they began to plunder the Jews, the Greeks, and even the Christians. Want was sometimes so severe and necessities so pressing, that they went even so far as to impose taxes on the property of churches and religious communities, which complained loudly at it. It was what the monks of the time called *delivering up the vine of the Lord to the fury of the Turks*, an abominable act deserving the pains of hell.

The revolution caused by the crusades exercised too much influence on the development of European institutions, not to lead to careful investigations into the means by which these expeditions to distant lands were supplied with food. At the beginning, as we have seen, enthusiasm sufficed : the volunteers supported themselves from the product of lands sold or funds borrowed; later, it was necessary to feed and pay them, for the inhabitants everywhere fled at their approach and left them only deserted places to travel through. There exists a singular letter of pope Innocent III to the leaders of the fifth crusade : " You are devoted," he said to them, " to the service of the crucified to whom the whole earth belongs. If any one should refuse you the necessary provisions, it would not appear unjust that you should take them wherever you can find them, *always in fear of God and with the intention of making restitution.*" The learned historian of the crusades who quotes this letter very sensibly adds : " It is unnecessary to say that the crusaders were naturally inclined to follow the advice of the pope, and that they did not wait for it before procuring the provisions they needed." Their practice of pillaging did not always keep them from famine, and the history of the crusades is full of accounts of their sufferings. There was no regularity in the supplies of provisions, except at the time when the expeditions were made by sea, with the intervention of the powers which bordered on the shore of the Mediterranean.

The results of the crusades have been looked at in

various ways, according to the point of view which the various historians have taken. Considered in their relation to human freedom, it cannot be denied that the crusades contributed to alleviate slavery, by enabling a multitude of the serfs of the nobility to pass into the more tolerable condition of dependence on the clergy. By weakening the fortune and the number of the lords, they made way for the coming in of the bourgeoisie. The continual consumption of soldiers they occasioned, rendered men scarce and led to good treatment of those remaining in the West. At the same time, the latter, invested with the local government in the absence of their masters, administered with moderation, and allowed the people to form habits which the barons, on their return, did not venture to oppose. Peace reigned in the rural districts all the time that the tyrants of the castles were making war in the Holy Land. *The truce of God*, a work of the clergy, which the expeditions into Palestine rendered still more sacred, placed under the safeguard of the church the husbandman and his plough, I might almost say his independence. We cannot say how far that alliance might have extended, if the serfs who set out for Jerusalem had thought of employing for their own emancipation the enthusiasm which was urging them on to the conquest of a tomb.

Insensibly the clergy took the place of the nobility in the administration of justice, protected the widows and orphans, the strangers, the poor, the *lepers*. They had become the guardians of all minors abandoned by heads of families; and, confining the penalty of their sentences to spiritual punishments, they substituted for the sword of the lords a weapon less dangerous and yet as much respected. Their supremacy, daily increasing, finally excited the jealousy of the barons, who, in the thirteenth century, formed a league against the clergy, *demanding that they render unto Cæsar what belonged to Cæsar*. The intervention of the popes was necessary to

reconcile this serious difference, which we shall see reproduced, and from which liberty will profit. Hence arose
parliaments, that bourgeois justice, offspring of the
clergy, which has rendered so many services to humanity
by keeping alive and making respected the old Roman
maxim, *Cedant arma togæ*. We must also recognize that
the necessity of looking out for the future, as well as the
great number of testaments and contracts that the pilgrims had to sign, made the importance of law and justice felt, and consequently seconded the progress of legislation and jurisprudence. But the progress was more
strikingly manifest in manufactures, navigation and commerce. At one time it seemed as if the navigators of
all countries had made a rendezvous in the Eastern
waters. Bremen and Lübeck made the acquaintance of
Genoa and Venice. The Baltic Sea, a mysterious retreat
of Norman pirates, was discovered and explored. The
Hanse towns, by putting liberty under the protection of
commerce, prepared in the North a confederation rivaling the Italian republics, which brought, like them, its
tribute of intelligence and wealth to the common centre
of civilization. Naval architecture increased the size of
vessels for facility in the transport of pilgrims. Fifteen
years after the third crusade, formidable fleets might be
seen leaving the ports of Venice and Genoa such as the
Mediterranean had never before carried. Navigators
from Barcelona published the first collection of maritime
laws which were authoritative in Europe. The *Assizes
of Jerusalem*[11] contain some provisions of this kind, and
history has preserved for us several regulations drawn
up by Richard Cœur de Lion for the maintenance of
order on board his fleets. Piracy was repressed. The
regulations for the government of the seas, rigorously
enforced by two or three powers interested in making
good order respected, contributed much to the progress
of commerce by giving it a commencement of security.
Convoys of ships followed the coasts of the countries

where the crusaders were fighting, and became rich by selling them provisions and munitions of war.

Manufactures profited no less than commerce from the impulse given to ideas by the numerous expeditions to the Holy Land. We know that the crusaders preferred to enroll men who had a trade or some mechanical employment. These industrial pilgrims did not always make a journey unprofitable for their country, and while their comrades were marching to the conquest of the Holy Places, the industrial arts had also their crusade and purloined from the Saracens and Greeks secrets and processes more valuable than victories.* The crusaders learned at Damascus how to work the metals and make cloth successfully; they found in the East manufactures of camlet, patterns of which excited the admiration of Queen Marguérite. Many Greek cities supported silk-looms, which gave rise to the cultivation of the mulberry tree in Italy and consequently to an immense extension of its graceful products. The glass works of Tyre aided in perfecting the fine glass fabrics of Venice, so justly renowned in the middle ages. There is nothing, even to wind-mills, the introduction of which into Europe was not due to the travels of the crusaders. Sugar-cane, which they saw for the first time at Tripoli, was transported by them into Sicily in the twelfth century ; a multitude of other plants not less useful,—among others, maize, since called Turkish wheat,—owe also to them their naturalization in the West. How much time and trouble have nevertheless been necessary, for their conquests to bear fruit, especially when we recall that the most eminent men of the time,—Sire de Joinville, for example,— supposed in their simplicity that pepper and cinnamon came from the terrestrial paradise and that spices were fished in the waters of the Nile whither they had been carried by the winds ! †

---

* Michaud, *Histoire aes Croisades*, vol. vi, page 346.

† *Mémoires de Joinville*, 2d part, p. 36, edition of Ducange.

On the whole, the crusades exalted the authority of the princes and introduced serious modifications into the feudal régime. The nobles who had become subjects, the bourgeois who had become merchants, and the cities which had become rich, assured to the public revenues new sources, fruitful and regular, which consolidated the power of the sovereigns. From this time, the third estate could be set against the nobility; and it became by degrees, under the auspices of royalty, a powerful and respected class. These results were not developed in the same degree or in a like manner in all the countries of Europe; but they had no cause more potent than the crusades. We shall examine later the true elements of the affranchisement of the communes; what is certain is that they did not receive a gleam of independence until after the great crusading expeditions. Commerce itself, whose rights the Barbarians had sometimes respected, would have succumbed under the weight of exactions with which feudal anarchy overwhelmed it, if the necessities of the Holy War had not caused a restoration of its former independence. Thus, while at Byzantium, everything,—bread, wine, oil, and eatables of every kind*— was reduced to a monopoly, provisions circulated freely in the Mediterranean and in the maritime cities under the auspices of the religious crusade. The Venetians caused the principles of commercial freedom to be adopted wherever their political influence extended. To them is due the establishment of the first general factories or trading-houses, which served as models to all those which the various nations to-day maintain in each others' countries. The kings of Jerusalem, who had need of these bold merchants, accorded them numerous privileges and even territorial possessions. Thus the colonial spirit was born in Europe, and with it the bloody rivalries, the industrial enterprises and financial contrivances in which the Jews, those shrewd economists of the middle ages, played a part which claims for a moment our attention.

---

* Heeren, *Essay on the Influence of the Crusades.*

CHAPTER XV.

Considerations on the situation and influence of the Jews in the middle ages.—Nature of the services they have rendered to political economy.—Were they the first founders of credit?—Origin of *bills of exchange* and *monts-de-piété*.

WHILE the feudal system was covering Europe with barriers, tolls, and restrictions of every sort,* commerce took refuge in the bosom of a proscribed caste and under its influence preluded the magnificent destinies which the crusades were to assure it. It was indeed a spectacle worthy of interest to see the rapid development of wealth in the midst of the perpetual troubles of feudalism, and in the hands of the men the most mercilessly harassed, in that epoch of pillage and spoliation. It will not be unimportant to political economy to trace rapidly how this remarkable fact took its rise and grew to the rank of the most decisive events, under the sway of circumstances least adapted to favor its appearance.

I will not recall on this subject the history of the Jewish people and their long tribulations. Proscribed by the heathens, proscribed by the Christians and by the Mus-

---

* To give an idea of the singularity and diversity of these tolls, it will suffice to mention a few. A duty called *pontaticum* was paid for passing under bridges, and that of *portaticum* to enter ports. The lords made the trading boats that sailed on rivers along lands under their dominion, pay on the river bank a tax called *ripaticum* ; they demanded another called *tranaticum* for according permission to carry merchandise on a sledge. The *mansionaticum* was paid to avoid lodgment of warriors, and the *pulveraticum,* for the dust raised on the roads by trading wagons. There was also the *teloneum,* the *paraverdum,* the *cespitaticum,* the *coenaticum,* and many others whose names are no less barbarous and whose object no less odious.

sulmans, the Jews seemed to have thrived by persecutions and molestations, silently indemnifying themselves by the worship of gold, for the affronts heaped upon their religion, and always reappearing the more powerful as they were the more hated. As early as the time of Charlemagne, we see them in request at court, although they have no civil status and are not considered as citizens. Under Louis the Mild, they are refused the *favor* of the the *judgment of God* and of trials by fire and water; but, in compensation, they obtain private judges, and there exists, in 828, a special magistrate, an illustrious person, clothed with the office of *Master of the Jews*, who judges them and protects them. Many of them also came into France under the kings of the second race, principally into the cities of the south, where the demands of commerce, facility in finding shelter while passing the frontiers, and the means they had of correspondence with their co-religionists of Asia, attracted a very great number. For a brief period, one might think they were going to become veritable mandarins; their *master* resided at the court and was the intimate counsellor of the sovereign; the princes and nobles sought their protection by rich presents, and even accorded them privileges envied by free men.

Under the feudal régime no rank was assigned the Jews: they were to submit to the common law of servitude and obey the lords of the lands on which they were found. Their character of heretics prevented them from being protected as much as other feudal subjects, and they reached the point of being exchanged, sold and lent like cattle. Nevertheless their existence was still supportable when the first systematic persecutions were directed against them in the reign of Philippe I, who drove them from his dominions in 1096. They returned, however, a few years after, on condition of paying for the privilege, and they would perhaps have been forgotten, had it not been for the crusades, which greatly increased religious zeal and consequently the severity towards them. They were forced to contribute to the expenses of more than one campaign in the Holy Land, by means of a multitude of vague and odious accusations, which obliged them day by day to purchase life from the fury of the people with exorbitant sums. Though momentarily favored by Philippe Auguste, they finally led miserable lives under his reign, exposed to all kinds of outrages, and were forced, later, to wear a distinctive garb which too often marked them for murder and pillage. St. Louis burdened them with the most intolerable laws, freed their debtors, forbade all prosecutions that would favor the Jews, and pushed his severity so far as to interdict them from making contracts.* An ordinance in 1254 expressly declared " that the Jews must cease usuries, blasphemies, and sorcery, and live henceforward by the labor of their hands and other tasks, without loaning money." These ordinances were executed with a severity so much the greater, because the king declared that he had issued them to relieve his conscience and provide for his salvation. They even went farther in 1239, and we find in the assizes of Brittany † an atrocious provision, in virtue of which it was forbidden to inform against any one who should kill a Jew. Later, in 1288, the parliament of Paris condemned them to pay a heavy fine for having sung too loud in their synagogues. Philippe le Bel proscribed them and recalled them, by turns, according to the need he had of their money. His successor treated their existence as a purely commercial matter, and allowed them to collect their debts on condition of paying him two-thirds of them. " If, by chance," says the ordinance, " they cannot recover their synagogues and their cemeteries, we will have dwellings and lodgings given them *at suitable prices.*" After the lapse of twelve years, the king could drive them out only on condition of granting them a year in which to carry

---

* *Ordonnances des Rois de France*, vol. i, pages 53 and 54.

† D'Argentré, *Histoire de Bretagne*, Book iv, chap. xxiii, p. 207.

away their effects. Finally, he guaranteed them a certain freedom of person and property, which did not, however, prevent their being pillaged and hunted down in 1321, before the expiration of twelve years, under pretext of their connivance with lepers and even with infidels. They were also accused, as usual, of having poisoned the springs of water, and a great number of them were consequently burned to death. Several councils forbade them to practice medicine, and threatened with excommunication any Christian who should dare have recourse to their services. We cannot to-day properly characterize such absurdities; and yet we imitate them in our colonies towards men of color, to whom certain occupations are still interdicted; so true it is that while times change, prejudices are slow to disappear!

The history of the Jews, therefore, presents only a monotonous succession of vicissitudes. In 1340, their debtors are forbidden to pay them; in 1346 the Jews are compelled to become converted or to depart from the kingdom. In Italy, in Spain, in Germany, there are the same outrages, the same persecutions, sometimes suspended when the governments need their money, but resumed as soon as those needs are satisfied. To the office of *Master of the Jews* succeeds that of *General Guardian*, in 1359, as if these men had formed a nation in the midst of a nation. Then comes the captivity of King John, whose ransom they help to pay, and that aid is followed by a shower of favors. Their cemeteries are restored to them; they are allowed to acquire houses; they are exempted from aids (a special tax) and the salt-tax; the judges of the king are forbidden to interfere with their business, and their affirmations as to what is due them, are to be received as authoritative. It was the States-general which had obtained for them these advantages. A happy and singular result, for those times, of the intervention of the people in the affairs of the nation! But these fine days were not of long duration, and we see the Jews again forced to buy with gold, one by one, so to speak, the liberties which they had already paid for so many times.   Charles VI drives them from France in 1393 and compels them to withdraw into Germany, where new vexations await them, to last longer than in any other country.   What is certain is that at no time were they popular.   The services they rendered to the various governments as money-lenders, were dearly paid for by the people, and tend to explain how they could be seen at almost the same moment so earnestly protected by some and so cruelly treated by others.   The isolation in which they were forced to live, and the prohibition, long continued, against acquiring real estate, directed their speculations toward commerce and manufactures, in which they soon obtained incontestable superiority.   Unfortunately, they devoted themselves to these with a mistrust and timidity which by degrees led them to seek in trickery a shelter from the abuses of power, and thus were they led to those shameful transactions, of which their history presents only too many examples.

Nothing is more curious to study than the commercial condition of that nation which had no territory of its own, nor ports, nor armies, and which, constantly tacking about on an agitated sea, with contrary winds, at last arrived in port with rich cargoes and immense wealth.   The Jews traded because it was rarely permitted them to employ themselves in any other way with security.   While the multiplicity of toll-houses and the tyranny of the feudal lords rendered all trade impossible except that of the petty tradesmen of the market-towns and cities, the Jews, more bold, more mobile, were dreaming of vaster operations, and were working silently to bind together continents, to bring together kingdoms.   They avoided the highways and the castles, carefully concealing their real opulence and their secret transactions under the appearances of poverty.   They went great distances for rare products of the most remote countries, and brought them within reach of well-to-do consumers. By wandering about and traveling from country to country, they had acquired an exact acquaintance with the needs of all places; they knew where to buy and where to sell. Some samples and a note-book sufficed them for their most important operations. They corresponded with each other on the strength of engagements which their interest obliged them to respect, in view of the enemies of every sort by whom they were surrounded. Commerce has lost the trace of the ingenious inventions which were the result of their efforts; but it is to their influence that it owes the rapid progress of which history shows us the brilliant phenomenon in the midst of the horrors of feudal darkness. Insensibly, the Jews were absorbing all the money, since this was the only kind of property which they could acquire and keep safely, and usury soon appeared to them as the surest means of enriching themselves. Free to fit out vessels and to undertake avowed speculations, they would perhaps have renewed the marvels of Tyre and of Carthage: slaves, and burdened with contributions, they became accustomed to getting back by usury what was taken from them by spoliations. In vain were severe laws proclaimed against loans at interest; these laws only served to make loans more difficult and consequently interest more onerous. Lenders knew then as now how to elude the prescriptions which interfered with their projects, and their discounts were so much the more usurious as the risks were more serious. Gradually, with the aid of a little capital, they became masters of all fortunes, and more than once the despair of their debtors massacred them as creditors rather than as heretics.*

This state of things lasted until the discovery of the Cape of Good Hope and of America, an epoch when European nations devoted themselves to enterprises much more important than the peddling from house to house

---

* Arthur Beugnot, *Les Juifs d'Occident*, 2d part, p. 35.

of the Jews, and their speculations on short loans. But, for more than five hundred years, it is in the history of that nation that we must study the progress of commerce and the more or less venturesome attempts through which it has risen to the rank of a political power. The Jews began by selling slaves under the first race ; they became also collectors of tolls (telonarii), and their abuse of that office was such that it had to be taken from them. Later, we find them established at Vienne in Dauphiny, in relations with Marseilles for the trade of the Levant. They obtain, in consequence of these relations, several diplomatic missions, and they fill them with ability. The monk of Saint-Gall mentions a certain Jew trader who had become the favorite of Charlemagne, and who went to countries beyond the sea in search of the most valuable commodities. The priests and bishops had become their tributaries, and more than once the sacred vessels were pawned to these heretics, to meet the ruinous expenses of the clergy. The Jews were the depositaries of the finest cloths known, and they traded in them at immense profits : they extended the use and at the same time the demand for them into castles and into abbeys. They also engrossed the trade in jewelry and in gold and silver bullion. Feudalism disturbed these lucrative occupations less than one might suppose : the lords put upon them strict conditions, but they had the good sense to treat them with respect. Besides, in the midst of the general terror which continually hovered around all highways and all travelers, the Jews, armed with safe-conducts, traveled over all Europe without inquietude, and in the tenth and eleventh centuries disposed like sovereigns of all the commerce of France. At that period, they had already greatly simplified commercial proceedings, and their correspondence would have done honor to the most able merchants of our great cities.

The appearance of the tradesmen of Lombardy, Tuscany, and other parts of Italy, completed the work of the

Jews and gave an energetic impulse to the commerce of the middle ages. The latter, from that time, traded in everything, and put in circulation real and personal property, such as horses, lands and houses. The historian Rigord goes so far as to say that the Jews were, at that time, real proprietors of half the kingdom. In vain royal ordinances fixed the rate of interest, regulated mortgages, the mode of prosecutions against debtors, and a multitude of other questions of an economic importance not less great; the Jews continued to loan and to sell, to those who needed loans and purchases, and who were only too careful not to discuss conditions. It is also claimed that it was at this time that the first bills of exchange appeared, the invention of which some trace to about the seventh century, and others, only to the middle of the twelfth. It is a point which has not yet been cleared up, and which is not of so much consequence as some have supposed. The date of such a discovery, even if it could be authentically fixed, would be of interest simply as a matter of curiosity ; but it appears destined to remain forever in doubt. It is thought, and with reason, that the invention is rather due to the Italian traders than to the Jewish brokers of this time, the latter not having had occasion as soon as the others to devote themselves to trade between different places, which probably suggested the idea. The very name of letter of exchange, which was primitively Italian, seems to indicate their true authorship ; and the first city where they were used, Lyons, then the entrepôt of Italy, is a further indication. It is probable that the Lombards and the Jews had an equal part in inventing them, and divined, from the beginning, the important consequences from their use.*

---

* M. Courcelle-Seneuil, in a learned article that he published in Guillaumin's Dictionary of Polit. Econ. (1853, 2 vol. gr. in-8vo.), traced the employment of this commercial procedure to antiquity. We reproduce here the historical part of that interesting study :

"It cannot be affirmed that the Phœnicians knew the letter of exchange. We know little of these people who brought writing to the Occidentals and who wrote little themselves, who purposely allowed an impenetrable mystery to

These ingenious contrivers later entered into a strife, and the history of the Italian republics of the middle ages is full of the debates which arose between them on the subject of privileges which some wished to exercise to the exclusion of the others. We see the Jews become intendants, stewards, procurators, bankers, and even agents in marriages, according as they are more or less forcibly driven from all the regular commercial positions by the bulls of the Popes or by the jealousy of competitors. Everything thus contributed to narrow them down to a vicious circle, from which they can only escape by usury and money negotiations. When envy has forced them to abandon a city, the interest of the inhabitants calls them back; their capital has become so necessary to

prevail in their industries and commercial processes, as well as in the discoveries of their navigators. Nevertheless, we can hardly believe that the numerous Phœnician trading-houses in the Indian Ocean, the Red Sea, the Mediterranean and even beyond the columns of Hercules, had between them neither exchange of credits, nor clearances followed by orders to ·pay at Asiongaber or at Carthage, everywhere, in short, where were found Phœnician traders having the same handwriting, the same language, and nearly the same laws.

"The Athenians, who were acquainted with orders, reckoning of interest, bank-deposits, and the negotiation of claims, were also acquainted with what may be called the elementary form of bills of exchange. In his plea against the banker Pasion, Isokrates, speaking in the name of a young man who had come from Pontus to Athens to see the world and learn commerce, expressed himself in these terms : ' As I wished funds from Pontus, I begged Stratokles, who was setting out for that country, to leave me his gold, which my father would refund to him. I thought it would be a great advantage to me not to have my funds pass over a sea infested with the pirates from Lacedæmon. * * * Stratokles being concerned to know who would pay back his money if my father did not act in accordance with my letters, and if I had left Athens on his return, I took him to Pasion, who promised to pay him, in that case, principal and interest.'

" Here is, in fact, a formal bill of exchange bought by Stratokles, and it is very probable that the trade of Athens, which had penetrated as far as India, and even to Serica, near China, and on the other hand as far as the Vistula, where it had encountered the Phœnicians, had experienced much earlier than the client of Isokrates, the advantage of the exchange of credits by means of which funds were transported, as it were, without being exposed to shipwreck or to the pirates of land and sea.

" The Romans, too, knew the bill of exchange under that form. ' Let me know,' writes Cicero to Atticus, ' if the money my son needs at Athens can be sent him by way of exchange or if it is necessary for it to be taken to him ' (' *permutarine possit, an ipsi ferendum sit.*') This passage, in which the letter of exchange is designated almost by name, does not permit a doubt of its existence in ancient times.

" It is true that neither the Roman laws, at least those which we possess, nor history, contain exact information in regard to the bill of exchange. But as we have already said, history, which, in our days, ordinarily neglects

these industrial cities that the orders of the authorities are disregarded to prevent the Jews carrying it elsewhere. Moreover, soon houses for loaning money are started even in the villages; and the Jews of Tuscany direct from a central point a multitude of branch-houses of their establishments at Florence and Pisa. Their opulence and their magnificence surpassed imagination, and aroused against them fanatical adversaries. We know the history of that famous Bernardin de Feltre, who carried his enthusiasm so far as to preach a crusade against them, and who on every occasion showed himself their most implacable enemy. He pursued them everywhere as usurers thirsting for the blood of the people : and, to ruin their establishments, he conceived the idea of opposing them by the formation of those houses for

---

commerce, concerned itself still less with it in those remote times. Besides, every branch of business, every council of state, and bankers at least as much as others, had colleges or fraternities, and their secrets, in all antiquity and during the middle ages. The operations of exchange, like other banking operations, were governed by laws of their own, by unwritten customs and usages of which the initiated alone had the secret, and of which legislators and society in general were entirely ignorant.

"We need not be surprised that the Jews preserved better than others the secret of the bill of exchange ; for, from the time of the first Cæsars, they were scattered over the whole empire, as the Acts of the Apostles bear witness, and they traded almost exclusively in the precious metals and in moneys. The Jews were obliged to carry with them bills of exchange, as well before as after their expulsion in 1181, a simple incident of the long persecution of which they were the object during fifteen centuries.

"In the middle ages, as previously, we find the bill of exchange wherever commerce is flourishing ; at Amalfi, at Sienna, at Florence, and in the Hansetowns of the Rhine and the Elbe. In 1255, says Mathieu Paris, Henry III, King of England, having need of money for his second son, Edmund, charged by the Pope to conquer the states of the house of Suabia in Italy, negotiated a loan with some merchants of Sienna and Florence. Its maturity having arrived and the king not knowing how to meet it, the bishop of Hereford, Egeblank, showed him a convenient way. He advised him to discharge the debt by drawing bills of exchange on the bishops of England through the Italian merchants, to the amount of the loan ; and this advice was followed. In vain the bishops protested and said they had done no act of commerce ; they were condemned to pay, by the tribunals of the Pope, who had approved the expedient. Such is the curious though scarcely commercial use that was made of bills of exchange in the thirteenth century.

"But neither in the middle ages nor in ancient times have we found any trace of endorsement and its consequences. 'The Jews,' says Savary, 'found a way to withdraw their effects, which they had confided to the hands of their friends, by secret letters couched in terms short and precise, and that through the mediation of travelers and foreign merchants.'

loaning on pledges, which are called *monts-de-piété*. At the beginning, everything was free in them, and the sums lent were without interest, while the Jews sometimes deducted beforehand an interest of 30 to 40 per cent. Moreover, their success was prodigious, and most of the cities of Italy had their *monts-de-piété*, which were one day to surpass in usurious exactions the boldest operations of the Jews.

However, these *monts-de-piété* could not fill the place of the establishments of the Jews, and this circumstance proves with what shrewdness the latter had truly divined the wants of the monetary circulation. Although the *monts-de-piété* loaned money almost without interest, the formalities which it was necessary to undergo in order to have a right to their help, the inevitable delays in their admin-

---

Thus these bills of exchange were not even drawn for the benefit of the bearer, like that of Stratokles, they were, to speak accurately, only advices for clearing the accounts, and we question whether the exchange relations introduced into Amsterdam by the exiled Lombards, were anything different.

"The formula of a bill of exchange of the 1st of February, 1381, which M. Nouguier adduces in his treatise, contains no name of the remitter, nor order, nor any mention whatsoever of protest or guaranty. It is a simple notice of clearing the account.

"As to the rest, it is sufficient to reflect one single moment on the situation of commerce in the society of that period and in ancient times, to comprehend that the modern bill of exchange, with the endorsement of its guaranties and the protest, could hardly have found a place there. Property, especially personal property, was so little respected then, that recourse to the tribunals was almost impracticable. The bill of exchange, if it had existed, could have had currency only between a very small number of bankers all well known to each other and of credit so assured as never to need the intervention of the tribunals.

"Thus, then, it was, that the bill of exchange entered into modern society. When Louis XI issued the ordinance of 1462, he made no law about bills of exchange : he simply authorized the merchants of the fair at Lyons to make use of them, as if that had been previously interdicted. The ordinances which established or rather recognized in 1549 the consular jurisdiction of Toulouse, and in 1563 that of Paris, attributed to these jurisdictions the knowledge of all contests relating to bills of exchange, and we must seek in these tribunals for the commercial law of the times, which was custom.

"The modern bill of exchange, with the endorsement and its consequent obligations, can have originated no farther back than the great commercial movement which marked the end of the fifteenth century, and it did not take its place in French law until the ordinance of 1673, at the very time when commerce was increasing in France in civil society and engrossing public attention." *Dict. de l' Econ. Pol.* Article, *Lettre de change.*
(Note of French editor.)

istration, the necessity of proving the legitimate possession of the articles pledged, and above all, the obligation on the part of depositors to make known their names, soon kept away borrowers, who could obtain funds at any time, in secret and without formalities, from the Jewish bankers. Rich and poor, lords and villeins, hastened to them, and their credit was so great at Leghorn, in the times of the Medicis, that the saying became proverbial : *" It is better to beat the Grand-duke than a Jew."* Pope Sixtus-Fifth had opened again to them all the sources of wealth which his predecessors had closed ; their goods were even exempt from every toll, the *sacro monte della pietà* ceased to compete with them, when the Christians in charge had surpassed the abuses of their rivals. After less than ten years of existence, the *monts-de-piété* had become what they are to-day, open pits under the steps of misfortune rather than asylums to escape it.

Everything then seems to warrant the belief that the Jews exercised a notable influence on the course of political economy in Europe, by keeping in charge, in the midst of feudal anarchy, the commercial traditions destined to become perfected and refined in the atmosphere of the fifteenth century. It is to the persecutions of which they were victims that we are indebted for the first attempts at credit and the system of circulation. They alone, perhaps, by concentrating on trade in gold and silver an attention which the prejudices of their contemporaries prevented them from giving to anything else, prepared the way for the great monetary revolution which the discovery of the mines in America and the establishment of European banks were to accomplish in the world. Thus the luminous trace of the future shines and is preserved, in the midst even of the darkest events ; and we shall follow it, still **more marked, in the history of the Hanse towns.**

CHAPTER XVI.

The Hanse towns.—Cause of their association.—Singular organization of their trading-houses.—Importance of the *entrepôt* of Bruges.—Origin of commission-trade.

WHILE the Jews were creating and extending commercial science in Europe in spite of feudal anarchy and the constantly renewed persecutions by which they were oppressed, a powerful association was forming in Germany and completing the work of the crusades after having anticipated it. The north and the south march thus in concert to the conquest of the great elements of public wealth, and the genius of production finds ever an asylum from the abuse of power and the exactions of tyranny. This progress is not easy to follow through the vicissitudes which incessantly agitate European society from the reign of Charlemagne to that of Charles V, but it is impossible to misinterpret the efforts which have been constantly made in one country or another, to restore to the laborer his rank and to labor its prerogatives. Even while crushing him, people have rendered homage to him ; and the history of the Jews, incessantly proscribed and recalled, is only a series of gropings, to the necessity for which the governments submit before arriving at the employment of credit, that is to say, an inviolable respect for their pledged word and for property. The establishment of the Hanseatic League is one of those laborious attempts. and must take its place in the history of political economy.

146

Of the first days of that celebrated association there exists no authentic monument from which one can determine the precise time of its formation. Most of the acts of accession to the Hanseatic Union have even disappeared from the archives of the principal cities which constituted a part of it. No record of the deliberations, no official report of the conferences has come down to us from the early days of these opulent cities, more occupied in acting than in speaking and writing. What is certain is that at the beginning of the thirteenth century, several maritime cities of lower Germany are found already united for their common defense, and above all, for the protection of their commerce. " Their beginnings were feeble," say the learned historian of these cities,* " their progress rapid, their success astonishing, and doubtless they were far from foreseeing that some day their opulence would have sovereign sway over the two seas of the north, and would weigh heavily in the political balance of Europe." The first treaties that they made with each other, aimed at the repression of piracy and the abolition of that brigandage known under the name of *wrecker's right*, then pitilessly exercised against all navigators. As their profits extended, it became necessary to protect them from the maritime depredations, which corresponded in cruelty with the exactions of the territorial barons. They obtained by purchase privileges which they could not obtain by good right or by force. By combining, they acquired more influence, and little by little they had placed upon solid bases numerous franchises which became the source of all kinds of prosperity.

The crusades soon offered active support to the spirit of enterprise of the Hanse-towns. Their ships took part in the expeditions to the Holy-Land and often visited the Mediterranean ; on more than one occasion, they landed bold passengers, who easily recognized the superiority of commerce from long voyages, over the poor

---

* Sartorius, *History of the Hanse Towns*, vol. i.

and restricted coast-trade of the Baltic. At the West and in the North Sea, Cologne, Bremen, Lübeck and Hamburg, obtained grants of important privileges. The favor had been accorded them of organizing themselves into a corporation in London, and of having there a commercial house and ware-houses, and they made such good account of it, that, in less than fifteen years, all the English commerce had fallen into their hands. In Sweden, Denmark, Norway and Livonia, their preëminence no longer knew any limits, and even to Novgorod the Great, the magistrates of Lübeck exercised a respected influence over the Hanseatic branch-offices. At the end of the thirteenth century, seven maritime cities of the Baltic are already uniting to defend some privileges which the king of Norway determined to contest with them in his ports : they arm a fleet to secure these privileges, and triumph over the opposition of the prince. In the following century, their preponderance is so great that most of the cities of the interior of Germany, as well as entire provinces, decide to join them. All wish to belong to that association where there are such large profits to be made and so few risks to run. The small cities are admitted into it with a right to protection on condition of bearing their part of the general expenses, as the price of their new independence. It is believed that the first act of general confederation was drawn up in an assembly held at Cologne in 1364, in which the league took the name of Hanseatic, or of *Hanse*, which signified, in the old language of the country, *corporation*. One thing is certain, namely, that from that time we no longer hear of the *traders of the empire*, nor of the *German navigators*, but of the trading houses and factories (buildings occupied by factors, who conducted trade in foreign parts.—*Trans.*) of the Hanse towns.

Unfortunately, this league bore within it germs of disorganization which would soon or late bring about its decadence and ruin. It lacked an executive power provided

with means sufficient to compel all the members to submit to the resolutions adopted by the majority ; it had
no chief appointed to direct its forces for the general
good. " It was a body with a hundred arms, without a
head." * In vain had they stipulated that refractory cities
should be cut off from the confederation, and that their
differences should be judged by a supreme council; these
essential clauses were never scrupulously executed, and no
idea of perseverance and unity ever guided the enterprises of the league. The spirit of anarchy which then
dominated in Europe had also breathed upon it, and
we cannot understand how each of the cities of which it
was composed could have kept the right of contracting
alliances with princes or states foreign to the confederation. Besides, it more than once happened that the interests of one or of several members of the league were
found to be in opposition with those of all the others,
and brought on wars disastrous to the entire association.
The kings of Denmark, Sweden and Norway, and all those
feudal powers accustomed to tributes and to pillage, at
last looked with unfriendly eyes upon the independence
of a few commercial cities and the insolence of the bourgeoisie which resulted from it. The latter, becoming by
degrees more powerful as they became more rich, could
take into their service the subjects of even their enemies,
and they opposed a commercial and moneyed aristocracy to the purely feudal aristocracy which made war
upon them. They were fortified, and could resist in
those times when artillery, as yet unknown, could make
no breach in their walls.†

---

* Schoell, *Cours d' Histoire des États Européans.* Vol. xv, p. 291.

† The names of all the Hanse towns have never been certainly known.
The most famous of those habitually designated in the official acts of the
confederation, were not more than forty or forty-five. They were Lübeck,
Wismar, Rostock, Stralsund, Greifswalde, Colberg, Anclam, Demmin,
Stettin, Kiel, Bremen, Hamburg, Mustargard, Culm, Thorn, Elbing, Dant-
zig, Kœnigsberg, Riga, Dorpt, Revel, Pernow, Cologne, Soest, Münster,
Osnabrück, Brunswick, Magdeburg, Hildesheim, Hanover, Lüneburg,
Utrecht, Zwolle, Deventer, Zutphen, Zierikzee, Briel, Middelburg, Dor-
drecht, Rotterdam, Amsterdam, Campen, Groningen, Harderwick, and

Their power was not slow in manifesting itself in the first contests they had to maintain, namely, against Waldemar, king of Denmark. They forced this king to flee from his dominions, and they spread such terror in the Baltic, that all the rival powers were humiliated before their triumphs. Thus disappeared the fleets of those redoubtable Northmen, who had held all Europe in check and founded kingdoms at more than five hundred leagues from their coasts. The squadrons of the Hanseatic League, commanded by senators from Lübeck, purged the seas of the North from pirates, and the treaty of Stralsund, in 1370, delivered into their hands for fifteen years the strong places of Scania, with the outlying districts. At this time, it may be said that the commercial law of maritime nations began its existence, and that commerce gave law to barbarism. Wherever the flag of the Hanse towns floated, respect for treaties was seen to succeed abuse of power. Commercial agencies, *entrepôts*, counting-houses and warehouses were established at all points where the exchanges could be of any importance. Russia was really discovered by these bold navigators, who were the first to open a route as far as Novgorod. The natural products of these vast, fertile, though badly cultivated regions, became, and have remained since then, the principal object of the commerce of the Baltic Sea. They were skins, hides, peltry, grain, hemp, tar, and timber of kinds which Europe lacked and which the Hanse towns furnished almost immediately in abundance. The most perfect freedom reigned among these cities in transactions which to-day are fettered by the exigencies of public policy, custom-duties, and all the delays caused by mistaken zeal for the interests of the public treasury.

If one transport himself in thought to our modern counting-houses in the Orient or in China, he will

Staveren. The others were designated by the general name of Hanse towns. Their full number may be estimated at eighty. (Note of French editor.)

recognize the traces of commercial usages which the Hanse towns made prevail in all Europe in the thirteenth and fourteenth centuries. In England and Russia, their traders enjoyed considerable privileges. They had at Novgorod a magistrate charged with maintaining order among them, and judging their cases according to the laws of the *Union*. This magistrate, assisted by a few experienced men, had the right to pronounce in certain cases heavy fines, and even the penalty of death, with appeal either to Lübeck, or to the Hanseatic Diet. The church and the factory of the *Union* were surrounded with an enclosure shut during the night and strictly guarded. The merchants of the *Hanse* had taken care to secure for themselves the monopoly of business. The Russians could sell only to them; and a statute of the confederation had forbidden the balances on accounts to be paid in specie. All the transactions were to be consummated by way of exchange. Hence arose contrabandage and interloping, now by Sweden, now by Finland, until the time when the English, having found the way to Archangel by the White Sea, annulled in fact the monopoly of the confederation. Besides, the bond was by degrees tending towards dissolution; and from this time, we see one city after another become detached from the Union, at the head of which Lübeck long shone with the greatest brilliancy.

To comprehend well the influence exercised by the Hanse towns on the development of the science of wealth, it is necessary to glance at the manner in which these cities had organized their branch establishments at Novgorod, Bergen, Bruges, London, and other places. All these were subject to the same rules, if we except a small number of local modifications. These branch-houses were composed of a series of buildings which were isolated and generally constructed on the sea-shore or on the banks of rivers, so that ships could easily approach to take in or to discharge their cargoes. Each body of buildings had a particular name and destination. The employés and the inspectors lodged within reach of the merchandise, which was distributed according to its nature, into granaries, store-houses, or cellars, as in the present docks of the city of London. Vast gardens served at need as a supplementary place of deposit and furnished the vegetables necessary for the consumption of the residents. During the winter, a common hall brought that numerous industrial family together about the same fireside ; vast dormitories received them afterwards for the night. No residents of the establishment could marry, and the infraction of that law was punished by the loss of the Hanseatic right and of the freedom of the city. Imagine the rules of a religious community applied to a commercial association, and you will have an idea of the constitution of these factories, the principal provisions of which are reproduced in our day, with some few differences, in those of the English at Canton.

As it is to-day* at Canton, it was forbidden the employés to visit, *under penalty of death,* the part of the city which belonged to the native inhabitants. The vicinity of the buildings was patrolled by sentinels during the night, and guarded by enormous dogs which threw themselves furiously upon every stranger who approached them. It appears, also, that the rules of the confederation did not permit the employés to do any trading on their own account; they were considered only as clerks acting in the name of their principals, and at the expiration of ten years, they returned to Germany, rich in experience and the knowledge they had acquired. To meet the expenses of the establishment, each commodity paid a light import and export duty. The avails of the fines for violation of statutes or of required forms, were applied to the same purpose ; and each confederated city was subject to a tax for the maintenance of these trading-houses.

The trading-houses extended their ramifications for

---

* *i.e.,* 1837.

a brief time throughout all Europe, and gave every-where an extraordinary impulse to commerce and manu-factures. The factory of Bruges became the *entrepôt* of all the productions of Europe, and the city contained as many as thirty-five thousand houses. During the finest days of their prosperity, the Hanse cities were mistresses of the fisheries, mines, agriculture, and man-ufactures of all Germany. The grain, wax, and honey of Poland, the metals of Bohemia and Hungary, the wines of the Rhine and of France, the wools and the tin of England, the linens of Holland, and the cloths of Bel-gium were exchanged in enormous quantities in their markets. The merchants of the south sent to the *en-trepôt* of Bruges the products of the Orient and of Italy, the spices of India, the silks, and the drugs, of which the consumption was very considerable. But soon the pros-perity of that city excited the jealousy of the other cities which contributed to the heavy expenses of her employés, and Cologne broke the bond which bound her to the league. The administrators of the grand factory had committed the error of establishing two categories of merchandise, of which one class was to be negotiated for only at the depository of the confederation, while the other was free from that condition. By degrees, an at-tempt was made to increase the number of free commodi-tics, that is, to make what is to-day called the *fictitious entrepôt* exceed the *real entrepôt*. The struggle which this effort occasioned decided several merchants to con-sign their merchandise to Flemish houses, to escape the demands of the *entrepôts*, and thus, from a protest against the arbitrariness of the tariffs, the commission-trade arose, the destinies of which were to be so bril-liant.

The English, in their turn, grew impatient of the privi-leges they had accorded to the Hanse towns, and in fact these privileges were excessive. It had been stipulated that suits between English and Germans should be sovereignly judged by two magistrates whom the king should appoint : the Germans had been removed from the jurisdiction of the court of the admiralty. A quarter in London had been left to them as sole proprietors, another in Boston and one at Lynn, and they were exempt from a series of custom duties and other taxes to which every other party was subjected. The quarrel began to grow bitter, when the English perceived that those from the Hanse towns were profiting by their privileges, to flood the country with cloths manufactured in Germany, and to monopolize all commercial operations. It was demonstrated that the Germans had imported in a single year forty-four-thousand pieces of cloth, while the English manufacturers had been able to dispose of but eleven-hundred. Later, Queen Elizabeth favored with all her influence the progress of the establishments which the *adventurers* * had founded to rival the Hanse towns, and she put the seal of her authority on those custom-house reprisals which may be considered as the prelude of the industrial struggles of the present time. From that moment, commerce rises to the rank of a political power : tariff battles are fought as well as artillery battles, and political economy makes its formal entrance into the councils of kings and into European law.

The Hanse towns rendered immense service to this movement so favorable to freedom and civilization, in uniting nations by the powerful bond of interests and trade. The establishment of the *entrepôt* of Bruges, which united the North and the South, had become the rendezvous of all the merchants of Europe and a place of the first rank in the circulation of specie and operations in credit. There were sixty-eight trade bodies there ; and at the commencement of the fourteenth century,† there existed in that city a marine assurance company

---

* It was under this name that a company of English merchants was formed, for destroying the commercial sway of the Germans.

† In 1310.

and brokers acquainted with the principal rules of ex. change.*   Hence went forth as from a common centre the orders of that commerce which would have awakened industrialism from the lethargy in which it was plunged, if the system of corporations, then in vigor throughout Europe, had not contributed to keep it in that condition. And yet, the Hanse towns created the system of the modern fisheries, both herring and whale, the merchant marine, the *entrepôts*, commission, and franchises of the kind which the Europeans enjoy in the Orient and in China, for lack of better.   They accustomed feudal bar. barism to respect labor to which it finally became tribu- tary, and they substituted the influence of industrial and economic intelligence for that of the cuirass and the sword.   They prepared the way for the emancipation of the common people of France and England, by making it evident on which side the power would be, whenever the commons would have an understanding and act in concert.   Finally, we owe to them the abolition of the first commercial barriers, and the first attempts at public credit, of which they set the example whenever the ne- cessities of the confederation compelled them to resort to it.   The representative and elective system which they propagated, the sort of hierarchy which they established between the allied cities, protected or in subjection, trained each one of them in. the defense of its rights, and led them to the conquest of new rights.   Thus the trace of economic progress continually reappears, in the midst of the vicissitudes of the nations which seem to have lost it, and the productive forces in man continually prevail over his destructive propensities.

---

* As the inhabitants of the Hanse towns were commonly designated in England under the name of Esterlings, and in sales it was stipulated that payment should be made in money of the Esterlings, it is probable that the denomination of pound *sterling* dates back to that period.—Fr. Ed.

"The term sterling seems to have been applied in consequence of its use among the Ripuarian Franks, sometimes called the Esterlings."—Chambers's Encyclopædia.

CHAPTER XVII.

The Affranchisement of the Communes and its influence on the course of economic and social progress.

WHILE the Hanse towns were organizing into a confederation in the north, the great work of the affranchisement of the communes was being accomplished in the south. The Roman traditions had become more deeply rooted there than in the rest of Europe, and even under the domination of the Barbarians, the great cities of Provence and Languedoc had never ceased to enjoy the benefits of a municipal government. Gradually, as the cities of the north acquired importance by their wealth, they made attempts to conquer their independence. They wished to be free in the disposition of their fortune, and to connect with it some privileges, as at that time it was considered an evidence of servitude not to have any. The bourgeois obtained that of being judged by their peers and escaping the oppressive, partial, and venal jurisdiction of the lords. They claimed the right of being taxed in a fixed and limited manner, of themselves making laws concerning their interests, and of maintaining order in the cities and market towns. "See," said the abbé Guibert, a chronicler of the twelfth century, " see what they mean to-day by this *new and detestable word commune ;* people subject to the villein-tax pay rent no longer to their lords more than once a year; if they commit any offense, they are cleared on the payment of a penalty fixed by law: and as to the levies for money that are usually imposed upon serfs, they are exempt from them." *

This was the aspect of the new-born freedom to a churchman. The church had reason to be alarmed at the universal conspiracy which broke out against all privileges, and which would soon attack its own. For it had by degrees substituted itself for the lords in obtaining exemption from taxes, and fiscal prerogatives of the highest importance. Every day its wealth was increased by donations, and its pretentions rose with its fortune to the point of even making kings uneasy upon their thrones. Louis IX himself, who was a saint, was obliged to bring them to reason ; and his successors, frequently excommunicated, had to maintain long struggles with the papacy, at all times the natural protector of ecclesiastical demands. Thus was continued that permanent, immortal protest of the human race in favor of a more equitable distribution of the profits of labor. The church had joined in it in the days of her misfortunes, and had furnished powerful weapons to the defenders of civil equality at a time when all the world was bending under the feudal yoke. But, as feudalism grew weaker, the church desired to become its heir, and to resume her old authority over the kings, who, consequently, threw themselves into the arms of the people and created the third estate from the affranchised communes.

This great revolution was not the work of a day ; we see its results, but we do not know the precise date. It is probable that the movement began in some opulent cities, and was insensibly propagated, according to circumstances, throughout all the towns ; some of which demanded the confirmation of the privileges they had long possessed, and the others argued of services rendered and deeds accomplished, in order to obtain a grant legalizing what they had already won by conquest. The first charters of emancipation are generally attributed to Louis le

---

* *Mémoires de Guibert*, Book iii, chap. 7.

Gros, because he was the first king who had recourse to the support of the bourgeois to resist the usurpations of the nobility. But it would be an error to suppose that at the time when the various cities constituted themselves into communes, they possessed no local institutions of the people, charged with watching over the interests of the inhabitants. They had mayors, aldermen, peers, jurors, and consuls. We know of the energetic and celebrated struggle which the inhabitants of Vezelai maintained against their abbot and his monks, who claimed the right to keep them forever under the feudal yoke. Nothing in history is more curious than that long quarrel between monks speaking in the name of the liberties of their church, and a few bourgeois who claimed on the other side the privileges of their commune—a serious dispute which lasted several years, and in which bishops, lords, the court of Rome, and the king of France, interfered for the ruin and enthralment of a paltry market town. The cities of Tournay, Noyon, Meaux, and Dijon, enjoyed very extended privileges, in the foremost rank among which always figure certain commercial liberties, and some special prerogatives in the matter of roads, moneys, corvées, and taxes. The abbé Suger, who was minister, and who wrote a biography of Louis le Gros, expressly * says that *the men of the parishes of the country* assisted this prince at the siege of Thoury. Later, Queen Blanche, during the absence of Saint Louis, entrusted the defense of cities to the bourgeois militia. The more one studies this subject, the more is he convinced that it was the accumulated wealth in the cities which gave rise to ideas of liberty and led to the affranchisement of the communes.

If these communes did not form, as in Germany, a general confederation, it was because they found a support in sovereigns as interested as themselves in humbling the

---

* Suger, *De Vitâ Ludovici Grossi ;* in Duchesne, Hist. franc. script. vol. iv. p. 301.

power of the barons. Royalty could do nothing entirely alone against that multitude of lords intrenched in their castles, who exploited the resources of France for their personal advantage. Neither could the communes do anything without the support of the kings; there was between them and the latter a virtual alliance, which contributed not a little to the foundation of independence and national unity. The Chronicles of Saint-Denis have celebrated the devotion of the cities of Corbie, Amiens, Arras, Beauvais, and Compiègne, which sent their contingents to the battle of Bovino. Royalty had the good judgment to declare free the cities subject only to its authority, and that intelligent resolve secured it a great amount of devotion, which was not always paid with ingratitude. I would not dare affirm that the kings and cities thought, in acting thus, that they were conforming to a system, and laying, by common accord, the basis of a new social order; but the movement was so rapid that history can scarcely follow its progress, and is still, in our day, endeavoring to investigate its causes.

We cannot, however, deny that this revolution was due to the influence of wealth and labor, which, later, took advantage of it to march on to new conquests. There was effected in Europe about that time a renovation, the dawn of which dates back to the first crusades. We might say that ideas were everywhere broadening and rising higher; the human mind was becoming emancipated under the protection of the great principle of association. In the south, people were uniting for the conquest of the Holy Land, and in the north for the security of commerce. Art and trade corporations, formerly unknown, were multiplied so numerously that it was soon necessary to make regulations concerning them, lest they should make war upon each other and become a dangerous power in the state. Everywhere labor was restored to honor; the municipal magistracies were veritable syndicates; the aldermen and the prevosts of the tradesmen were the equals of the lords, and controlled public opinion and the power of the cities. Read the ordinances of the first five or six kings of the third race; you will find a great number devoted to matters of political economy, fairs, markets, moneys, exchanges, sales and purchases, weights and measures, freedom of trade, and especially to the privileges of the communes. Royalty governs seriously: it puts its hand to all affairs, and the science of administration is principally manifest in the new and bold manner in which it approaches economic questions. We shall soon see with what firmness Saint Louis stated them, if he did not have the time or the good fortune to resolve them: and one will be surprised at the immense work accomplished in his reign, notwithstanding the external preoccupations of the crusades and the internal struggles of the feudal spirit against royalty. " We know that kings have long hands; " said Abbé Suger in his life of Louis le Gros; and Saint Louis had still longer ones than his predecessors.

We experience a lively interest in seeing thus arise from the darkness of the middle ages the first rays of that bright fire of the arts and manufactures, which was at the same time the effect and the cause of our municipal liberties. The communes took the names of *conjuration, friendship, confederation,* and *fraternities,* which indicated clearly the aim of their existence and organization. They each provided themselves with a tower with a belfry, to give the signal for assembly or for battle: they gave themselves a guard and magistrates: they had a municipal treasury and a communal seal, distinctive marks of their power and individuality. They interdicted the erection of any fortress capable of disturbing them, within reach of their walls; and in all cases, they exercised local sovereignty. The example of the Italian republics and that of the Hanse towns, which were also communal powers, taught them how to make that sovereignty respected. To properly comprehend the *economic*

importance of communal affranchisement, we must consider to what hard necessities the inhabitants of the cities
and market-towns were subjected. The lords had the
pretention to claim unlimited credit from all the bourgeois : often, too, they took whatever suited their convenience, without ever paying ; and, as every one knows,
this was the one of their old habits which the aristocracy
found it hardest to give up. We see the bourgeois (those
of Soissons among others) stipulate in their charter that
the inhabitants of the city shall not give more than three
months credit to the bishop, and that, if he does not pay
at the time agreed, all farther credit shall be refused him.
The trade associations, which have appeared since then to
present a purely industrial character, were bodies essentially devoted to the maintenance of the liberties of the
commune : their aim was, to escape from annoyances by
the nobility and to defend themselves against the forced
loans, which, under the appearance of liberty, would have
renewed for them all the miseries of servitude.

The communal privilege differed from municipal franchises in that the royal sanction was necessary to it and
conferred upon it great power. Sometimes it was acquired by composition with the feudal lord, who granted
it for a money compensation ; but as this privilege involved serious modifications in the financial situation of
the cities, either by reducing or suppressing the payments
they had to make to the barons, the latter frequently
offered much resistance to the attempts of the bourgeois,
who were obliged, from time to time, to resort to shrewd
management in order to conquer them. We read in a
communal charter accorded to the inhabitants of Dour-
lens, " that this charter is granted because of the injustices
and annoyances practised by the powerful against the
bourgeois of the above-mentioned city." Philippe-Auguste said, on granting a charter to the city of Saint-Jean
d'Angely, that he favored it with all his heart, in order that
the inhabitants might better defend and guard *his rights*

*as well as theirs.** This fact is certain, that freedom advances with the same step as labor, and no epoch has been more fruitful at the same time in industrial developments and in social conquests, than that upon which we are entering.   M. Guizot has observed,† as a striking proof of the general movement of minds toward reforms, that, in the twelfth and thirteenth centuries, there were found two hundred and thirty-six government acts relating to communes, viz., nine under Louis le Gros, twenty-three under Louis VII, seventy-eight under Philippe-Auguste, ten under Louis VIII, twenty under Saint Louis, fifteen under Philippe le Hardi, forty-six under Philippe le Bel, six under Louis X, twelve under Philippe le Long, and seventeen under Charles le Bel.   Now, if one considers that kings were not the only ones who gave charters and intervened in the affairs of the communes, it will be easy to conceive the importance of the change which had taken place in the condition of the people.

This revolution, for it was one, was the direct and immediate result of the immense creation of wealth due to the industrial cities of the middle ages.   The barons, possessors of the soil, disdained to engage in any laborious occupation and left to the bourgeois the care of providing for their needs and their pleasures.   By degrees, the money obtained by these lords, by means of taxes or pillage, became heaped up in the coffers of the city people, in exchange for wools, silks, gloves, helmets, and articles of luxury, for which the aristocracy were eager. "The lords were prodigal ; the bourgeois, on the contrary, passed for being very avaricious ; " ‡ and it is not surprising that by their savings they thus created a considerable amount of capital which acquired great value, thanks to the security strengthened by the affranchisement of

---

* " Ut tam nostra quam sua propria jura melius possint defendere, et magis integre custodire."

† *Cours d'Histoire Moderne*, vol. v, p. 132.

‡ Capefigue, *Histoire de Philippe-Auguste*, vol. iv, p. 243.

the communes. One finds evidence of it in Joinville : "There were so many malefactors and thieves around Paris, that the whole. country was full of them. The king, who took great pains that the poor be well cared for, knew the whole truth: he ordered an investigation throughout the kingdom in order that 'good and strict justice' should be done, which should spare the rich no more than the poor. The land then began to improve, and people came on account of the good administration of law, and so much was business increased and improved, that sales, seizins, purchases and other things were worth double when the king took the lead."

We see communes almost simultaneously established throughout Europe, in Italy, Spain, Germany, France, and England. They are everywhere, because everywhere manufactures and commerce resume their importance. Genoa, Florence, Venice, Barcelona, Bremen, Lübeck, Hamburg, Bruges, Paris, Lyons, Marseilles, London and Bristol seem for a time governed by the same laws. In them personal property stands proudly side by side with landed property and claims its rights. The land, henceforth incapable of sufficing by itself alone for the needs of the new social condition, begins to lose its prestige, and to behold a part of the power of the landholders pass into the hands of artisans. Democracy appears, strong from the spirit of association and all the resources of organized and disciplined labor. The third-estate is established : the middle class, dreamt of in olden time by Plato and by Aristotle, becomes a deliberating body, grants or refuses subsidies, judges itself, guards itself, governs itself. Population increases with the means of subsistence. Arts and manufactures become improved, commerce gives the signal for the general bringing of nations nearer to one another, and the strong castles become tributary to manufactures. There is very remarkable evidence of this in the contemporary royal legislation. The first volume of the collection of these ordinances, for the third race, embraces more than a hundred, all devoted to ques tions of work and the industrial arts, of monuments, commerce, and exchanges. These ordinances, unquestionably, leave much to be desired, for they are generally drawn up for fiscal and oppressive ends; but their number and variety even, demonstrate the importance already attached to the matters which they attempted to determine. We shall explain their spirit and the principal facts, with a few details, because, taken together, they form the first official starting point of economic science in Europe.

CHAPTER XVIII.

The economic legislation of the first kings of France of the third race.
—Ordinances regarding the Jews.—Moneys.—Against the export of coin.—
Trade in grain.—Sumptuary laws.—Official origin of our commercial preju-
dices.

THERE exists, we have said, authentic evidence of the
prodigious impulse given to the production of wealth,
through the influence of the crusades and by the trade
of the Hanse towns, from the twelfth to the fourteenth
century: it is the collection of the ordinances of the first
kings of France of the third race. We find among these
ordinances more than a hundred provisions, all relating to
industrial and commercial matters, principally upon usury
and the Jews, coins, workmen, weights and measures, and
even some attempts at a *maximum* price and sumptuary
regulations. The whole political economy of the time is
revealed in these remarkable documents, the study of
which appears to us to merit particular attention, because
they afford a complete summary of the ideas of our ancestors upon several questions which to-day still divide us.
Certainly, if commerce and the industrial arts had not at
that time become considerably extended, we should not see
the contemporary administrations so seriously occupied
with their affairs that under the single reign of Philippe
le Bel fifty-six ordinances were issued simply in reference
to royal and seignorial coins, and more than ten on the
Jews and Italian tradesmen.

An attentive examination of these monuments of the

economic legislation of the middle ages, enables us to judge with some accuracy of the nature of the influence exercised by the government upon questions of finance and manufactures, at this interesting epoch.   Such a study is so much the more curious, as most of our present commercial prejudices have no other origin than the exclusive and intolerant legislation of the thirteenth century.   Thus our laws upon usury, so deeply at variance with experience, good sense, and the general interest of lenders and borrowers, are only a relic of the ordinances issued against loaning at interest, and especially of those against the Jews under Louis IX. and his successors.   Our bad custom-house laws, so exclusive, so hostile to foreigners, are the fruit of the narrow habits of nationality and egoism general at a period when national unity needed them to become consolidated rather than enriched. ، The intervention of the government in the purchase and sale of goods, and the attempts at *maximum* prices, renewed under the terror of 1793, date from the day when Philippe le Bel* thought it his duty to fix the price of wheat and oblige the traders to keep the markets supplied with it, however scarce it might be.   All our legislation in grain is traceable to the ordinances which forbade its export, and the first errors of the system of *the balance* are found in the ordinance of the 28th of July, 1303, which prohibited the export of gold and silver.   Who can say how far these continually repeated prescriptions may have contributed to strengthen deplorable prejudices in the minds of the people?

Let us examine rapidly and in chronological order the ordinances issued from the accession of Philippe-Auguste to the time of Charles le Bel, *i. e.*, for a period of about two centuries.   Of all the kings who occupied the throne during these two hundred years, there was not one but thought he must manifest his power or his orthodoxy by severe measures against the Jews.   We constantly come

* Ordinance of March, 1304, in the Louvre Collection, vol. i, p. 426.

upon ordinances against these pariahs of the middle ages, who were considered as preëminently subjects for taxation. Philippe-Auguste issued four celebrated ones, the first of which threatened them, the second despoiled them, the third drove them from the country, and the fourth freed their debtors. Louis VIII also proclaimed his. He suppressed all interest on money, and caused the sums due the Jews to be paid for the benefit of the lords. We have already seen that Saint Louis was no less severe in regard to them: Philippe le Bel and Louis le Hutin continued the system of their predecessors.

After the Jews come the moneys, and no reign passed without the royal authority issuing more than one ordinance on this subject. Saint Louis decreed that the coin of his government should be substituted everywhere for that of the lords; and that prescription, already attempted by his predecessors, would have had favorable results, if, later, kings had not abused their right by artificially multiplying their resources by fraudulent alterations of the coin. These alterations were repeated with unheard-of perseverance, notwithstanding the bad results which followed nearly every one of them. Now, it was forbidden those whose income was less than six thousand francs, to possess gold and silver plate: again, those who had any were enjoined to carry a third of it to the mint, where the manipulators of the crown bought it at the old price, to sell it again at a profit under the form of debased coin.* The king was himself obliged to ask pardon for this of his own subjects, and he promised to indemnify them in the future.†

---

* *Ordonnance de Philippe le Bel*, in the Louvre Collection, vol. i, page 324.

† We give an extract from that curious document: " Nostrum facimus quod pro ingruentibus nostris negotiis, temporibus istis monetam fabricari disponentes, in qua forsan aliquantulum deerit de pondere, alleio, seu lege * * * ne propter hoc monetam recipientes eamdem in posterum damnificari contingat aut lædi, praesentium tenore promittimus, quod omnibus qui monetam hujusmodi in solutum, vel alias recipient in futurum, in quod de ipsius valore, ratione minoris ponderis, alleii, sive legis deerit, in integrum de nostro supplebimus, ipsosque indemnes servabimus." *Ordonnances des Rois de France*, vol i, page 325.

The regulations about grain occupy a notable place in the collection of ordinances. A war, a famine, a bad harvest, was sufficient to bring about a prohibition to export provisions, with heavy penalties; but these prohibitions almost always resemble reprisals, and they are generally accompanied by a corrective. "Considering," it is said, "that our enemies might profit by our provisions, and that it is also important to leave them their merchandise, we have ordered that the former shall not be exported nor the latter imported." It was therefore the thought of war which caused foreign commodities to be rejected in 1304, by Philippe le Bel, and in 1793 by the National Convention; and to-day in a time of complete peace and full civilization, the same system still prevails, supported by the same arguments!

Sometimes, however, the ordinances were marked by a wise and thoughtful solicitude, as when they prescribed that statistics be obtained of the supply of grain in the cities and provinces, for the purpose of restoring confidence among the citizens and enlightening the magistrates. The edict of February, 1304, due to Philippe IV, shows also, in other matters, remarkable penetration and accurate views. "Let persons be sent into all the cities and villages of the viscounty of Paris, to ascertain everywhere how much grain, as wheat, meslin (a mixture of wheat and rye,—*Trans.*), rye, barley, oats and every other kind of grain there will be, and how much in each city and territory, and how much will be needed to keep them alive until the new comes and to furnish grain for sowing; and whatever is in excess shall be brought to the markets within that viscounty, *not all together, but by degrees*, so that the grain can last until the next season; and it must not be allowed to be taken out of the said viscounty, without especial leave. Any one who wishes can buy the grain, if he pays the money at once, but let no one buy grain to store in a granary, under penalty of losing it."

But in spite of these precautions which aimed at the

same time to prevent popular alarm and monopolies, this very prince was obliged to promulgate, the following month,* an ordinance concerning the *maximum*, in virtue of which no one could sell, under penalty of confiscation of his property, a *setier* of the best wheat, Paris measure, for more than forty Parisian sols (a coin worth about a half-penny.— *Trans.*), and a *setier* of grain of an inferior quality, proportionately.   A *setier* of the best beans and the best barley, Paris measure, was to bring thirty sols; the best oats, twenty sols ; a *setier* of the best bran, ten sols.   Whoever had more grain than he needed for provision and for seed, must send it to market ; and if, after the proclamation was made, any persons were found to have more than the necessary quantity, all was confiscated for the benefit of the king.†   Who would then

---

* In March, 1304.

† It may be well to quote that ordinance here, as also those decreed by the National Convention, which proclaimed the *maximum*. The following is the ordinance of Philippe le Bel :

Philippus Dei gratia, Francorum rex, Ballivo Viromandensi salutem. Sicut, in subjectorum nobis populorum tranquillitate et prosperitate ventura gloriamur uberius, sic et in ipsorum afflictione et adversitate noxia, et oppressis compatimur, et condolemus afflictis vias exquirentes et modos, juxta datum nobis a Deo potentiam, quibus et eorum succuratur indigentiis, dispendiis obvietur.

Cum itaque victualium omnium et præcipue bladorum, pisoram, fabarum, hordei, avenæ, cœterorumque granorum, quibus sustentari consuevit populi multitudo, adeo in regni nostri partibus Domino permittente caristia invaluerit his diebus, quod *humilis plebis copia innumerabilis, nisi eis indilato succuratur remedio*, diutius, absque gravi totius vulgi dispendio, non poterit sustentari.

Generali condolentes excidio, *præsertim cum necessitatis tempore omnia fere communia jura publicé proterantur*, consulte duximus ordinandum, quod baillivias, vice comitatus, prepôsituras, et alia loca regni nostri, de quibus expedire viderimus, faciemus publice proclamari, ac etiam inhiberi, sub omni amissione bonorum, ne quis subditorum nostrorum sextarium frumenti melióris, ad mensuram parisiensem, ultra summam quadraginta solidorum parisiensium, vendere, vel emere, seu vendi, aut emi facere, quoquomodo præsumat, et sextarium frumenti, seu bladi minoris, pro minori pretio, vendi, aut emi descendendo, præcipimus, habita consideratione ad valorem et pretium melioris sextarii, aut pisorum meliorum, ad mensuram prædictam similiter, pro quadraginta solidis parisiensibus et minora pro minori pretio descendendo, vendi præcipimus, ut est dictum.

Fabas quoque. et hordeum, pro triginta solidis, avenamque pro viginti solidis, et furfur pro decem solidis parisiensibus, sextarium, ad mensuram parisiensam, de melioribus et de aliis pro minori pretio descendendo, ac cœtera grana, habito respectu ad meliora, juxta eorum qualitatem, vendi volumus, modo quo superiùs est expressum.

have supposed, that after that threatening ordinance, the famine would increase and the markets be barren? This is what actually happened, because then as to-day every similar law must bear its consequences. In vain had Philippe IV taken care to add that *people could securely bring every kind of bread* to market, with a royal safe-conduct, without any one having power *to stop or to take away horses and carts :* his infraction of the eternal laws of trade was not long in aggravating the evil which it aimed to prevent, and he was obliged to revoke the ordinance concerning the *maximum*, almost immediately after having issued it. The terms which he employed on that occasion are so remarkable that we reproduce them literally ; they belong, besides, to the history of science, which rarely finds a frankness so explicit in the language of kings.

Vobis itaque præcipimus, et mandamus quatenus in civitatibus, oppidis, bonis villis et aliis locis bailliæ vestræ, de quibus expedire videritis, ordinationem, et statutum prædictum publicè et solemniter proclamari, et in qualibet sui parte faciatis firmiter observari. Si quem vel quos ipsius transgressores inveneritis, animadversione in eosdem expressa punientes, nemini in hac parte parcendo, nisi de nostra speciali licentia, seu mandato.

The following is a statement of the reasons for the law on the *maximum* presented to the Convention by Coupé, of the Oise, in the name of the committee on subsistence :

" I hasten to present to the National Convention the result of the discussions of your commission on the *maximum* to be fixed upon for the various commodities of prime necessity, except wood and charcoal, which you taxed yesterday by a special decree.

" This law is awaited with the greatest impatience ; and malevolence and cupidity, combining their detestable operations with those of our enemies from without, do not permit us to defer it.

" We have felt the number and extent of the difficulties connected with it : the law has even seemed to alarm some of our colleagues : only a small number of us have remained, and these are sustained less by confidence in our strength than by our good intentions.

" In ordinary times, the prices of things are naturally formed and adjusted by the reciprocal interest of buyers and sellers : this scale is infallible. It is useless, even under the best government, to interfere with it. However enlightened, however well-intentioned, the government may be, it never finds so just a scale, and it runs a risk by interfering to produce a change.

" But, when a general conspiracy of unexampled malevolence, perfidy, and rage, combines to break this natural equilibrium, to famish us and rob us, the *safety of the people becomes the supreme rule.*

" Society has the right to resist that war of commerce and tyrants, and to reëstablish and secure with a firm hand the balance which should exist between our productions and our necessities.

" Philippe, by the grace of God king of France, to the bailiff of Senlis, greeting: Whereas, in order to *restrain the common tempest* and necessity of these days, on account of the high price of wheat, peas, beans, barley and other kinds of grain by which the mass of the people are sustained, we lately ordered and established and caused to be proclaimed and forbidden throughout our kingdom that any of our subjects, under penalty of losing all his property, should venture to sell the best wheat at more than forty sols, beans and barley at more than thirty sols, oats at more than twenty sols, and bran at more than ten ; from which statute and ordinance we hoped that the greatest alleviation and comfort would come to our people, which has not yet come.   However, since, on account the new circumstances, it is advisable to change our council and ordinances :   We, in order that the necessities of the people may be more promptly met, *have*

" Then, too, intelligent calculation is necessary. We must be satisfied with establishing, by a *maximum*, salutary limits, beyond which it will not be permitted to pass.   It is advisable to leave further action to legitimate commerce, and to attend to the relations of interests ; and they are innumerable throughout all the localities which France embraces, and still more in all the circumstances of a hundred different wars, and the unprecedented conspiracy of all parts of Europe against us.

" Your commission has seen what an endless task, what an inextricable labyrinth it would be to descend into all the details of particular kinds of provisions, and the reports of localities, and moreover that the law would become endless and impracticable.

" They have, therefore, endeavored to get hold of a general and simple principle, which could be applied everywhere at the same time, according to the various necessities in buying and selling.

" For that, they have chosen a basis which represents these needs in their natural and spontaneous condition : they have chosen the respective values of provisions as they were in 1790.

" Then everything was at its rate, according to the relations of producing countries to consuming countries, and the apportionment of the differences necessary to activity of commerce was found ready made ; there was nothing more to do except to add an increase proportioned to the more or less aggravating circumstances in which we find ourselves."

Then follows the decree of which the following is the first article :

" The articles which the National Convention has judged to be of prime necessity, and of which it has deemed it best to fix the maximum or the highest price, are :   Fresh Meat, Salt Meat and Bacon, Butter, Sweet-Oil, Beef-Cattle, Salt Fish, Wine, Brandy, Vinegar, Cider, Beer, Fire-wood, Charcoal, Mineral-Coal, Candles, Lamp-Oil, Salt, Soda, Soap, Potash, Sugar, Honey, White Paper, Leather, Iron, Cast, Lead, Steel, Copper, Hemp, Flax, Wools, Stuffs, Linens, Prime Materials for manufactured goods, Wooden Shoes, Shoes, Colza and Rape, Tobacco."

recalled, (revoked) and *do recall* the prices we have put for the said kinds of grain, and have ordered and established that whoever in our kingdom has any of the above-mentioned grain, may sell it in market at such a price as he can get for it.   And we will and command that people shall be allowed to come to market securely and quietly, without fear for their horses or carts."

Thus an experience of a few weeks had sufficed to demonstrate the inutility of violent means in the matter of supply of provisions.   The ordinances of Philippe le Bel are very instructive in this respect, because they form, as it were, a little economic drama, where the play begins, progresses, and ends, precisely according to the rules of science, that is to say, to the advantage of freedom.   It is somewhat difficult to comprehend why it was that after experiments so decisive, the struggle was repeated under several reigns, and even at the end of the eighteenth century, between Galiani and Turgot ; between the administrators and the *economists*.   This is not all :   Philippe le Bel, disabused by these unfortunate attempts at a *maximum*, went farther than we have yet done at Paris, at the time when I am writing.   A year after the revocation of his ordinances and the restoration of free trade in grain, he freed the consumers from the monopoly of the bakers, and permitted every citizen to supply himself with bread in whatever way he pleased.   " We ordain and decree that each Parisian or person residing at Paris, may make bread for the supply of his own house and to sell to his neighbors, if he makes sufficient and reasonable loaves and pays the customary duties.   We ordain and decree that every day of the week, any one who wishes, may bring bread and grain and every other kind of provisions to Paris and sell them safely and peaceably. We likewise decree that the community may have any of the provisions coming to Paris that shall be offered in open market, at whatever price the wholesale merchants pay for them."   Strange to say, nearly five hundred years later, Saint

Just was obliged to acknowledge in the National Convention in almost the same terms as Philippe le Bel, the in-
efficiency of the *maximum* to conjure famine. " The various laws that you recently passed in reference to means
of subsistence would have been good," he said,* " if men
had not been bad. When you passed the law for a *maxi-*
mum, the enemies of the people, richer than they, bought
above the *maximum*. The markets ceased to be supplied,
through the avarice of the sellers : *the price of provisions*
had been lowered ; but the provisions were scarce. The
commissioners of a great number of communes competed
for the purchase of them, and as uneasiness nourishes and
propagates itself, each one wished to have store-houses
and prepared for famine so as to be preserved from it."
Who can help being struck by the similarity of these ac-
knowledgments, notwithstanding the five centuries which
separate them ?   But at no epoch has one been able to
violate the essential laws which govern the production of
wealth, without feeling almost immediately the fatal effects of that violation ; and history is replete with similar
lessons, which do not, however, prevent the same errors
from being repeated.

One finds a striking proof of this in the indefatigable
persistence of sovereigns in overthrowing, at their capri-
cious pleasure, the legislation in reference to coins. We
can scarcely comprehend the patience of the people in
bearing with those perpetual changes in the official value
of gold and silver coins, veritable sophistications of which
commerce was the victim, and which can be considered
only as evidences of bankruptcy. At one time it pleased
the king to declare that the small sovereigns (*royaux*)
should be current for eleven Paris sols ; again, that there
should be a return to the good coin of the time of *Mon-*
sieur Saint Louis, and that no one should presume to pay
otherwise ; then the employment of foreign coins was interdicted ; and finally, that of copper coin. After having

---

* The *Moniteur* of Oct. 14, 1793. p. 92. 3d column.

thus made a disturbance in prices, it was necessary to interfere in contracts, leases and rents ; and finally it was ordered that payments be made each year, or each half year, *in current money.** No one, from this time forward, could count on any regular income, and the king himself was obliged, in order to sell his woods which nobody wanted, to make the *amende honorable* and declare that those who bought *in the time of good coin* should pay in good coin, and those who should buy of the same wood *in time of weak coin* should pay in weak. Each ordinance of alteration was followed by a catastrophe which it was supposed could be remedied by tyrannical regulations. This struggle is interesting to study, because it demonstrates the danger and inutility of sovereign intervention in transactions to which government owes simply liberty and security. In departing from these fundamental doctrines, the kings of France opened the way for commercial crises, and commenced the long and painful series of experiments which fill the first epoch of our economic history. How many attempts there were to prevent the export of gold and to cause the precious metals to be brought from every direction to the mint, where the workmen of the crown transformed them night and day into debased coin ! Even pilgrims were hardly excepted from the severe rule forbidding the exportation of money. It seemed as if by retaining it, wealth was being retained ; people did not yet comprehend the simplest laws of the circulation, and they were laying the foundations of that worship of gold of which the *exclusive system* was to become later the final expression. Some were obliged to sell their silver plate, others to have their necklaces and rings melted for coinage. There was a belief that wealth was multiplied by making of one good coin two bad ones ; and when prices rose in view of these assignats of royal

---

* " If bargains are made for a sum or quantity to be paid *in different years* for *five thousand livres*, for example, or for more or less, *to be paid in ten years*, every year so many thousand livres, they shall be paid *in such money as shall be current according to our ordinance*, at the time when each payment shall fall due."—Ordinances, vol. i, p. 444.

fraud, no other corrective was found to that inevitable consequence than to proclaim sumptuary laws and impose limits on consumption.

" We decree," says an ordinance of 1294, " that every manner of people who have not an income of six thousand Tournish livres shall not use, and will not be able to use any gold and silver plate, for drinking, for eating, or for any other use, and that no person, under penalty of fine and imprisonment, shall practice any fraud about it : and from the above mentioned silver, we decree that our coin be made for the *common profit of our kingdom.*"

Another ordinance of the same year prescribed as follows :

" No bourgeois woman shall have a chariot.

" No bourgeois, man or woman, shall wear green, or grey, or ermine, and they shall dispose of those they have, by a year from Easter next. They shall not wear, nor will they be able to wear, gold, precious stones, or coronets of gold or silver.

" The dukes, counts, and barons of six thousand livres in land, or more, may have four robes a year and no more, and the women as many.

" A knight who has three thousand livres in land, may have three robes a year and no more ; and one of these three robes will be for summer.

" No one shall have at the principal meal but two viands and a pork soup, and let him not deceive about it, and if it is *fasting season*, he shall only have two herring soups and two dishes.

" It is ordained that no prelate or baron shall have a robe for his body of more than twenty-five Tournish sous a Paris ell."

Who would believe that all these injunctions, worthy of the worst utopias of Sparta, and *these herring soups*, not less ridiculous than the black broth of the Lacedæmonians, belong to a time when an effort was everywhere being made to revive manufactures, and when the Hanse

towns and the Italian republics had already risen to a
very high degree of riches and splendor! But the sight
even of that wealth, suffices to explain the blind perseverance of kings in prohibiting the export of gold.
France had at that time little to offer in exchange for
the products she needed ; and it was in vain that ancient
ordinances forbade to trade otherwise than by exchange
of commodities, since on the one side there was only
money, and on the other products. It was absolutely necessary that money should go, and it went, to be swallowed
up in the coffers of the Italian governments, which we
shall soon see maintaining armies of mercenaries with the
gold of the nations tributary to their commerce and
manufactures. In vain, from time to time, the royal wrath
lays hold of these intrepid merchants, under the stigma
of Lombards, usurers, and *Caorsins ;* general interest has
rendered them necessary, and they continually reappear,
eager for the quarry,' sowing in the heart of the people
the first distrusts, still ineffacable, of the exportation of
gold.* Such was the true origin of our prejudices in
political economy, which arose from political resentment,
as when all commerce with the Flemish † was interdicted ;
or from religious fanaticism, as when the Jews were persecuted. The prejudices have been perpetuated from age
to age in the administrations and the spirit of the people,
and they still bear sway, invested with the supreme sanction of governments. This explains why so much difficulty is to-day experienced in destroying them in spite of
the refutations and solemn protests of experience and
history. Such is the power of everything that has been
strongly organized ; and nothing has been so with more
talent and ability than the rising industrial arts, whose
beginning under Saint Louis we are about to study.

---

* " And as we have learned that several Italians are in our kingdom,
who are carrying on trade in merchandise and are making contracts *which
are not honorable,* our intention is, not to give to such Italians the above-
mentioned franchises and liberties."—Ordinance of Louis Hutin, July 9,
1315.

† See another ord'nance of Louis le Hutin of February 28, 1315, and the
sixty to eigh y ordinances issued against the Jews in less than four reigns.

CHAPTER XIX.

Organization of Corporations under the reign of Saint Louis.—The *Book of Trades*, by Etienne Boyleau.—General view of the System of the Corporations.—Its past benefits and present disadvantages.

THE reader has been able to judge, from the ordinances which we have quoted, of the state of anarchy which existed in European society at the end of the twelfth and in the thirteenth century. There was neither rest nor stability except for landed property; it alone had all the enjoyments, all the privileges, all the liberties. But already by its side was arising personal property, created by the labor of the democracy; and in vain the rank to which it aspired and which it was soon to occupy, was refused it in the state. By degrees it became emancipated in the cities, which it either bought or had adjudged to itself, the bourgeoisie; every day saw new edicts declared in its favor, and its power became consolidated by the very efforts made to ruin it. The communes were already emancipated when they obtained the concession of their franchises, and the persecutions against the Jews, who were continually proscribed and always recalled, already proved the importance of the possessors of capital. Legislation became humane in proportion as the villeins acquired wealth. They were protected in the fairs, on the markets: they were granted tribunals composed of their peers, and were exempted from a multitude of exactions from which they had previously suffered. But at the time of their emancipation, a remarkable fact occurred, which characterizes in a striking manner the feudal spirit of the times: it was the hierarchical organization of laborers under the system of corporations. It came into the mind of no one to free man as man; the principle of equality did not yet exist. There were to be masters and apprentices as there were lords and vassals, and a soil for agriculture. No one conceived of free labor; it was absolutely necessary that the workman work for a master as the peasant for a lord. This was the price of freedom; the king sold it as an article of food, but it was not without purchasers. And how could it have lacked them, in the midst of that industrial army which suddenly arose from the darkness of feudalism !

It will always be greatly to the honor of Louis IX that he was the first who thought of subjecting such an army to the yoke of discipline.* It gained thereby in

---

* It is now known that the organization of trades was anterior to Saint Louis. Here is what M. Levasseur says on this subject in his excellent History of the Working Classes. (1859, 2 vols., in 8vo, Guillaumin.) "Certain corporations doubtless trace back to the Roman colleges, although it is impossible to follow their traces in history from the fifth to the eleventh century. We need not be astonished at the silence of the chroniclers and of the archives, on such subjects, at a period of grossness and of ignorance, when manufactures were of so little consequence and when events the most important left so few traces. But as soon as the practice of writing became more common, the proofs of the ancient existence of some corporations begin to appear. The *marchands d'eau* at Paris, are probably the direct descendants of the Parisian *nautes*. It was always necessary that a company of bargemen should transport the provisions and merchandise necessary for the supply of Paris. History, after the fall of the Roman empire, had lost trace of them : it finds it again under Louis VII, who in 1121, accords them privileges as a company already ancient. At the commencement of the twelfth century, it was not known how far back originated the corporation of butchers at Paris ; a charter of 1134 speaks of ' their ancient chopping-blocks : ' another of 1162 recalls ' the antiquity of the customs the butchers have long enjoyed,' and orders their reëstablishment.

" If we had charters for industrial organization anterior to the eleventh and twelfth centuries, it is probable that we should see figure in them the *marchands d'eau* and the butchers, who, being always necessary to the city of Paris, were not exposed to perish like so many others, in the wreck of civilization. The trade bodies which reconstituted themselves, were obliged to do it so much the more promptly, as the city, on account of being inhabited by artisans, was the more industrial and populous. The trade body preceded the commune, but we cannot say by how many years, and there must have been in that pacific and secret reorganization of labor still more of diversity than in the more noisy reorganization of the communes. The eleventh and twelfth centuries appear, nevertheless, to have been the time

power and vitality what it appeared to lose in independence, and it is since that epoch that manufactures have taken a start which will no more be arrested. We can but be struck with admiration at the keen penetration with which everything was classed in that curious monument of legislation, called " Establishments of the Trades of Paris," which has come down to us entire from the reign of Saint Louis.*

It was to Etienne Boyleau that Louis IX intrusted the care of putting into execution his grand conception of giving to the industrial arts and to commerce protective regulations and a discipline capable of securing their prosperity. The " Establishments " exercised too great an influence on the development of public wealth and the destinies of manufactures, not to occupy a place in the history of political economy, and we shall devote to it a special examination. A simple quotation from the preamble will give a general idea of it.

" Etienne Boyleau, guard of the prevostship of Paris, to all the bourgeois and all the residents of Paris, etc., greeting: Because we have seen at Paris in our time much jocularity and unbridled lust which is becoming corrupt, and likewise the nonsense of the young and

---

when the artisans began to feel the need of combining and formed their first associations. It appears that the statutes of the chandlers of Paris date from 1061. In the *Register of the Trades* prepared by order of Etienne Boyleau, the artisans often plead the privileges which Philippe-Auguste had given or himself confirmed to them, and which consequently, could not be subsequent to the year 1223. In 1160, Louis le Jeune grants to Theci, wife of Yves and to her heirs, the grand-mastership of the five trades of cobblers, *baudroiers* (belt-makers ?), sweaters, leather-dressers, and purse-makers. Each of these trades must have been previously organized. At Rouen, the shoemakers and cobblers constituted a corporation to which king Henry I, who died in 1135, had granted certain rights.

" The trade bodies, then, existed before the thirteenth, and even before the twelfth century ; but it was not until about 1260, when the communal movement to which they had given birth, had in its turn communicated to them a new activity, that one sees them established in a complete and regular manner —Vol. i, p. 193, et seq.

* ..ree or four manuscripts of it are in existence. The most ancient belongs to the imperial library. The archives of the prefecture of police possess a good copy. The *Register of Trades* by Etienne Boyleau, is published in the unedited documents on the History of France, by M. Depping, 1837, in 4to.— Note of French editor.

ignorant, among the young foreigners and those of the
city, who neither have nor practice any trade, because
they had sold to strangers no things of their trade so
good or so loyal as they should be * * * our intention is to include in the first part of this work, so far as
we shall be able, all the trades of Paris, their regulations,
the manner of initiation (*entrepresures*) into each trade,
and their fees.   In the second part, we intend to treat of
the causeways, *tonlieus* (sums paid for standing in market),
conduits, shores, market dues, weights, boating dues,
machinery, and all other common matters.   In the third
part and in the last, of courts and jurisdiction, for all
those who have courts and jurisdiction in the city and
the faubourgs of Paris.   This we have done for the profit
of all, including the poor and the strangers who come to
Paris to buy commodities, that the commodities may be
so loyal that they will not be deceived by there being
some defect ; and to punish those who shall receive dishonest gain or through lack of sense ask it and take it,
contrary to God, to law and to reason.   When this was
done, collected, brought together and arranged, we had
it read before a great assembly of the wisest, most loyal,
and most venerable men of Paris, and those who know
most about these things, who all praised this work much ;
and we commanded all the trades of Paris, all the tax-
collectors and all the commoners that they should not
act or go contrary to it."

Thus the king had especially in view the termination
of the numerous frauds committed to the detriment of
buyers, and the drawing up special regulations for each
trade.   A few manufacturers remained free ; several
were bound to the payment of certain duties, and a
small number could be carried on only by receiving the
privilege from the sovereign.   Such were (who would
think it ?) the occupation of cobbler and that of huckster
of onions and garlic.*   The most minute prescriptions

---

* " No one can be cobbler unless he purchases the trade from the king.
" No one can be a huckster of fruit or of greens, that is, of garlic, onions,
or eschalots, if he does not buy the trade from the king."—Extracts from
Book of Trades.

obliged the workmen to conform, under penalty of a fine, to a great number of observances laid down for them in the " Establishments." Spinners were forbidden to mix the fibre of hemp with that of flax. The baker, privileged by the king, could sell salt-water fish, cooked-meat, dates, grapes, common pepper, cinnamon and licorice; but the cutler had no right to make the handles of his knives. The porringer-maker and the makers of troughs would not have been allowed to turn a wooden spoon. The single business of hat-maker had five different trades. In thus establishing division of labor, Saint Louis contributed much to the perfection of manufactures, and, by guaranteeing to the purchasers honest goods, he encouraged commerce more than his successors did in ten reigns.

The " Book of Trades" contains regulations for more than a hundred different occupations, whose number and variety suffices to demonstrate the importance that the industrial arts had acquired in the cities.* Most of

---

* The following are the names of the principal kinds of business organized by Etienne Boyleau, just as designated in his " Book " : Lamp-makers, Barrel-Makers, Pewterers, Fullers, Dyers, Shoe-makers, Potters, Coppersmiths, Hawkers, Guagers of wine, Tavern-keepers, Sellers of Cerevisia (a beverage, — *Trans.*), Hucksters of Salt and of Sea-fish, Hucksters of fruit and of green herbs, Goldsmiths, Rope-makers, Toy-men, Cutler-Smiths, Cutlers that make handles, Locksmiths of *laton*, Beaters of iron-wire, Makers of iron-buckles, Makers of iron-wire buckles, Drawers out of brass-wire, Dress-Cutters, Workers of flax at Paris, Workers of flax outside of Paris, Traders in hemp and hemp yarn, *Chanevaciers*, Pin-makers, Carvers of crucifixes and of knife-handles, Painters and Carvers of images, Workers in silk fabrics, Makers of thread bracelets, Those who work on silk cloth, Smelters of ore, *Fermaillers de laton*, Makers of chaplets, shoe-buckles and dress buckles, Weavers of silk kerchiefs, Carpenters, Masons, Makers of cross-belts, Cordwainers, Dealers in sheep-skin or *Chaveteniers de bazenne*, Weavers of knotted carpets, Cobblers, Leather-dressers, Makers of leather straps, Dealers in hay, Flower milliners, Cotton-hat makers, Felt-hat makers, Weavers of cloth, Herring-dealers, Farriers, Locksmiths, Bakers, Millers of Grandpont, Corn-Chandlers, Measurers of grain, Dealers in oil, Tallow-chandlers, Sheath-makers, Makers of scabbards for swords, Casket-makers, Comb-makers and lanthorn-makers, Makers of writing-tables, *Oyers* and Cooks, Poulterers, Dicers, (Makers of gaming dice,) Makers of sewing thimbles, Button-makers, Barbers, Bath-keepers, Mercers, Old-clothes women who sell old linen in the new markets, Drawers out of iron-wire, Dealers in fastenings, Inn-keepers, Dealers in chaplets of bone and horn, Makers of coral chaplets, Makers of amber chaplets, Enamelers of jewelry, Dealers in diamonds, Beaters of gold to thread, Tin-beaters, Beaters of gold-leaf, *Lasseurs* of thread and silk, Girls who spin silk on great spindles,

these rules, which would be unendurable in our day, produced a genuine revolution in the arts which they aimed to guard and perfect. Soon the numerous frauds which dishonored the workshops and paralyzed commercial speculations were observed to disappear. Even if the organization of corporations had rendered only this service to labor, the good which resulted from it would be immense ; but the workers grew strong by undergoing discipline. The *esprit de corps*, in other times so disastrous, arose among them and gave to their association a serious character and a solid existence. These brotherhoods, these *universities* of workmen did not, afterwards allow the privileges so dearly bought to be easily wrested from them. They put themselves under the protection of the saints, adopted sacred banners, standards of their independence, and persistently avenged the least offence done to any of their members. They had their syndics, their chambers of discipline, their councils, their defenders. The honor of the various corporations being thus placed in the safe keeping of all those who belonged to them, raised the laboring classes to the rank of the social powers, such as the clergy, nobility and magistracy. Their hierarchy was not less strict than in the high ranks, and the lords of the castle were not more respected by their vassals than the masters by their apprentices. The habits of domination passed very quickly from the castles to the workshops; there was a shop-despotism by the side of the tyranny of the manors.

Saint Louis was far from foreseeing all the consequences of his organization of the trades, a work of policy quite as much as of political economy. He, in fact, only laid the first stone of this grand edifice of corporations,

---

Makers of thread and silk fringes, *Escuelliers*, Weavers of swaddling-bands, Weavers of Saracen tapestry, Dealers in old furniture, Makers of leather purses and trusses, Saddlers and painters of saddles, *Chapuiseurs* Painters of armorial bearings, Harness-makers, *Conréeurs de Cordoües*, *Couratiers de Cordoües*, Peacock-feather milliners, Furriers and trimmers of hats, Surgeons, Furbishers, Makers of artillery-bows, Fishers (with a rod), Dealers in fresh-water fish, Dealers in salt-water fish.

and we might sum up his system in two lines : " Every
man shall work at his trade and nothing but his trade, in
order to do well and cheat nobody." But, as the provost
Boyleau had carefully provided against all cases of fraud,
and indicated the best processes of labor, it came to pass
that the *Book of Trades* became a treatise on manufactures, and the model according to which every one directed his efforts. The *Grand Chamberlain of the King*
obtained the supervision of the corporations, and secured
the royal sanction for all measures which could be of advantage to them. Henceforward a lively emulation was
established between the artisans : assembled in the same
quarters,* placed under the eyes of each other and before
consumers free to choose the most worthy and skillful
among them, they soon acquired qualities which would
have remained very rare under the preëxisting anarchical
régime.

It was reserved for the successors of Louis IX to complete his work and to complicate, while desiring to resolve
them, the difficult questions which soon or late were to
arise from it. Saint Louis had, in fact, regulated too
minutely the task of each workman, for there not to arise
numerous conflicts between the different arts. How
could discords have been avoided between hat-makers,
some of whom had the right to make only cotton hats
and the others only felt hats? Who could answer for
harmony always reigning between the cutlers who made
handles and those who made blades? Who does not see
the difficulty of recognizing, in the making of candles,
the mixture of old wax with new? The spinners could
no longer mix hemp and flax ; the cobblers had no right
in mending shoes to renew more than two-thirds of them,
under penalty for encroaching upon the prerogative of
the shoemakers. Master-saddlers out of work were permitted to make shoes, but shoemakers could not make
saddles. The joiners had functions carefully distin-

* Joinville, p. 152.

guished from those of the carpenters. Scarcely, therefore, had these brotherhoods become established, when
the workers ceased to live as brothers. Powerful against
attacks from without, the corporations had to maintain
continually in their own midst a civil war, and their discords were not long in delivering them over, bound hand
and foot, to the arbitrary power of the crown. From
Saint Louis to Louis XIV, there was not a sovereign
who did not impose restrictions, taxes and new regulations upon them: the courts overpowered them with
judgments and fines without diminishing their ardor or
calming their hatreds. The founder of trade corporations
had desired to create order ; his successors only saw in
them a means of making money.

   An ordinance of Charles VI, in 1407, begins to modify
the prescriptions of Louis IX relative to the sale of merchandise. The edict of Henry III, in 1581, imposes a
heavy tax on corporations, under the form of a royal
duty, and multiplies the rules concerning apprenticeship,
the reception of masters and the election of wardens.
Another edict, by Henry IV, issued in 1597, confirms the
preceding and adds to it some new provisions more oppressive. At length, Louis XIV, by his edict of March,
1673, establishes corporations in all the cities and market-
towns of the kingdom, and creates more than forty superfluous offices. Thus mutilated by the hand of ten kings,
the corporations no longer bear scarcely any resemblance
to what they were under Louis IX, and there remains
almost nothing of the high conception which originated
them. They now present nothing but a vast arena where
ignoble mercantile combats take place, to the advantage
of the new feudal power, which exploits, under the name
of comrades and apprentices, the unfortunates who had
escaped from the glebe of serfdom. Monopoly invades
industrial society. The number of trades is strictly
limited, to secure to some privileged individuals the advantages of mastership. Artificial obstacles are placed

in the way of the genius who is in advance of his age ; and interminable delays prolong under the name of apprenticeship, the childhood of man. This apprenticeship itself is only a disguised slavery. But still it is slavery. During its whole period, the unfortunate apprentice is the property of his master, who is invested with the right of making him work, even by beating him. There are redhibitory vices for him as for animals. At one time, this period of hard trial lasts eight years; at another it terminates at the end of seven, and the *apprentice* rises to the dignity of *comrade*. He is the freedman of those times, the mulatto of those internal colonies. A person who had served at Rouen five years of apprenticeship and as many as a journeyman, could not enter a corporation at Paris or Bordeaux, without becoming again an apprentice,—a requirement as absurd as it would be to oblige an officer to become again a soldier on changing his regiment.

The long sufferings of the working class under this régime of monopoly and exploitation have been too much forgotten. What rendered them more horrible, was that the tyrants came from the work-shops, and seemed the more pitiless by reason of their common origin with the apprentices. When the hour came for a journeyman to pass to a master, he encountered for judges those whose interest it was to put him aside as a rival. They asked of him a *masterpiece* to prove his talent, but a masterpiece executed according to certain rules, so that his genius was constrained to stop at the level of their mediocrity. No one could deviate from the received processes, under penalty of a fine ; and this was a time famous for fines, which were imposed for the slightest forgetfulness as well as for the gravest offences. A cooper was obliged to put his mark on his casks, and to pay a fine for a hoop badly set. The locksmith was liable to imprisonment for his locks, the draper for his cloth, the tanners for their leather. The sergeants were continually passing in the streets armed with a long pole with parchment ribbons, scrawled over with decrees against the bakers, the masons, the goldsmiths and other artisans.   The collectors had no other occupation and the crown no better revenue. One is astounded at the abuses which were daily committed, to the detriment of the laboring classes, when he reads with attention the immense quantities of decrees issued upon debates originating in the jealousy of corporations or their differences with the crown.   At Paris, the expenses of these suits rose, about the middle of the seventeenth century, to more than 500,000 francs a year. Modest corporations had them which cost 25,000 francs. The statutes of all the corporations are still in existence, and may be found either in the City Hall Library or in the archives of the police; but it is difficult to discover them under the confused mass of edicts, decrees and sovereign decisions which were daily called forth by the least incident.   The *esprit de corps* combined with the demands of private interest to prolong their duration, and there are examples of fierce rivalries that no one had succeeded in harmonizing after a struggle of more than a hundred years.

Thus, Louis IX had intended to establish order, and his successors brought about industrial anarchy notwithstanding the absolute oppression under which the subaltern workmen groaned.   Who would believe that women were excluded from the corporation of embroiderers?   The journeymen could not marry before having attained to mastership, and, as we have said, that mastership was for them the land of Canaan, which they were permitted to see, but rarely to enter.   Besides the execution of the accustomed masterpiece and the double delays of apprenticeship and comradeship, enormous expenses awaited the daring one who would cross the boundary : registration, royal fee, reception fee, police fee, fee for opening a shop, honorary fees to the dean and the wardens, payment of the usher and the clerk of the

corporation, gratuities to the masters who were called to
the ceremony ; nothing was lacking there, and often the
unhappy journeyman could not pass to the degree of
master, for want of the capital necessary to throw a sop
to his judges.   How many feelings of despair must
have agitated the souls of the workmen during this long
period of oppression !   Everything was interdicted, even
to the power to dispose of themselves ; as if freedom
to work was not the most sacred of all rights !   But
the last expression of the system of corporations has
been proclaimed only in England, where the law but
lately punished with death a workman-deserter, even
when his country had no work to give him.   Etienne
Boyleau, *provost* though he was, did not think of that.

However, in spite of their numerous vicissitudes, the
corporations organized by Saint Louis with the idea of
order, discipline and probity, produced results well worthy
the attention of economists and statesmen.   They accustomed the workmen to patience, accuracy and perseverance ; they gave renewed security to commerce, and also
a tremendous impetus to this important element of public wealth.   From the time consumers were certain of being no longer deceived about the quantity or the quality
of the products, they made more considerable demands,
and hence procured more extended means of subsistence
for the laboring classes.   There were also some advantages in that strict hierarchy which considered the master-
workman as the family head of his workmen, with powers
almost as extended as those of a father over his children.
The limit fixed to the number in each trade kept competition within bounds doubtless somewhat narrow and consequently infected with monopoly, but it hindered those
rash enterprises which too often give to the industrial
struggles of our time the character of a deadly warfare,
where the vanquished becomes bankrupt without the
conqueror making a fortune.   In delaying the marriage
of workmen without capital or position, the rule of the

corporations might pass for a blessing, at a time when
paternity seemed to be only the gift of creating unfortunates. But who will absolve that feudalism of the
workshop from all the scourges it brought in its train?
If it rendered some services in times now remote, how
many ravages did it not cause in the subsequent centuries? How many men of genius did it not stifle in the
cradle? What fatal habits of servitude did it not keep
up? The most significant thing that can be said on this
subject, is that corporations have been modified or unsettled at all epochs when civilization has taken a step
forward, and that they have been re-demanded whenever
the humanitarian movement has appeared stationary or
retrograde. Turgot suppressed * them and his fall recalls them : the Revolution and the Empire destroy them
beyond recovery, and in 1814 a famous petition solicits
their re-establishment.†

We are, however, not consistent, when we refuse to the
founders of this system the tribute of honor which is
their due. The establishment of corporations, if one excepts its fiscal abuses, was in harmony with the political
constitution of the times in which it originated. There
were few trades, but there were customs duties between
the provinces ; few productions and few markets. The
interior customs duties secured to local manufacturers
the sale of their articles, and the convents offered bread
and an asylum to unoccupied workmen. By the celibacy
of the monks and of the workmen, population was restricted within limits proportioned to the means of subsistence in those times. The apprentice earned nothing ;
but, after a few years, his maintenance fell upon his
master. Competition did not lower the rate of wages,
and commerce did not experience those sudden and fre-

---

* See the edict of Turgot of 1776, and the report of Dallarde to the Constituent Assembly, session of Feb. 15, 1791.

† This petition, extremely curious, and drawn up by M. Levacher Du-
plessis, has been printed in 4to.

quent variations in prices which with us disconcert the shrewdest speculators. We have emancipated labor, but, strange to say, its condition, in many respects, has become more hard and more precarious. It is because we have very imperfectly executed the great work of freeing the workers : we have proclaimed unlimited freedom of pro duction, but we have denied ourselves the liberty of allowing our products to flow abroad. Our system of free competition is incomplete ; and, since the destruction of the work of Saint Louis, we have only attained the power of encumbering ourselves : tariff-wars have succeeded the contests of the corporations.

CHAPTER XX.

The impetus given to political economy by the Italian republics of the middle ages.—Increasing influence of labor.—Increase of personal property.—Resulting changes in the social condition of Europe.—Foundation of credit.—Bank of Venice.—Origin of the modern prohibitory system.

WHOEVER attentively studies the history of the last days of feudalism, cannot fail to be struck with the efforts made in different parts of Europe to secure to all pro ducers a juster proportion in the distribution of the profits of labor. The affranchisement of the Communes in France, the establishment of the Hanseatic League in Germany, the creation of the Italian republics, in the middle ages, are only episodes in this great work of emancipation which is pursued from age to age with steady perseverance. The organization of corporations, in the reign of Saint Louis, in its turn powerfully contributes to it. Wherever artisans and tradesmen combine, they endeavor to create an existence independent of the caprice of lords and governments. The ease with which they conceal their wealth or remove it when the storm gathers, their tendency to collect together, and the need there is of their services, secure to them franchises which were nowhere more extended than in Italy, where they were even given the monopoly of sovereignty.

In the year 1282, the industrial arts were so powerful at Florence, that the citizens of that republic elected a magistracy composed exclusively of merchants, under the name of *Priors of the Arts*. These delegates of the people, united in a supreme college of six members, were invested with the executive power and lodged in the palace of the nation. Their functions only lasted two months, but they could be reëlected at the end of two years. The priors were chosen by their predecessors and the heads of the *major arts*, and a certain number of notables. At Sienna, the citizens did the same, and the fifteen lords who governed that little republic were replaced by nine bourgeois, exclusively selected from the tradesmen. At Genoa and at Venice, commercial fortunes took the place of the landed aristocracy and created a power more absolute than that of the feudal barons. In most of these republics, it was necessary to work at some art or trade, in order to remain a citizen or to be able to aspire to the government of the state. The merchants considered themselves ennobled by their business itself ; there was a *silk nobility* and a *wool nobility*, and the latter soon thought they had a right to look down upon the former.* At the commencement of the fourteenth century, we observe in all Italy infinite shades of diversity among the various republican constitutions ; but they all agree in this, that nowhere did the aristocracy prevail over the industrial and commercial bourgeois. Soon, fire-arms and printing, by bringing physical forces and human intellects more nearly to a level, gave a last blow to the power of the castles.

What man of the people must not have felt his heart beat with hope at the sight of the daily increasing progress of Italian liberty! Never had the republics of Rome and of Athens enjoyed a freedom like that. At Rome and at Athens the contest was for the sovereignty of a few ; in the Italy of the middle ages, the independence of all was defended. The magistrates were taken from the counting-houses, from the way-side shops : the nobles were kept at a respectful distance. Every one worked for himself, not for masters. There were few vexations and few imposts, absolute freedom of trade and

---

* Daru, *Histoire de Venice*, vol. i, p. 505.

vigorous organization of the industrial arts. The custom
of having public and private assemblies soon gave rise to
orators and statesmen ; and experience in mercantile affairs gave an impetus to the first financial ideas which
became popular in Europe. We need not suppose that
these governments of merchants were exclusively occupied with commerce : * their policy was often more liberal
than that of the lords whose place they had taken. They
accorded to the fine arts every species of encouragement,
and multiplied with most praiseworthy solicitude institutions of benevolence, instruction, and public utility.
Thirty hospitals with a thousand beds for the sick and
the poor; more than two hundred schools where ten
thousand children were learning to read ; and splendid rewards lavished on the genius of painters, architects, and
sculptors, all testify to the enlightened zeal of the administrators of Florence in the fourteenth century.

Their commercial prosperity was not less worthy of
remark. There were estimated to be two hundred manufacturers of woolen goods, producing every year about
eighty thousand pieces of cloth, the sale of which secured
wages to more than thirty thousand workmen. Eighty
counting-houses were devoted to banking business, and
their numerous branch establishments everywhere favored
discount and credit, already familiar to the inhabitants of
that country, before the rest of Europe had become acquainted with them. Florence then equalled in wealth
and productive power the republic of Venice, which surpassed most of the other states. Its public revenues
amounted to three hundred thousand florins. Villani
compiled quite a complete list of them at that time,†
which is followed by the budget of expenses, a financial

---

* Sismondi, *Histoire des Républiques Italiennes du Moyen Age.* Vol. iv,
p. 166.

† This important document has been quoted by M. de Sismondi, in his
excellent history of the Italian republics.   I reproduce it entire, as the only
complete budget of these times which has been preserved for political economy.

monument quite worthy of meditation, when one considers the little progress the most renowned nations had then made in the art of finance. One is surprised to see in it that the republic accorded no salary to its public functionaries, unless they were foreigners. The militia took the place of the army during peace, and the mercenaries in the pay of the state figured only among the extraordinary expenses of war. The indirect taxes far exceeded in number and value the direct ones, especially

---

Revenues of the city and republic of Florence, from 1336 to 1338, in gold florins of the weight of 72 grammes at 24 carats.

	FLORINS.
Port duties, or import and export duties on merchandise and provisions, farmed out by the year at	90,200
Import on the sale of wine at retail, ⅓ of the value.	59,300
Estimo, or land tax on the country places.	30,100
Tax on salt sold at 40 sols a bushel to the bourgeois, and 20 sols to the peasant.	14,450
Revenue from the property of rebels, exiled and condemned.	7,000
Tax on lenders and usurers.	3,000
Dues from nobles invested with territorial possessions.	2,000
Tax from contracts (inscriptions like mortgages).	11,000
Tax on butcheries for the city.	15,000
" " " country.	4,400
Tax for rents.	4,050
Tax on flour and mills.	4,250
Imposts on citizens appointed podestats in a foreign country.	3,500
Tax on indictments.	1,400
Profit on the coinage of gold pieces.	2,300
" " copper pieces.	1,500
Rent of lands of the corporation, and tolls.	1,600
Tax on cattle-dealers in the city.	2,150
Tax on the verification of weights and measures.	600
Street sweepings and rents of the deposits of Orto San-Michele.	750
Tax on country rents.	550
" tradesmen.	2,000
Fines and sentences from which payment is obtained.	20,000
Defaults of soldiers (for exemption from military duty).	7,000
Tax on doors and houses in Florence.	5,550
Tax on fruit-women and old-clothes women.	450
Permission to carry arms, at 20 sols per head.	1,300
Tax on sergeants.	100
Tax on woods floated on the Arno.	100
Tax on the examiners of guarantees given to the corporation.	200
Share of the state in duties collected by the art-consuls.	300
Tax on citizens who reside in the country.	1,000
Tax on possessions in the country.	
Tax on battles without weapons.	
Tax of Firenzuola.	
Tax on mills and fishing.	

The total exceeds fl. 300,000

upon the land contribution, which was twice smaller than the single revenue from drinks. The amount of the fines and convictions plays a great part in the budget of receipts, a sad evidence either of little respect paid the laws, or of severity in their execution. What else were the profits on the minting of gold and copper coin, than a concession of the same kind as the alterations in money, of which our history is full, from the time of Philippe Auguste to Charles le Bel? Nevertheless, the account of the expenses and revenues of Florence testify strongly to the simplicity of the governmental régime of the republic; happy would it have been, if the rivalry of the new

Expenses of the Republic of Florence, from 1336 to 1338, in Florentine livres, a gold florin at 3 livres and 2 sols.

LIVRES.

Salary of the podestat and his family (his archers and sbires[12]). .	15,240
" captain of the people and his family. . . .	5,880
" executor of the orders of courts.	4,900
" guardian, with fifty horses and 100 foot soldiers (an extraordinary office soon abolished).	26,400
Judge of appeals on the rights of the corporation. . . .	1,100
Officer charged with repressing the luxury of the women. . .	1,000
Officer of the market of Orto San-Michele.	1,300
Office of paying troops.	1,000
Office for payments to invalid soldiers.	250
Treasurers of the corporation, their officers and notaries. . .	1,400
Offices of the land revenues of the corporation.	200
Jailors and guards of prisons.	800
Table of the priors and their family at the palace. . . .	3,600
Wages of the *donzels*[13] of the corporation and of the guardians of the towers of the podestat and of the priors.	550
Sixty archers and their captains in the service of the priors. . .	5,700
Notary of reforms, with his assistant.	450
Lions, torches, light and fire at the palace.	2,400
Notary at the palace of the priors.	100
Wages of the archers and tipstaff.	1,500
Trumpets of the corporation.	1,000
Alms to monks and to hospitals.	2,000
Six hundred night-guards in the city.	10,800
Flags for festivals and horse races.	310
Spies and messengers of the commune.	1,200
Ambassadors.	15,500
Castellans and guards of fortresses.	12,400
Annual provision of arms and arrows.	4,650

Florins 39,119 at 3 liv., 2 s. per florin=liv. . 121,630

Labors on the walls, bridges and churches form the extraordinary expenses, with the pay of military men. In time of peace, the republic kept in its pay seven-hundred to a thousand dragoons and as many foot-soldiers.

nobility and too often the oppression of the people by patricians originating from themselves, had not opened the way to civil discords and exposed the frontiers to foreigners! The Italian republics of the middle ages may be considered as great commercial houses, administered with ability and economy. The revenues created by labor were rarely touched by taxation there, and they daily gave rise to new capital, which the freedom of transactions allowed to be advantageously increased. The city of Hamburg and that of Geneva, so rich notwithstanding the scantiness of their territory, to-day give us a pretty accurate idea of the prosperity of those great municipal cities of the middle ages. Their environs, covered with country-houses and delightful villas, where opulence reposes from the fatigues of commerce, are a faithful representation of the sumptuous abodes of the Italian merchants, who were then almost all lodged in palaces of which their present successors cannot even maintain the accessories. They had also become the lenders of funds to the principal powers of Europe : they were in request as intendants of domains and administrators of finances. It was to them that sovereigns in distress always applied : it was their gold florins that the kings of France took especial delight in altering, and of which they changed the value from ten sols to thirty. Edward III of England had chosen his two bankers at Florence, and the loans he made through them so far exceeded his repayments, that the Bardis found that they had advanced to him one hundred and eighty thousand marks sterling, and the Peruzzis one hundred and thirty-five thousand, together amounting to sixteen millions three hundred and eighty thousand of our francs, at a time when money was five or six times dearer than in our day.* The citizens of the Italian republics controlled at that time the best part of European commerce Their workmen were eagerly sought everywhere as the most

---

* Sismondi, *Hist. of Ital. Repub.*, vol. v, p. 261.

skilful, and their products as the most perfect. They had
become arbiters in matters of taste and the sole merchants
renowned for tissues, fashions, arms and furniture. Their
capital procured for them also immense profits, not to
mention their gains as ship-chandlers, as bankers, and as
partners in all enterprises of any importance. The laws
which they made in their capacity of legislators invested
with supreme power, favored in the most liberal manner
all commercial transactions; and they were the first to
prove, in theory and in practice, the advantages, still only
partially understood, of the most unlimited freedom of
trade. Genoa and Venice had no other element of greatness.

We must here take note of the important part which
the Italians took in the foundation of the first credit institutions. Their immense trade had early made them
feel the necessity of simplifying the contrivances of every
kind of which that branch of production is composed;
and at the end of the twelfth century, Venice had seen
arise in its midst a bank of deposit which opened credit-
accounts with money-lenders, to facilitate payments and
transfers of indebtedness. The bank retained no duty
for safe-keeping nor for commission, and paid no interest;
but its certificates of deposit performed the same functions as money. By means of a fund (*It. cassa*), called
cash, they paid at sight in specie the bills that were presented; and they chose for these payments the best
money, which became that of the bank. It was ruled
that the bank should only pay and reckon in good
ducats, whose standard was finer and alteration less common than that of other specie. From this time, the paper of the bank had the advantage over all bills of the
merchants, of being exchangeable for standard money,
and the credit of the establishment was placed on a solid
foundation. By degrees, the government introduced the
custom of making its payments in orders on the bank,
instead of in specie, and it thus added a new element of

success to those the bank already possessed. Finally, the opening of a debt and credit account, which permitted the owners of funds to transfer their credits, completed the working facilities of the bank, and soon gave rise to several similar institutions.*

The position of Venice made the perfecting of the industrial arts and of commerce a necessity to her from the very beginning. Venice was a republic without territory, and her capital a fleet of vessels at anchor. From commerce she was obliged to seek not fortune, but life itself. Therefore, the whole policy of the government had for its constant aim the increase of her commercial liberties and her financial franchises among all nations. For lack of more valuable products, the Venetians began by selling salt ; then they exported the agricultural products of the north of Italy, and went to the Black Sea for those of Turkey, Russia, and Persia. At the fair of Pavia, as early as the time of Charlemagne, they had dazzled purchasers by magnificent exhibitions of valuable carpets, silk goods, gold tissues, pearls and precious stones. Sumptuary laws obliged them to economize their capital and to sacrifice to unproductive consumption only a part of their revenues. Placed between the East and the West, they had imitated the industry of a part of their neighbors and the economic simplicity of the others. Their privileges at Constantinople had somewhat of the insolence of conquest, and their colonies in the Mediterranean would to-day almost form a kingdom. Venice maintained her consuls, and, in general, all her commercial employés,in truly royal luxury. She required them to have a numerous retinue in a state to worthily represent the republic and to appear imposing to strangers. The podestat of Constantinople was for some time on the footing of a sovereign. He judged, in final appeal, the differen-

---

* M. Daru published, in the 7th volume of his *Histoire de Venise*, in the proofs and illustrations, sect. 2, paragraph 5, a memoir on the Bank of Venice, under date of June 30, 1753, extracted from the correspondence of the Abbé of Bernis, then embassador from France.

ces between natives of Venice ; he wore scarlet buskins, a mark of imperial dignity, and always appeared in public surrounded with guards.   It was by thus honoring the commercial profession and favoring in all ways the citizens who devoted themselves to it, that the Venetians so much increased the preponderance of their country and the consideration for the merchants who were making its fortune.

The republic also employed, in the fifteenth century, in the single dock-yard of Venice, six thousand workmen and thirty-six thousand marines.   The government sent every year to the principal ports squadrons of four to six large galleys, which received the merchandise destined for private individuals.   The object of this was to keep the navy in practice and also to make it useful in time of peace, to make the national flag respected, and to provide means of transport for those who were not in a condition to arm vessels on their own account.*   The commercial marine maintained not less than three thousand vessels employed in the importation and exportation of the products of all the countries in the world.   These ships explored in turn the ports of the Black Sea, those of Syria and Egypt, and they went from harbor to harbor to visit all the places of the Peloponnesus, of Asia Minor, Cyprus, Candia, and the Greek Archipelago.   One fleet, the most important of all, set out every year for the coasts of Flanders, coasting along Sicily, Africa, and Spain, with great vessels which could not have had crews of less than two hundred men, and which trafficked in succession on all the coasts in such merchandise as the inhabitants needed.   Commercial treaties secured the most advantageous intercourse in every port to the Venetian merchants, who had correspondents at Bruges, Antwerp, and London, with the merchants of the Hanse towns. Venice had at that time already given a great impetus to her manufactures, and the richest packages of her expe-

* Sandi, *Storia Civile di Venezia*, lib. v.

ditions were composed of mirrors, crystal-glass, cloths of fine wool, and elegant silk goods, made by Venetian work-men. The most enlightened governments of our time have never shown as much solicitude as did that republic for the interests of commerce and the industrial arts.

Some authors* have thought they saw in these long voyages made in the interests of commerce on vessels belonging to the state, the model of the companies which the Dutch, English and French subsequently organized for trade with the Indies: we cannot coincide in that opinion. Without doubt, the private citizens who rented the vessels from the government, for their own trade, enjoyed some privileges; but these privileges were not permanent, and every galley was separately rented at a price so moderate, that one cannot reasonably attribute to mercenary motives the system followed in that regard. Commerce was for a long time free at Venice; and the republic only began to decline when its government had caused the source of its prosperity to be exhausted by monopoly. At first all the young patricians were sub-jected to the most severe ordeals of a commercial train-ing. They were often sent as novices on board state-vessels to try fortune with a light venture, so much did it enter into the views of the administration to direct all citizens toward industrial occupations! The only re-proach that can be brought against the Venetians, is the effort to exclude foreigners from all competition with them. Although commercial jealousy had not yet erected prohibitions into a system, and the ports of the republic were open to all the merchandise of the world, yet the Venetians only permitted its transporta-tion in their own ships; and they reigned as absolute masters over all the Mediterranean. War had given them security from the Pisans, the Sicilians and the Genoese. Spain, long occupied by the Moors, gave them little occasion of offence. France disdained commerce;

---

* Among others, Count Daru, *Histoire de Venise*, vol. iii, page 107.

England had not yet begun to think of it; the republic of Holland was not in existence. Under cover of the right of sovereignty on the gulf, which she had arrogated to herself, Venice reserved the almost exclusive right to navigate. Armed flotillas guarded the mouths of all her rivers, and allowed no barque to enter or depart without being rigorously examined. But what profited that jealous solicitude for the interests of her navigation? A day came when the Portuguese discovered the Cape of Good Hope, and all that structure of precautions and mistrust suddenly fell to pieces.

Here begin the first wars of customs-duties, and political economy receives from history valuable instruction. The Venetians had levelled all obstacles, but for themselves alone, and to the exclusion of other nations. Their legislation was very strict in respect to foreigners, in the matter of commerce. The laws forbade a merchant who was not a subject of the republic to be even received on board a vessel of the state. Foreigners paid customs-duties twice as high 'as natives. They could neither build nor buy vessels in Venetian ports. The ships, the captains, the owners, must all be Venetian. Every alliance between natives[14] and strangers was interdicted; there was no protection, no privileges and no benefits save for Venetians: the latter, however, all had the same rights.[*] In Venice itself, and there alone, was it permitted to negotiate with the Germans, Bohemians and Hungarians. As national manufactures acquired importance, the government departed from the liberal policy it had hitherto pursued, and the manufacturers obtained an absolute prohibition of such foreign merchandise as they produced. In vain, in the seventeenth century, did declining commerce urge the reëstablishment of former liberties and the freedom of the port: the attempt was made for a brief moment, but the spirit of restriction won the day, and the prohibitory régime early prepared the way for the death of the republic.

---

[*] Sandi, liv. vi, chap. i.

The people of Italy, however, pardoned the Venetians for their commercial intolerance, because of the moderate price at which they delivered all commodities.   The Jews, Armenians, Greeks, and Germans flocked to Venice and engaged with safety in speculations, which were always advantageous, because of the security which the credit institutions gave and the recognized probity of the merchants.   But soon Venice saw numerous manufactures spring up in Europe rivaling her own, and her commerce encountered most formidable competition in that of the Portuguese, Dutch, Spanish and English.   The discovery of the Cape of Good Hope took away from her the monopoly of the spices of the Indies.   The taking of Constantinople, by Mahomet II, had already deprived her of the magnificent privileges which her subjects enjoyed in that rich capital of the Orient.   But the discovery of America and the vigorous reprisals of Charles V, who, at the commencement of his reign, in 1517, doubled the customs-duties which the Venetians paid in his states, completed the ruin of that fortunate monopoly which had made all Europe tributary.   Charles V raised the import and export duties on all Venetian merchandise to twenty per cent ; and this tariff, which would to-day appear moderate, sufficed then to prevent the Venetians from entering Spanish ports.   Such was the origin of the exclusive system, the fatal invention which the republic of Venice was so cruelly to expiate.   So long as she sought fortune only in the free competition of the talent and capital of her own citizens, she increased from age to age and became for a moment the arbiter of Europe ; but as soon as she wished to rule the markets by the tyranny of monopoly, she saw a league formed against her commerce, formidable for a very different reason from that of Cambray.

We could wish no other argument in favor of free trade than the prodigious development of Venetian industries during the long reign of that freedom.   It had not been

necessary to have recourse to protection to secure to the
republic, in its finest days, skilful architects, ship-builders,
and civil engineers who would meet all the demands of
her service. Her goldsmiths passed for the most renowned in all Europe. She had manufactures of silks
unrivaled even in Italy, where that branch of industry
early made rapid progress; and these manufactures
brought her, from the first, more than five hundred thousand ducats a year, being nearly three millions in our
francs. The most ingenious workmen from abroad
received encouragement of every kind to establish themselves at Venice, and the state inquisition pursued with
its homicidal threats the native workmen who were so
bold as to expatriate themselves. "If any workman or
artist," it was said,* "transports his art to a foreign
country, to the detriment of the republic, an order to return will be sent him. If he does not obey, his nearest
connections will be put in prison, in order to force him
to obedience by the regard he bears them. If he returns, the past will be forgiven, and an establishment at
Venice will be obtained for him ; if, notwithstanding the
imprisonment of his relatives, he persists in his determina-
tion to remain in a foreign country, *some emissary will be
charged to kill him*, and after his death, his relatives will
be set at liberty." The inevitable result of these atrocious
provisions was to retard the development of the industrial arts, by preventing workmen from going to foreign
countries to study the secrets and the improvements
which the arts needed. By making a mystery of their
already old inventions, they accustomed their artisans to
them, and shut the workmen up, so to speak, within a
narrow circle. Everything around them was progressing,
while they were remaining stationary, and the products
of their manufactures kept somewhat of a market within
the republic only by favor of the prohibitory laws. The
decline began with protection.

---

* Art. 26 of *Statutes of State Inquisition.*

Venice had, however, commenced her industrial career under the most favorable auspices. A tribunal had been created there, as early as 1172, for the regulation of the arts and trades. The quality and the quantity of materials were strictly examined. Every workman was forbidden to perform more than one kind of work, in order to execute it with more care. Manufactures, by the end of the fourteenth century, had therefore attained a very high degree of perfection. The making of cotton cloths was known at Venice about that time. The finest linens in all Italy were made there, and it was known how to print colors renowned for their brilliancy and solidity. Berthollet reports* that it was at Venice, in 1429, that the first published account of the processes employed in dyeing, appeared. Chemistry was then more advanced there than in any other country, and the Venetians were in almost exclusive possession of the trade in drugs. They prepared and gilded leather in a manner recognized as superior to that of any other people. Their laces, known under the name of *point de Venise*, were eagerly sought after. Their hardware and their sugar refineries scarcely sufficed for the needs of European consumption; and, when painting was still in its infancy among their rivals, with them it had risen to the first rank among industrial arts. They had established numerous manufactures, which have since been surpassed in France and in the rest of Europe; but to them belongs the honor of having served as a model to all the others. The Venetians, therefore, were distinguished not only in commerce, but also in the industrial arts; they for a long time united to the advantages of transportation, the profits of manufacture. The prudent and ingenious use which they had made of the contrivances of credit, had by degrees extended throughout the Italian republics, and had developed manufacturing and commercial wealth in them upon a vast scale.

---

* *Eléments de l'art de teinture.*

There is in existence a remarkable discourse, delivered
in 1421 at the Grand Council, by the doge Thomas Moncenigo, upon the financial resources and the extent of commerce of the republic of Venice.* After an exact and detailed exposition of the profits of national labor in foreign
markets, and of the part of it which reverted to the state
treasury, the old doge dwelt principally on the danger
there would be in disturbing that magnificent prosperity,
in order to ward off a war then eagerly demanded by the
restless spirits of the period. " You are the only ones,"
he said, " to whom land and sea are equally open. You
are the channel of all the wealth ; you provide for the
entire world. The whole universe is interested in your

---

* This discourse is literally quoted by M. Daru in his *Histoire de Venise,*
vol. ii, pp. 293–314. The following extract seems to me worthy of figuring
beside the budget of the city of Florence :

" I have prepared," says the doge Moncenigo, " a statement of the products of our commerce :

DUCATS.
" Every week there comes to us from Milan seventeen or eighteen
    thousand ducats, which makes per year   .   .   . 900,000
From Monza, a thousand per week, and per year . . 52,000
"   Como, two   "   "   " . . . 104,000
" Alessandria, one   "   "   "   . . 52,000
" Tortona and Novara, two thousand per week, and per year . 104,000
" Pavia, two thousand per week, and per year . . 104,000
" Cremona, two thousand per week, and per year . . 104,000
" Bergamo, fifteen hundred "   " . . 78,000
" Palermo, two thousand   "   " . . 104,000
" Piacenza, one   "   "   " . . 52,000

1,654,000

" What evidently establishes the truth of this result is the acknowledgment of all the bankers, who declare that every year the Milanese has to
pay us sixteen hundred thousand ducats. Do you find this a pretty fine
garden which Venice is enjoying without its occasioning her any expense ?

DUCATS.
" Tortona and Novara use per year six thousand pieces of cloth
    which, at fifteen ducats a piece, make . . • . 90,000
Pavia, 3,000 pieces . . . . • • 45,000
Milan, 4,000   "   of fine cloth, at 30 ducats • • . 120,000
Como, 12,000 " at 15 ducats . • . • 180,000
Monza, 6,000 "   "   " • • • . 90,000
Brescia, 5,000 "   "   " . • • • 75,000
Bergamo, 10,000 " at 7 " . • • . 70,000
Cremona, 140,000 pieces of fustian at 4½ ducats . • • 70,000
Parma, 4,000 pieces of cloth at 15 ducats • • . 60,000

900,000

fortune. All the gold of the world comes to you. Fortunate, so long as you hold to pacific ideas, while all Europe is on fire ! As for me, so long as there remains in me a breath of life, I will persist in this, that we must love peace. I have always tried to take measures that the interest of the loans and all public expenses be promptly met every six months, and I have had the good fortune to succeed. It only remains for you to maintain the happy state of our affairs, praying the All-Powerful to make you persevere in the salutary system thus far pursued. If you continue in this course, you will become formidable and the possessors of all the wealth of the Christian world. Keep yourselves, as from fire, from

"In all 94,000 pieces ; and the import and export duties, at simply one ducat per piece, bring us 200,000 ducats.

" We have a trade with Lombardy estimated at 28,800,000 ducats. Do you think Venice has there a pretty fine garden ?

	DUCATS.
" Then come the hemps for the sum of	100,000
The Lombards buy of you every year 5,000 lbs. of cotton for .	250,000
20,000 quintals of thread (or perhaps of spun cotton), at 15 to 20 ducats per hundred	30,000
2,000,000 lbs. of Catalogne wool, at 60 ducats per thousand .	120,000
As many from France	120,000
Cloths of silk and gold for	250,000
3,000 lots of pepper at 100 ducats per lot	300,000
400 loads of cinnamon at 160 ducats per load . . .	64,000
200,000 lbs. of ginger at 40 ducats a thousand . . .	8,000
Sugars taxed from 2 to 3 to 15 ducats per hundred . .	95,000
Other commodities for sewing and embroidery . . .	30,000
4,000 thousands of dye woods at 30 ducats a thousand . .	120,000
Grains and plants for tinctures	50,000
Soaps	250,000
Slaves	30,000
	1,817,000

" I do not count the product of the sale of salt.* Acknowledge that such a commerce is a fine estate. Consider how many vessels the movement of all this merchandise keeps employed, either in carrying it to Lombardy or going for it to Syria, Romania, Catalogne, Flanders, Cyprus, Sicily and all parts of the world. Venice makes two and a half or three per cent on the freight. See how many people live from this movement : brokers, workmen, sailors, thousands of families, and finally the merchants, whose profit does not amount to less than 600,000 ducats.

" That is what your garden produces. Have you a mind to destroy it ? No, indeed : well, you must defend it against whoever may come to attack it."

* Count Filéasi, in his _Researches on the Commerce of Venice_, p. 270, values the salt product at a million ducats.

touching the property of others and making war unjustly: God will punish you for it. *Then those who had ten thousand ducats, will have no more than a thousand; those who had ten houses will be reduced to one, and so on. No more property, no more credit, no more reputation. From the masters that you were, you will find yourselves subjects, and of whom ? Of military men, of soldiery, of these bands whom you are keeping in pay.* Foreigners have often rendered homage to your wisdom, by taking arbiters from among you : continue then, for your own sake and for the happiness of your sons, in the system which has procured you so much prosperity."

One can scarcely fail of being touched by the grandeur and the wisdom of this language. People then even at that remote time already comprehended that commerce was essentially the friend of peace, and that nations were jointly and severally responsible for each other in good as well as in bad fortune. "What will you sell to the Milanese," said the doge, "when you shall have ruined them ? What will they be able to give you in exchange for your products ? And your products, what will become of them before the exigencies of a war which will encroach upon the capital you need to create them ? " Simple good sense indicated then to eminent men what experience has since put beyond doubt, and what theory to-day teaches, supported by the authority of facts.

In the other Italian republics, where the industrial and commercial spirit had prevailed over feudal despotism, as at Florence and Venice, the prosperity was not less brilliant, nor the progress of every kind less astonishing. Every one knows of the wealth accumulated at Genoa through the boldness of her navigators and the ability of her merchants. Genoa had counting-houses in the Archipelago and the Black Sea, and her merchants came to the ports of the Hanse towns to share the profits with Venice. The bank of St. George, which originated in

1407 from loans contracted to meet the public * necessi-
sities, soon became a rival to that of Venice, and rendered
the same service as its rival.   However, the Genoese †
did not hold as long as the Venetians to the principles of commercial freedom, and their government furnishes the first example of exclusive privileges granted to
a company, on payment of subsidies.   At Milan, in the
year 1260, the government was occupied with the recen-
sion of the lands, and in that capital of the Lombard republics, it was necessary to put more than a hundred
mints in operation, to meet the immense demand for
money, necessitated by the development of business.   In
whatever direction we turn our eyes, we are struck by
the devouring activity which reigns in all these republics,
and by the penetration with which each of them adapted
its institutions to the needs of manufactures and commerce.   To them we owe the creation of the first institutions of public credit, whether it was the invention of
banks, or the conception of loans.   They had already organized industry, before Saint Louis had founded corporations.   The power of their governments seems to have
had no other mission than to protect the interests of labor ;
and, while everywhere else taxes were being levied on
peasants and villeins, at Venice, Genoa, Florence, Pisa,
and Milan, these same villeins, enriched by commerce and
the industrial arts, were disposing, like masters, of the
sovereignty.

The Italian republics, then, not only served the cause
of liberty by reviving the noble rivalries of the old Greek
republics in independence, but, by placing labor everywhere in honor, they changed the face of Europe, and
prepared the way for the advent of the liberal doctrines
whose triumph we shall one day behold.   It was among
them that the great economic experiments were made,
from which science was to come forth all armed.   These

---

* Gilbart, *History and Principles of Banking*, p. 10.

† Count Pecchio, *Histoire de l' Économie Politique en Italie*, p. 6.

republics tried, in turn, before the other nations, free trade and prohibition. They confronted the first perils of credit, and laid the foundations of the modern system of loans. While the rest of Europe was covered with donjons and thatched huts, Italy was building marble palaces and temples ; she was fitting out thousands of vessels, laden with the products of her manufactures. She was organizing labor, and calling all the citizens, without caste distinction, to honors and fortune, when, on account of knowledge or capacity, they were worthy of it. Happy if aristocracy had not glided into her midst, by favor of wealth, like prohibition following manufactures, and like monopoly on the steps of commerce ! How many lessons for us in that immense variety of events ! Experiment there preceded science, and showed the first example of a broad application of the theories of trade to the practice of government. Administration was there presented under the simple and regular forms of an industrial management, where all the resources were put to work with order, intelligence and economy. One might call these governments vast enterprises, strong in assured credit, which dispatched rich cargoes to all ports, and which were constantly occupied with supplying, by unwearied production, the wants of an immense consumption. It was, in fact, in the Italian republics that the most ingenious arts and the most advanced financial doctrines of which history makes mention at that time, took their rise ; and we cannot say to what degree of splendor these states might still have risen, but for the fatal accession of Charles V, who changed at once the face of Europe and that of political economy.

CHAPTER XXI.

The change in the course of political economy brought about by Charles V.—The spirit of conquest substituted for the commercial spirit.—Official establishment of the restrictive system.—Slave trade.—Financial operations. —Convents and pauperism.—Opposition of Protestantism.

CHARLES FIFTH, a child of Flanders, emperor of Germany, and monarch of Spain, united in his person, in the highest degree, all antipathies to Italy. He came from a country where the manufacturers of Venice, Milan, and Florence had found formidable competitors; he was, in his character as emperor of Germany, the highest personification of the Ghibeline party, so abhorred in Italy; and, as king of Spain, he was to become the most injurious rival of the Italian bankers, who could oppose no serious resistance to the fortunate possessor of the mines of Mexico and Peru. Hardly had he ascended the throne, when he put into the commercial balance, beside the weight of the sword, that of the new world and of a great part of the old. In politics, in religion, in the industrial arts, his power would suffer no rival; and, from the age of twenty years, he was prepared to raise all questions and to overturn all kingdoms.

It is not without reason that historians agree in considering the reign of this prince as the point of departure of a new social order in Europe. Dating from his reign, in fact, a rapid and profound change takes place in the course of civilization. Ideas are as much disturbed as empires, and for the first time for many centuries, the world seems summoned to the definitive struggle between despotism and liberty. The discovery of America, the expulsion of the Moors from Spain, the Protestant reformation, the trade in blacks, are events contemporary with Charles V, and each of these events bears the germ of twenty future revolutions. To the municipal régime which had been established under the influence of labor, in all the free cities of Germany, Belgium, Spain and the Italian republics, succeeds the domination of a few powerful monarchies, which divide Europe among themselves, after having ruined it. Charles V was the principal instrument of that revolution, the consequences of which were to be so fatal to political economy, by putting under the protection of force the worst doctrines which have afflicted humanity.

The necessity of carrying on the constantly renewed wars, reduced this monarch in the first years of his reign, to financial expedients which deprived productive industries of the greater part of their capital, and swallowed it up in the gulf of sterile consumption. His treasury was always empty; his troops were badly paid, and they acquired the habit of living by pillage, extortions, or arbitrary taxes. Violent and oppressive measures everywhere supplanted the regular system of taxation established by Italian financiers. Then began extortions of every kind, quartering of soldiers on the people, and excessive taxes on consumption, which augmented the price of hand-work to the detriment of manufactures. Import duties were increased upon raw products. For the free practice of the arts, was substituted the monopoly of trades and of commerce. Everywhere arose, flanked with privileges, imperial or royal manufactures, from which it was necessary to purchase licences in order to have a right to work. All these restrictive measures became by degrees incorporated in the laws and established by custom; then came sophists who embodied them in doctrines; and thus all the economic heresies with which Europe is still infested have become so much the more difficult to destroy, since they present themselves with the sanction of time and the character of authority. Charles V rendered them more harmful by organizing them and making them penetrate the administration, of which they were to become the rule of conduct and the inviolable dogma.

A more deplorable result of the Austro-Spanish imperial system was the restoration to honor of the aristocracy of parchment and of the sword, which was beginning to disappear before the notabilities of manufactures and commerce. The nobility of the Italian republics, of the Hanse towns, and of the great Belgian, French, and Spanish mercantile cities, worked, at least, and took pride in having descended from working people ; but Charles V began to sell titles in order to have money, and the Castilian prejudice, which makes nobility consist in idleness, spread like a plague through all Europe. So one single reign sufficed to put public liberties back to the worst days of feudalism. Every day some great industrial enterprise withdrew from the arena, where it was no longer able to maintain itself without derogation. The lords had ceased to plunder the passers-by on the highways, as their predecessors did from the height of the old donjons : but they retrenched themselves in privileges which secured to them the best part of the profits of the labor of their fellow citizens. Multitudes of farmers of the revenues caused the farming of them to be adjudged to themselves ; and one of the governors for Charles V, in the conquered countries, dared respond to the royal orders : " The king commands at Madrid, and I at Milan." There was no more public discussion, no more recourse to justice possible ; no more consular jurisdiction, no more credit : all the protecting forms had been abolished to make room for the absolute régime of Spanish pachas.

But it was not alone in Italy and in the states of Charles V that people had to deplore this sudden change in the course, and above all in the doctrines of governments. To any one who remembers the scrupulous fidelity of the Venetians, the Florentines, the Genoese, and the Hanse towns, in keeping their engagements, the hazardous expedients to which the policy of the emperor of Germany accustomed and forced the other princes by his example and his continual wars, will appear more disastrous than the immediate damage which resulted from it. Nothing contributed more to paralyze social development, than the fear and uncertainty which extended to all relations which needed guaranties and security. Upon what basis could one henceforth found the best speculation, when the principal sources of the public revenues were alienated in advance for several years, and the coins changed either by boldly debasing them with alloys, or by spoliating decrees? Money also, for which no profitable and sure investment could be found, soon deserted the industrial arts and became immobilized in purchases of lands. Agriculture, vitally injured by the decline of commerce, was soon ruined under the influence of legislation which prohibited the export of grain. To complete the misfortune, the numerous changes brought about in the administration of the states overpowered by the war, afflicted Europe with a plague revived from the Lower Empire: we mean the law-suits and quarrels of every kind, with their usual *cortége* of rapine and of lawyers. The dazzling splendor of the fine arts never atoned to Italy for the decline which followed the loss of her freedom; and the continual decrease of her population has sufficiently demonstrated, since then, that the true elements of the prosperity of states consist in useful arts rather than ornamental ones.

The reign of Charles V was especially adverse to the progress of political economy, because he turned Europe violently away from the regular paths of production, to precipitate it into the hazards of war and the old system of exploiting men, which was engendered by feudalism. All the false doctrines and injurious prejudices which we to-day have to combat, we owe to his government, continued and made worse under his execrable successor. Freedom of trade was going to be established in the world and to rally in a common solidarity the interests of the south and of the north : Charles V substituted for it restrictions and prohibitions. The banks of Venice and Genoa had just founded credit : Charles V began to make debased coin ; and, although the treasures of the new world were so open to him as to bring him in nearly fifty millions of francs a year, he flooded Europe, about 1540, with a considerable mass of debased coin of Castilian gold. This detestable example found only too many imitators ; and there was a time when, according to the expression of M. Ganilh, " Italy was as much noted for her bad moneys as for her excellent works upon money." Wealth was no longer sought in labor and the intelligent employment of capital, but in the accumulation of specie, the export of which was prohibited by draconian laws ; as if it were possible to buy the commodities one no longer produced himself, and to keep the money which served to pay for them. Then came about the first attempts at those strange theories the invention of which belongs entirely to the Spaniards, and which an economist of their country summed up so naïvely, two hundred years later, in this remarkable passage : " It is necessary rigorously to employ all the means which can lead us to sell to foreigners more of our productions than they will sell us of theirs : *that is the whole secret and the sole advantage of trade.*" *

---

* Ustariz, *Théorie et pratique du Commerce*, chap. iv, p. 13, of the French edition. That author added : " If we could at least remain on a par of exchange, it would still be enough to keep in Spain the greater part of the wealth which comes from the West Indies to Cadiz, instead of which it cannot to-day be to us of any utility. On the contrary, these treasures become injurious to the monarchy, if, from the very port where they arrive, they pass at once into the hands of people who are our rivals, who carry them in great quantities into the countries under the dominion of the Turks. Thus, besides the misfortune of being deprived of our silver as soon as it arrives at Cadiz by fleets or gallions, and the disagreeable circumstance of seeing it carried away by nations little friendly to us who make use of it to increase

Such is the system which has given rise to the innumerable wars of which Europe has been the theatre since the accession of Charles V, and which still unconsciously dominates the commercial policy of almost all modern governments. All have used their strongest efforts, from that time, to retain money and to proscribe foreign merchandise; all have thought they saw in importations a cause of ruin, without perceiving that importations were becoming so much the more necessary as interior production diminished, among each people, exactly in proportion to the restrictions imposed in order to give it increased activity. It was besides, pursuing a chimera, to attempt to sell without buying, and to aspire to the monopoly of manufactures, while abandoning the great works of industry for the product of the mines. Spain has since cruelly expiated that fatal error of Charles V: she lost her manufactures because of having attached too much importance to the gold of her colonies, and later, her colonies escaped from her, because she had too much neglected her manufactures.

But this bad system was not the only error to which Charles V gave currency in Europe. Humanity can seriously reproach his memory for having reëstablished, on an immense scale, slavery, which was just dying out, and the exploitation of human beings, which was near its end. The trade in negroes was organized during this reign as a legitimate and regular institution, and the fatal doctrine of the Greeks and Romans was revived, by virtue of which the profits of social labor belonged of right to a few privileged individuals. Millions of men perished in America, victims of this detestable prejudice, and Africa has not yet ceased, after three hundred years, to pay its tribute of blood and tears to the system which has been

their commerce and their opulence, we have the pain of knowing that a great part of these millions *pass to the Turks and other infidels to increase their power and our losses.* These baneful consquences merit the greatest attention and the most secure measures to prevent them."

And yet Ustariz wrote these lines in 1740, and he had been a minister!

the result of it.   One can form no idea of all the absurdities which were invented at that epoch, to secure to
the men of the metropolis the benefits and revenues of
the new colony: never was the audacity of privilege
manifested in a manner so tyrannical. The metropolis
imposed all its products on the colony, and forbade it to
procure them for itself, even on its own soil. The Americans were forbidden to plant flax, hemp and the vine, to
establish manufactures, to build ships, and to have their
children educated elsewhere than in Spain.   At the same
time certain useless articles of consumption were prescribed for them, and they were subject to exactions the
history of which would to-day seem fabulous.   The whip
of the commander represented at that time the whole of
Spanish civilization.

While the maxims of the government of Charles V
protected in America the establishment of slavery and of
the most odious monopolies, in Europe they encouraged
in every way despotism and idleness.   Convents were
multiplied and endowed at the expense of agriculture
and labor.   The inquisition lighted its thousand funeral piles against civil and religious liberty ; magnificent but useless monuments succeeded those numerous
constructions of public utility which had so brilliantly
distinguished the administration of the Italian republics.
One would have said that no one in Europe was to be
provided with an abode, except five or six demi-gods in
the temples ; the human species might esteem itself happy
to crawl under thatch.   This was the epoch of all bad
ideas, of all bad systems, in arts and manufactures, in
politics, and in religion.   We do not to-day commit a single error, nor follow a single industrial prejudice, which
was not bequeathed to us by that mischievous power
which was strong enough to convert into law its most
fatal aberrations.   No, never will science find terms strong
enough, nor humanity tears enough, to stigmatise and to
deplore the ill-omened acts of such a reign !   Philip II,

of unfortunate memory, only carried them to their re-
results; it was Charles V who laid their foundations.
But the crimes of the son ceased with his life, while the
doctrines of the father hinder still, after three centuries,
the progress of civilization.

Noble and sublime protests have nevertheless been
offered against these grave attacks upon the imprescriptible rights of humanity. Spain still religiously preserves
the remembrance of the heroic attempts of Padilla and
the municipal towns of the Peninsula which followed the
impulse of his patriotism. It was a fine reflection of the
ancient independence of the communes, and one can
judge by what they asked, what Charles V had made
them lose. " We ask," said the chiefs of the provincial
league, in their celebrated remonstrance to this prince,
" that the people no longer furnish gratuitous lodging for
troops ; that all taxes be reëstablished as they were at the
death of Isabella ; that in the states which shall maintain
the succession, each city send one representative of the
clergy, one of the nobility, and *one of the third estate*,
each elected by his order ; that no member of the states
receive either office or pension from the king, whether for
himself or for persons of his family, under *penalty of death*
and confiscation of his property; that each city or community pay its representative a salary suitable for his
support during the time he shall be present at the states,
and *that the lands of the nobles be subject to all the public taxes, the same as those of the communes.*" * Such was
the political economy of the liberal party of that time ;
but the death of Padilla † and the defeat of the Spanish

---

* Robertson, *History of Charles V*, book iii.

† Sandoval, History, vol. i, p. 478, has preserved for us the admirable
letter which Padilla wrote to the city of Toledo the night before his execution. We must reproduce a few of the last thoughts of this martyr of communal franchises. " To thee the crown of Spain and of the entire world ;
to thee who wert free, from the times of the powerful Goths, and who by
shedding the blood of strangers and of thy own people, hast regained liberty
for thyself and for the neighboring cities : thy legitimate child, Juan de
Padilla, informs thee how by the blood of his veins thou oughtest to renew

insurrection permitted Charles V to lay the weight of his iron yoke upon the greater part of Europe, henceforth delivered up to the pillage of his troops and to the contagion of his doctrines. France even was obliged to descend into the arena,* where she fought long with glory, if not always with success, until the powerful diversion of protestantism in Germany again placed all liberties under the protection of a principle.

Thus, from whatever point of view we look at the history of Charles V, we cannot help recognizing that this monarch hindered the magnificent development of wealth and prosperity created by the emancipated bourgeoisie of the middle ages. By attempting to reconstruct the universal monarchy of Charlemagne and to take away from the various European states their physiognomy as well as their independence, he condemned them to the scourge of standing armies and anticipated-taxes. He reëstablished slavery in America, then nearly abolished in Europe. He concentrated in his single person and in that of a few princes, his allies or his rivals, the power of the sovereignty, which the middling classes had begun to share. These are, without doubt, grave charges, in the eyes of posterity ; but there are still graver ones, the consequences of which were not less deplorable. The government of Charles V was one of those which have contributed most to spread over the world the hideous evil of pauperism. Did he not, by destroying the freedom of the industrial arts and of commerce, turn towards the con-

thy ancient victories.   If fate has not decreed that my acts should be placed in the number of the successful and famous exploits of thy other children, it must be imputed to my bad fortune and not to my will.   I pray thee, as my mother, to accept the life I am about to lose, since God has given me nothing more valuable which I can lose for thee.   *   *   *   I will write thee no more about it : for at this very moment I feel the knife near my bosom, more touched at the grief that thou wilt feel, than at my own wrongs."

* " In one of these numerous wars, in 1552, a French army of 44,000 men, commanded by the constable of Montmorency, invaded the three bishoprics, preceded by a manifesto in French and German, the frontispiece of which represented a cap with two poniards, surrounded by the word LIBERTY." Schoell, *History of European States*, vol. xv, p. 160.

vents a multitude of beings condemned to choose between a contemplative life and one of beggary? Did he
not, by creating the colonial system, accustom one part
of his subjects to live at the expense of the other? Did
he not favor the establishment of the society of Jesuits,
so fruitful in inventions fatal to labor and to freedom?
Was it not he that made such a melancholy funeral for
the Italian republics?

But the bad genius of a single man could not prevail
against the eternal destinies of the human race. While
fortune seemed to smile on Charles V and to crown all
his enterprises, there arose in old hard-working Germany
a power which was to destroy the fruit of his victories
and prepare great humiliations for his successor. Freedom of inquiry reappeared at the voice of an irritated
monk. The germs of independence, scarcely stifled in
the Hanse towns, were starting anew under the hot
preaching of protestantism. Oppressed peasants flew to
arms ; most courageous writers preluded by bold essays
the eloquent manifestoes of the eighteenth century.*
Smuggling and interloping deadened the effect of the
nascent monopolies. The annoyances caused by the
farmers of the revenues, the venality of the offices, and
the weight of the taxes, made people feel the value of
order in the finances and the need of consideration among
the magistrates, and strengthened the education of the
people by hard experiences. The spirit of enquiry which
emanated from the protestant reformation had just penetrated all social questions : it is important to study
its economic consequences before touching upon those
which followed the discovery of America, for these two
words, *reformation* and *new world* are full of memorable
instruction.

See *Le Contr'un,* by La Boëtie, p. 125.

CHAPTER XXII.

The Protestant Reformation and its influence upon the course of political economy.—Secularization of the monks.—Sale of church property.—Importance of such property in England at that time.—Poor-laws.—Increase of working-days.

THERE is something truly providential in the advance of labor and of liberty. Persecuted at one point, they take refuge in another: arrested in their onward course, they start forward the more earnestly for the future as soon as the way is again open. To Greek and Roman slavery succeeds barbaric independence: the latter, in its turn, scarcely changed by feudal servitude, reappears more brilliant and more strong in the affranchised communes. The glebe succeeds the mill-stone, and corporations precede freedom of labor. When one experiment has had its season, it returns to the darkness of the past and suddenly the new experiment begins, charged with transmitting to posterity the principal and interest of all which have preceded it. The protestant reformation is one of these grand revolutions in the majestic development of humanity. Its beginnings were very humble; but its results have changed the face of Europe. Leo X had seen in it only the revolt of a monk, and Charles V only an infraction of the dogma of passive obedience; but under the revolt of the monk was hidden a protest against the exploitation of Christendom by the bishop of Rome, and the appearance of Luther at the diet of Worms was only the prelude of the League of Smalkalde, that is to say, of the first confederation of small states against the despotism of the great ones.   Moreover, from the first lightning flash of that tempest, it became evident that the thunder-bolt would strike institutions supposed to be consolidated by time, but which time had undermined. As the discovery of the Cape of Good Hope had just wrested from the Venetians the monopoly of commerce, the establishment of protestantism took from the Pope and emperors the domination of Europe.   The Guelphs and Ghibelines were put out of consideration, and social questions appeared in an entirely new light.

One cannot help recognizing a sort of consoling and marvellous correlation between these great contemporary events, such as the trade in blacks and the Protestant reform which was destined to put an end to it; the universal monarchy of Charles V and the formation of the German states, which were joined later by all Sweden under the lead of the great Gustavus Adolphus, and by the United Provinces of Holland, immersed in blood by Philip II.   But we have to consider them only from an economic point of view, and although, for that examination, most historians are not very safe guides, the results present so pronounced a character, that they need but be indicated, to make their importance perceived.   It was at first only a refusal to pay for the indulgences by means of which Rome was obtaining money in even the smallest villages; * but this refusal became the era of a first reform in the system of taxation, and it is not so far as one may think from that reform to the financial discussions of modern constitutional parliaments.   In Germany, the petty princes had soon comprehended all the advantages they could derive from the religious enthusiasm, to lead on their people to resistance to the ambi-

---

* I have had in my hand the original of a certificate of plenary indulgence accorded for the sum of one franc, fifty centimes in our money (less than thirty cents.—*Trans.*).   It there says literally : " Veniam damus Joanni N. pro omnibus peccatis, præteritis, præsentibus et *futuris*, quantumcumque enormibus."   * * *   The beneficiary had added in the margin, perhaps imprudently, the name of his wife, who thus found herself included in the indulgence, over and above the bargain.—*Author's Note.*

tious projects of Austria. Besides, the allurement of the
treasures of the clergy, which each protestant sovereign
added to his fiscal resources ; and that of independence
and intimate union, which the common cause established
between all the confederates, decided the most timorous
to run the risks of the league and to found the first
efficacious coalition of free states against the preponderance of their oppressors.

The first result of the struggle, and the one most important to political economy, was the secularization of
the monks and the sale of the property of all the religious
communities, or its addition, pure and simple, to the
public domain.   This property had already great value,
and it acquired considerably more by passing into laboring hands, on coming forth from the unproductive régime
of mortmain, to which it had been long subject.   The
nobility had their share of it as well as the sovereign
princes, and one portion was applied with more or less
equity and discretion to the maintenance of worship, of
the poor, and of public educational institutions.   When
the reformation penetrated into England, the change was
still more sensible, and it was effected there on such
bases, that it may be considered a virtual revolution.
There the clergy possessed seven-tenths of the landed
property,* and the thousand and forty one religious
establishments in the kingdom, in the time of Henry
VIII, enjoyed a revenue of about six millions of francs
in our money, an enormous sum for that period, by reason of the scarcity of money and the smallness of the
national revenue.

The suppression of a great number of days improperly
made holy days, restored to labor millions of hands accustomed to lying idle, and furnished new elements of increase to public wealth.   But, at the same time, that enormous mass of laborers, voluntary or forced, thrown
into circulation on coming forth from the convents which
had defrayed the expenses of their idleness, occasioned

* J. Wade, *History of the Middle and Working Classes,* p. 38.

unforeseen modifications in the social organization and made pauperism appear under a new aspect. There were two sorts of poor: those who under the preceding régime had been accustomed to àsk alms, and those who had given to them. Their number even became so large that it was necessary to have recourse to legislation to restrain them, and to regulate the hard conditions which the reform of the convents had imposed upon them. Most of them obstinately refused to labor, and those who resigned themselves to it, did not always find work. What was to be done with that adventurous and nomad population, with those unhappy *roundsmen*, seeking bread and work from door to door, most frequently without finding either! Catholicism had created that pest by multiplying convents : protestantism aggravated it by suppressing them. Who would have thought it when the work was begun !

Besides, that epoch was more fruitful than any other in legislative and administrative measures of every kind, to compel vagrants to have a permanent abode, and to make idlers work. The annals of England are full of these measures ; and in looking them over, we know not whether to be more astonished at their powerlessness or their multiplicity. In 1531, Charles V had published in the Netherlands a long edict on this subject as sterile as all the analogous ordinances of the kings of England. He had forbidden any person except the monks and pilgrims to beg under penalty of flogging and imprisonment. Those known to be needy were to be maintained by means of regular collections at the doors of the churches, hospitals, and houses of refuge, and the magistrates were authorized to take collections in the churches or in private houses once or twice a week for the same object. Recalcitrant idlers * could be compelled to work. But all these severe measures in Belgium, England, and Germany, only served to make more evident the absurdity there was in decreeing, by ordinance, public prosperity.

* Anderson. *History of Commerce*, vol. ii, page 55.

This strange pretention was pushed in England and in the protestant countries to the extreme limits. The suppression of convents in them, converted, at one stroke of the pen, more than five thousand monks into miserable pensioners of the state, and threw them, without being accustomed to labor or to the world, into the midst of the needs and seductions of an industrial society. Corrections, chastisements and tortures were of no avail to these men inured to idleness, and who besides had not all at their disposal the means of labor. How was compulsory idleness among them to be distinguished from that which was voluntary? That question is not yet settled in Europe, although it has been propounded for several centuries, and it daily becomes complicated in the progress of industry and civilization, by a multitude of difficulties, which render it more and more difficult of solution. In vain did protestantism produce in contrast to the blind charity of the catholics, the severity of the poor laws; there has been only one result from them, which is, that the poor of protestant countries are obliged to hide their poverty, while those of catholic countries can exhibit it without fear; but the wretchedness is not the less real in the two camps. Who knows, indeed, whether the poor-tax has not contributed to multiply them more in England than in Spain, by securing to them, at the expense of the parishes, a regular and compulsory revenue, instead of the precarious resource of alms!

One has, however, no right to blame protestant influence for the consequences of the principle it has laid down. The suppression of monasteries and the sale of their property were wise means and dictated as much by reason as by necessity. At another time, too, when personal slavery and also serfdom were suppressed, one might have been disposed to calumniate liberty on seeing the embarrassment which those *prolétaires* without property and suddenly emancipated and delivered up to themselves, experienced in regard to means of subsistence.

Liberty imposed upon them the necessity of earning their livelihood by the sweat of the brow, and of justifying their dignity as free men, by work, which is its distinctive sign and essential condition. This was a condition which protestantism required of all its citizens, as the numerous and varied wants of our present civilization demand more work, because they produce more enjoyments. It would not then be just to make either religion responsible for the existence of an evil inherent in human nature and which has continually been reproduced under all religions and all régimes. It suffices to know at that time what was the mode of life of the working people, to form an idea of the miseries which awaited the indigent without work and even the farmer on his land. Erasmus tells us that most of the houses were yet without chimneys, and that the people in them trod the bare ground for lack of tiles or bricks ; the beds consisted of a heap of straw rarely renewed, and a badly-hewn block of wood served as a pillow, Fortescue, who traveled over France at that time, said of our peasants : " They drink water, eat apples, make rye bread of a dark color, and do not even know what meat is."

The definitive establishment of protestantism in Europe contributed much to change this sad state of things. If the suppression of convents did not resolve the question of pauperism which their multiplicity had complicated, it at least forced a part of the idlers to seek means of subsistence in labor. Too great a number of holy days were a loss to production ; the protestants reduced it to suitable proportions, and soon the countries where the reforms had triumphed presented striking contrasts to the catholic countries. As far as the population could no longer live by alms, they contracted more industrious and more regular habits, which still remain, and which distinguish them in a very remarkable manner in Europe. It is since the schism of Henry VIII and the abolition of convents that England has progressed,

through the most cruel vicissitudes, to its present development.   Germany also owes like results to protestantism, and this very day the catholic part of that fine country is inferior in civilization, wealth and intelligence to
the protestant part.   Look at Geneva and the Swiss reformed cantons ; how different from the catholic cantons !
The prosperity of Holland, after its revolt against the
Spanish monopolists and persecutors, was attributable to
no other cause.   In France itself, when later, Louis XIV,
under an evil inspiration, signed the famous revocation
of the edict of Nantes, the protestants, banished from
the territory, went abroad giving lessons in the industrial arts to all Europe.   Flanders, Switzerland, England
and Prussia * were enriched by the fruit of their labors.
Their ardent and strict proselytism attracted many generous minds and made them accept sacrifices which the
indolent and luxurious ease of catholicism would have
always rejected.   The simplicity of their worship and of
their dress saved to industrial enterprises an immense
amount of capital, which, throughout catholic Europe,
was consecrated to maintaining the majesty of the temples and the luxury of the prelates.

The revolution was not less decisive in everything which
closely appertains to the social questions debated since
the beginning of the centuries.   The spirit of association
led the catholic ranks to attack, and the protestant ranks
to defend themselves.   Printing, which had just been
invented, was a new weapon which served both parties
to their advantage, and took its rank among the powers.

---

* " At the accession of Frederick William to the regency," says a German
writer, a prince of the house of Brandenburg, " no hats, stockings, serges, or
any woolen cloth, were made in this country : the industry of the French enriched us with all these manufactures.   They established works for making
cloth, serges, bunting, small goods, druggets, caps, and stockings woven
upon stocking frames ; beaver, goat-skin, and rabbit-skin hats, and dyes of
all kinds.   Some of these refugees became merchants and sold at retail the
products of the others.   Berlin had goldsmiths, jewellers, clockmakers and
sculptors, and the French who settled in the Netherlands cultivated tobacco
and brought excellent fruits and vegetables into the sandy districts, which,
under their care, became admirable kitchen gardens."

The purely intellectual struggle which was established at the outset, forced the dissenters to study and reason; and the light born from errur and trouble, finally extended to subjects which appeared most foreign to these disputes. One reform led to another: philosophy was substituted for scholasticism, and the morality of the casuists vanished before that of the gospel. Every body began to work, and beside the greatest modifications in religion there came about unlooked-for industrial changes. Thus, the simple suppression of the days of abstinence prescribed by the command of the catholic church, led to a considerable diminution in the number of vessels devoted to fisheries. Holland consumed more meat in proportion as she consumed less fish. Her mariners became agriculturists, and they raised cattle instead of fishing for herrings. The reaction of the protestant reformation produced also other effects of a higher order, although more indirect. When Philip II seized Portugal and closed the entrepôt of Lisbon to the Dutch merchants accustomed to buy there merchandise from the East, the latter went directly to the Indies and there laid the foundations of their colonial power. A religious caprice of this bad prince caused the Spanish to lose the empire of the sea.

But it was given to protestantism to assume a higher character and to exercise a more general influence, when it had borrowed the help of the French language, which had just become popular in Europe. From this time, the reformation became an auxiliary to politics; and the religious wars which have desolated our country, sufficiently prove that doctrines and their consequences had been taken into serious consideration. The poor masses began to comprehend the importance of a change which relieved them from ecclesiastical tithes, and the higher classes did not view without interest the religious movement which restored to them freedom of investigation and independence of thought. The property of the church, previously exempt from taxation, reverted to the public domain and relieved the tax-payers from the burden of the innumerable taxes by which they were overwhelmed. A part of it went back to the aristocracy and attached them to the new ideas, by increasing at the same time their importance and their fortune. The petty princes of Germany had welcomed these ideas as a means for rallying the people against the domination of Charles V ; the noblemen of France became attached to them to increase their local influence and because protestantism accorded perfectly with their provincial habits. There was a time when Europe was divided between protestant federalism and catholic unity. It would now be covered with great, free cities like the Hanse towns, or small independent states like the Italian republics, if the Calvinistic principle had completely triumphed ; it would have been absorbed into two or three great monarchies, perhaps into one alone, if this principle had entirely disappeared. What would have become of civilization, in either event ? We cannot say ; but the prosperity of the protestant countries permits no doubt that the reformation would have given much activity to the development of public wealth ; we should not have seen the social revenues of Europe devoured by three or four belligerent powers, more occupied with the interests of their aggrandizement and their policy than with the well-being of the people.

Protestantism must have contained within it fertile germs of the future, since wherever it has become established, people have contracted more regular habits, stricter morals, and a more pronounced inclination to labor. Compare Holland and Portugal, England and Spain, Lutheran Germany and Catholic Germany : what a contrast in respect to intelligence, wealth and morality ! What a difference between the life which reigns on the one side and the apathy in which the others vegetate ! One can well judge of it in future in \merica, where

civilization seems to have established its two extremes:
the United States of the North have attained the highest
degree of prosperity under the influence of free investigation and with a protestant population; the republics
of the South, notwithstanding the natural advantages of
their climate and the richness of their soil, have not yet
been able to establish a regular government because of
their catholic prejudices.   Idleness and beggary reign
there always, as formerly in their parent country, while
the labor of the Americans in the North has brought the
forests under cultivation and peopled the deserts with
opulent cities in less than fifty years.   Unfortunately,
protestantism, so successful in multiplying wealth, has
not yet found the secret of distributing it with impartiality among all the classes which produce it.   It has
broken the bond which united Christian nations, and substituted national egoism for the universal harmony to
which catholicism was tending.   There is no longer any
common thought in Europe to-day in a position to rally
minds and convictions.   In the industrial arts, in politics,
in philosophy, in religion, ideas float, swayed by the
breath of revolutions.   Each day undoes the work of the
preceding.   People dispute with each other for the markets, and enter into competition, instead of associating
themselves together under the guidance of their necessities and for the exchange of their respective products.   I
desire before all to be just, but I cannot help acknowledg-
ing that if the former catholicism did not know how to
put itself at the head of the production of wealth, we
cannot reproach it with that barrenness of doctrines, in
virtue of which distribution takes place in a manner so
little equitable in protestant countries.   Science, then,
must to-day assume the functions of this great priest-
hood, by preaching peace and solidarity to nations, and
by demonstrating to them that their interests are one,
notwithstanding the apparent opposition which they
present.   This truth will appear more striking after a
rapid examination of the colonial system.

CHAPTER XXIII.

Consequences of the discovery of the New World. The European colonial system in the two Indies.

THE large profits which the Venetians derived from their trade with India, had for a long time excited the emulation and the jealousy of other nations. During all the fifteenth century, the Portuguese had been unremitting in their search of a route by sea to the countries whence the Moors brought to them, across the desert, ivory and gold dust. It was in this search that Vasco de Gama proceeded from port to port along the coasts of Africa, as far as the Cape of Good Hope, and discovered the shores of Hindustan, in 1497, after a voyage of eleven months. Five years previous, Christopher Columbus touched America and endowed his country and the world with a new hemisphere. Europe then finds herself suddenly and without preparation, launched in the way of colonial conquests, which were to exercise so profound an influence over her destinies.

One cannot exactly compare the system she pursued in regard to them, with that which guided the Greeks and Romans in their settlements of the same kind. The Greek colonies had generally been peopled by citizens compelled to expatriate themselves, by the violence of factions or by the impossibility of finding a sufficient subsistence in their country. We have seen that these colonies enjoyed a certain independence, and that most of them became virtual empires. The Roman colonies had risen upon different bases : their internal administration, less independent than that of the Greek possessions, wa? modeled on the régime of the metropolis, which con sidered them at the same time as asylums for poor or dis contented citizens and as military outposts in a foreign country. Nothing similar is found in the thought which inspired the Spanish and Portuguese expeditions, and which has directed, since, all the settlements of the Eu. ropeans in the two Indies. It was in search of gold and wealth that Vasco de Gama and Christopher Columbus, those preëminent adventurers, were sailing with heroic perseverance, when they arrived on those shores where their appearance was to cause so much blood to flow and so many tears to be shed. One has only to read the recital of their first exploits, to be convinced that their aim was neither to civilize, nor even, although they may have said so, to convert the population, but to rob them, exterminating them, if necessary.

When Christopher Columbus returned to Europe and was presented in great pomp at the court of Castile, that which most agreeably impressed his illustrious hosts, was a collection of plates of gold, gold bracelets, bits of gold, mingled with some bolls of cotton, which he brought with him from the newly-discovered countries. Fernando Cortez and Pizarro sought for nothing else in their bold expeditions to Mexico and Peru, and we know their sur- prise and joy at the sight of the treasures they went to conquer. It was love of gold which led these courageous filibusters to the ends of the earth and made them sur- mount the most formidable obstacles. Wherever they set their foot, they asked information about gold, and they reëmbarked when there was none to ravish. To this cause must be chiefly attributed the slow progress of the Spanish colonies. The gold and silver accumulated by the natives were soon exhausted, and the waves of emigrants which followed the conquest employed all their activity in labors, generally unproductive, in the mines.

It was only after long and fruitless attempts in that hazardous career, that it was perceived that the American soil contained rich resources productive in quite a different way from its mines of gold and silver.

But the prejudices engendered by that fever for the precious metals did not disappear with the circumstances which had given rise to them. Every one knows the dream of Sir Walter Raleigh of the golden city and the country of Eldorado. More than a hundred years after the death of Sir Walter, the Jesuit Gumila was still persuaded of the existence of that marvelous country, and he expressed with much warmth how happy he should be to be able to carry the light of the gospel to a people who could so generously reward the pious labors of the missionaries.* Every Spaniard thought he was embarking for the promised land in setting sail for America. The cupidity of the multitude was continually excited by exaggerated reports, to which we must pardon them for having given credence, in consideration of the treasures which they continually saw arrive from these romantic places. By degrees the entire Spanish nation became accustomed to the idea of making a fortune without working, and they not only scorned agricultural occupations, which might have changed the face of America, but those which were necessary to themselves to prevent the decline of their own country. Every Spanish citizen believed himself a nobleman invested with his fief in the New World, and the colonial legislation soon strengthened this fatal prejudice. America was considered as national property of the parent country, and the latter imposed on it rules, the tyrannical absurdity of which became equally disastrous to the two countries. We have already mentioned some of them in our rapid sketch of the political economy of Charles V.

Such was the origin of the colonial prejudices which so long hindered the prosperity of the world and made the

---

* Adam Smith, *Wealth of Nations*, Book iv, chap. vii.

discovery of the new continent sterile in the hands of its authors.   Negro slavery, that shame of civilization, is only one episode of them; and although it still exists, we hope its last knell will soon be sounded.   But there are other vices which will long be incurable, because their origin dates back to the early days of the conquest, and because they have profoundly penetrated our colonial morals.   People of every rank have been too much accustomed to living at the expense of the workers; and while in Mexico and Peru the colonists pitilessly exploited the unhappy natives, the parent country, not less unmerciful, was taking from the colonists the fruit of their rapine, under the names of tariffs, tithes, *alcavala* and twenty others similar.   This bad economic policy infested Europe and prepared the way for the industrial and commercial rivalries from which almost all modern wars have arisen.

Before entering upon an account of these deplorable events, it may be proper to point out here one of the most curious results that the discovery of the New World has given to science.   When the Spanish were weary of experimenting on the mines, they gave themselves to some attempts in agriculture, such as the cultivation of sugar-cane and cotton.   Then people witnessed the phenomenon of a population, in command of more land than they could cultivate, being obliged to grant very high wages to workmen who were themselves in a condition to become proprietors and to pay wages, in their turn, to other workmen soon rich enough to leave them.   The liberal reward of labor encouraged marriages, and contributed to the increase of population.   Thus the United States have seen, in less than half a century, the number of their inhabitants increase from one million two hundred thousand souls to more than fifteen millions,* while the Spanish colonies of South America, devoted to idleness, and equally the prey of civil and religious corpora-

---

* Probably now (1879) not far from fifty millions. — *Trans.*

tions, have constantly deteriorated. Even to-day, when restored to their independence, they still sadly struggle in the swaddling-bands of the past, under the weight of the vices and incapacity of their early founders.

The great error of this system, invented by the Spanish, lay in seeking to isolate from the rest of the world a people who had more than three thousand leagues of accessible coasts. The Spanish too soon forgot that it was in hatred of Venetian monopoly that the Portuguese had sought to win a fortune by maritime discoveries, and that they themselves supposed they had sent Columbus to the East Indies, when he discovered the West Indies. The common name, applied to colonies so different, testifies strongly of the spirit which then animated the voyagers from the Iberian peninsula. Why then did they depart so positively from the spirit which had made them undertake so many and so great enterprises? We have answered:—the spirit of monopoly, in hatred of which the Spaniards discovered America, and which their government established there on bases so odious, was a necessity of the warlike policy of Charles V. Constantly reduced to expedients, and pressed by want of money, that prince saw in America only a mine of gold, and worked it without pity because he was without resources. All his legislation had for its sole aim to rob the natives by means of the colonists, and the colonists by means of tariffs. Notwithstanding his great penetration and his great experience in affairs, Charles V had never a suspicion of the advantage he might have derived from his rich conquest, if he had wisely administered it, instead of inconsiderately oppressing it. His successors killed the hen with the golden eggs: but he had already opened its entrails.

This bad example, given by the Spanish, was unfortunately imitated by all the European nations in their relations with their colonies. There was not a single one of them which dreamed of the immense benefit it might

have derived from free trade, by putting it under the
protection of its flag. Every metropolis considers itself
the proprietor of its colony, and the time was at hand
when the slavery of nation to nation was going to succeed
personal servitude. Portuguese, French, English, Dutch,
Swedes and Danes, all yielded to the same prepossession
and they have since cruelly expiated it, by their irrepara-
ble mistakes. Brazil has become independent of Portugal ; France has lost St. Domingo ; England has been
driven out from the United States ; Holland is reduced
to the island of Java, and Spain has now only Cuba and
the Philippine Islands. It is not that the colonial system
of these nations was absolutely the same. Some among
them administered their colonies directly, as Spain and
Portugal ; others gave up the government of them to
privileged companies, as did England, France, Holland
and Denmark. But if there were some differences in the
methods of proceeding among all these administrations,
there were none in the idea which directed them. Everywhere there was a desire to make use of the conquest in
the Greek and Roman manner ; and, in order to succeed, rules, restrictions, prohibitions, and too often cruel
punishments, were multiplied. The privileged companies worked their monopolies with the most merciless
severity. The colonists were obliged to sell them all
their superabundant products. The monopoly fixed the
prices at the highest rate when it sold, and at the lowest
rate when it bought. It was often the interest of the
company even to depreciate the value of the colonial
products and to arrest their increase in quantity, so that
the price could be kept very high in Europe. A passion
for this desolated a part of both hemispheres, and the
Dutch in the Moluccas, as we have seen, set fire to plantations of spice trees, to prevent their rivals from profiting by them.

Other nations, without according privileges to exclusive
companies, restricted colonial commerce to one single

port of the metropolis, from which no ship was permitted to set sail, either alone or in convoy, without a special authorization, except at a time determined. This circumstance obliged the ship-owners to have an understanding with each other, and often to associate themselves together, so as not to injure each other by competition: and the effect remained the same with regard to the colonists, who were always obliged to buy dear and sell cheap. The most liberal parent countries sometimes modified the form of these regulations, but they never ceased to consider the colonies as possessions rightfully subject to an exceptional justice. Notwithstanding the revolutions which have at various times protested against that oppression, all European nations still persist in the same system. There is a special legislation for the colonies in France, in England, in Holland and in Spain. What is legitimate in Europe, ceases to be so in Asia, in Africa, in America. Negro slavery has come in, to complicate in the New World that régime already stained with more than one radical vice. The colonists have compensated themselves, at the expense of that unfortunate race, for the outrages they endured from the high and powerful lords of the mother country; and thus the colonial régime has become the school of all the immoralities with which industrial and commercial civilization is still afflicted.

The fatal principle of monopolies even penetrated establishments where the mother country had no right to exercise sovereignty. In Japan, in China, and at some points on the shores of the Mediterranean, where, for want of colonies, they were reduced to tolerated trading-houses, these latter were secured to privileged companies; and it is only within a few years that the English have abolished the monopoly of the India Company for Chinese trade, which is henceforth open to all British citizens. It is now beginning to be comprehended that it is not necessary to be master of a country in order to estab-

lish advantageous relations with it. When, after the
American war, the English government saw itself forced
to sign a peace with its emancipated colony, there was a
general commotion in the ports of England. The city
of Bristol addressed a petition to parliament, to entreat
it to refuse its sanction to that fatal peace which would
bring ruin upon British commerce; and a few years after
the signing of the treaty, the same city asked an authorization to excavate new harbors for its ships, the number
of which had doubled in consequence of its relations with
the United States. By losing its possessions which had
revolted, the English nation saved the expense of keeping and administering them, and its commerce gained in
extent and importance much more than colonial despotism could have given it. If Spain had had the good
judgment to make peace, at a suitable time, with the
republics of South America, and to profit by the advantages resulting from the uniformity of the language,
habits and wants of the two peoples, she would not to-
day be without resources, and her industries would have
regained some traces of their former splendor.

Who cannot now comprehend the difficulties in governing a country two thousand leagues away, with ideas
in opposition to the character of its inhabitants and with
the enormous expenses which all distant operations ne-
cessitate? The power falls in this case into the hands of
viceroys, proconsuls, or governors. The government of
the mother country only sees through their eyes, only
acts upon their advice, and is too often a dupe of the reports made to it. "Dependent colonies," says J. B. Say,[*]
"have always been as badly settled as badly governed.
People go to them only with the expectation of resurn-
ing; that is to say, to return to Europe with a fortune
well or ill acquired." Moreover, see what, after three
hundred years of domination, was the condition of most
of the colonies which are to-day at length emancipated!

---

[*] *Cours Complet d'Economie Politique*, vol. i, page 629.

They will long bear the scars of the plague-spots which the tyranny of their parent-countries brought upon them, and the long influence of their fatal principles will blast in them for a century to come all attempts at regeneration. They are under the common law of the individuals, fortunate if they have an education, unfortunate if it is neglected. Europe has accumulated in these regions of privilege all the abuses and all the vices of her worst governments. She has there reorganized slavery on an immense scale, to such a degree that in several colonies the black population has outrun the white aristocracy. St. Domingo has given the signal of reaction, which already is faintly heard in Louisiana and Brazil, and which the abolition of slavery in the English Antilles will inevitably precipitate, if the recalcitrant colonists do not finally open their eyes. When one hears the revelations * which each day brings, of the internal administration of the colonies, he ceases to be surprised at the languishing condition in which they have been, and at the despair which has driven them to revolt. Never has appeared a more audacious contradiction to the designs of the Creator. Never have more brows, bowed to the dust, entreated a more merited reparation or one more tardy in coming.

However, the colonial system was maintained in all its vigor only as a temporary evil, from which Europe was to receive, at a more or less remote future, the most brilliant compensation. The privileges of the companies were never granted for perpetuity, but only renewed either by legislative acts, as in England, or by royal ordinances, as in other countries. No one could ever at the outset have dared to proclaim the perpetuity of a régime so monstrous, even though politics and necessity seemed to justify its establishment. It was to be, like all monopolies, only a temporary measure, indispensable to strengthening the rising colonies, and which would right-

* See work published in 1826, in London, under the title: *Noticias Secretas de America, por don Jorge Juan y don Antonio de Ulloa,* in 4to.

fully cease as soon as they should be well established. By degrees, however, the lease having become emphy-teutic, ended by taking the character of a perpetual grant; and its duration would never have been interrupted but for the intervention of revolutions. It had already been very much prolonged at the time of the discovery of the special products found or naturalized in the New World, such as cochineal, Peruvian-bark, sugar, coffee, cotton, cocoa, indigo, dye-woods and the other articles of which European nations wished to have their share, even at the cost of contrabandage, interloping, and war. Hence arose a new system of commercial law, eminently exclusive, each wishing to keep for himself the monopoly of the products in favor, or to take it forcibly from more fortu-nate rivals. Complications were especially manifest when most of the European powers had founded settlements under the same parallels of latitude, or when they had naturalized in them the cultivation of commodities for which the demand was great. Sugar was soon exported from San Domingo, Jamaica, Cuba, and all the Antilles belonging to various masters. Coffee was planted in Brazil and Martinique. Cotton enriched the plains of Lou-isiana, Georgia, and Carolina. Indigo came at the same time from Calcutta, Guatemala and Caraccas. Sugar from India competed with that from America, both to-day be-ing threatened by that of the beet. The gold was ex-hausted; but there remained in America mines more valuable, and these were the only ones which the blind parent-countries had not known how to work.

The great error of Europe lay in seeking profit in high prices resulting from the rarity or the monopoly of colonial products, rather than in their abundance. At the commencement, the first comers attempted to prevent their rivals from coming; they even tried to con-ceal the way to the Indies, as misers conceal their trea-sure: then, the way being once known, they forbade for-eigners to land on their possessions; and when, in spite of

force and threats, they had to resign themselves to having competitors, tariff-wars created distinctions between productions from the same soil. Sugar and coffee cost more or less according as they were imported by foreign or native vessels. A certain American colony near the mainland was obliged to have its grain brought from Europe, at the risk of dying of starvation in case of delay in arrivals. All this absurd legislation is to-day in force.*
England has strengthened it in her famous navigation act: France by all her tariff laws; Spain by respect for her own invention. Lands separated a few hours distance by an arm of the sea, are as foreign to one another, under the sky of the Antilles, as if the Atlantic Ocean extended between them its fifteen hundred leagues of breadth. We ourselves sacrifice the general interests of national commerce to two or three isles less populous than a single one of our departments. The consequences of the system adopted by the founders of the colonies, have, on the whole, been only the trade in blacks, tariff-wars, maritime wars, enormous naval expenses, even in times of peace, and the necessity of paying dearly for provisions which to-day all Europe would have cheap, if it had employed in the fertilization of the colonies a tenth part of the treasure expended in ruining them. Some day it will be difficult for our posterity to believe that this system could have lasted so long, and that the people of Europe would have borne such great sacrifices for the maintenance of a state of things so opposed to their real interests. It has been said in explanation that the exclusive commerce of the colonies, by preventing competition, did not risk being affected by those perturbations which more or less menace commerce between independent nations: but besides competition being a real advantage, we must consider that monopoly can only be maintained in colonies of small extent and easy to guard. All the British marine would to-day no longer suffice to

---

* See note on chap. xxix.

protect the coast of the American Union against contrabandage, if this country still belonged to Great Britain,
and if there were profit in carrying products there. The
severe regulations of the Spanish government, its custom-officers and its coast-guards, have not prevented
South America from being flooded with European merchandise. Nor is it true that the mother-countries owe
to the prohibitory system the regularity of their supplies
of colonial provisions. Prussia, Austria, Saxony, Switzerland, Bavaria, and all the states which have no trans-
atlantic colonies, have never lacked for sugar, coffee or
cotton ; on the contrary, these articles have always been
cheaper than in the countries with possessions beyond
the sea. Having no monopoly to support, these states
choose the places where they can procure for themselves
the provisions they need, on the most advantageous
terms, and experience has proven that they have always
been supplied with them more cheaply than the maritime nations.

On the whole, the colonial régime has only ended in
creating between monopolies and their dependencies a
reciprocity of prejudices and wrongs, and the commerce
of the colonies has been, on both sides, only a source of
vexations and impoverishment. With the purest blood
of their veins have the people of Europe paid for the
honor of founding settlements in the two Indies. These
settlements are, in the eyes of attentive observers, only
like children who have imposed great privations on their
families up to the time when, arrived at maturity, they
are in a condition to maintain themselves. Sometimes,
in that case, gratitude attaches them more strongly to
the authors of their days : more frequently the latter
have to complain of their indifference or ingratitude ; but
it is folly to suppose that independence will not come
with age, and that after three hundred years of tutelage,
this age has not arrived for all the colonies. To prolong
their childhood, is to continue to support people who can

take care of themselves, or to oppress citizens worthy of living free. To-day, when all the chimeras on gold and silver have vanished, and when a conspicuous failure has discredited the last attempts at working mines in America, we must seek for wealth from different sources. But, before indicating them in detail, we will take a glance backward and present a rapid account of the monetary revolutions which preceded and which followed the discovery of the New World.

CHAPTER XXIV.

The various Monetary Systems which prevailed in Europe from the ancients to the discovery of the mines of the New World.—Economic consequences of the discovery of these mines.—General view of the works which have been produced on coins.

THE ancients appreciated as well as the moderns the true functions of money. Aristotle said of it: " It is an intermediary commodity, designed to facilitate an exchange of two other commodities." Xenophon* is not less explicit: " In most of the other cities," he says in speaking of Athens, " a trader is obliged to take commodities in return for those he brings, because the money used in them has not much credit outside; with us, on the contrary, the foreign merchant has the advantage of finding a multitude of objects which are everywhere in demand, and, besides, if he does not wish to encumber his vessel with merchandise, he takes pay in ready money, which of all negotiable articles is the safest and most convenient, as it is received in all countries, and besides, it always brings back something to its master, when the latter judges proper to dispose of it."

The functions of money have not changed since Xenophon and Aristotle; money is still an intermediary commodity designed to facilitate the exchange of other commodities. How is it then, that its history, which it would seem ought to be very simple, is the most exceedingly complicated and difficult of all those of which a general view constitutes the annals of political economy?

---

* *Essay on the Revenue of Attika.*

How comes it that all nations have had their particular money, instead of entering into an arrangement for the selection of a uniform standard? And, above all, why does each century offer us the spectacle of a monetary revolution, that is to say, of a subversion of the value, form, weight and standard of the principal element of circulation, the one which should remain the most unchangeable of all? Why, in short, do we see so many good coins and so many bad ones appear, by turns, in the markets of the world, some of almost pure metal, others almost made up of the alloyage? An exact and well-developed answer to all these questions would demand volumes, and these volumes exist; I will limit myself to indicating some of the most important, not to extend the examination of the subject investigated in them farther than comports with the limits of this history.

The question of moneys is one of those which the moderns have complicated most; the same confusion reigns there as in languages, and for the ingenious simplicity of the ancients has been substituted contrivances so complex, that we have lost the hope of returning to it, even though all Europe should make a compact to this end. Let us lay down a few principles to guide us in this study. The essential property in money is that it should retain its value from the time it is received until it is paid out; otherwise, people, in exchanging what they sell for what they buy, would not receive a commodity equal in value to that with which they parted. Another property of money is, that its value is measured, like that of any other object, by the quantity of things that some one consents to give in exchange; if, for an ounce of gold money, one consents to give fifteen times more grain or any other commodity, than he would give for silver money, it is easy to see that gold money, of equal weight, is worth fifteen times more than silver money. Consequently, we can understand the folly of the attempts made at various times to alter the coins, that is, to give them perforce a value which they did not possess. In proportion as these changes were effected, the prices of commodities rose, because every one refused to give an equal quantity of them for a less value in metal. Moreover, it was necessary to proclaim a *maximum* whenever it was desired to obtain any results from these grand spoliations. When crown pieces containing an ounce of silver were reduced to contain only a half ounce, under Louis XIV, they could purchase, instead of sixty pounds of wheat, only thirty. At all other periods in our history, much before and long after Louis XIV, the same causes produced the same results.

The more or less fraudulent manipulations of the coins which have been practiced from ancient times down to the present, proceed from an error of governments, still quite widespread, which has led people to suppose that money has a character of fixity which it does not possess. People have erroneously imagined that the monetary unit, in its character of measure of values, had itself an invariable value, and that when one paid at one time more, at another less for any commodity, it was necessarily the commodity which changed in value, and not the money. This error has served as a pretext to the cupidity of several princes, who were imprudently persuaded that it depended only on them to double their resources by declaring that one hundred thousand crowns were worth six hundred thousand francs, as if they would not be punished the very day after their fraud by the increase in the prices of everything, and by the necessity of doubling the taxes to meet it. We must then give up the idea of comparing with certainty the value of the income of any business at times remote from ours with that of similar occupations to-day, because it is impossible to find for the purpose a common measure, like the metre for lengths and the litre for capacities.

Many as have been the changes to which money has been subjected, all nations have had recourse to it as the commodity to effect their exchanges. The Lacedæmonians had iron money, and the Romans of the early days of the republic, money of copper. Shells, nails, cacao beans, and pieces of leather, have been, in various countries, employed for that purpose; but, from the most ancient times, gold and silver have enjoyed the almost exclusive privilege of serving as material for money. The unchangeable and homogeneous character of these metals, their extreme divisibility, their native purity, equal in all places, their resistance to wear by the aid of a few particles of alloy, perhaps also their natural beauty, sufficiently explain the universal [16] suffrage they have obtained at all times and in all countries. Besides, whenever one speaks in a general way of money, it is understood that it is of gold and silver money; and the first historic fact in which he becomes interested is, to learn what, at different periods of the world's history, was the quantity of these metals in circulation. Who does not comprehend the advantage derived from an intermediate agent in exchanges, of so small a volume, everywhere sought for and everywhere welcomed, while, with simple barter of commodities, commerce would always have remained in its infancy? But it is found that what we would have so much interest in knowing, is precisely what we have most difficulty in ascertaining. We do not even know to a certainty the amount of money at present in circulation in our country, although an exact account has been kept of all the pieces coined for many years. We are unacquainted with the number and value of those which have been melted or exported: we do not know the quantity of coins still existing of old mintages. The small copper coins, which have survived all recoinages and all reforms, also constitute a portion difficult to estimate of our monetary wealth and of that of other nations. " I have found in our provinces," says J. B. Say, " some of these copper pieces which have been in circulation from the time when we were under the dominion of the Roman emperors. They pass for one liard, two liards, one sou, two sous, with the effigy of those masters of the world."

The rapid multiplication of bills of exchange, banknotes, paper money having forced currency, and in general that of all commercial effects, has contributed much to render more difficult an estimate of the amount of money in circulation. But it is not necessary to know all the facts, to draw inferences from them of practical utility. The essential point is, to know by what signs abundance or scarcity of money is manifested, for these signs are sometimes very deceptive. Thus, in countries where great commercial activity reigns, money is almost perpetually in circulation; and less money than one would suppose, is needed for the demands of business; * while in other countries, where money abounds, but where there are no transactions, one might suppose money to be very rare, because it does not circulate. In proportion as the means of the people increase, a portion of the precious metals is employed for gold and silver articles, and ceases to perform the function of money. In other circumstances, money diminishes in value because of its abundance, and many mines cease to be worked, until there is profit in resuming their exploitation. In the study of monetary questions, it is necessary to take into account all these variations; but an exact knowledge of the coin possessed by all nations is useless in that solution.

There is no doubt that in the finest days of the Roman empire, when the annual revenue of the state was estimated at nearly a milliard, there was an enormous mass of money in circulation, and yet manufactures did not exist. The money came by way of pillage, and was ex-

* For an account of the London Clearing-House, whereby transactions to the amount of many millions daily are settled without the intervention of a single bank-note or sovereign, see H. D. Macleod's *Principles of Econ. Phil.*, vol. i, chap. vii, § 73. On payment of French indemnity to Germany, see vol. ii, chap xv, § 12, of the same work.— *Trans.*

pended in prodigalities. The little that the Romans obtained from the mines was due to the labor of slaves, as in Greece ; and it does not appear that much importance was attached to them, even when their exploitation was farmed out to grantees, and regulated to the profit of the emperors. But the increase in the quantity of money was already felt in prices, and we have some difficulty in comprehending the enormous rate to which a great number of articles in general demand had risen at Rome even in the time of Cicero. Later, imperial avidity, breaking all barriers, obliged the citizens to work in the mines, as enterprises of public utility, like the *corvées* of the middle ages ; * and this régime was so hard, that under the emperor Valens entire legions of miners joined the Goths in their invasion into Dacia. Meanwhile, the enormous accumulations of capital which the heads of the Roman aristocracy enjoyed, were not without influence on the magnificent development of the prosperity of the empire, and we cannot doubt that most of the cities which rose, as if by magic, in all parts of the territory, owed their prosperity to that cause. Tiberius † was rich enough to distribute to those who had suffered by fire the sum of about twenty millions in our money. Adrian expended nearly eighty millions in our francs in gratuities to secure to Commodus the succession to his throne ; and the emperor Severus did not pay less than thirty-five millions of francs in liberalities at his accession.

One single circumstance seems to us, however, of a nature to shake the faith that has hitherto been given to the marvelous tales of the historians who have transmitted to us accounts of the millions heaped up by the Romans ; it is that nothing has been found in the ruins of Herculaneum or Pompeii which could justify these exaggerated statements. Almost all the utensils found have

---

* Jacob, *On Precious Metals*, vol. i, page 174.
† Suetonius, *Life of Tiberius*, chap. xx.

been of iron or bronze, even those we usually make of silver; and yet the wealth, and the sumptuousness of the paintings, the furniture, and the statues, would sufficiently demonstrate that we had penetrated into dwellings anciently inhabited by opulent families. Could there have been such differences between the money and the metal employed that people would always convert the latter into specie, or must we reduce to more modest proportions the metallic wealth of the Romans? It is certain that this wealth was very considerable, because the transfer of the seat of empire to Constantinople sufficed to weaken seriously the riches of the West. Capital emigrated in the train of the great families with their armies of slaves; and Italy, which was the garden of Rome, beheld her country-houses deserted for the ruins of the Bosphorus. Mr. Jacob * has published on this subject, a table of the monetary decline of Rome from the time of Augustus to near the end of the fifth century, from which it would appear that a diminution of specie took place from the beginning of the Christian era down to the year 482, in the ratio of nine milliards to two milliards of francs. The movement transferring specie from the West to the East, which continues in our day, had just commenced and has never been arrested.†

From the year 482 to the end of the ninth century, the specie diminished from two milliards to less than one milliard of francs and even to eight hundred and twenty-five millions, according to the calculations of Mr. Jacob. The appearance of the Mohammedans sufficed to suspend all labors in the mines: at the same time, the horrible confusion which prevailed in Europe from the time of the

---

* In the *History of the Precious Metals* by the same author, there is a price-current list of about four hundred articles of consumption in the reign of Diocletian, in 301, prepared by Vescovali and William Banks. This document contains details valuable in the study of money and prices.

† For information on the successive depreciation of money, see the work of M. Leber : *Essai sur l'appréciation de la fortune privée au moyen âge*, 2nd edit. 1847. Guillaumin.—*French Editor.*

invasion of the Barbarians, does not permit us accurately
to trace further the metallic wealth. Prices become
lower and lower, either through the influence of servitude,
which forced to unremunerated labor a multitude of men
such as are to-day paid wages, or on account of the increasing scarcity of specie. We hear nothing more of the
rich and abundant mines which existed in Austria, Hungary, Bohemia, Saxony, and the Tyrol. Sovereigns
receive in kind from their vassals the tributes which to-
day are paid in money. We have seen that Charlemagne
watched with the most bourgeois solicitude, over the
administration of his domains, and that the greater part
of his revenue was composed of the material products
he obtained from them through his farmers. The mass
of the people had more limited demands, and the articles they bought consisted principally of purchases for
food. We can readily see that not much gold or silver
would be needed to pay for a piece of bread which cost
a liard (less than a farthing—*Trans.*) or a bunch of
vegetables, the maximum price of which rarely rose to a
sou (about a half-penny—*Trans.*). This explains the
immense quantity of small change which served for the
circulation in those little prosperous times : gold and silver pieces were very rare, and their value diminished
from reign to reign until they were as thin as a sheet of
paper. The happy possessors of those precious metals
were objects of adulation and envy, as, for example, the
Jews, whose economic history we have sketched and
whose persecution we have recounted. Nobles and
villeins equally solicited their benevolence—the nobles
especially, who were more eager for pleasures, and who
purchased the means of procuring them, by all sorts of
acts of complaisance, and even by presents to the wives of
these accursed heretics.*

The precious metals were principally employed in the
service of the churches, where shone magnificent vessels,

---

* Agobardus, *De Insolentia Judæorum*, page 144.

enormous candelabra, lamps, balustrades and statues, of gold and silver. The ornaments of the priests also consumed considerable quantities, and there really remained very little for making and renewing the coins. These coins were generally very badly stamped, and one might say, to see the progress in goldsmithing contemporary with that decline in coinage, that gold and silver were only designed to serve for jewelry and in the construction of sacred vessels. Saint Eloi is known to have been a great goldsmith of the time of king Dagobert, as was Alan of Walsingham among the English of the middle ages, and the celebrated Benvenuto Cellini in Italy, in a century nearer ours. When Richard was prisoner in Germany,* Saint Louis in Egypt, and King John in England,† their ransom could be effected only by bringing into requisition the plate and jewels of the nobles and the churches. The historians of the Saxon period, in England, often speak of a *living money*, which was authorized by law, and which consisted in paying for every kind of commodities in *slaves* and in *cattle*. Later, as money again appeared, living money was no longer allowed, except by special contract; and in this case, horses, cattle, cows, sheep and slaves could only be given in payment according to an agreed valuation. The fines imposed by the state or the church were alone excepted and payable at will, either in coin or in *living beings*. We must, however, do this justice to the church, that, to discourage the trade in slaves, she finally refused to accept

---

* Historians estimate the ransom of Richard at five millions in our francs. Almost all the metallic riches of the barons and the churches were employed for it.

† The ransom of king John was fixed at more than thirty millions of francs in our money. The first fifth was paid down, which appeared so enormous that it would have been impossible to meet it, if recourse had not been had to the Jews, accompanied by the assurance that privileges would be granted them. The successor to King John was so poor that he was obliged to pay the expenses of his household in money of lead lightly plated with silver. The times of the payment of John's ransom were successively postponed, and France still owed the last fifth forty years after the treaty, when a new war with England broke out.

any in payment. Doctor Henry has left us a history of England in which are found several curious estimates of prices in our money, corresponding to the living money According to his calculations, the fine of a slave would have been in the year 997, about 70 francs ; of a horse, 45 francs; of a cow, 8 francs; of a sheep, one franc, fifty centimes. We know, by the accounts which have been preserved in the Strasbourg cathedral, that the daily wages of the masons employed in the construction of that edifice were from three to four * centimes in our money.

In the reign of Charlemagne, the silver pound was composed of twelve ounces of metal : it was divided into twenty *sous*, each of twelve *deniers*, and the denier corresponded to about six sous in our present money. A four pound loaf of bread was sold for less than five centimes, which will give a pretty correct idea of the small quantity of money then in circulation. By degrees the pound of Charlemagne fell from 80 francs to 10 francs, to which it had fallen by successive alterations, during the reign of King John. But the crusades made a part of the precious metals which had taken the route for the East, flow back toward the West. The taking of Constantinople by the crusaders, gave rise to an immense division of the spoils, and Gibbon asserts that the Emperor Alexis paid the Marquis of Montserrat the enormous sum of sixteen hundred pounds weight in gold. However, there is reason to believe, that, at the time of the foundation of the kingdom of Jerusalem, the revenues of the country were insufficient for the maintenance of the government, and that Europe was obliged to contribute considerable sums every year to provide for it ; which renders very difficult an exact estimate of the money in circulation at that time. All that we know is, that after the impetus which resulted in the great movements of troops and provisions to the Holy Land, things resumed their accustomed course,

* Less than one cent, U. S. money.

and the diminution of specie continued to be felt in all the countries of Europe.

The discovery of the mines of the New World abruptly arrested this diminution. The mass of metal which these mines poured into the circulation, rose in a few years to twelve times the amount of all the preëxisting money, especially after the discovery of the mines of Potosi, the most prolific of all, in 1545. Immediately prices rose rapidly, and the average product of the mines from 1546 to 1600 may be estimated at more than sixty millions of francs a year. From 1600 to 1700, this product increased to about eighty millions annually; and from 1750 to 1800 the importation of specie from America into Europe regularly exceeded the sum of one hundred and eighty millions a year. But the increase was by far the most considerable from 1800 to 1810, for it has been estimated, from the best authorities, at two hundred and fifty millions of francs. One would suppose, at first thought, that such a rapid increase must have produced a corresponding rise in prices, and suddenly changed the condition and the wages of labor; but it was not so. The progress in arts and manufactures contemporary with the discovery of the mines, necessitated the employment of a greater quantity of money, and so much the more was needed as its value diminished from its very abundance. A competency having become more general, many persons were able to convert their savings into articles of gold and silver. The discovery of the Cape of Good Hope, by opening direct communication with the Asiatic continent, which was accustomed to importations of gold and silver, prevented the new monetary revolution from bringing about a reaction in prices that would have be-come dangerous in Europe but for that diversion.

Consequently, as the mass of money increased, demand for it became more keenly felt; transactions which up to that time had been very difficult or even impossible, employed a greater quantity and prevented its value diminishing in the same proportion as its abundance had in-creased. Economists are not agreed as to the increase in the price of commodities from that fall in the value of money. Adam Smith* estimates it as threefold, while the Marquis de Garnier rates it at twice as much. By a truly remarkable coincidence, at this very time most of the sovereigns chose to raise artificially the value of coins. Royal edicts had raised, in France, the nominal value of the coined silver mark to 16 and 18 livres instead of the 8 to 10 livres at which it was counted in the first years of that century. The effect of these two causes, which acted simultaneously on the nominal price of all provisions for general consumption, produced a rise which made them appear ten to twelve times dearer than they were previously. People could not explain this commer-cial phenomenon, which became the subject of a memorial presented to Catherine de Medécis, and printed at Bor-deaux in 1586, under this title : *Discourse on the excessive-ly high prices, presented to the Queen, mother of the king, by a faithful servant of hers.*‡ The author of this dis-course here passes in review, in the greatest detail, the prices of different kinds of grain, meats, fruits, vegetables, forage and other commodities of daily consumption, the rate of salaries, wages, day's-work of mechanics in winter and in summer, just as these prices were sixty or seventy years before; and he shows that at the time when he writes most of these prices have become ten to twelve times higher. " As to landed property," he says, " let one examine houses, fiefs, seigniories, arable lands, mead-ows, vines and other property to which nothing has been added for sixty years, and he will find that to-day they will sell for six times more than they did formerly.† "

---

* *Wealth of Nations*, Book i, chap. v.
‡ *Notes de la traduction d'Adam Smith ;* by Garnier, vol. v, p. 191.
† The same lamentations were heard at that time in England. We ob-serve in a sermon by Bishop Latimer, in the reign of Edward VI, these singular words : '' The physician, if the poor man be diseased, he can have no help without too much ; and of the lawyer the poor man can get no

This increase in the price of things manifested itself in all the countries of Europe, in proportion as the gold and silver of the New World was distributed in them through the agency of the Spaniards. We find in the *Secret des Finances*, attributed to Froumenteau, that from the end of the reign of Louis XII to the year 1581, when that book was printed, that is to say within a period of seventy-five years, the public tributes had more than quintupled in France : the same increase having been experienced in other countries, there was a strong demand for labor to provide for them, and it was perhaps as much from this cause as in consequence of the development of civilization, that prices, momentarily increased, ended by maintaining themselves within reasonable limits, notwithstanding the artificial increase of the sum total of the money by alterations, and its real increase by importations. All the habits become changed ; bold enterprises are executed, new demands are created with the possibility of satisfying them ; greater means of exchange facilitate commerce and speculations. If, however, America had not been discovered, gold and silver pieces would have been less numerous, but they would have had more value ; there would have been relations between commodities and money very

counsell, expedition, nor help in this matter, except he give him too much. You landlords, you rent-raisers, I may say you steplords, you unnatural lords, you have for your possessions yearly too much. Poor men, which live of their labour, cannot, with the sweat of their face, have a living ; all kinds of victuals are so dear, pigs, geese, capons, chickens, eggs, etc ! These things with others are so unreasonably enhansed ; and I think verily, that if thus continued, we shall at length be constrained to pay *for a pigge a pound.*"

We find the same grievances in the Spanish writers. Father de Sancho, author of a work entitled : " Restauracion Politica de España," which sums up quite well the political economy of those times, thus expresses himself on this subject : " Es verdad, que antes del descubrimiento de las Indias solia comprarse por un quarto lo que ahora por seis reales ; valia el cobre tres tanto mas que ahora la plata, pues pesaba un quarto lo que ahora un real de à dos ; y ansi, mas rico estaba uno con cien reales en quartos que ahora con cinco mil. Y con la abondancia de plata y oro ha baxodo su valor, y conseiguientemente ha subido el de lo qua se compra con la moneda ; y asi se introducen altos precios en todas las cosas, y faltando la plata y oro, quedan los hombles obligados à tan grandes gastos, imposibilitados de alcanzar las grandes cantidades que son menester parà ellos ; porque antes que hubiese tanta plata, un pobre hallaba un quarto en ocho blancas, mas facilmente que ahora dos reales en diez y siete quartos."

different from those which exist to-day: more things would have been obtained with less money; but production would have been long in a languishing condition for lack of capital, and civilization would have remained stationary with production. What proves this is that the impetus given to labor by the augmentation of the precious metals did not stop at this first step. Soon the specie no longer sufficed: bills of exchange, notes of banks of deposit and of circulation, and all the institutions of public and private credit came in to increase the number of means of exchange, and consequently to stimulate labor to the highest degree. It is not necessary to confine ourselves to abstractions: abundance or scarcity of money cannot remain an isolated fact; there is a constant tendency towards an equilibrium. When metallic money abounded in Spain, it excited there a keen desire to consume, by affording the citizens of that country the necessary facilities for procuring in foreign countries whatever could gratify their tastes or satisfy their wants. Europe began to produce for them, and for nearly a century, they alone commanded labor, and were the most powerful promoters of the industrial arts. Through their hands was brought about an immense distribution of wages, and mechanics dared to indulge a faint hope of obtaining, by means of their pay, something more than the poor bit of black bread on which they had hitherto subsisted.

But such a great change could not be brought about without suffering. At first, before the increase of farm-rents and salaries had come into harmony with the rise in the price of things, it was hard for all those who lived on a fixed income or a limited salary. The increase of money acted in that case like the invention of a machine, which at first causes a withdrawal of a certain number of mechanics, until the demand for the products, called forth by the lowering of prices, has restored employment to them. This explains how it was, that, instead of rejoicing at a circumstance, which, according to the common ideas, was to enrich the whole world, the contemporaries were only impressed by the increase in prices which rendered life harder for them.   We have seen the state of opinion in that regard in France, England, and Spain ; and a very curious book could be made of all the jeremiads inspired by this phenomenon of the rise of prices, at which people were the more alarmed because they did not all comprehend it.*   And in fact it was difficult to explain how provisions and other commodities could thus have increased in price, since they were neither more rare nor more in demand.   The same quantity of grain exchanged at all times for a cow or a certain number of sheep ; but, when it was necessary to measure these commodities by means of money, the proportions were no longer the same ; the buyer complained of being obliged to give more money, forgetting that when he became seller, he also received more.   However, the one who produced more than he consumed, saw his profits increase when he estimated them in money, while he who found himself in the contrary condition, the simple consumer, perceived with bitterness his own ruin, in the face of an income that was unchanged while prices were rising.   But as in organized society everybody is a producer at the same time and almost in the same proportions as he is a consumer, the discomfort became daily less considerable, and the equilibrium brought about prosperity.   Money was not long in diminishing in value while increasing in quantity, and the prediction of Bishop Latimer that a pig would soon cost more than a guinea, was completely fulfilled.   There happened in Europe what happens in all countries when the influx of specie causes enterprises to be undertaken which would not have been dreamed of if that influx had not permitted them to be executed.

---

* The most remarkable of these writings is that which appeared in 1581, during the reign of Elizabeth, under this title : *A brief conceipte touching the commonwealthe of this realme of England.*   It has the form of a dialogue in which figure a landed proprietor, a farmer, a merchant, a manufacturer, and a theologian.

M. de Humboldt has estimated the product of the mines of the New World from the discovery to our time, at the enormous sum of thirty milliards of francs. Without confidently admitting a figure so high, we think that nothing less than the fecundity of these mines would have sufficed to meet the wants of the circulation, as soon as labor had been stimulated in Europe by the importation of the first products. The prosperity of England, Holland, Germany, France and even Russia must be attributed to the industrial impetus which these different countries received from the shipments of American bullion in exchange for their raw products or their manufactured goods. When the war of independence, by suspending the labors in the mines of Mexico and Peru, reduced the production of the precious metals to a third of what it previously was, Europe made up the deficiency by improvements in credit and the multiplication of effects of every kind which aim to take the place of money or to supplement its services. This revolution of an opposite character to that which followed the early days of the discovery, is continuing to-day,* in consequence of the increasing diminution in the

---

* Since the author wrote these lines, important changes have taken place in the production of the precious metals. The discovery of gold in California in 1848 and in Australia in 1851, and the consequent extensive mining operations, and also the increased working of auriferous deposits in Russia, in addition to the silver product of the Mexican and South American mines, so augmented the total of the precious metals, as to cause a depreciation of the value of money in general and especially in the value of gold as estimated in silver. Levasseur, (*La Question de l'Or*, Paris, Guillaumin, 1858, p. 192, et seq.) estimates that in France, money had in 1856 lost 29 per cent, or about two-sevenths the value it had in 1847. His estimates are based upon the rise in prices of articles of ordinary consumption : and making allowance for such other causes as existed, he attributes twenty per cent of the depreciation in the value of money to the increased supply of the precious metals.

A. J. Warner (*Appreciation of Money*, p. 10) says : " The quarter of a century from 1848 to 1873 has been pointed out by economists as being the period of greatest activity in the production and distribution of wealth of any period in the whole history of the world. During these twenty-five years, about thirty-six per cent was added to the stock of precious metals in the hands of man ; and during these same years the trade and commerce of all civilized and commercial nations increased at a rate never known before— the commerce of the United States and Great Britain being increased by from 300 to 400 per cent, and national wealth in a corresponding degree."

supply of the precious metals. Indeed, if one compares the mass of commodities at present in circulation with that of twenty years ago, he will see that an increase of specie of at least ten per cent would have been necessary to maintain the same prices. Far from any such increase, specie is diminishing, and the population as well as the demand for money is increasing. A sudden and extraordinary cause has also coöperated since 1815 to increase the demand. The governments which had issued a considerable quantity of paper money during the long wars of the Revolution and the Empire, wished to redeem it after the peace. The very American states from which Europe derived its specie, have lived mostly by loans since that time; and luxurious habits have become so general among us, that quite an important sum of gold and silver is employed every year for artistic or for household objects; 30,000,000 of francs are thus devoted

---

Ernest Seyd (*Fall in the Price of Silver*) estimates the addition to the existing stock of money between 1848 and 1875, *i.e.*, in 27 years, at 40 per cent.

Now, (in 1879), the tide is again the other way, and we have been witnessing for the past five years an appreciation of money similar to that existing when Blanqui wrote the above pages. The present universal fall of prices as measured in either gold or silver (as exhibited in carefully prepared tables of more than forty articles of prime necessity) shows that the increase of the world's volume of currency has not kept pace with the increase of population and business. This fall in prices—a crucial test of appreciation of money—is not confined to America and Europe, though probably greatest in the United States, Germany, and England, but extends to India and China. J. Hector, Deputy Secretary and Treasurer of the Bank of Bengal, in his pamphlet, *Currency considered with special reference to the fall of Silver and Consequences to India,*" (Blackwood & Sons, Edinburgh and London, 1877), shows by tables of prices of exports from India and of prices of food there in five principal cities, that general prices in India were lower in 1876 than in 1872, though wages had not moved, either up or down.

The London Economist of Dec. 28th, 1878, says : "It is a fact which will scarcely be disputed, that the purchasing power of gold is now considerably greater than it was in the three years 1872-3-4. The assertion may readily be corroborated by an appeal to the market price of commodities then and now : and the result, which yields *an average fall probably exceeding twenty per cent*," etc.

The causes of the present appreciation of money are principally the German demonetization of silver and the consequent limitation of its coinage in the States of the Latin Union and in the United States, and the withdrawal of a large amount of paper money from circulation in Germany, France and the United States. Diminished production at the mines is another cause.— *Trans.*

in France, and Humboldt reasonably thinks that we may estimate at four times that amount, or 120,000,000, the like consumption which takes place in Europe.   Mr. Huskisson informs us that in the year 1828, the amount of the charges in England for assaying was 2,625,000 francs, which supposes in that country alone, a manufacture of articles of gold and silver to the value of more than 100,000,000 of francs.

Thus the waves of money which have not ceased to flow over Europe since the end of the fifteenth century, are beginning to retire.   The reaction is doubtless taking place slowly, but steadily ; and already the countries most advanced in manufactures and commerce are obliged to ask of credit what the mines have ceased to furnish to supply their needs.   Gold and silver tend to play henceforth the part in transactions which reserves do in banks of discount.   A universal clearing-house will sooner or later be established, to settle all accounts by compensation in credits, and we shall see realized the utopia of Ricardo, that money is in its true condition, when it is in the state of paper.   Do we not already find proof of it in the operations of the banks of France, England, and the United States ?   What an establishment is that which carries on operations in discount to the amount of seven or eight hundred millions a year, by means of a capital stock of one hundred millions in specie, one-fourth of which would suffice to meet its demands ?   Metallic money, as we see, henceforth plays only a secondary part, and although it would seem that its value must increase by the reduction of the product of the mines and by the increase of the demands of trade, paper money tends to depreciate it, and to take its place in all the markets of of the world.   The bill of exchange circulates everywhere in preference to coin, because it is more convenient and runs fewer risks in circulation.

This monetary revolution, almost accomplished in Europe, will permit no more recurrence of the alterations

and frauds of which the history of nations presents such
numerous examples. By experiments and misfortunes,
people have at last arrived at a comprehension of the necessity of an inviolable respect for all the elements which
concur in the security of the exchanges. Nations and
kings to-day are cured of the fatal mania of seeking the
precarious resource of debased coin, a resource always as
disgraceful as it is sterile. But who can number the mis-
deeds of this kind of which history is full, since the discovery of the New World? They who had no mines,
imagined they could find the equivalent of them by reducing the standard or weight of their coins, and the
false money became to the governments a two-edged
sword, with which they wounded themselves while attempting to make use of it against their enemies. Thus
it was with the Dutch, in their revolution against Spain,
and with the French, in the seventeenth century, in their
war against the Spanish. Venice and Florence likewise,
those opulent republics, did not reject these ignoble
means of supplementing their revenue ; and one may rank
among the principal causes of the decline of the Florentines the habit acquired by their merchants of devoting
themselves to traffic in specie moneys rather than to the
cultivation of the arts which had made the fortune of
their ancestors. The evil was not long in taking deep
root, and there were not only bad moneys, but innumerable books upon money. This is perhaps the economic
subject on which most has been written. Every one
thought he had found the philosopher's stone. Davan-
zati wrote in 1582: "Gold and silver are instruments
which make the property of mortals circulate over the
whole globe, and which may be considered as secondary
causes of a happy life." Serra published, in 1613, his
work entitled: *A short treatise on the causes which
make gold and silver abound in kingdoms*, and he devoted himself to proving that in his eyes the only wealth
was gold and silver. Montanari issued. in 1680, his

VARIOUS WORKS ON MONEYS. 261

Treatise on Moneys, in which we find, with the prepossessions of his predecessors in favor of the precious
metals, very just reflections on the phenomena of circulation. A century previous, Gaspard Scaruffi, of Reggio,
had addressed to Count Tassoni a " Discourse on
Moneys," full of views very broad, and still worthy of
interest to-day, after the excellent writings which have
appeared on the subject. It was Scaruffi who first proposed the gold and the silver mark, adopted since in all
Europe, to serve as a guaranty in the goldsmith's trade.
The other Italian writers on political economy, Broggia,*
Neri,† Carli,‡ Beccaria,§ Vasco,¶ have thrown much light
on all questions relating to moneys, the whole of which
the French economists have summed up with more or less
order and perspicuity. Boutteroue, Leblanc, Abot de
Bazinghen, Dupré de Saint-Maur, Boizard, and Poulain,
have left us writings more complete than those of the
Italians, but in which we do not find the same breadth of
view and the same originality. In Holland, England,
and Spain, the question of moneys has given rise to thousands of books, more or less tinged with the prejudices
of the times, but which can henceforth have only an importance arising from curiosity, since modern economists
have thrown light upon that subject by the most brilliant
and conscientious labors.

The foolish attempts, which were repeated for many
centuries, against the integrity of the monetary system,
are forever ended. Of all the causes pending before the
tribunal of science, there is not one that she has judged
with more experience and maturity, and upon which her
judgment is more invulnerable. Every one to-day knows
that the real advantages which Europe has derived from

---

* *Treatise on Moneys*, 1751.
† *Observations on the Legal Price of Moneys*, 1751.
‡ *Treatise on Moneys*, 1760.
§ *On the Confusion in the Moneys, and the Remedies*, 1762.
¶ *Political Essay on Moneys*, 1772.

the discovery of the mines of the New World, do not come exclusively from the abundance of the precious metals, but from the cultivation of the commodities for consumption, which constitute the basis of our exchanges with that country. Gold and silver have disappeared; cotton, sugar and coffee remain. The single discovery of the potato was worth more than that of the mines of Mexico and Peru.

CHAPTER XXV.

Some evil consequences of the discovery of the American mines.—The first appearance of paupers in England.—Ministry of Sully.—His financial reforms.—His erroneous ideas on manufactures and trade.—He is the most ardent propagator of the *mercantile system*.—His proneness to sumptuary laws.—His severe attacks on financial abuses.—Definitive results of his administration.

IF, in our examinations, we were limited to the surface of things, there would perhaps be reason to deplore the discovery of the New World. The great importation of specie which resulted from it, seems, in fact, to have only served to throw Europe into extreme confusion, and to disturb minds as well as all business affairs. Charles V and Philip II took advantage of it to satiate their ambition, by arousing on every side bloody and ruinous wars; the other princes saw in it only an opportunity to get hold of the money of their subjects, in order to fight with equal arms against the possessors of the new land of promise. Everywhere the money-grasping spirit was awakened at the sight of the masses of gold and silver which came to us from America; and the first result of that inundation was to suspend the activity of the people and the kings, who ran after the wealth of the mines rather than encouraged that which came from labor. We have seen the surprise of some and the expedients resorted to by others, at the appearance of those uncomprehended phenomena of the sudden rise in the prices of things without increase in the rate of wages. In vain were new palliatives adopted against the incidents of each day; the evil reappeared under a thousand unforeseen forms, continually more threatening and more incurable. Debased coin, increased taxation, exactions of every kind, could not bring relief, and the most frightful anarchy for a time came near desolating Europe.

Let us transport ourselves in thought back to the time of our civil wars, under Henry III, when on all sides the old catholicism, shaken to its very foundations, was attempting to grasp again a power which was about slipping from its hands. This was the most brilliant period of the American mines; each year gallions were returning from Mexico, loaded with heavy piasters ; and nevertheless, poverty was reigning everywhere, in spite of the new-born elements of opulence ; and, from one extremity to the other, Europe was a prey to discord and misery. "The country," exclaimed a contemporary French writer,* "is devoured not only by *gendarmerie* and *gabelleurs*, but every hour soldiers come out of the fortresses, who go forth on marauding expeditions, with so great insolence and violence that there is not a village or house which, one, two, or three times a week, is not compelled to deal out portions to satisfy the appetite of this rabble ; when the soldier departs, the sergeant enters, and the houses are ordinarily so full of *gensdarmes*, soldiers, collectors of *tailles*, *gabelleurs*, and sergeants, that it is a great marvel when an hour of the day passes without a visit from such people."

The same state of things existed in England, Flanders, Italy, and Germany. One might say that whole armies of soldiers had been thrown upon the public, and that the people were condemned to give henceforward their sweat and their blood to the last drop to satisfy that thirst for gold and silver which was devouring their oppressors. Instead of seconding the natural resources of each country, the precious metals served at first only to exhaust them, and nearly three centuries of experiments and misfortunes were necessary to teach us that their

* Froumenteau: *Le Secret des Finances*, edition of 1581.

true destination was to support industry rather than war. The mines of America were discovered a hundred years too soon: they should not have poured their treasures into Europe until after the long religious wars from which resulted freedom of investigation, order in finance, and security for labor. In the hands of a king like Philip II, their effect was more murderous than that of powder, and it was by them, or because of them, that France, Spain and England were so long afflicted. The princes who had no mines, sought for their equivalent in the purses of their subjects, without suspecting that by thus attacking capital as well as income, they were striking production at its source and the state at its vitals. Moreover, when we study the history of these deplorable times, we hear only of provinces exhausted, houses destroyed, and unfortunates wandering about the country. When the states of Blois assembled, there was presented to them an enumeration of these scenes of despair and ruin; and in all the dioceses, after every recital of the losses in money, were named the number of priests murdered, of monks, soldiers and bourgeois massacred, and of girls and women violated, without this supplement to the budget of miseries being ever forgotten.

The most horrible confusion prevailed equally in England; and the reign of Elizabeth, the results of which were to be so glorious for her country, had commenced under very lugubrious auspices. Henry VIII had seized the property of the churches, under pretext of relieving his subjects from the weight of taxes, which they nevertheless continued to pay. Elizabeth prosecuted mendicancy with an inflexible hand, and instead of restoring a few thousand workmen to society, she infested England with robbers. Under the reign of Henry VIII, according to the testimony of Harrison, more than 72,000 had already been put to death, and under the reign of Elizabeth, there was not a year passed without three or four hundred being sent to the gibbet. These unfortunates, wandering in bands of several hundreds, pillaged farms, plundered travelers, and from the depths of the forest braved the prosecutions of the government. After having tried all kinds of punishments, Elizabeth was obliged to put the burden of their support upon the parishes, and to create the famous poor-tax, which was insufficient to maintain them, but not to prevent their multiplying. Thus, in Spain, the mines of the New World had turned the administration and the people from the true paths of wealth, by securing to them, almost without effort, an income independent of labor : in France, they had just forced the king to multiply taxes and exactions of every kind, in order to sustain himself against the competition of the Spanish ; and in England, they gave rise to the poor-tax, one of the worst inventions of modern times.

It is not impossible, however, to recognize in the midst of this chaos, the dawn of a more prosperous epoch and of a more regular order of things. In vain the sovereigns tried to retain the gold and the silver, to extort it from their subjects, and to favor its importation and forbid its exportation ; gold escaped from every pore and went wherever great transactions, that is to say, great profits,* called it. By degrees, too, governments perceived that the collection of taxes needed, in order to become productive, to be subjected to strict rules ; and these rules appeared in legislation. The parliament in England and Sully in France were the originators of this reform, from which financial science was soon to arise, and with it a remedy for the bad systems born of contemporary ignorance and the incapacity of governments. Here begins a new era for political economy, and we see at length a system arise from the midst of the frightful anarchy which devastated Europe during the long religious wars.

History has justly recognized in Sully the most com-

---

* " Money," says Mengotti, " is essentially rebellious to the orders of law: it comes without being called, it goes without being arrested, deaf to advances, insensible to threats, attracted solely by the allurement of profits."

plete personification of this system, which we cannot better make known than by a rapid recital of the principal acts of the administration of this celebrated minister. They are not all in conformity with true principles, for Sully had no fewer prejudices than his contemporaries ; but he was the first administrator resolved not to proceed at hazard, and his acts are all remarkable for a spirit of order and consistency which exercised the greatest influence over the political economy of Europe. Hardly was he invested with the confidence of Henry IV, when he began to study carefully the burdens and the resources of France ; and he prepared the first budget which served as a basis of public accounts. His investigations revealed a debt of about three hundred millions of francs towards the end of the year 1595, and he at once unremittingly applied himself to the creation of ways and means necessary to extinguish it. His principal maxim was, to apply a fixed part of the receipts to each part of the expenses, without ever permitting it to be diverted to any other use. He put a restraint on the collectors of the revenue, who were exploiting the country with such audacity, that of the 150,000,000 of francs demanded of the tax-payers, scarcely thirty millions entered the public treasury. The receivers were prohibited from seizing, under any pretext, the cattle and farming implements of cultivators in arrears, and the most severe penalties were inflicted on soldiers who should annoy a peasant, either during their marches or when they had arrived at their quarters, which annoyance was, as we have seen, one of the most horrible pests of that time. It required no less firmness to repress the avidity of the provincial governors, who had pushed license so far as to levy contributions on their own account and by their authority alone. The duke of Epernon, who obtained, by such abusive measures, an income of sixty thousand crowns, ventured to resist Sully, *who defended as a soldier his operations in finance.**

---

* Forbonnais, *Recherches sur les finances.* Vol. i, p. 38.

The courageous minister, after having brought to their senses all these plunderers, from high to low, soon comprehended, and he asserted it often, that to enrich a prince, it was necessary to enrich his subjects. All his efforts were then directed toward the improvement of agriculture, which he considered the prime industry of the country.* He lavished on it encouragement of every sort, and in a few years the lands which had fallen into neglect in consequence of the misfortunes of war, had been again brought under cultivation. He abolished the restrictions most embarrassing to the circulation, and he suppressed the little favors of every kind which the cleverness of courtiers had obtained from the king. Thus the duke of Soissons had procured a grant authorizing him to levy a duty of fifteen sous per bale on commodities exported from the kingdom. Henry IV supposed he had granted a gratuity of a few thousand crowns ; the courtier had derived a revenue from it of three hundred thousand francs. Sully caused these usurped revenues to be restored to the treasury. Unfortunately, this great minister did not, in all his life, comprehend the importance of manufactures. There was in him at the same time a sort of aristocratic aversion to mechanical labor and a philosophic indifference to all articles of convenience and luxury. Sully was a nobleman with a stoic soul, a true Roman patrician of the fine days of the republic. We know the long quarrels he had with Henry IV on the subject of the plantations of mulberry trees encouraged by that prince, which came near embroiling him with his minister. Sully shrank from the idea of the introduction of silks into France. " What are you doing," he said,† " by presenting to the people the cultivation of silk for an employment ? You make them leave a hardy and laborious kind of life, such as that of the fields, for another which does not fatigue by any violent

---

* " *Labourage et pâturage*," he said, " *sont les deux mamelles de l' Etat.*"
† *Mémoires de Sully.* Vol. ii, p. 289, edit. in 4to.

exercise. It has always been remarked that the best soldiers are always taken from the families of robust laborers and sinewy mechanics : substitute for them these
men who are only acquainted with a kind of work which
children can do, you will find them no longer adapted to
military practice, which the situation of France and her
political condition make it indispensable for her to preserve and maintain. At the same time that you will
enervate the people of the rural districts, who are, in
every respect, the true props of the state, you will introduce by those of the city, luxury with all its train, voluptuousness, effeminacy, and idleness, which are not to be
apprehended for those who have little and who know how
to content themselves with little. How now ! have we
not already in France a sufficiently large number of these
useless citizens, who, under a coat of gold and scarlet,
hide the manners of women?" A Roman censor could
not have spoken better ; but a minister of agriculture and
commerce should have other ideas.

It was this philosophic prepossession against luxury *
which inspired in Sully most of the bad regulations which
his administration imposed on commerce and manufactures. All consumption of foreign products seemed to
him a larceny committed against France and an attack
aimed at her morals ; every exportation of money a calam-
ity which it was necessary to prevent by energetic measures. He was thus led to adopt the first theories of the
mercantile system, of which we may consider him the
most ardent propagator. Never had any one displayed
greater severity toward smugglers, especially toward
those who exported gold or silver. To confiscation of
the specie seized, he caused to be added confiscation of
all the property of the offenders, and the king declared

---

* Sully, besides, preached by example : " He ordinarily went clothed in
grey cloth, with a doublet of satin or taffeta without pinking or embroidery.
He praised those who dressed in this manner and ridiculed the others, who
wore, he said, their mills and their woods of full-grown trees upon their
backs."—*Péréfixe*, 3d part.

on oath that he would never grant any pardon for crimes of this sort. The money coined by the different princes of Europe had been current up to this time, and had been employed in France indifferently with the money bearing the stamp of the sovereign: people were now forbidden to make use of any of it, except that of Spain, the employment of which was too general to be suddenly suppressed. But this prohibition was a fatal blow to commerce, and restricted the circulation of capital, because people preferred to keep the proscribed specie rather than carry it to the mint, where enormous seigniorage duties awaited it. Sully thought he could enforce this system by sumptuary laws which aimed at the compulsory reduction of all public and private expenses, and which would, as he thought, bring about wealth and prosperity *by privation.* "It is still more necessary to do without the commodities of our neighbors," he said,* "than without their money. The necessity people impose on themselves of dressing in certain materials rather than others, is only a fault of our fancy; but the price we pay for it is a wrong done to ourselves with full knowledge of the case." The silk merchants of Paris having come to protest to Sully against this course, in the name of the commerce of the city, the minister received them with ill-temper, and allowed himself to address to one of them outrageous language, which he should not have employed.†

Nor would he ever suppress the custom-house of Vienne, better known later under the name of *customs of*

---

* *Mémoires.* Vol. ii, p. 390.

† Sire Henriot, charged with the address, having bent his knee before commencing, Sully raised him up brusquely, and after having turned him around on all sides to contemplate at leisure his dress of the antique style, lined with silks of various colors, according to the custom of his calling, said, "How now, my good fellow, do you come here with your company to complain? Why, you are *finer than I*! How is this? Here is taffeta, here is damask, here is brocade;" and he ridiculed the deputation, without hearing it, in so cruel a manner that the confused merchants said, on going away: "The valet is harsher and more self-asserting than the master."

Valence, the avowed object of which was to render impossible any trade between France and Italy. This fatal
toll-house established on the Rhone, seemed to have
made of it an impassable river, and forced the trade to
take another route, to the great detriment of our interests. Forbonnais reports the speech of a deputy from
Lyons to the states of Dauphiny, in 1600, in which the
sad consequences of the stubbornness of Sully are energetically described. "This custom-house," said the deputy, "was established for the reduction of the city of
Vienne ; and although the city of Lyons had, from the
beginning, appreciated the danger from it, it hoped that
as it had been created for urgent and temporary necessities, there would be an end to it before there was occasion to complain. But as things which appear at their
commencement mild and easy become in time harsh and
intolerable, this toll has become a reef which cannot be
encountered without shipwreck. Since the passage of
the Rhone has been brought into discredit, and the merchants have preferred to try any other risk rather than
expose themselves to every sort of injustice, the city of
Lyons recognizes that from the celebrated and flourishing
city which it formerly was, it will become a desert, if freedom of trade is not reëstablished. All the merchandise
which came from the Levant to Marseilles and thence to
Lyons, has already left the old way and sought other
routes, which, though longer and more difficult, are more
secure.* Do not think, gentlemen, that we are so little
instructed in the science of obedience, *the best and most
fortunate possession of subjects,* that we thought of opposing the intentions of the king, or of diminishing his revenues. The taxes from which the people suffer, however
great they may be, are always accounted holy and just ;
but they are in the state what sails are to a vessel, to

---

* From that time, the trade of Italy with England and Flanders, which
had been carried on by transit across France, took the sea route, which
it has never abandoned.

guide it, secure it, but not to burden and submerge it."
The historian Mathieu, who has preserved this speech,
acknowledges that the complaints were general, and that
they were not regarded.

Sully, continually misled by the same prepossessions
which made him dread foreign commerce and internal
manufactures as causes of impoverishment and ruin,
imagined he ought to increase the restrictions which
former kings of France had put on freedom of labor. We
know that Henry III had ordered, in 1581, that all merchants, traders, artisans, and mechanics with a trade, residing in the cities and market-towns of the kingdom,
should be incorporated, with master and warden, without
any exception. A second edict, in 1583, had declared a
permission to work a royal and domanial right: in consequence, the period of apprenticeship, the form and the
quality of the masterpieces, the formalities for the reception of masters, and all the old legislation of Saint Louis
had been so reviewed and corrected, that labor had become a sort of privilege. Sully did not abuse the royal
and domanial right, but he began to sell letters of mastership, which exempted the titularies from apprenticeship and tests ; and, creating privileges in the very midst
of privileges, he did what Saint Louis would not have
dared to do, notwithstanding the difference of time and
circumstances. He acted thus from a profound and conscientious conviction, persuaded that manufactures were
a parasitical branch of production, injurious to agriculture, and of which he would have said with Xenophon:
" What shall be done with people, most of them seated
all the day and bound down to trades whose products
enervate the consumers and make us spend money?"

The dominant thought of Sully, in taking all these
measures, was to supply the wants of the state and to
have always on hand a considerable quantity of money.
No opposition seemed to him tolerable, when there was
danger of being trammeled in the execution of this diffi-

cult task. Now he replied to recalcitrant parliaments :
" The king cannot consider unjust what is advisable in
his affairs : " again, he caused to be constructed in the
Bastille numerous vaults destined to receive masses of
money, of which he thus deprived the circulation, but
which he thought as necessary to the security of the state
as magazines of powder to its defence. Henry IV supported these measures from time to time by studied discourses, like that in which he explained in a council extraordinary the motives he had in making a reserve of
funds to satisfy the exigencies of an unforeseen war or
guard against the demands of a stormy minority. Sully
was preoccupied all his life with that financial disquietude,
to which he more than once sacrificed principles which
were dear to him ; but his errors were rather those of his
time than of his judgment, and he was able to say this
in justification of himself, in his memoirs, that abundance
began at last to reappear, and that the peasants, *delivered
from all their tyrants in finance, the nobility and the militia, sowed their fields and reaped their harvests in security*.[*]

Then it was that he planned the execution of those
great works of which the canal of Briare was to be the
first, and which he had so much difficulty in making
Henry IV understand, little accustomed as he was to anticipating advantages so far ahead, he who had lived by
expedients and encroachments on the future.

Sully himself summed up his economic doctrines in a

---

[*] It was not without difficulty that Sully had succeeded. He himself relates how every day he had to fight some battle to defend the interests of his
country. " The king," he says, " had just allowed twenty edicts to be drawn
from him, and I was setting out to make an attempt with him, *in favor of
the people*, when I met the marchioness of Verneuil, who asked me what the
paper was which I held. ' What are you thinking of doing with that ? ' she
said to me. ' I am thinking, madam, of remonstrating with the king.'
And for whom, pray, do you suppose the king would do anything, except
for those who are his cousins, relatives and mistresses ? ' ' All that you say,
madam,' I replied, ' would be well if his majesty took the money from his
purse : but to raise it from tradesmen, artisans, farmers and shepherds, does
not appear so ; *they are the ones that support the king and us all ;* it is
enough for them to have a master, without having so many cousins, relatives,
and mistresses to support.' "

written statement sought from him by that prince, and
which he has reproduced in his memoirs. "To see if my
views corresponded with his," he says, "the king desired
me to give him a memorandum of everything which I
thought capable of overthrowing a powerful kingdom,
or merely of dimming its glory. I present it here as
a brief of the principles which have served me as a
rule. 'The causes of the ruin or weakening of monarchies are unreasonable subsidies ; monopolies, principally in grain ; *neglect of commerce*, traffic, tillage, the arts
and trades ; a great number of public offices ; the expenses of these offices ; the excessive authority of those who
fill them ; the expenses, delays and iniquity in the administration of justice ; idleness, *luxury, and everything which
has connection therewith ;* debauchery and corruption of
morals ; *the confusion of ranks ;* variations in the money ;
unjust and imprudent wars ; the *despotism of sovereigns ;*
their *blind attachment to certain persons ;* their prepossession in favor of certain ranks and certain professions ; the
cupidity of ministers and people in favor ; the *degrading
of people of quality ;* contempt and forgetfulness of literary people ; toleration of evil practices and the infraction
of good laws ; and a multiplicity of embarrassing edicts
and useless regulations.'" Sully was not always consistent with these doctrines, in all his long administration.
We find it difficult to reconcile what he said of the importance of the arts and trades with his efforts to prevent the establishment of silk manufactures and especially with his system of *privations*, which naturally closed
every sort of market for manufactured products. Since
neglect of commerce and variations in the money seemed
to him so prejudicial to the general good of the state, he
ought not to have kept up the custom duty at Vienne
and disturbed the monetary régime. But his prejudices
explain his contradictions. He could not make the development of manufactures accord with his horror of
luxury and with the necessity of providing for the finan-

cial exigencies of each day. We may say that these two feelings were the keenest and most active of his whole life. The exactions of lawyers and of the administrators of the finances particularly excited his indignation, and his ministry was a long combat against their rapacity. The truly heroic campaigns he directed against abuses of every kind and the boldness of the reforms which the death of Henry IV prevented him from carrying into execution, are not sufficiently well known. In closing this chapter, I will give an idea of them, that one may judge of the intellectual movement which was, at that time, already taking place in matters of political economy.

In the ecclesiastical government, lists were to be prepared of all the benefices with their names and revenues,* so as to render an account of the importance of that part of the national wealth. Among the nobility, a census was made of all the lands and of the revenues they brought to the proprietary noblemen ; in the case of the commonalty, the necessary precautions were taken to avoid the least outrage on the part of the soldiers and the nobles toward agriculturists, artisans, and merchants. Sully at the same time pursued with his anathemas all extravagant expenses. " One may be assured," he said, " that if I had been considered, I would have tolerated neither carriages nor other inventions of luxury, save on conditions which would have cost vanity dear. Special regulations should prescribe that the procurers-general prosecute and punish as examples those who by the scandal of a prodigal and dissolute life are prejudicially known to the public, to private citizens, or to the procurers themselves. The means given to enable them to do it would be to connect with them, in each jurisdiction, three public persons, called *censors* or *reformers*, chosen every third year in a public assembly, and authorized by their position, with which should be connected all sorts of exemptions, not only to denounce to the judges all fathers,

---

* No beneficiary could have more than ten thousand livres of income.

young men with families, and such other persons as are accused of carrying a dissolute life beyond the bounds of honor, and superfluous expenses beyond their ability, but also to oblige the judges themselves, to apply the remedy prescribed against excesses of both kinds, prosecuting them in case of refusal. Two admonitions should pre-cede every criminal prosecution; but at the third there should be entered a sort of action for guardianship, by which the bad households would see the management of their goods and effects pass into hands which left them only just two-thirds, and reserved the other third for the payment of their debts. No condition of life should be exempt from the requirement, and no citizen should be able to avoid that censorship, with any appearance of the truth, because it would have itself to respond for its actions to a superior tribunal, the ministers of which should, as well as this, be kept to their duty by the threat of a punishment corresponding to the dishonor. It should be decreed at the same time that no person, of whatever quality or condition he might be, should borrow a sum deemed considerable in proportion to his means, nor any other lend it to him, under penalty of losing it, without this fact was declared in the contracts or obliga-tions in which he pretended to employ that loan. It should besides be forbidden, with the same view, to all fathers of families, to give to one of their children, in establishing him, a sum greater than was just, consider-ing their present means and the number of those children born or to be born; excepting the single case which per-mitted despised or wounded paternal authority to punish a vicious and unnatural child."

One might think he heard, on reading these lines, a Saint-Simonian sermon of our day; and the resemblance between the doctrines is still more striking in the threat-ening provisions of Sully, to destroy, as he expressed it, the *contemptible art of chicanery*. In law-suits between relatives, the plaintiff was held, before everything, to

make an offer and even a summons to put all his differences to the arbitrament of four persons, chosen among
the relatives or friends of the parties, two by each : an
umpire named by the arbiters was to give the casting
vote. "In regard to judges' fees, salaries, vacations and
other expenses, as well as *all the different subterfuges of
chicanery, and all the other abuses of the bar in pleas
and deeds*, of which complaints are heard everywhere, the
king thought he could do no better than to put all these
details into the charge of twelve men chosen from those
best informed in affairs, to be discussed and regulated."
Sully would then have had the civil code drawn up two
hundred years sooner. Henry IV was so preoccupied
with the desire for these reforms, that the day when Sully
sent him the programme of them, made out by his own
hand, the king had him immediately called, *to talk together of them*, and as soon as he saw him, he cried out,
" Let my mass be delayed, for I must talk with that
man, who is not a man for mass." The death of
Henry IV prevented the execution of these projects,
most of which were doubtless impracticable, but which
nevertheless expressed the economic thought of Sully,
such as we find it in the acts of his administration. The
principal merit of this great minister was that of having
reëstablished order in the finances and having by that
means alone facilitated the return, or rather creation, of
the elements essential to public prosperity. His canal of
Briare opened the first hydraulic way in France, to which
he soon added the establishment of public barges on the
rivers, as he had organized post-houses on the highways
with relays of horses for travelers. He had found France
three hundred millions of francs in debt, which would be
nearly a milliard to-day : he left her entirely free. He
reduced the taxes, improved the highways, the fortifications, the material of war, the public domain, and furnished the treasury a reserve in specie of fourteen millions
deposited in the Bastille.   Twelve years had sufficed to

bring about these results, which prepared the advent of the fine days of the reign of Louis XIV, and which definitely installed political economy in the councils of kings.

CHAPTER XXVI.

The ministry of Colbert and its economic consequences.—Edict and tariff of 1664.—Its real aim.—Edict of 1667.—Encouragements to marriage.— Fine instructions to ambassadors.—The real doctrines of Colbert.—He is erroneously considered the founder of the prohibitory system.

BETWEEN the administration of Sully and that of Colbert, was that of two priests, Richelieu and Mazarin, both wasteful of their means, though from different motives, the wholly selfish aims of whom have nothing in common with political economy; but there was also the reign of Elizabeth in England and the development of the commercial power of the Netherlands, magnificent episodes in the history of science and of the world. The lofty genius of Colbert rises above these two events; and the splendor which rendered them conspicuous in Europe pales before the recital of the grand deeds accomplished by the minister of Louis XIV. Colbert was, in fact, the only minister who had had a system, settled, complete and consistent in all its parts; and it is to the eternal honor of his name that he made it triumph in spite of obstacles of every kind. Although this system was far from being irreproachable in all its parts, it was an immense progress at the time of its appearance; and we have had nothing since then which can be compared with it, for breadth and penetration. Its organization seems to have maintained something of the respect connected with religious establishments: it made a sect; and that sect counts to-day perhaps as many faithful adherents as the great church which has taken for its banner the immortal principle of commercial liberty.*

It was, moreover, the need of restoring order in the finances, which gave rise to the attempts at amelioration made by Colbert. This illustrious minister soon comprehended that the surest way to increase public fortune was to favor private fortune, and to open to production the broadest and freest ways. His principal merit consists in having brought into perfect harmony all the elements which could insure its success. One of the first acts of his ministry, the reëstablishment of the taxes on a uniform basis, is an homage rendered to true principles; and one cannot doubt that all the others would have been in conformity with this glorious precedent, if the science of wealth had been, at that time, as advanced as it is to-day. Colbert would certainly have carried out in France what Mr. Huskisson had begun in England at the time of his sudden death. It was he who commenced most of the reforms the completion of which is still our aim through difficulties which he also created ; for he often gave with one hand to withdraw with the other, and he was obliged to make more than one concession to the prejudices of his contemporaries and the exigencies of his position. But his work remains none the less worthy of our homage, as the finest monument raised to science by the hand of civil power, and also as a proof of the resources economic theories can offer to a statesman.

Even before his entrance into affairs, the needs of manufactures and commerce had already found eloquent organs. It may not be amiss to rapidly narrate their grievances in order to better appreciate the immensity of the task devolving upon Colbert, and his merit in accomplishing it. We have seen that Sully, notwith-

---

L'Histoire de la Vie et de l'Administration de Colbert, by M. Pierre Clément, 1846, Paris, Guillaumin, is a work so highly esteemed as to have obtained for its author admission to the Academy of Moral and Political Sciences.

standing his sound sense and his force of will, did not succeed in destroying a multitude of internal taxes which interfered with commerce between the provinces, and some of which, like the *duty of Valence*, had become real pests. His successors had increased most of these taxes and had created new ones accompanied by the most vexatious formalities and the most odious coercive measures. Never was collection more harsh; it much resembled the extortion of oriental tax-gatherers; and many merchants had renounced trade to get rid of it. Others had left France; and those who had been able to hold out, exhausted by the fiscal demands, saw their resources daily diminish and their capital encroached upon. Agriculture itself, so well protected by Sully, had become greatly discouraged. Many lands lay uncultivated; the live-stock was neglected, and France was beginning to be covered with vagrants and beggars. We find a faithful picture of this state of things in the petition presented to the king, January 26, 1654, by the six bodies of merchants of the city of Paris. "Sire," said the petitioners, "experience teaches that excessive taxes have never increased the revenues of a state, because they cause a loss on the whole of what is gained on the parts. In fact, only commerce and manufactures attract the gold and silver by which armies subsist. * * * If our workmen profit by their industry, it is not without the help of foreigners, who furnish us all the fine wools, for we have only coarse ones, as well as the drugs for dyes, the spices, sugars, soaps and leathers, which we cannot dispense with and which are not found in the kingdom. Foreigners will not fail to retaliate, by laying heavy duties on all these commodities; whence it will come to pass that we shall obtain no more, or that they will prohibit the admission of our manufactured products: consequently our workmen will be without employment, and the number of useless ones and of beggars will increase."

Colbert had soon sounded the depth of this evil, and

the measures he adopted prove that he had at heart its removal. The edict of September, 1664, reduced the import and export duties on merchandise to suitable limits, and suppressed the most onerous. " It is our intention," said the king, " to make known to all our governors and intendants in what consideration we hold *at present* everything that may concern commerce, and why we wish them to employ their authority to have justice rendered to the merchants, that they may not be diverted from their trade by chicanery. * * * We have invited all the merchants by circular letters, to apply directly to us in all their needs: we have invited them to depute some among them to bring us their propositions; and, in case of difficulties, we have appointed one person of our suite to receive their complaints and to present all their requests: we have arranged that there shall always be in connection with our suite a commercial house to receive them; we have resolved to use every year a million livres for the reëstablishment of manufactures and the increase of navigation; but as the most solid and most essential means for the reëstablishment of commerce are the diminution and the regulation of the duties which are levied on all commodities, we have arranged to reduce all these duties to one single import and one export duty, and also to diminish these considerably, in order to encourage navigation, *reëstablish the ancient* manufactures*, banish idleness, and, by honest occupations, turn away a great number of our subjects from an inclination to a groveling life, under appointment to various offices without duties, which degenerate into a dangerous chicanery infecting and ruining most of our provinces."

At the same time Colbert prohibited the seizure for the *tailles* (villein-tax) of beds, clothes, bread, horses and cattle serving for labor; or the tools by which artisans

---

* In 1658, 80 millions of livres worth of French manufactures had been exported to England and Holland alone. v. *Mémoires de Jean de Witt* (vol. vi, p. 182.)

and manual laborers gained their livelihood. The register of the survey of lands was revised, so that property should be taxed only in proportion to its value and the actual extent of the land. The great highways of the kingdom and all the rivers were then guarded by armies of receivers of tolls, who stopped merchandise on its passage and burdened its transportation with a multitude of abusive charges, to say nothing of the delays and exactions of every kind. An edict was issued ordering the investigation of these degrading charges; and most of them were abolished or reduced to just limits. But while bringing about these useful reforms in the present, Colbert prepared others for the future by instituting a council of commerce, the members of which were to give an official exposition of the needs of their branch of business and of manufacturing industry in general. An investigation into the public offices sold resulted in the discovery that there were then in France more than forty-five thousand families employed in services for which six thousand would have sufficed. An enormous amount was thus expended every year to the detriment of the working population; and Colbert mercilessly prosecuted its reduction. This minister professed the most profound contempt for the class of fund-holders and also for that of office-holders, whom he considered as parasites living on the labor of the community at large, and he devoted himself to reducing the number of the latter, either by abolishing the offices or limiting their salaries.

The lease of customs duties being about to expire, Colbert improved this occasion to revise the tariff; and although this fatal measure has since been considered as the finest monument of his administration, we think we should present it in its true aspect, which seems to us to have been invariably misapprehended. Colbert's aim in revising the customs was to make them a means of protection for national manufactures, in the place of a simple financial resource, as they formerly were. Most articles of foreign manufacture had duties imposed upon them, so as to secure to similar French merchandise the home market. At the same time, Colbert spared neither sacrifices nor encouragement to give activity to the manufacturing spirit in our country. He caused the most skilful workmen of every kind to come from abroad; and he subjected manufactures to a severe discipline, that they should not lose their vigilance, relying on the tariffs. Heavy fines were inflicted on the manufacturers of an article recognized as inferior in quality to what it should be. For the first offence, the products of the delinquents were attached to a stake, with a carcan and the name of the manufacturer; in case of a second offence, the manufacturer himself was fastened to it. These draconian rigors would have led to results entirely contrary to those Colbert expected, if his enlightened solicitude had not tempered by other measures what was cruel in them. Thus, he appointed inspectors of the manufactures, who often directed the workmen into the best way, and brought them information of the newest processes, purchased from foreign manufacturers, or secretly obtained at great expense.   Colbert was far from attaching to the customs the idea of exclusive and blind protection that has ever been attributed to them since his ministry. He knew very well that these tariffs would engender reprisals, and that, while encouraging manufactures, they would seriously hinder commerce. Moreover, all his efforts tended to weaken their evil effects. His instructions to consuls and ambassadors testify strongly to his prepossessions in this regard. He recommended to them to smooth over all difficulties which our merchants might encounter in foreign countries, and to make their privileges respected in every possible way. We cannot read without admiration the despatches he sent to M. de Béziers, ambassador of France at Madrid : " In case the subjects of the king," he said, " receive any bad treatment from the governors or other officers of the catholic king, whether in their persons, or in their vessels or merchandise, you will make known to the council of Spain that His Majesty is resolved not to suffer his subjects to be molested in any manner, and that *we shall be able to bring about an abandonment of the practice adopted hitherto of not rendering them any justice.*" We are to-day very far from manifesting a spirit so bold. " I pray you," he added, " to look into the matter and see if anything can be done agreeable to the merchants, to facilitate their commerce and to increase it. As the affairs which they have in Spain usually remain long undecided, for want of being looked after, it is necessary to place some person there who has intelligence, and can apply himself solely to the support and relief of the merchants."

On another occasion he wrote to M. de Pompone, ambassador to Holland: " The maritime commerce of the whole world is carried on with about twenty thousand ships. In the natural order, every nation should have its share in proportion to its power, the number of its people and the extent of sea coast; the Dutch have fifteen or sixteen thousand of this number, and the French perhaps five or six hundred at the most. The king employs all sorts of means which he thinks to be useful, in order to come a little nearer the number that his subjects ought naturally to have." And in order to succeed, Colbert granted prizes for navigation in the Baltic and for fishing in distant seas: he suppressed the right of *aubaine* (a prerogative by which the kings of France claimed the property of foreigners who died in their kingdom, without having been naturalized.—*Trans.*) at Marseilles, in order to attract foreigners there; and soon opulent houses from the Levant were established in that city, where they constructed a great number of vessels. At the same time, the edict of August, 1669, declared maritime commerce compatible with nobility, and per-

mitted any nobleman to be directly or indirectly concerned in it without derogation. The creation of entre
pôts served as a compensation for the rigors of the tariffs.
He gave also all foreign merchandise an opportunity of
transit through France. His attention extended to
even the least details for its security. "Take good care,"
he sent word to M. de Sonzy, " to do nothing which can
interfere with or diminish commerce. You did well to
have the clerk of the office at Mortagne arrested for retarding the passage of the charcoal boats ; it is of very
great consequence that merchants should not be annoyed
on any pretext whatsoever. Never decide any case without having heard them. *Rather be a little duped by them*
than to embarrass commerce, because this would annihilate products. Nevertheless, always present the strictness
of the ordinances."

This is how Colbert understood the administration of
the customs. We should be very fortunate to-day if it
were understood in the same manner, in its aim and
its means of execution. As an instrument of protection, he did not separate it from an indefatigable activity in manufactures, and it is easy to see that this
protection was in his view only a temporary measure,
such close watch did he keep lest it should degenerate
into a premium given to carelessness, and into annoyances prejudicial to commerce. One would say he asked
pardon of France for it in all the despatches he addressed
to his ambassadors. He said to his son: "You must
feel as keenly all the disturbances which occur in commerce and all the losses the merchants experience *as if
they were your own.*"

Not content with having established entrepôts in the
ports, he designated them for stopping places for foreign
merchant-vessels, ordering that any duties they should
have paid should be refunded to them, when it suited
their convenience to re-export their merchandise. At
that time the West India Company found itself no

longer in a condition to maintain its exclusive privilege. The colonies were lacking necessary things, and the low price at which their products were taken was driving the inhabitants to despair. Colbert decided to render commerce free, and caused an announcement to be made in all the ports that every person should henceforth have a right to devote himself to it. The more one studies the administrative acts of this great minister, the more one is convinced of his lofty sense of justice, and of the liberal tendencies of his system, which has hitherto been generally extolled as hostile to the principle of commercial liberty. In vain the Italians have hailed it by the name of *Colbertism*, to designate the exclusive system invented by themselves and honored by the Spanish: Colbert never approved the sacrifice of the greater part his fellow citizens to a few privileged ones, nor the creation of endless monopolies* for the profit of certain

---

* M. Henri Baudrillart, in his work on *Jean Bodin and His Times, a representation of the political and economic theories in the 16th century*, a work which throws much light on the beginning of political economy in France, has noted the true historical origin of the prohibitory system in our country. We read there on page 14: "The real sponsor of the prohibitory system in France was the minister of Charles IX, René de Biragues, keeper of the Seals in 1571, and Chancellor of France from the death of L'Hopital to 1578. He was the first one to lay down as a principle the double prohibition against exporting from the country materials suitable for manufacture, and importing the products of foreign manufacture. We will quote the preamble of the edict of January, 1572, on foreign commerce and the regulation of the kingdom: "In order that our said subjects," we read in the the collection of old French laws, vol. xiv, "may better devote themselves to manufacture and working in wools, flax, hemp and yarns, which are increasing and abound in our said kingdoms and countries, and may make and realize the profit from them which foreigners do, who come here and buy them usually at a low price, transport them and work them up, and afterward bring the cloths and linens which they sell at a very high price; we have ordered and do order that it shall hereafter be allowable to no one of our said subjects and foreigners, for any cause or under any pretext whatsoever, to transport out of our said kingdom and country any wools, flax, hemp or yarns. We also very expressly forbid all entrance into this our said kingdom of all cloths, linens, gold or silver laces and ribbons, as well as all velvets, satins, damasks, taffetas, camlets, linens and all sorts of stuffs striped or having in them gold or silver, and likewise all harness for horses, belts, swords and dirks, stirrups and gilded, silvered or engraved spurs, under penalty of confiscation of said merchandise. * * * Besides, we forbid the entrance into our said kingdom and country of any sort of foreign tapestries, of whatever material and fashion they may be, under the same penalties as above." One finds by the side of this, inspired by the same spirit,

branches of industry. We may reproach him with having been excessively inclined to make regulations, but
not with having enfeoffed France to a few spinners of
wool and cotton. He had himself summed up in a few
words his system in the memorial he presented to the
king : " To reduce export duties on provisions and manufactures of the kingdom ; to diminish import duties on
everything which is of use in manufactures ; and to repel
the products of foreign manufactures, by raising the
duties.* "

Such was the spirit of his first tariff, published in September, 1664. He had especially aimed at facilitating
the supply of raw materials in France, and promoting the
interests of her home trade by the abolition of provincial
barriers, and by the establishment of lines of custom-
houses at the extreme frontiers. The opposition he encountered in many localities for a long time paralyzed the
effect of his good intentions ; but with perseverance he
succeeded in making every part of France share the benefit
of his reforms. The only reproach that can be justly
made against him is the abuse of the protective instrument he had just created, by increasing in the tariff of
1667 the exclusive measures directed against foreign
manufactures in that of 1664. It was no longer then a
question of manufactures, but of war, namely, with Holland ; and this war broke out in 1672, after long and unavailing negotiations. The new tariff excluded a quantity
of Dutch goods : on her refusal to admit them, France
immediately saw her own wines, brandies and manufactured products interdicted. Agriculture, already condemned to hard suffering by the prohibition to export
grain, one of the errors of Colbert, experienced a severe
check from the new prohibition, which affected its most
important products. From the same epoch date the first

an edict on the manufacture of cloths (March 2d, 1571) and another (June,
1572) on the regulation of the rate of interest at six per cent. (*Note of
French Editor.*)

    * Forbonnais, *Considérations sur les finances*, vol. ii, page 434.

wars of commercial reprisals between France and England, hostilities which were to cost both nations so much blood and so many tears. Manufactures were then seen to prosper and agriculture to languish in France, under the influence of this system. I know not whether Colbert also feared he would see the population diminish; but he issued in November, 1666, an edict on that subject which is hardly in accord with the theories of Malthus. In virtue of this edict, every head of a family, who was the father of ten children, was exempt from taxes for the remainder of his life. If he was a nobleman, the king granted him a pension of a thousand francs, and two thousand francs, if he had twelve children. The favor of exemption from taxes for five years was extended to young people who married at twenty years; and by way of compensation, a tax was levied upon male celibates of twenty years, even under the paternal roof. At the same time, Colbert endeavored to put a limit to the development of religious communities; private citizens were forbidden to bequeathe to them, or to sell by a sinking fund their inheritances or any kind of property whatsoever. But all these combined were not effective. The measures by which Colbert opened new sources of wealth in the country, were worth more than his premiums of encouragement to the fecundity of noblemen, for he was obliged to renounce the latter in 1683, after they had engendered more abuses than citizens.

The treaty of Nimeguen forced France to renounce the system of exclusions organized by Colbert against foreign manufactures. Each day, each event, thus brought about a modification of what was too absolute in the ideas of this minister; but his prohibitory doctrines had been given to a land where they were to be religiously kept under the auspices of personal interest. The French manufacturers became accustomed to consider as a right the protection which had been accorded them as a favor; and that which, in Colbert's mind, was to be only tempo-

rary, became in their eyes final.   The prodigious industrial development which followed his system, the regulations promulgated to sustain it, and the renown of its author, all contributed to propagate the fatal doctrine of
the natural hostility of manufacturing nations.   Hence
have arisen those expressions now proverbial, though de-
void of sense, of the danger *of becoming tributary to foreigners, of letting our market be invaded by foreign commodities, of allowing our gold to be ravished from us*, and
a thousand others similar, as if all buyers were not tributary to sellers, and the latter in their turn, to buyers; as
if, in short, a people would not receive in exchange for
their commodities the commodities of their neighbors,
unless they gave them gold.   If it were so, there would
be no more commerce; for what trade could there be,
where one was willing neither to let gold be exported,
nor commodities imported? Europe will have to suffer a
long time from this prejudice, which has given birth to
so many wars, and which has thrown all nations into the
dangerous way of having privileged branches of industry.
No, Colbert was not to blame for it, and it is in vain that
some honor his memory and others reproach it, on this
ground: Colbert was a man of exalted probity, an enemy
of all monopolies, and the sternest adversary to privileges
of every kind.   Never would this minister, who already
dreamed of a just distribution of taxes, and who knew
how to tell his master stern truths, have organized from
bottom to top the bad system which some have wished to
baptize with his name.

    We only mention as a memorial the great works he
caused to be constructed to increase the viability of
France, and the Languedoc canal, that fine imitation of
the canal of Briare, which so far distanced its model.   It
is for us to make known the dominant thought of Colbert,
and not the details of his works; and a simple narration
of his economic labors ought to be sufficient to reveal it.
During his whole ministry, Colbert committed no other
errors than those which were imposed upon him, or that

an exaggerated sentiment of love for his country inspired in him in some rare instances. Such were the high duties he established in his tariff of 1667, with the intention of securing to France the production of such articles as she obtained from abroad ; and yet, need we say, this tariff contained no absolute prohibition. Colbert had wisely judged that the prohibition to import was sufficiently represented by the customs, especially when they rise to a certain rate. Then, if manufacturers do not know how or will not, with the high premium which the tariff accords them, gratify the taste of consumers, the latter have still the choice of foreign manufactures, by paying a voluntary tribute from which the state profits, for rejection of home products. This restricted liberty awakens an industrial emulation between different nations, which, on the contrary, national monopoly stifles.* Colbert certainly was far from supposing that, at some future day, after French industry had taken its rank in Europe, his tariff would be judged insufficient and be guarded by prohibitions which he had not found necessary for its protection, when it was only just adopted. It was reserved for our epoch, so justly proud of the progress of its manufactures, to demand at the same time medals to reward them and prohibitions to sustain them. We should be fortunate, in this respect, to go back to Colbert and to return to his tariffs ; more fortunate still, if our ambassadors sometimes received some such famous instructions as he sent to M. de Béziers and to M. de Pompone ! Let people then cease to claim the sanction of Colbert's name for the numerous monopolies with which France is to-day beset. These monopolies are the work of the unhappy times through which the present generation has passed : they are all subsequent to the treaty of 1786, and the issue of the great wars of the revolution and of the empire. Reëstablished as instruments of hatred and of extermination, they ought not to have survived the war : we hope they will not survive peace.

---

* M. Bailly, *Histoire financière de la France.* Vol. i, p. 454.

CHAPTER XXVII.

Political economy under Louis XIV.—Commercial ordinances.—Navigation.—Streams and forests.—Black code.—Councils of prud'hommes.—Poor-laws.—Creation of foundling-hospitals.—Creation of commercial companies.—Opinions of contemporary economists: Vauban, Boisguilbert, the Abbé of Saint-Pierre.

IF, as one of our statesmen * lately wrote, "Laws are always the monuments the most important and the most instructive to the historian," there is no legislation of more interest to the political economist than that of the reign of Louis XIV. We have already made known the dominant thought of the great minister to whom this reign owed so much of its renown; it is time to point out the acts which were its expression, which together compose the finest structure which has been raised by any government to economic science. Alone, in the midst of the ruins of the past, this edifice remains; and it still towers in all its height above our institutions, which have not lost, notwithstanding the shock of revolutions, the impress of its imposing originality. To Colbert belongs the honor of having given a dowry to France, by being the first to comprehend, in their full extent, the resources of production. Sully had wished to keep France within the narrow limits of an exclusively agricultural and patriarchal system; he had opposed with all his power the development of manufactures, and he had seen in commerce only a dangerous opportunity for the exportation of specie. His severe economic policy had been

* M. Thiers, *Law, Encyclopédie Progressive.*

continued under the reign of Louis XIII, by sumptuary laws and ordinances, of a character hostile to progress in wealth. Colbert opened a career for national labor in a regular and judicious manner ; and we cannot question that his legislation preceded by a century at least the theories of modern political economy. Through him, France enlarged her borders and was brought into relation with the world ; she ceased to be exclusively agricultural, and became enriched at the same time by the new value given to her territory and to her inhabitants.

This epoch will forever remain celebrated in the annals of science, because it demonstrated the intimate union between material and social progress. How many kinds of commercial stocks owe their existence to those fine ordinances on navigation, on trade, on manufactures, of which Colbert was the dispenser and the organ! When we study them attentively, it is easy to recognize that they created a formidable rivalry to the landed aristocracy, by giving to all citizens an opportunity to rise to fortune by the influence of labor alone. The forces of the nation were thereby doubled, and Louis XIV was able, during his long reign, to raise our country to the first rank of powers; happy if he had not abused the immense resources accumulated by his minister! Our time, so fertile in hazardous attempts, has nothing which can be compared to the boldness of the creations of that epoch ; one would say that they were all cast at a single heat, with so much judgment were they arranged and directed towards the same end.

The condition of the poor first attracted the attention of the government. While in England they were scourged and mutilated under the draconic laws of Henry VIII, Colbert caused an edict to be issued for the establishment of a house of refuge at Paris, where the needy should be received " as living members of Jesus Christ, and not as useless members of the state." * An-

---

* Edict of April, 1656, in the *Collection of Isambert.* Vol. xvii, p. 326

other edict in June, 1662, ordains that a hospital be
founded in every city and market-town of the kingdom
for the invalid poor, the mendicants and orphans, "who
shall be instructed in the trades for which they are capable of being qualified." Premiums of encouragement
are offered to men who will marry orphans of the asylum
of mercy; the king orders that, in this case, they be
granted the mastership without expense. The ordinances
issued during his reign testify to the constant efforts of
this prince to extirpate from his states the pest of mendicancy, a grave question in every age, and one which
ours has as yet been able to resolve only by imprison-
ments and prosecutions. At the same time, the solicitude of the government was establishing the first houses
for foundlings,* houses which have since then become
more fatal to children than would be utter abandonment;
and our progress is still limited to counting the victims.†

I have told what Colbert had done for manufactures.
He carried too far his mania for making regulations, and
we to-day can scarcely comprehend that excess of penalties for errors in chemistry or mechanics, as if they were
crimes against morals. However, such rigor was perhaps
necessary to success in the industrial arts, as strict rules
are to rising communities; and Colbert compensated for
it by so many benefits that one can hardly reproach him

---

* Edict of June, 1670.

A foundling hospital was established at Paris in 1462, and it is probable
that they existed in the sixth century. Mention is made of them in the
capitularies of the Frankish kings. One is known to have been established
at Milan in 787; at Montpellier, in 1070; at Eimbeck, in 1200: at Rome,
in 1212: at Florence, in 1317, and in Nuremberg, in 1331.—(*Trans.*)

† MacCulloch states that in the foundling hospital, at Dublin, of 12,786
abandoned children, 12,561 died in less than six years, from 1791 to 1797.—
(*Polit. Econ.* p. 232.) (*Author's note.*)

The official report of M. Gasparin, at Paris, in 1837, showed that the in-
fant mortality was appalling there, and that those who survived, constituted
a large proportion of the thieves and prostitutes of the country.

An official report made to the prefect of the Seine in 1857, says: "Of
3,507 infants born and admitted in 1844, 2,659 died before their twelfth
year, a ratio of 75.81 per cent. Also, of 3,573 infants born and admitted
in 1845, 3,700 had died at the end of twelve years, or 75.77 per cent.—
(*Trans.*)

with it.   It seemed to him that discipline in the work-shops was the surest means of defending them against the perils of foreign competition ; and he inflexibly adhered to this position.   Consequently, French products acquired a good reputation throughout Europe, and their supe-riority was soon established in the markets of the world. By its masterpieces, French industry began the brilliant career which it has continued to pursue, and we still live by the glorious traditions of its illustrious founder. Throughout the country, a peculiar and lofty impetus controlled the movements of production, which were disciplined like an army ; and if sometimes individual genius encountered obstacles in the strict conformity of the rules, the mass of the laborers gained much by their promulgation.

Besides, everything was consistent in the general views of Colbert.   His genius protected with a common solici-tude the interests of agriculture, of manufactures, and of commerce.   There lies his true glory ; and while we still discourse on the relative importance of these three ele-ments of public prosperity, he encouraged with equal ar-dor all the branches.   The declaration of January 25, 1671, forbade the seizure of the cattle of the farmers,* as Sully had interdicted the seizure of implements.   The ordinance of July, 1656, prescribed the drainage of the marshes.   A decree of the council, of the 17th of Octo-ber, 1665, favoring the reëstablishment of the studs, laid the foundations of that entirely agricultural institution, from which we should long since have derived good re-sults, if all the administrations had been actuated by the spirit of its author.   Finally, the grand edict on the waters and forests, which cost Colbert eight years of labor, became the basis of our forest code.   But it was not sufficient to remove the natural difficulties in the way of agricultural production ; of what advantage would this

* " He did not wish," says Necker, " that misfortune should be punished by lack of power to repair it."

new fertility have been, deprived of markets for the sale
of the products?

Colbert had thought of the importance of the roads,
and he had them repaired with all the luxury of resources
which the fortune of France permitted. The opening of
the canal between the two seas, the project of the canal
of Bourgogne, and all those bold lines, so understand-
ingly traced since on the map of our country, are striking
testimonials of his solicitude in that regard. His predecessors seemed to have thought only of isolating the
French provinces from each other, and France from the·
rest of Europe; Colbert's system was, to break down
barriers and to multiply transactions. In manufactures,
he created the councils of *prud'hommes;* * in commerce,
he published in succession his declaration † on the *drawing and negotiation of bills of exchange*, and his immortal ordinance of March, 1673, our first commercial code;
but navigation especially owes him the most eminent
services. Before the *navigation ordinance*,‡ which for

---

* *i.e.*, "Mixed councils of master tradesmen and workmen for the decision of disputes between persons of both these classes."—*Sp. and Sur.
Fr. Dic.*

† August, 1669.

‡ January 9th, 1664. I will simply quote the preamble of this ordinance,
to give an idea of the broad and independent manner in which Colbert looked at all questions :

"Louis, etc. After the various ordinances which we have made to regulate by good laws the administration of justice and of our finances, and
after the glorious peace with which it has pleased God to crown our late victories, we have thought that, to complete the happiness of our subjects,
nothing more remained except to procure abundance for them by facilitating
and increasing commerce, which is one of the principal sources of the happiness of nations ; and as that which is carried on by us is the more considerable, we have taken pains to enrich the coasts which surround our
states, with a number of harbors and vessels, for the security and convenience of navigators who now land in all the ports of our kingdom ; but, because it is not less necessary to strengthen commerce by good laws, than to
render it free and convenient by the excellence of the ports and by force of
arms, and because our ordinances, those of our predecessors, and the Roman
law, contain but very few provisions for the decision of the differences which
arise between merchants and seafaring people, we have judged that to leave
nothing to be desired for the good of navigation and commerce, it was
important to fix the hitherto uncertain jurisprudence of maritime contracts,
to regulate the jurisdiction of the officers of the admiralty, and the principal
duties of seafaring men, and to establish a good police in the ports, coasts

the first time settled definitely its essential rules, there was scarcely any maritime commerce in France. Colbert alone gave it impetus and life. The East and West India Companies, worthy rivals of the Hanse towns, were established under his auspices. A colony, a part of La Rochelle, went to people Cayenne ; another took possession of Canada, and laid the foundations of Quebec ; a third became established in Madagascar. The commerce of the Levant received new life, that of the north was opened, and that of the colonies extended. The Senegal Company, first organized as a monopoly, soon beheld its commerce become public property ; and the Black Code * was the first constitutional charter of that unfortunate race which enlightened Europe was one day to set free.

We know not which most to admire, the *ensemble* of that vast economic legislation, or the purity of the considerations on which its decrees were based. Colbert took care to surround himself with all the men versed in the matters to which his vigorous hand was going to bring reform ; he questioned them, listened to their objections, and very often modified his opinions by theirs. He caused a nursery of trees to be planted in the faubourg of Roulers, and established barges on the Seine. He created the receiving-house (petite poste) † and perfected the general post-office ; he deepened the channel of the Marne, and he made of Dunkirk a frée port. Regulations, edicts, declarations, letters-patent, and ordinances, had, in less than twenty years, furnished a solution to all the difficulties raised by commerce in grain, wine, tobacco, and the precious metals. We might say that France had not yet known herself and that the minister of Louis XIV revealed her to herself, so many important works arose in her midst, and so numerous were the fleets which set sail from

and roadsteads which are within the extent of our dominion. For these reasons," etc.

    * March, 1685.

    † May, 1653.

her ports. Although the great Colbert never had occasion to formulate his ideas into a system,* and to publish what in our day is called a programme, it is easy to recognize in him one of the most resolute innovators of which history makes mention. Born from the working class, and having attained by merit alone the highest of honors, he never ceased to work for the amelioration of the fate of the greater number; and the testimony of contemporary writers confirms the opposition he courageously made to the prodigality of Louis XIV.† France had become so beautiful, before this prince had consumed all the resources with which Colbert had enriched her! Never had it been more clearly recognized what the genius of a great people can do, when it is governed by men worthy of comprehending and directing it.

Moreover, even after the reverses which followed the old age of the king, even after the revocation of the Edict of Nantes, France did not descend irretrievably from the elevated position which she had attained. That was doubtless a dreadful blow to her which took away five hundred thousand of her most industrious children, for that cruel loss has never been repaired; but the habits of order and of labor with which they were imbued spread throughout all Europe, and thus the great renovation wrought by Colbert ceased to have the narrow character of nationality which perhaps it would have otherwise maintained. Every nation had a share in the benefits of

---

* See Forbonnais, *Considérations sur les finances de France.* Vol. i, p. 271.

† Colbert expressed himself in strong terms about it to the king himself, in a memorial from which I extract the following :

" In regard to the expense, *although that is no affair of mine,* I simply entreat your majesty to permit me to say that, in war and in peace, your majesty has never consulted his finances to determine his expenses, which is so extraordinary that assuredly there is no precedent for it : and if he would be so kind as to have the present times and past years compared, for the twenty-five years that I have had the honor of serving him, he would find that, although the receipts have greatly increased, the expenses have far exceeded the receipts : and perhaps that would convince your majesty to become more moderate and retrench the excess, and by this means bring about a little better ratio between the receipts and the expenditures."

that statesman : Germany, England, Switzerland and Holland received with our exiles the heritage of our manufactures, and unfortunately that of the exclusive ideas which had prevailed at their establishment. No one suspected that Colbert had only meant to grant to manufactures a provisional protection, to give them time to grow and become consolidated. People sought progress by prohibition, while he desired it by competition ; and prohibition continues still, under forms more or less restrictive, because it is easier to exclude rivals than to surpass them. That is how the system of Colbert became European ; but it was fatal to France only because it exposed her to the reprisals of her neighbors, at the very time when the revocation of the Edict of Nantes left our industry disarmed. Colbert had sown : foreigners reaped.

We cannot attach too much importance to the study of these facts, without which the history of political economy under Louis XIV would be inexplicable. Colbert himself was more than once reduced to undoing his own work by the misfortune of the times and the necessity of meeting the exigencies of events. Money, which his tariffs had aimed to retain in France, went out in millions during the long persecutions of the protestants, and with the latter also went most of our arts, of which they carried the secrets abroad. We thus lost at the same time an immense amount of capital,* and the manufactures which could indemnify us for its loss. From these calamitous times dates the origin of the most brilliant foreign manufactures and that thirst for monopolies which characterizes the mercantile system. There was a brief period when no books were written except those to demonstrate the advantage of monopolizing money and the danger from allowing it to be exported. The Dutch, too, when they had become manufacturers, ardently proclaimed the regime of prohibition, and contemporary writers in Great

---

* Macpherson (*Annals of Commerce*, vol. ii, p. 617) estimates at nearly one hundred millions of francs the metallic wealth imported into England by the refugees.

Britain speak only of the disadvantages of exchange, whenever, in their country, it involved exportations of specie. "The surest means of enriching the nation," wrote Thomas Mun,* " is to sell every year to foreigners more commodities than we consume of theirs." Charles Davenant, Sir Joshua Child and Sir James Steuart, his fellow countrymen, Melon and Forbonnais in France, Genovesi and his school in Italy, and Ustariz in Spain, have maintained the same opinion ; and it is not surprising that all Europe has sanctioned prejudices stamped with a certain color of patriotism.

From the first, however, the irresistible power of principles modified that exclusive tendency of governments in reference to manufactures. Almost all the ruling powers tempered, by commercial treaties, that is to say, by a virtual concession of privileges, the rigor of the new tariffs. One would say that they felt the need of mutually compensating one another for the wrong that the prohibitory system could not but cause them. And already, under Louis XIV, it was not alone upon such questions that controversy was raised : political economy was entering upon higher and more perilous discussions. The prodigalities of the latter part of this reign had brought public misery to its worst. All the resources which the genius of Colbert had created were exhausted. He was himself obliged to have recourse to oppressive expedients to satisfy the exigencies of his master ; and more than once, in the despair of his soul, he had increased taxes against which his heart and his reason equally protested. " Five sous should be saved in unnecessary things," he said to Louis XIV, " and millions expended when the interest or the glory of the country is in question. A useless repast of 3,000 livres gives me incredible pain, but when the question is of raising millions of gold for Poland, I would pledge my wife and children and go on foot all my life to furnish it." Such was the man

---

* *England's Treasure by Foreign Trade,* p. 11.

whose funeral was disturbed by a blinded people and whom it was necessary to bury at Saint-Eustache by night, like a public enemy.

But this noble heritage of franchises was well received after his death, and generous voices were found which dared take up the defence of the principles and of the people. The marshal of Vauban * did not hesitate to speak stern truths, in his "Project of a Royal Tithe." "From all the investigations I have been able to make," said he, "during the many years which I have devoted to them, I have expressly observed that in these latter times, nearly a tenth part of the people are reduced to poverty, and, in fact, to beggary; and that of the nine other parts, five are of those who are not in a condition to give alms to the former, because they are themselves reduced within a very little of the same unfortunate condition; of the four parts which remain, three are in very straightened circumstances, and embarrassed with debts and law-suits; and in the tenth, in which I put all the soldiers, lawyers, ecclesiastics, all the nobility and the men in military and civil offices, the good merchants, the bourgeois who have incomes and are most comfortable, one cannot reckon over one hundred thousand families, and I think I should not be telling a falsehood if I should say that there are not ten thousand of them, small or great, that can be said to be in very easy circumstances."

The marshal of Vauban had been impressed, like Colbert, by the unjust apportionment of the taxes, which was the greatest evil of the time; and he deplored the abuse of privileges in virtue of which the richest classes were exempt from imposts. The idea occurred to him that the revenues, obtained from the people at so great an expense, could be advantageously replaced by one simple, general, and justly apportioned tax on real estate, fixed at one-tenth of the income in kind for the fruits of

* Blanqui recognizes Vauban as the real author of the " Royal Tithe," falsely attributed, he says, to Boisguilbert.

the earth, and in money for other property, and which he called for that reason the *royal tithe*.

We find numerous points of similarity between his economic views and those which Turgot was to make prevail a half-century later. He demanded the suppression of internal customs-duties and the lowering of the tariffs on foreign products; a réduction of a half in the salt-tax and the abolition of indirect taxes, including the ecclesiastical tithe. There were in his project of reform many impracticable ameliorations; but the fundamental maxims on which it was based, do like honor to his judgment and to his heart. "No state," he said, "can sustain itself, if the subjects do not sustain it. Now, this support comprehends all the needs of the state, to which, consequently, all the subjects are under obligation to contribute. From this necessity there results, first, a national obligation for subjects of every condition to contribute in proportion to their income or their business, without any one being reasonably exempt; secondly, that it is sufficient authorization for this tax that one be a subject of this state; thirdly, that every privilege which tends to exemption from this contribution is unjust and abusive, and neither can nor ought to prevail to the detriment of the public."

But not alone on these financial generalities are the superior reason of Vauban * and his ardent love for humanity conspicuous: we find, in the smallest details, the able administrator and the enlightened economist.

It is sufficient to read, in his *Royal Tithe*, the chapter that he devoted to the salt-tax, where considerations the most profound are mingled with the most familiar and popular details. "Salt," according to him, "is a manna *which God has bestowed upon the human race*, and upon which, consequently, it would seem that one ought not to lay a tax." Then he adds: "The high price of salt

---

* The finest analysis of the ideas of Vauban is found in Steuart's *Investigation of the Principles of Polit. Econ.* Book v, chap. ii.—(*Note of Author.*)

makes it so rare, that it causes a sort of famine in the kingdom, deeply felt by the humble who cannot salt meat for their use, for lack of salt. There is no household which cannot support a pig; which, however, is not done, because there is nothing with which to salt it ; they do not even more than half salt their pot, and often not at all." Would not one think, in reading these simple reflections, that he was listening to a writer of antiquity? And yet the book of Vauban is little known, although it contains the principal bases of economic science, whose modern founders we daily glorify.

Another economist, equally forgotten, of the century of Louis XIV, Pierre de Boisguilbert, has traced in the liveliest colors the sufferings and the needs of his contemporaries, in a writing entitled " Detailed account of France under Louis XIV." In it he unreservedly points out the causes of the decline whose symptoms were becoming manifest to all eyes ; and he insists, like Vauban, on the injustice of a bad apportionment of taxes, against which the great Colbert himself had protested in vain. The custom-duties are no more spared in it than in the book of Vauban. "They cause," he said, "nearly the same effects as the *aids*, and still more evil, by banishing foreigners from our ports and obliging them either to go elsewhere for what they came to us to obtain, or to learn our manufactures by attracting away our workmen." The same rectitude of judgment was observable in all the estimates of the condition of France at that time, a deplorable condition, which drew tears from all generous men, and which had impressed with a like disquietude economists and poets, Boisguilbert and Vauban, Fénelon and Racine ! The population was everywhere continually decreasing. "The common people have diminished much in these latter times," said Vauban, "by war, by diseases, and by the poverty of these latter years, which have caused a great number to die of hunger, and reduced many others to beggary."

One cannot, however, deny that the reign of Louis XIV, so much decried, opened the way for reforms important in the history of political economy. Manufactures, strictly organized, gave birth to masterpieces, and doubled our productive forces; commerce rose to a height hitherto unknown, under the control of the fundamental institutions which were to increase its splendor. The wrong of the king lay in expending more money than the taxes furnished him, and preventing the formation of capital which would have completed the work of Colbert. Profits were absorbed before being created, and there was already opening, under the auspices of Louvois, the gulf of the loans which were to change the science of finance and perfect the study of credit. France had become an immense workshop, from which we already see appear the questions of pauperism, notwithstanding the small development of machinery and the obstacles which the system of corporations put in the way of manufactures. The project of the Abbé of St. Pierre for perpetual peace, considered an utopia, contains many acute perceptions on these difficult social questions, and the great *Economist* school of the eighteenth century is already completely revealed in these remarkable words of Boisguilbert: "Although magnificence and abundance are extreme in France, as they exist only among a few private individuals, and the greater part are in the extremest poverty, that fact cannot compensate for the loss which the state experiences for the greater number."*

---

* *Détail de la France sous Louis XIV*, chap. vii, 1st part.

CHAPTER XXVIII.

Propagation of the mercantile system in Europe, under the name of Colbertism.—It is neutralized by contrabandage.—Influence of contrabandage on the solution of economic questions.

IT is an error to regard Colbert as the founder of the *mercantile system:* we have seen that this system, which aims at continual selling without ever buying, came from the Spanish, and was the work of Charles V. It was already obtaining recognition throughout Europe before it had a name; and Colbert was not an advocate of it in the earlier days of his ministry, for all the ordinances of that period were favorable to freedom of trade. It was only when he determined to give an energetic impulse to our manufactures that he reflected on the advantage that might be derived from the prohibition of foreign products. All manufacturers interested in raising the prices of commodities became henceforth his auxiliaries, and ardently took up the defence of a system which assured them immense advantages. At the same time, the public treasury had its share of the duties to which the imported articles were subject, and this alliance contributed also to strengthen public prejudice. No one would have dared disapprove an expedient so happy as to enrich at the same time private citizens and the state.

In fact, the true nature of the damage inflicted on the country by the adoption of this system, was not immediately recognized. Manufactories were seen to spring up on every side, the high price of their products brought considerable profits to the manufacturers, and increased their capital by accumulation. The French manufactures in silks, mirrors, cloths, and carpets no longer knew any rivals, and all Europe had become tributary to them ; but there came a time when foreigners began to employ reprisals and to reject French supplies. To the tariff of 1667 the Dutch responded, in 1671, by the prohibition of French wines and brandies ; and that quarrel, wholly commercial, was nevertheless one of the principal causes of the war of 1672, since it was necessary to moderate the tariffs at the treaty of Nimeguen. However, the contagion had reached all nations, and tariff wars have not ceased to afflict the world since that period.

Another disastrous consequence of the mercantile or restrictive system, was the absolute subjection of laborers to capitalists, and the increase of individual poverty in the presence of general wealth. This terrible contrast has not ceased since then to alarm modern society. An artificial and intense production has taken the place of the regular and quiet labor of previous times ; and by a strange contradiction, governments have restricted the means of selling by limiting the power of buying. The mercantile system originated in the false idea that a nation grows rich by exporting and poor by importing, a fundamental error, the bad consequences of which have been put henceforth beyond doubt by economists of every country. As a simple historian, I will not review the memorable debates which have arisen on that serious question ; it will suffice to recall that the complications of which it is full, owe their origin to the privileges lavishly bestowed by Colbert on French manufactures, and that the manufactures of other nations have, in their turn, had concessions granted to them.

There is reason to think that if Colbert had been better acquainted with the true laws of production, he would have led neither his own country nor Europe into the perilous path which they still pursue. Following the example of the Spanish, this illustrious minister was too much preoccupied with the influence of money, and he did not see that, on the whole, every nation pays with its own products for those it obtains from foreigners, whether the foreigner sends gold or delivers merchandise. He shared the prejudice common * at a period when the recent discovery of the mines of America had procured for their happy possessors a supremacy envied by other nations. It was to obtain her part of the gold distributed in Europe, that France determined to have her accounts settled in specie, in spite of the train of vexations of every kind by which that resolution was to be accompanied.

Never, it must be said, was any paradox received with more enthusiasm than that on which rested the whole theory of the mercantile system. In France, in England, in Germany, in Italy, and in Spain, all the writers were unanimous in lauding the marvels of industrial isolation without considering that this system was destroying itself by becoming general, and that the hope of selling without buying would be lost whenever every nation should wish to force its neighbors to buy without selling. The most learned economists became the propagators of that doctrine, and their number was so great that the mere mention of their writings will occupy several pages of this work.† Administrations were not slow

---

* Don Bernardo de Ulloa has pointed out with great clearness the general error of his countrymen on the subject of metallic wealth :

" When we saw ourselves masters," he says, " of the New World and its mines, we confidently thought this vain title would secure us forever the enjoyment of these treasures ; we seemed to see the nations come to us in humble dependence to seek the superfluous portion of our wealth. Deceived by that flattering chimera and satisfied with the beauty and cheapness of foreign fabrics, we abandoned care for our manufactures : foreigners profited by a negligence so favorable to increase their own, and soon, by this means, took away from us not only all the gold and silver which the Indies had produced for many years, but even our valuable raw materials, which their manufactures could not do without."—*On the Reëstablishment of the Manufactures and Commerce of Spain*, p. 3.

† The French editions of Blanqui have an analytical bibliography at the end of the work.— *Trans.*

in adopting their ideas, which have given rise to all the obstacles waiting for the grand commercial reformation whose dawn we are beginning to discern.   If great private interests have been created under the control of this prejudice, this is not a reason for despairing of the ameliorations imperiously demanded by general interest. "The disbanding of an army," says Adam Smith, "involves also some inconveniencies : must we then remain in a state of perpetual war, for fear of dismissing a few soldiers?"

The mercantile system has lived thus long only because it was, at the outset, clothed with a dogmatic form. Wealth, it was said, is money : with money one commands labor, and furnishes subsistence to laborers. Money is the sinews of war and the source of power. Whoever possesses it, commands those who have it not. All the efforts of a good government must then aim to procure the most possible for the nation ; and as the quantity in each state can only be increased by the exploitation of mines or by importations from without, people must either have mines or get possession of foreign money by export trade.   From the point of view of this system, home trade is of scarcely any importance, because it does not increase the mass of specie, and the result of the exchanges give no favorable balance in coin. What one loses, the other gains, but there is no increase in wealth.   Foreign commerce, on the contrary, presents the immense advantage of an opportunity to settle the transactions in money ; and for this reason they must be so regulated as to export much and import very little. The beau-ideal would be to import nothing at all, but they limited themselves to requiring that a nation should make no other exchanges than those which procure a payment in specie ; and, in this case, they said the balance of trade was favorable to it.

The consequences of this system are easily deduced, so that foreigners may not carry off our gold, we must buy nothing of them to be paid for in coin, and we must sell them all we can so as to have their money. But suppose they take a notion to manufacture in their turn and to do without us ? In this case, we have the resource of prohibiting the export of our raw materials, in order to prevent them from working and to force them to leave us the profits on the manufacture. Such are the necessities of that political economy which involves prohibitions of imports and prohibitions of exports, and favors obstructions and poverty at every point. Unfortunately, *the patent for that fine invention has expired,* to use the expression of Mr. Huskisson. All nations have in turn prohibited the export of raw materials and the import of manufactured articles; they are henceforth obliged to turn back upon themselves and seek a refuge in home trade, after having exhausted all the artifices of treaties and suffered all the reprisals of tariffs. What have they gathered on this battle-field as a trophy of victory ? Pauperism, tariff-wars, commercial crises, a high price for all the products which Providence had scattered, so to speak, along our path. And yet the mercantile system has survived the concert of maledictions with which it was overwhelmed by the *Economists* of the eighteenth century ; it still reigns in our day in the councils of governments, and it maintains under the mask of an interested patriotism all the monopolies from which Europe suffers and of which she complains.

However, it is in the nature of bad institutions never to be respected, and to give birth to protests which end in bringing about reform : *smuggling* was to the exclusive system the most constant and the most expressive of these protests. Smuggling has become in our day a veritable half-commercial, half-military power, which has its leading stations and its official rates, its veteran soldiers and its experienced chiefs. It is as exact in its deliveries as the most scrupulous merchants ; it braves the seasons and defies the best guarded lines of custom-houses, to such a degree that assurance companies which protect it, count upon fewer losses than any others. Smuggling is, in fact, the only means which remains to the various industries to procure for themselves the prohibited products whose use is indispensable to them. It has not ceased to increase with the expansion of general business, and at many places in Europe, it is systematized with truly marvellous skill. It is owing to smuggling that commerce did not perish under the prohibitory régime : while that régime condemned people to supply themselves from the most distant sources, contrabandage made the distances less, lowered prices and neutralized the disastrous action of monopolies. An invisible and constantly renewed competition kept the privileged ones alive and indemnified consumption for the rigor of the tariffs. Although its very existence is an offence to the law, smuggling has nevertheless contributed to the solution of almost all the questions of political economy relative to exchanges. While savants discuss and commerce entreats, contrabandage acts and decides on the frontiers; it presents itself with the irresistible power of actual facts, and freedom of trade has never won a victory for which smuggling has not prepared the way.

If we carefully examine the periods when contraband trade has prospered, we shall be easily convinced that it has always been in the countries and at the times when the mercantile system was in vigor. The Spanish colonies in America were always a centre for it. When Napoleon decreed the continental blockade, Russia, Germany and Holland became covered with smugglers ; the emperor himself was obliged to authorize the fraud by means of licenses, which became an irregular source of so many fortunes. The war of 1812, declared against Russia, originated principally in the opposition of the Russians to the demands of French prohibition; and there was a time when smuggling was the only resource of European commerce. If, in this cursory view of the revolutions of economic science, it were permissible to cite special recent facts, we could easily demonstrate that to contrabandage alone must be attributed the modifications imposed upon the exclusive system. Our manufacturers of muslin obtained the conditional importation of foreign-spun cotton only after having long provided themselves with it by fraud; and our tariffs on horses were moderated only after a public acknowledgment * that the smuggler mounted his merchandise and galloped off with it. How many commodities to-day rare and dear, would have their tariff lowered, if the smuggler could take them on his saddle and cross the boundary with them! A notable perfecting of the fraud would be sufficient to overthrow all the tariffs in the world and oblige each nation to maintain itself by the kind of production peculiar to its soil or to the genius of its inhabitants.

The mercantile system was no more fortunate in its persistent attempts to attract money from foreign countries than in excluding their commodities. In vain, laws prohibited the export of gold under severe penalties: in vain, as in England, governments attempted to make the balance incline in their favor, and published tables of exports greater than those of imports: England did not keep one guinea the more on that account, and she is to-day the country where there is the least specie. Spain, that classic land of prohibitions, has constantly furnished gold to all Europe. Paper-money has driven out coin wherever its presence has diminished the value of coin, in spite of the penalty of death inflicted on the smugglers. The fear of paying for foreign commodities with the precious metals is a vain fear; the precious metals never go from one country to another to pay pretended balances, but to seek the market where they will bring the most. It is always well for us to consume the products which a foreign country furnishes of a better quality

* The acknowledgment was made in one of the sittings of the parliamentary session of 1836.

or at a lower price than our own, and we may rest assured that the foreigner will always be paid in things which we produce more cheaply than he. " I say that he will be paid thus, because it cannot be otherwise." * History is full of the contradictions which events have given to government policy, when the latter has attempted to interfere in the interests of exclusion or of resentment. When Philip II, after having become master of Portugal, determined to forbid his new subjects all communication with the Dutch, the latter, excluded from the entrepôts of Lisbon, where they had been accustomed to provide themselves with merchandise from India, themselves went to the Indies for these goods ; and that which had been done to cause their ruin, was the origin of their greatness. Later, the National Convention of France having prohibited the importation of undressed leathers from Spain, under pretext that they would injure those of our country, the Spanish, obliged to consume their raw leathers, began to tan them themselves, and that business passed into Spain with a good part of the French capital and workmen. The same thing took place in the kingdom of Naples, where the duties increased by us on wools from that country, forced the producers to close to our cloths a market of the highest importance.

The evils of the mercantile system have been convincingly shown by the writers of the *Economist* school, and unanswerably proven by Adam Smith,† J. B. Say,‡ and the most renowned authors. This system is to-day maintained only on account of difficulties which owe their existence to its long continuance. No enlightened man in Europe any longer believes in the marvels of the balance of trade ; but the grave complications to which the system has given rise cannot be resolved without clashing with numerous interests with which the over-scrupulous

---

* J. B. Say.   *Treatise on Polit. Econ.*, vol. i, p. 257.
† *Wealth of Nations.*   Book iv.
‡ *Traité d'Economie Politique.*   Vol. i, p. 218–80.

prudence of governments refuses to interfere. Being intimately connected, besides, with the fiscal receipts, the doctrine of high tariffs finds protectors in the statesmen who fear lest they may compromise at the same time public revenues and private enterprises. It will be by the advance of public credit that the mercantile system will perish; whenever its consequences shall have been carried to their extreme limit, and produced a general obstruction in industries, it will be necessary to return to the system of freedom, which alone can reëstablish an equilibrium between production and consumption.

CHAPTER XXIX.

The first contest between the Mercantile system and Free-Trade, between England and Holland.—Disastrous effects of that contest.—Navigation Act. —Éloquent phillippic of M. d'Hauterive against the Restrictive System.

THERE was a time when, in Europe, the mercantile system and that of free trade came into collision, under the flags of two powerful nations, England and Holland. When the former country defied the latter, the latter had risen to a very high degree of wealth and splendor by the free development of the wealth of its inhabitants and without the aid of any restrictive law. The Dutch presented to the world a striking example of what the genius of a hard-working people can accomplish, when it is seconded by commercial institutions founded on the principle of liberty. Their territory produced scarcely any cereals, and yet scarcity was so unknown among them, that Europe applied to them in her extremity. "Let famine prevail elsewhere," said the author of "The Riches of Holland," "and you will find wheat, rye, and other kinds of grain at Amsterdam: they are never lacking there." By their organization, the Dutch had necessarily become the universal intermediate agent in commerce. Sir William Petty estimated, in 1690, the tonnage of their vessels at more than nine hundred thousand tons, which was nearly half of all the tonnage of Europe; and nevertheless they had no product of their own to export. Their country was the general storehouse for all products of industry, and their ships, as Sir William

Temple said, the carriers of the ocean.   Division of labor was practiced by them with admirable intelligence;
not only merchants, but entire cities, were exclusively occupied with one single branch of commerce.   Middelburg,
for example, carried on the trade in wines; Flushing,
that with the West Indies; Saardam was peopled with
ship-builders; Sluys, with fishers of herrings.   In each of
these branches, there existed an active competition, and
all were conducted with an ability and economy worthy
to serve as a model.   When, after the treaty of Aix-la-
Chapelle, the stadtholder made a sort of investigation for
the purpose of learning the useful projects which could
be proposed to him by his fellow-citizens, the experienced
business men whom he consulted classed in the first
rank among the causes of the former prosperity of Holland, the maxims of toleration, that is to say, of political
and commercial freedom, which the confederation had
made their law.   If, later, that country descended from
the high position to which that liberal policy had raised
it, we must attribute it only to the introduction of monopolies, notably that of the India companies, which
became the most shameful source of abuses, I might almost say, a nursery of crimes.

It was then that England undertook to oppose the
prosperity of the Dutch by her famous *Navigation Act*,
which secured for English vessels the monopoly of transportation, by absolute prohibitions in certain cases, and
by heavy fines in others, on foreign navigation.   All vessels, of which the proprietors, masters, and three-fourths
of the crew, were not English subjects, were forbidden to
trade in the establishments and colonies of Great Britain,
or to carry on a coasting trade along her coasts, under
penalty of confiscation of vessel and cargo.   Other restrictive measures completed this system of exclusion,
from which arose the most fiercely contested maritime
war of which history makes mention.   France played
her part in it against the Dutch by the announcement

of the tariff·of 1664; and from that time the most enlightened nations of Europe have constantly vied in their
efforts to injure one another, instead of trading together
on loyal bases. These reciprocal hindrances have nearly
annihilated all regular trade on a large scale between
them, and put into the hands of smugglers the principal
part of the importation of English merchandise into
France, and of French merchandise into England. Commerce, long given over to the monopoly of privileged
companies, has degenerated since then into exactions
and rapine of every species. Thus our fathers saw three
great companies dispute with each other by most violent
measures the spice-trade of the Indies. The Dutch with
sacrilegious harshness destroyed the clove trees of the
Moluccas, to prevent their rivals from sharing in the
crops. The sole idea which preoccupied these companies was to exclude competition, to grasp for themselves the monopoly of certain articles, and to limit the
supplies of them, so as to raise the price enormously
high. If any one wishes a striking proof of the ruinous
influence of this system and of its tendency to restrict
the natural limits of the field of commerce, he will find
it in the fact that American merchants who trade freely
to-day with the possessions of the Netherlands, in the
Eastern archipelago, employ more ships than did the
Dutch monopolists. The recent abolition* of the privilege of the English East-India Company has nevertheless contributed to increase the relations of England with
the peninsula of Hindustan. One simple fishing station
has become, under the influence of free trade, an establishment of the first order, in less than twenty years.

Wherever the principle of liberty has had a struggle
with that of monopoly, the same results have been manifest. It is vain to pretend that the Navigation Act was
the source of the industrial development of Great Britain:
that act can be considered only as a sacrifice imposed on

---

* 1833 was the year when the trading privileges were taken away. *Trans.*

commerce, in favor of policy. Adam Smith justified it only on this ground ;* and yet to-day we may doubt, looking at the definite results of its adoption, whether that act was a work of wise policy. The principal result of its vigorous enforcement was to daily reduce more the trade of England with other European nations, and to oblige that empire to seek in its colonies markets which the exclusion of foreigners had made it lose among them. The fortune of Great Britain began from that time to rest on artificial bases; it was necessary for her to maintain considerable fleets to protect distant settlements, whose independence continually threatened to strike at the heart of her industries, which had become accustomed to the system of monopolies. Hardly ten years ago, Mr. Huskisson pointed out in parliament these dangerous probabilities; and still neither England nor Europe are yet cured of the pernicious doctrines of Charles V.† These doctrines accustomed nations to

---

* " As defence is of much more importance than opulence, the navigation act is, perhaps, the wisest of all the commercial regulations of England." *Wealth of Nations*, Book iv, chap. ii.

† The great commercial revolution which took place in England under the influence of the Free Trade League has carried away also the Navigation Act, at least in its essential features. We borrow from an article by M. Henri Baudrillart, inserted in the *Dictionnaire du Commerce et des Marchandises* (Guillaumin, 1859) the history of the gradual modifications which ended by the entire abolition of that famous act :

" For more than 130 years, the Navigation Act subsisted without sensible alteration. The independence of the colonies of North America gave it the first blow. Henceforth separated from the parent state, North America could no longer claim to trade with British ports in virtue of its old colonial privileges ; and on the other hand, the act formally excluded, in the trade with America, any foreign flag. It was impossible, however, that the new state should remain under the ban of such an exclusion ; never would it have consented to abandon to English ships all the carrying trade ; the Navigation Act was therefore obliged to yield. After quite long negotiations between the United States and England, in which various systems were proposed and debated, it was agreed that the vessels of the new state, although coming from America, should be admitted, against the tenor of the law, to the ports of Great Britain, on the same conditions as those of the old established states of Europe. Later similar relaxations were allowed in favor of the former Spanish and Portuguese colonies of South America, as fast as they became independent of their mother countries, as well as in favor of the black republic of Hayti. Moreover, the English Antilles, which were accustomed, in case of pressing need, to count upon supplies from the North American colonies, found themselves, in consequence of the separation of the United States from Great Britain, unexpectedly left unprovided for ;

consider as useful measures all those which presented a character of hostility to their neighbors ; they made pass into all codes a new law of nations, in virtue of which the good of each seemed to have for its principal element the evil of some other. Whatever revolutions have since agitated the world, this fatal prepossession has remained the same, during the war of the United States of America, during the French Revolution, after the emancipation of the Spanish colonies, after that of Greece, and even after the conquest of Algiers. In vain have privileged companies perished, one after another ; in vain monopoly has brutalized and decimated the population of South America, while in North America freedom has enriched them and multiplied them tenfold : the mercantile system pursues its ravages and receives from the most advanced governments only weak and ill-

---

it was then necessary to allow, in their interest, new derogations from the Navigation Act. It thus became gradually broadened and moderated by the concessions of commercial treaties founded on the principle of reciprocity, until its entire suppression in 1849.

"It is not for us to recount in detail the history of these successive derogations from the primitive act of Cromwell, which were wrung from British policy by the force of circumstances. * * * The incessant tariff laws between North America and England after 1792, the time when the United States, not being able to obtain from its mother country the adoption of the principle of reciprocity, made its congress adopt a Navigation Act corresponding in certain respects with the English act, although more elastic. as it authorized the government to suspend its effects whenever arrangements concluded with other nations should require ; these tariff-laws, we say, ended in 1815, at the conclusion of a treaty of commerce and navigation founded this time on the principle of reciprocity and equality of rights. An analogous treaty was concluded in 1823 with Prussia, not without a strong repugnance on the part or the English government and people, who consented to it only under the influence of demands which were taking a threatening form, and which tended to become general. A first amendment of the navigation act in 1825, under the ministry of Mr. Huskisson, who inaugurated the tariff reform, and a second amendment in 1845, under the ministry of Robert Peel, who was to complete that reform, added so many exceptions to the principal clauses of the Navigation Act, that it had almost disappeared, while seeming, on account of the pains taken to respect its primitive form, to subsist as in its finest days, To Lord John Russell belongs the honor of having triumphed over the last opposition of a traditional attachment, and having called forth the repeal of the act itself. Some of the restrictions it contained still exist, it is true, in the executory law of Jan. 1, 1850, which has taken its place ; but the object of the English government in obtaining them was to take away the occasion for new facilities for smuggling, rather than to act with a view to protection. Thus the restrictions in everything concerning coasting trade, and those concerning

directed blows. "The theory of prohibitory laws," says M. Hauterive,* "is written in letters of blood in the history of all the wars which for four centuries have everywhere brought industry into conflict with power; which oppress the one, corrupt the other, degrade political morals, infect social morals and devour human kind. The colonial system, slavery, the hatreds born of avarice, called commercial wars, have caused a flood of errors to issue from that Pandora's box;—false maxims; excessive, corrupting and badly distributed wealth; poverty, ignorance and crimes, which have made of human society, at some epochs in the history of modern nations, a picture so odious that one dare not stop to gaze at it, for fear of having to pronounce against the development of industries and the progress even of civilization."

---

* *Elements of Polit. Econ.*, p. 199.

inter-colonial trade are maintained, except the special authorizations, and finally those which relate to the formation of English crews."

With the prohibitory and restrictive laws fell also the colonial system. In the session of the House of Commons, on the February 8, 1850, Lord John Russell thus expressed the new principles which were henceforth to guide the conduct of Great Britain in regard to her colonies; "In what concerns our commercial policy, the entire system of monopoly is no more. The only precaution that we have henceforth to take, is, that our colonies grant no privilege to one nation to the detriment of another, and that they impose no duties on our products sufficiently high to be equivalent to a prohibition. I think we have a right to make that demand in return for the security we afford them." * * * "We ought not to attempt to go back, in any respect, from that decision" (referring to the substitution of free-trade for monopoly. — *Tr.*), "but that you shall trade with your colonies on the principle that you are at liberty to obtain productions from other countries, where they may produce better or cheaper than in the colonies, and that the colonies should be at liberty to trade with all ports of the world, in the manner which may seem to them most advantageous. That, I say, must in future be a cardinal point of our policy.

"In conformity with the policy on which you have governed your British North American colonies, you should, as far as possible, proceed upon the principle of introducing and maintaining political freedom in all your colonies. I think whenever you say political freedom cannot be introduced, you are bound to show the reasons for the exemption, and to show that the people are a race among whom it is impossible to carry out free institutions—that you must show that the colony is not formed of British people, or even that there is no such admixture of British population, as to make it safe to introduce representative institutions. Unless you can show that, I think the general rule would be that you should send to the different parts of the world, and maintain in your different colonies, men of the British race, and capable of governing themselves; men whom you tell they shall have the full liberty of governing themselves : and that while you are their repre-

However, in spite of this sombre picture, the prohibitory system carried in itself the germs of a renovation which has greatly diminished its disastrous effects. The incontestable impetus which it gave to production, in England, France and Holland, especially at the beginning, contributed much to raise the rate of profits in all the protected branches of industry, and made immense amounts of capital flow in, which also soon became insufficient. Consequently the bank of Holland and the bank of England were called to provide by credit for the daily increasing needs of the industry and commerce of the two countries. The fortune of these banks is intimately connected with the Navigation Act and with the establishment of manufactures,* and it is explained in a

---

* " The act establishing the Bank of England (July 27, 1694) is thus entitled in the primitive charter of concession : *An act for granting to their majesties several duties upon tonnage of ships and vessels, and upon beer, ale and other liquors, for securing certain recompences and advantages in the said act mentioned, to such persons as shall voluntarily advance the sum of fifteen hundred thousand pounds, towards carrying on the war with France."* Gilbart, *History of Banking*, p. 27.

sentative, with respect to all foreign concerns, you wish to interfere no farther in their domestic concerns than may be clearly and decidedly necessary to prevent a conflict in the colony itself.

" I believe these are the sound principles on which we ought to proceed. I am sure, at least, they are the principles on which the present government intends to proceed. * * * I believe not only that you may proceed on those principles without any danger for the present, but there may be questions arising hereafter, which you may solve, without any danger of such an unhappy conflict as that which took place with what are now the United States of America. On looking back at the origin of that unhappy conflict, I cannot but think that it was not a single error or a single blunder which got us into that contest, but a series of repeated errors and repeated blunders —of a policy asserted, and then retracted—again asserted, and then concessions made when they were too late,—and of obstinacy when it was unreasonable. I believe it was by such a course we entered into the unhappy contest with what were, at its commencement, the loyal provinces of North America. I trust we shall never again have to deplore such a contest. I anticipate indeed, with others, that some of the colonies may so grow in population and wealth that they may say : " Our strength is sufficient to enable us to be independent of England. The link is now become onerous to us ; the time is come when we think we can, in amity and alliance with England, maintain our independence." I do not think the time is yet approaching, but let us make them as far as possible, fit to govern themselves ; let us give them as far as we can the capacity of ruling their own affairs ; let them increase in wealth and population, and whatever may happen, we of this great empire shall have the consolation of saying that we have contributed to the happiness of the world."

One may consult on this great economic revolution, RICHELOT, *Histoire de la Reforme Commerciale en Angleterre*, 1855.—*French Editor.*

natural manner by the advantages which resulted from them for the companies, which, sheltered by credit, were in a position to defy the slowness of the return voyages from the two Indies. It was also from credit that Louis XIV, when dying, demanded a reparation of the errors and prodigalities of his reign, which engendered, as every one knows, the system of Law.

CHAPTER XXX.

FEW revolutions have exercised such an influence on the course of civilization as that of the foundation of credit in Europe. This was a new conquest of the genius of man, and an immense force added to all those at his disposal. Whence came that force? By what combination of circumstances did it manifest itself, at the very moment when it seemed as though the discovery of the mines of America would render it superfluous? How, after so many benefits, did it become so fecund in catastrophes that enlightened minds even went so far as to curse its existence? Its real source is lost in the night of time. We know that there were bankers at Rome and at Athens, that there were such also in the middle ages, and that public banks were founded, in 1157 at Venice, in 1349 at Barcelona, at Genoa in 1407, at Amsterdam in 1609, at Hamburg in 1619, and in 1694 in England. Such are the facts and the dates: it remains for us to explain them.

The first effect of the discovery of the New World was to give a truly feverish impulse to speculations in America. Capital, attracted by the allurement of enormous profits, flowed toward speculative commerce, to the detriment of many other branches of industry, more useful, and above all, less venturesome. Raw materials hitherto unknown, such as sugar, cotton, tobacco, and spices, entered into consumption and became the objects of an immense trade. Numerous ships set sail from all the ports of Europe, to return with rich cargoes; but it was necessary to await their return in order to reap the profits, and the length of the voyages necessitated considerable advances. Hence the first banks were all established in maritime cities. Later, the prohibitory system, by calling toward manufactures a part of the capital which had been devoted to foreign trade, caused the necessity of credit to be daily more felt, and new banks sprung up from the needs of labor.

Nothing is more simple and more ingenious than the fundamental principle of these banks, the establishment of which separates ancient from modern political economy, as two very distinct epochs. Among the ancients, production had no resources but in the labor of slaves and the capital of money-lenders ; among moderns, it had for support freedom of the workman and the facilities of credit. As soon as it was perceived that the money which merchants were obliged to keep on hand to meet their payments, was, while in their hands, unproductive capital, people reflected how they could make it productive, by substituting the promise for the money and creating banks. "The gold and silver money which circulates in any country," said Adam Smith * on this subject, "may very properly be compared to a highway, which, while it circulates and carries to market all the grass and corn of the country, produces itself not a single pile of either. The judicious operations of banking, by providing—if I may be allowed so violent a metaphor—a sort of wagon-way through the air, enable the country to convert, as it were, a great part of its highways into good pastures and corn-fields, and thereby to increase very considerably the annual produce of its land and labor. The commerce and industry of the country, however, it must be acknowl-

* *Wealth of Nations*, Book ii, chap. 2.

edged, though they may be somewhat augmented, cannot
be altogether so secure, when they are thus, as it were,
suspended upon the Dædalian wings of paper money, as
when they travel about on the solid ground of gold and
silver."

This passage from Smith characterizes in an exact and
picturesque manner the true properties of credit. But
the first banks of Europe did not risk a flight on Dædalian
wings, and their timid attempts were far removed from
the hazardous operations of the banks of our day. They
modestly called themselves banks of deposit, and their
coffers always contained in specie, sums equal to the
amount of their notes. These notes were only certificates
transferable by indorsement, like our bills of exchange,
and they presented at first no other advantage than
economy in the transportation of specie. Each paper
florin had its guaranty in coin ; only, the coins were of a
certified weight and fineness, so as to relieve the holders of
commercial paper of all uncertainty, and to give the bank-
money a stability which should render it superior to any
other. In vain the neighboring states altered their money
or allowed themselves to be invaded by depreciated coin :
the simple stipulation of payment in an order or *transfer*
on the bank of deposit protected by the state, secured to
this standard a decided superiority, and soon all payments
were stipulated to be made in bank-money. However, the
certificates of deposit were limited by the amount of the
sums paid in, and the circulation, in being made by means
of paper, had only the advantage of being more convenient
and more speedy.

The Bank of Amsterdam was the first one based on
this simple regulation ; for what we know of the
Bank of Venice and that of Genoa does not permit a
doubt that these banks were anything but great administrative agents of the government for the collection of its
revenues. The spirit which ruled at the foundation of
the bank of Amsterdam was entirely different. The

able business men who originated it, had wisely considered that every saving in the expense of maintaining the *fixed* capital of a country is a source of advantage to its revenue. Now, everything that is not retained
in this immovable capital, belongs to the *circulating* capital, which provides raw materials and the wages of labor,
and gives activity to all branches of industry. The substitution of paper for gold and silver money, was one
way of substituting a more simple and economical commercial instrument for an extremely expensive one. This
advantage would be the first to impress merchants as
intelligent as those of Amsterdam ; but it was not the
only one which the organization of the bank from which
they were to derive so large profits, offered them. Holland was then flooded with a great quantity of foreign
money, worn down and clipped, which her extensive trade
brought in from all the countries of Europe, and which
had reduced the value of current money to nine per cent.
below good new coin. Besides, the latter was melted
and exported as soon as it appeared in circulation, and
traders knew not where to obtain specie to pay their
bills of exchange, the value of which became from day
to day more variable, to the great detriment of their interests.

This was the first object of solicitude to the founders
of the establishment. The bank only received good or
bad foreign coins and the coins of the country itself
according to their intrinsic value, and it decided to exchange them for good standard money, by simply deduct-
ing the expense of coinage and of management. The
bank-money from this time obtained a marked favor over
current money, and this circumstance considerably increased the demand for the bills. The city of Amsterdam was responsible for their payment, and the facilities
which the employment of these notes afforded to commerce, raised their price sensibly above their real * value.

* *i.e., par* value.   Blanqui seems to have shared the common belief that

However, this superiority was recognized only in so far as the corresponding coin remained on deposit in the coffers of the bank, from which, besides, one could withdraw it only at a disadvantage, since it was necessary to pay a certain sum for the expense of guarding, or rather of withdrawing it. Later, the bank gave credit on its books, in exchange for deposits of gold and silver bullion, and this contrivance added new facilities to those which its bills of credit already presented. We readily perceive that, as the value of these bills depended entirely on the presence of the coin given in exchange, it was necessary for the bank to carefully guard its coffers and for the government to be able to resist taking supplies from them in time of need. Hence, the direction of the establishment was entrusted to four magistrates, renewed every year, who, under oath, verified the condition of the treasury on entering upon their official duties, and compared it with the condition of the books. It is a fact generally known, that when, at the approach of the French, in 1672, the bank decided to have the amount of the deposits distributed to the parties having claims, the specie taken from its vaults still bore the traces of a fire which had broken out some years previously. Public and private credit began thus to be founded on confidence; and we should honor the men who gave this noble example to modern associations. Economic science had now taken an immense step. It was demonstrated that metallic money was unnecessary in order to develop industry and commerce, since a few millions of flying leaves sufficed to take its place in all transactions. Credit thus became truly capital in the hands of the workers and prepared the way for their emancipation, by investing them with a sort of unlimited property, the most respectable of all, because it is founded on the ser-

there is such a thing as *intrinsic* value. On "Error of the expression Intrinsic Value," see H. D. Macleod, *Economical Philosophy*, vol. i, chap. v, § 2. (Longmans & Co., London.) *Trans.*

vice of labor and respect for engagements. Nothing will henceforth arrest the effect of human intelligence, as in the unhappy times of Roman usury and feudal servitude; and history, far from contradicting the theories of political economy, will only confirm them each day.

The Bank of Amsterdam and the other banks of deposit established on a similar basis, were, however, only a first attempt in the ways of credit. They undoubtedly gave to gold and silver a more active power of circulation, under the form of transferable certificates; but, except the profit resulting from the *agio* (premium on the bills.—*Trans.*), the value of monetary capital was not augmented by its transformation into bills of credit. Europe remained with the simple resource of its money, augmented by all the gold and silver imported from America; but this was insufficient to respond to the demands of production which this new element of wealth had called forth. A great step had been taken; a still greater was needed, and the banks of deposit became banks of circulation. Since the certificates of the former were accepted as money, by reason of the confidence had in the guaranty of the deposits, why might not that confidence be carried a little farther, by increasing the number of bills to a sum greater than the amount of the deposits? What disadvantage could result for the holders of these effects, who were certain of being paid in specie whenever they manifested such a disposition? Did not one see every day the notes of a banker circulate with all the privileges of money, even to bearing interest like money itself?

All that was needed was to determine, by sure calculations, what, on a given amount of business, would be the quantity of notes presented for redemption, in order to have always on hand the sum of money necessary to meet them. Any economy, however small, in the reserve funds, became an advantage to labor, and might serve to give support to new manufactures. It could be exported, if people were so disposed, to increase the capital devoted to foreign commerce. It was as if the general wealth of the country had been increased by so much at the cost only of the printing or the engraving of the bills which were substituted for the silver. Here the perfect justness of the comparison of credit to the wings of Icarus, so poetically conceived by Adam Smith, begins to be manifest. No one can affirm the ratio that exists between the sum of money in circulation in a country and the total value of the annual product which it puts in circulation. Ought the banks of circulation to reserve a third, a fourth, a fifth, or a half of their capital in specie, in order to be always ready to redeem whatever part of their issues should be presented for conversion into coin? Was there not perpetual danger of being confronted by continual calls for redemption? For it is principally by discounting bills of exchange, that is to say, by advancing money on that security, that banks issue their bills. The profits consist in the interest on these bills until the maturity of the bills of exchange. The payment alone brings a return to the bank of the advances which it has made, with the profit of the interest it has previously deducted. What would happen, then, if, after having given its notes in exchange for commercial bills, these effects were not paid at maturity! What resource would remain for the holders of notes of the bank, if the security of its creditors perished in its hands?

From this point of view, especially, banks of circulation are far from presenting the same ground of security as banks of deposit. They render more services than the latter; but they offer fewer guaranties. Their directors do not know how to guard against the natural tendency to discount, that is to say, to realize an assured, immediate and palpable profit, by means of a simple bill which is only a promise. Most banks have been ruined by the abuse of their peculiar principle, and on account of not having taken sufficiently into calculation, that, by multiplying their discounts, they exposed themselves to the loss of their reserves. Adam Smith, James Steuart, J. B. Say, and M. Storch, and especially M. de Sismondi have explained, in the clearest and most admirable manner, all the complications which can result, either to the public or the banks, from errors of calculation or of avidity in their stockholders. They have completely demonstrated that every excessive issue of notes obliged these establishments to hoard money in so much the greater proportion as the uneasiness of the holders made the run on the banks greater. The necessity of purchasing specie, in such cases, imposed on the banks sacrifices greater than the profit they had realized from the discounts, and they were often compelled to call back from foreign countries, at great expense, the money whose exportation had been caused by their excessive issues. Europe has witnessed memorable examples of these crises of the circulation, within a century: the suspension of payments by the bank of England and the ruin of the provincial banks in that country, to say nothing of the system of Law, and later of the assignats, in ours; an immense revolution, which we will study by itself, because of the sober instruction its history furnishes.

Meanwhile, credit has survived all these tempests, like the gunpowder which opens ways through the heart even of rocks, in spite of the perils connected with its use. When one to-day compares the circulation of paper with that of specie, he is convinced that credit has wrought a profound revolution in the relations of peoples. Every day reveals to us new materials which production takes hold of by means of credit, and which credit alone permits to be sent to the ends of the earth. The colossal enterprises of which our century opens the career, the spirit of association which extends like a net-work over the face of Europe, the struggle everywhere going on between civilization and the relics of barbarism, are wholly the work of credit; all come from that idea so fecund and so simple which gave birth to banks of circulation and principally to the Bank of England. Every man has, since that time, been able to carry his head high with the pride which the hope of an honorable independence gives. Landed proprietors have seen the workshops of industry rise by the side of their castles; the seas are covered with ships, and foreign shores with European colonies. Everything has advanced with rapid pace, and the world has made more progress within two hundred years than it did in the previous ten centuries. History bears evidence that this power of credit will henceforth decide finally the great contests of the world; as witness Holland, which at last humiliated Louis XIV, and England, which sent Napoleon to die at St. Helena.

The beginnings of this power were, however, very modest, even in England, where the first bank of circulation seemed at its commencement to be modeled after those of Venice and Genoa, and was, for a long time, only a department of the treasury. In 1694, it lent its entire capital to the government and required from it interest at eight per cent.; then, in 1696, doubled this very capital; and lent it again, in 1708, after having doubled it a second time. In vain its shares lose half their value; in vain its bills suffer a depreciation of 20 per cent, and temporarily cease to be paid: people never grow weary of subscribing to new shares, in spite of the enormous depression of the former, because it is the state which is the principal debtor of the bank, and because the influence of the national guaranty already makes itself felt on the public loans. People soon comprehend the importance of such a solidarity, and the public confidence attaches itself to the fortune of the state as to the best anchor of safety. The Bank of England has made, since that period, great mistakes, and even one day, in 1797, ventured totally to suspend its payments in specie, without losing at all its importance, notwithstanding that declared failure. The nation ratified the decision

of parliament which authorized bankruptcy, and the bank-
bills, having become paper-money, veritable assignats,
continued to circulate as if they were still redeemable in
coin. The government received them in payment of taxes,
and those were exempt from imprisonment for debt
who discharged their obligations by means of them. One
would suppose that from this time these notes would
have multiplied beyond measure; but the acts* of parliament, and the public prudence restricted their issue to
wise limits, and England was able for twenty years to do
without the larger part of her specie, without ceasing
to be the foremost commercial nation in the world."

Finally, the famous act of Mr. Peel brought about the
resumption of specie payments, towards the latter part
of the year 1819," and five years after, in 1824, it has been
estimated there were seven hundred companies† organized or near being so, with a capital of ten milliards, a
fourth of which were established, in 1827, with two milliards five hundred millions. In this short space of time,
Great Britain had lent to foreigners one milliard two
hundred and fifty millions of francs. Such are the marvelous effects of credit‡ and its influence on the develop-

---

* No limit upon the issue of notes by the Bank of England was prescribed
by Parliament during the suspension of specie payments. *Trans.*

† v. "*A complete view of the joint-stock companies formed during the years*
1824 *and* 1825," by Henry English.

‡ I have been obliged to confine myself to briefly indicating here the
revolution wrought in Europe by the establishment of banks of deposit and
circulation, and the principal bases on which these banks were founded. All
the details of their organization have been fully explained in Adam Smith's
Wealth of Nations, Book ii, chap. 2, and Book iv, chap. 3; in the 4th
book of Steuart's *Investigation of the Prin. of Polit. Econ.*, and in M. de
Sismondi's *New Principles of Political Economy*, vol. ii, the latter a declared enemy of banks; these are the three authors to be read in preference
on this important subject. M. Storch, J. B. Say, Malthus, and Ricardo
himself, must have borrowed from them, especially the two former, the fine
analyses they have given of the functions of banks. To any one who desires to go deeply into the subject, " *The History of Banks*," by Mr. Gil-
bàrt: the famous pamphlet of Cobbett, entitled, "*Paper against Gold*," a
true masterpiece of dialectics and financial clearness; the work of Mr.
Thornton, "*An Inquiry into Public Credit;*" and the public investigation by
the parliament of England on the occasion of the renewal of the privilege
of the bank, are indispensable documents to consult. The whole science of
credit is there. One may also consult, but reservedly, the work of Mr.

ment of production, that, notwithstanding these considerable exportations of money and the enormous capital
engaged in mining enterprises, lighting, steam-boats, spinning mills and forges, England still finds, in our day,
means to devote five or six hundred millions to her railroads. She directs the works of peace with as much
energy as she prosecuted, twenty-five years ago, the works.
of war. And yet England is the European country which
has the least metallic money, so that, there at least, one
might believe that economic adage of Ricardo: "Money
has arrived at the maximum of perfection, when it is in
the condition of paper." I do not explain, I relate; before believing Ricardo, let us see what Law attempted.

Joseph de Welz, entitled : *La magia del credito svelata* (*i.e.*, The Magic of
Credit revealed.) 2 vols. in 4to, Naples, 1824.—*Note of the Author.*

To these works may be added the *Traité théorique et pratique des opérations de banque de M. Courcelle Seneuil*, 3d edit. 1857, and *Du Credit et des
Banques*, by Ch. Coquelin, 2d edit. 1859.—*Note of French Editor.*

The Theory and Practice of Banking, by H. D. Macleod, and *Elements
of Banking*, by the same author (Longmans, Green & Co., London, 1876),
are excellent works on banking.—*Trans.*

CHAPTER XXXI.

The system of Law.—The circumstances which gave rise to it.—Principal causes of its failure.—Its influence on the course of political economy.

At the commencement of the eighteenth century, a
profound change had been wrought in the political economy of Europe. The extraordinary expansion of foreign
trade and the establishment of the restrictive system had
concentrated capital on navigation and manufactures.
We might say that the earth had been abandoned as a
sterile element, and there was no longer any talk save
of privileged companies, for trade either in the East- or
the West-Indies, or for the manufacture of cloths, carpets, or glass. All funds were soon employed in these
enterprises, because of the favor and profits which monopoly assured to them. Every nation, moreover,
thought that by entering upon the way of tariffs, it
would protect its products against the competition of its
neighbors, and find its elevation in their downfall:
Spain, by means of prohibitions; England, by excluding
foreign vessels; France, by imposing upon them differential duties. All the benevolent habits of reciprocity
had given way to repellent measures, the very image of
war in the midst of peace.

To complete the misfortune, wars too real arose from
these pernicious doctrines, of which the *Navigation Act*
and the tariff of 1664 were only the prelude. To the internal injury which nations did to themselves by the
abuse of the protective system, were soon added the

frightful evils which resulted from an open struggle,
maintained with equal intensity on either side. We
have seen what the competition of England and Holland
produced in this way, and by what catastrophes the last
years of the reign of Louis XIV were disturbed. The
finances of all nations were exhausted; there was no
longer any capital to carry forward the war, nor to restore
manufactures. One nation alone, in the midst of these
disasters, had preserved a proud and indomitable attitude, as later did the English before Napoleon: this
was the Dutch; and they had found resources, next to
their patriotism, only in their credit. We have shown
what intelligent views directed the foundation and the
rapid development of the bank of Amsterdam, notwithstanding the limit imposed on its issues of notes by the
necessity of possessing an equivalent capital in specie.
Soon the banks of circulation, and especially the bank of
England, gave a more active impulse to all industries,
and labor entered upon a new era.

France alone, among these great nations, had remained
behind; and her badly-inspired government had given itself over to the excesses of the *Revocation*, while England
and Holland, under the auspices of credit, gave birth to
marvels. Vauban and Boisguilbert have described in
pathetic terms the sad diminution of the productive
power of France in these deplorable times. " *There only
remained to them eyes to weep*," said they of our fathers;
and we are compelled to believe in the reality of their
misfortunes, confirmed by such high testimony. It was
in this condition that Louis XIV left our country at his
death. Up to the last moment, his ministry had lived
by miserable expedients. It had been reduced to multiplying ridiculous offices in order to obtain money from
the new titularies; and while England and Holland were
borrowing at three or four per cent, the farmers of the
revenue made the king of France pay ten, twenty, and
even fifty per cent for money. The enormity of the

taxes had exhausted the rural districts, which were deprived of their laborers in consequence of the demands of war; commerce had become almost null; manufactures, decimated by the proscription of the protestants, seemed condemned to lose all the conquests due to the genius of Colbert.

Such was the situation of France when Louis XIV died. The public debt amounted then to more than three milliards, and bankruptcy seemed imminent. It was even proposed to the regent, who nobly rejected the proposition, and set himself about establishing a commission, (the famous commission of the *visa*), to examine the validity of the claims of the various creditors of the state. It was at this time that John Law made the proposition of a bank of circulation and discount, and laid the first foundations of credit in our country. We shall be obliged to set forth, at some length, the ideas, so high and so long misunderstood, of this celebrated man, who committed the error common to all men of his stamp, of being right a hundred years too soon, and of dying without being comprehended. His early youth had been adventurous, but occupied with special studies on public credit in England and Holland, at the source of large business negotiations. He had had a near view of what activity of circulation can do for a country, and his imagination, exaggerating the benefits of credit, had made him believe that an abundance of money was the principal cause of the wealth of states, since money alone brought about the development of their manufactures and of their prosperity. This was, in some respects, a general opinion in Europe at the time when he lived, and contributed not a little to favor the adoption of his views. It seemed to him that by assuring to a country the possession of a quantity of money sufficient to command labor, it could be made to attain the highest degree of wealth and power. Now, banks of circulation allowed the place of money to be supplied by credit, which procured for paper the value and utility of coin ; and, as there were no limits to the issue of paper money, the public wealth appeared to him henceforth protected against all obstructions.

Such was the error of Law : the exaggeration of a good principle.   He had taken the effect for the cause, by attributing to credit results of which credit is only the consequence.   He had not considered that money, whether specie or paper, must always be proportioned to the quantity of values in way of circulation by exchange, and that money could not give rise to manufactures among a people, without pre-existing labor.   The increase of money, without a corresponding increase of exchangeable values, would only cause the prices of things to rise, instead of increasing the real wealth of a nation.   But the vast and sure genius of Law had comprehended from the beginning the necessity of furnishing capital to labor, at a low rate.   He had observed that private credit, that is to say, that of bankers and money-brokers, was often injurious to the industrial arts, because of the despotic control exercised by lenders over the workers ; and he wished to substitute the advances of state credit for those of private credit.   " Do not forget," said he to the regent, " that the introduction of credit has brought about a greater change among the powers of Europe than the discovery of the Indies ; that it is for the sovereign to give it, not to receive it."

All his ideas, therefore, from the first, turned towards the means of securing to the government the direction of public credit, by putting into its hands the administration of a general bank charged with collecting all the revenues of the state, and managing all the monopolies with which it should be invested.   But, either because theories in finance were then comprehended by few people, or because the novelty of the project alarmed people's minds, Law obtained only the right to establish a private bank, exactly similar, in many respects, to the present Bank of

France. Its capital stock was six millions, divided into twelve hundred shares of five thousand francs each. This bank was authorized to discount bills of exchange, to keep accounts with merchants, and to issue bills payable to bearer, in coin of the denomination and weight of the coin of the day. Scarcely was this bank founded when credit appeared again on every side,* confidence gained over even foreigners, and usury ceased to exercise its ravages. The government added its sanction to that of the public, by receiving as specie the notes of Law's bank. It was the first trial made in France of this new money; and we may venture to affirm that its use would have become general, had it not so quickly degenerated into abuse. In fact, so soon as the regent had issued the edict of April 10, 1717, which obliged the collectors and receivers of taxes to pay the bank-bills in specie, whenever they were presented to them, these bills acquired considerable importance; silver ceased to travel about and took refuge in the coffers of the provinces, or in those of the bank, to meet the disbursements, which were so much the less demanded, as paper was more convenient and of less expensive transportation. The suc-

---

* Dutot thus describes, though with some exaggeration, the effects produced by Law's bank :

"Abundance soon spread through the cities and the rural districts : it released both from the oppression of debts which poverty had caused to be contracted ; it awakened industry, it restored the value of all landed property, which had been suspended by those debts ; it made the king able to clear away and remit to his subjects more than fifty-two millions of the taxes of years previous to 1716, and more than thirty-five millions of duties, extinguished during the regency ; it lowered the interest on public funds, it crushed out usury, it raised the value of lands 80 to 100 per cent, it caused edifices to be erected in city and country, and the old ones which were falling to ruins, to be repaired, lands to be cultivated, values to be given to materials derived from the earth, which previously had no value ; it called home our citizens whom poverty had forced to go elsewhere for means of livelihood ; finally, that abundance attracted foreign wealth : jewels, precious stones, and everything that could accompany luxury and magnificence, came to us from foreign countries. Whether these prodigies or these marvels were produced by art, by confidence, by fear or by chimeras, if one chooses to say so, we can but acknowledge that that art, that confidence, that fear, or those chimeras had wrought all these realities, which the old administrative management would never have produced."—*Réflexions politiques sur les finances et sur le commerce de France.* vol. i.

cess was so complete and so decisive, that the bank could issue as many as fifty millions of bills with a capital of six. The deposits of gold and silver daily increased with the demand for bills. They were even more in demand than they are to-day, when bank-bills have so much difficulty in circulating, as soon as they have crossed the boundary of Paris.

Thus Law had realized in less than two years the most brilliant utopias of public and private credit. He had obtained, on an immense scale, results which are still, after a hundred years, centered in a few commercial cities ; he had reached, at one single stroke, the end of a course which would have seemed to require several successive generations. It will be to the eternal honor of his memory to have organized entirely, without omitting any essential wheel, a mechanism so complicated as that of banks of circulation, and to have familiarized his contemporaries, the victims of so many financial deceptions, with the system of confidence and of bills. Who can tell his joy at seeing the prompt success of his work, labor encouraged, hope reborn, and France smile on his efforts ! But these days of triumph were to be of short duration, and Providence had in reserve for him in the very near future cruel compensations. We shall profit by them, as by a serious lesson worthy to figure in the history of the science.

The bank of circulation established at Paris no longer sufficed for the ambition of Law. He pursued continually the first object of his desires, viz., the establishment of a national bank, charged with collecting the public revenues and exercising the commercial privileges which it should please the government to grant it. The possibility of issuing bills for a sum ten times greater than the reserves in specie, seemed to him henceforth too limited. He had conceived the idea of combining into one common association all the capitalists of France, and putting under their control, as a loan,[16] all the elements of public wealth, from landed property to the uncertain ventures of colonial trade. What could be a finer mortgage than France! And what value such a security would acquire, when the credit assured to the most humble proprietor would give an unlimited scope for improvements of every kind! But Law could not present this project to the public in its majestic simplicity; national confidence was not sufficiently enlightened to permit it. It was necessary for him to graft, so to speak, his universal bank on some institution adapted to the prejudices of his contemporaries; and, as misfortune would have it, the mania for colonization, which was then general, afforded him an opportunity to found a commercial company on the banks of of the Mississippi. Thus was born the West India Company, with a capital of one hundred millions, composed of two hundred thousand shares of five hundred francs each, under form of notes transferable by endorsement. To favor realizing from them, Law thought all the stockholders should be authorized, by the edict making the grant, (August, 1717), to pay one-fourth of the amount of their subscription in specie, and the other three-fourths in certificates of *rentes*, known under the name of *billets d' Etat* (government bills), then greatly depreciated. This circumstance gave them some favor, and sensibly raised public credit; but the safety of the enterprise really depended on the success of the colonial trade of the company; and, however credulous contemporaries may have been, the dividends were in fact never derived from any other source than from the interest of the *billets d' Etat*, paid by the government to the shareholders. Soon a formidable opposition, arising from parliament, pretended to contest the right of the new bank to collect taxes and make public payments, and the treasury clerks were forbidden to pay specie for the notes which should be presented. A *lit de justice* (*i.e.*, a sitting of the parliament of Paris in the king's presence—*Trans.*) was necessary to restore order, to say nothing of the competition of the Pâris brothers, who organized **the** *anti-system,** under the influence of the parliamentary party.

Finally, December 4, 1718, two years and a half after its foundation, the bank of Law was declared a royal bank, and the capital was paid back to the stockholders. The king took upon himself henceforth the responsibility for the security of the notes, the issue of which amounted in a few months to more than the capital of the previous bank. Unfortunately, in order to give credit to the new bills, Law thought it necessary to obtain of the regent an edict forbidding the transportation of money between the cities where the bank offices were. This was giving a forcèd currency to his paper money ; and this was not the only error of Law. It was in his destiny to import into France, with the most useful employment of credit, the most disastrous of its abuses, agiotage, (*i.e.*, specula tions on the rise and fall of public funds—*Trans.*). The agiotage arose from the relations of the royal bank with the West India Company. The shares of this company having fallen considerably, Law, who wished to maintain them, engaged to buy them below par at a given time, and to pay a premium equal to the difference between the market-price and their par value. Everybody wished to run the chance of the profit which would result from it, and the shares rose. They rose still more when Law, being in favor with the regent, had caused the monopoly of the East Indies to be added to the privileges of the West India Company, with authority to issue new capi tal sufficient for that association. Well-managed con trivances, because they were new, made specie flow into the coffers of the Scotch innovator. He gave time to the stockholders to pay the amount of their shares, with-

---

* The name *anti-system* was given, from its opposition to the ideas of Law, known under the name of *the system*, to the association formed by four brothers named Pâris, from Grenoble, to break down the bank of Law by means of a capital of a hundred millions, the interest of which, being better secured than that of the bank, would naturally make the shares of the latter fall.

out dreaming that time would be lacking to him to complete his work, and that he would soon be reproached with the ruin of the country; he gave them time, of which the Americans of our day have the saying, "Time is money." The speculators bought at once shares and expectations; and Law redoubled his efforts to give value to both. The silver, great quantities of which were poured into the coffers of the state, inspired in him the idea of a recoinage of the money. He caused the exclusive privilege of coining it to be accorded him by an edict, which favor cost the bank fifty millions. Then began those reciprocal concessions between the government and *the system*, the former always granting and the latter constantly promising, with the same want of reflection and the same heedlessness of the future. There were, however, enormous advantages obtained by the recoinage, and if the India Company had furnished its part of the dividends, the royal bank would have been established on impregnable foundations. The avidity of courtiers and the folly of speculators decided the matter otherwise.

The shares had already risen to a rate which neither the securities offered by the company, nor even the most exaggerated chances of profit, justified. Operations were no longer anything but gambling; and their history is too well known to enter into its details here. Suffice it to say, the rise of shares improvised fortunes truly fabulous, and brought about, in property, changes which were not without advantage to the general prosperity of the country. The landed aristocracy, weary of possessing lands whose modest incomes could not be compared with the dazzling products of agiotage, exchanged their meadows and woods for shares; wages rose to a rate hitherto unknown, and the merchandise which encumbered the stores could not suffice for the eager haste of buyers. Law seemed to have attained the consummation of his desires. If any badly-inspired rivals bought his notes, to make him uneasy by loud demands for their redemption in coin, he caused an edict to be issued which reduced the value of specie, and he disconcerted coalitions by the boldness of his alliance with the government. Never, we must say, have bolder experiments been made with such promptitude and on such a scale; never have theories more adventurous had at their service a power more absolute. There remained only one last attempt, the most dangerous, it is true, but the most seductive of all; namely, the payment of the public debt. This would meet with fewer obstacles than any other, on the part of the regent; but it had the defect of being executed without precaution and in a premature manner. Fifteen hundred millions could not be thus lightly displaced in a country less accustomed to the vast operations of credit than England and Holland. It was also hazarding much to substitute the shares of the India Company for the titles of state creditors, and to make the latter barter off as people said in those times, their certificates of *rentes*, (*i.e.*, public funds) for the fogs of the Mississippi. Nevertheless, the measure could have succeeded but for the fury with which people rushed into the speculations of which it became the signal. The shares, almost as soon as issued, rose to three, four, and even ten times their nominal value. One would have said that the French were at a loss where to invest their money, so eager were they to obtain at any price titles to the new loan. The second issue resulted in one hundred thousand shares of five hundred francs, realizing at five thousand livres. There was a general frenzy, encouraged besides by the latitude accorded to subscribers to discharge the debt by ten monthly payments. It was sufficient to give *earnest money*, as M. Thiers * so ingeniously says, to secure ten shares instead of one. The creditors of the state were not the last to lend themselves to their own spoliation; and the history of the system is full of the brigandage which worthily opened the career of agiotage in our country.

---

* Article on *Law*, in *L'Encyclopédie Progressive*. p. 80.

We can here only briefly state the results of that great financial revolution, which caused great evils, like all revolutions, but which also produced great permanent blessings, in compensation for passing evils. Public morals, principally, received some rude shocks, too capable of turning worthy people from the long and thorny path of labor. " The variations of fortunes were so rapid," says M. Thiers,* " that stock-jobbers, receiving shares to sell, by keeping them one single day, had time to make enormous profits. A story is told of one, who, charged with selling some shares, did not appear for two days. It was thought the shares were stolen : not at all ; he faithfully returned their value ; but he had taken time to win a million for himself. This power which capital had of producing so rapidly, had brought about a traffic ; people *lent the funds by the hour*, and exacted unprecedented rates of interest. The stock-jobbers found, moreover, a way to pay the interest demanded, and to reap a profit themselves. One could even gain a million a day. It is not then astonishing that valets became suddenly as rich as lords ; one is mentioned, who, meeting his master in bad weather, stopped his carriage and proposed to enter it." The folly went so far, that shares rose to thirty times the capital, and speculations in public funds absorbed, as a gulf, all the savings of rich and poor, in less than a few months. There were soon not enough gold and silver laces at the stores to deck the new aristocracy which sprang from this effervescence of the purse ; and the six hundred thousand shares of the India Company came to represent more than ten imaginary milliards. One should have been a witness of some financial infatuations of the present time, to have an idea of the delirium of the time of Law, and the complete blindness into which the mania for speculation had plunged the most reasonable people.

Meanwhile, the moment of the crisis was approaching,

---

*Article *Law*, previously quoted.

without any one daring to prophesy it, not even Law himself, who seemed to believe in an indefinite duration of his system. There was no longer any security possible for a capital carried up to more than ten milliards; and even if the Mississippi had been a veritable Eldorado, four hundred millions would have hardly sufficed to insure an interest of four or five per cent on the ideal figure of the shares. It was soon necessary to impose by authority a multitude of measures which should have been the result of confidence; and from this moment confidence was shaken. Law supposed the bank notes could be sustained by edicts which forbade their conversion, at Paris, into gold and silver; then he caused an order to be issued that taxes should be paid in bills; and, finally, that creditors should have the right to demand also, in bills, the payment of their dues. But these vain expedients only hastened the consummation of the catastrophe. The most prudent were eager to realize, *i.e.*, to convert into lands, furniture and houses, the amount of their shares or their notes; and then was seen a phenomenon just the contrary of that already described, the bearers of effects running after all the solid values, while previously they seemed only too happy to get rid of these values to have stocks. Prices rose almost suddenly to a rate hitherto unknown, and the run upon the bank to obtain redemption of the notes in specie daily increased. An attempt was made to provide against this danger by giving forced currency to the bills, and announcing, in order to maintain the wavering confidence, dividends which could not be paid. Then came senseless measures: a prohibition against wearing gems and diamonds, lest people should buy them in exchange for bank-bills; the confiscation of old specie and domiciliary visits for the purpose of discovering it. The decline in the shares went on, nevertheless, rapidly, to the great despair of the unfortunates who had exchanged real estate for fictitious wealth, and amid the noisy saturnalia of all the newly-enriched, who had consolidated their fortune by purchases of land or by investments in foreign countries. The famous edict of March 5, 1720, completed that structure of violent measures, which has brought upon the system of Law the somewhat biased censure of posterity. This edict, assimilating, by astute combinations, the bank-bills with the shares of the India Company, that is, values obtained in exchange for serious titles, with values eminently fictitious and speculative, was a veritable bankruptcy, which no historian has attempted to conceal. It is difficult for us to-day to comprehend to what sad expedients Law felt obliged to descend, after this last stroke. The desperate edicts he caused to be issued, recall some of the measures of the terror of 1793,[*] and included the informing against possessors of gold and silver, and the perturbation of the monetary system. Science has nothing to do with these aberrations of a man of genius at bay, except to regret that he was brought to them, so to speak, in spite of himself, by the necessity laid upon him, of subordinating his operations to the exigencies of the court and the distressed condition of the finances.

Dutot, Forbonnais, Steuart and M. Thiers[†] have given a complete exposition of the last days of *the system* and the false combinations which determined its fall. It is now certain that the bank of Law would have rendered immense service to France, if the regent had not made of it an instrument for collecting taxes, a docile financial machine, instead of leaving to it the independence of a commercial institution. When we reflect that this bank,

---

[*] It was forbidden to keep more than four or five hundred francs in specie, under penalty of a fine of ten thousand francs. Nothing made of gold was to weigh over an ounce. The weight was fixed for all articles made by goldsmiths, as dishes, sugar bowls, and candlesticks. The ridiculous vied here with the odious.

[†] *Réflexions politiques sur les finances et le commerce ; Recherches sur les finances de France ; Recherches des principes de l'économie politique ;* article *Law,* already quoted.—*Note of author.*

The principal writings of Law have been inserted in the first volume of the *Collection des Economistes,* of Guillaumin, with *Notice historique sur Jean Law, ses écrits et les opérations du système,* by Eugène Daire.—*Fr. ed.*

established with a view to giving activity to the circulation, had come to the point of interdicting the circulation of gold and changing the values of coins, it is difficult to reconcile such an end with the prosperous beginning which permitted no one to foresee it. From May 21, 1721, the shares of the India Company and the notes of the royal bank were gradually reduced : this was decreeing bankruptcy, in place of waiting for it and submitting to it ; it was saying to the creditors of the government that they had been dishonorably deceived, and that now their eyes were being audaciously opened. But the public reaped, in truth, what they had sown. Was it not they who had caused the prices of shares to rise to an exaggerated figure, and who had thus artificially increased their value, so as to render impossible the payment of interest proportionate to a capital so enormous ! There happened to the bank of Law the same thing that was seen in America, at the time of the crisis which recently agitated that country. Most of the banks were ruined through having multiplied their issues too largely ; that is to say, through having speculated too much on the rise of lands and on the progress of a civilization which can advance only with the step of man. From whatever point of view one looks at *the system*, he will be convinced that if Law had remained faithful to the true principles of credit which he had so well developed in his *Considerations on Money*,* he would have raised France, a hundred years ago, to the first rank among financial powers, and perhaps prevented the terrible catastrophes by which the latter part of the eighteenth century was agitated. He is the only one, since the existence of banks, who has been able to put with impunity ten times as many notes in circulation as the specie capital his bank contained ; and, notwithstanding

---

* In this writing, translated into French, and reprinted in 1790, Law explained clearly his ideas on credit. Many economists have obtained from it useful information, without rendering its author the justice due him.—*Note of author*.

the imprudence of his conduct in reference to the India Company, he nevertheless has the honor of having been the first to create industrial values in France.

This single creation was a high and grand thought. The smallest capital henceforth found investment, and workers hitherto condemned to the uncertainty of wages, were henceforth admitted to the privileges of property. The shares of the bank and of the India Company offered to economical persons the advantages of a savings bank, with the chances of profit of a great commercial association. The conception of Law seems to us admirable in this respect. Public credit was substituted for private credit. The interest of money fell to the lowest rate; and consequently the most efficacious cause of inequality of conditions disappeared. Unfortunately, the Scotch financier shared the error common to several of his most illustrious contemporaries, in supposing that all that was needed to make the interest on money diminish, was to multiply the money; and he aggravated that error by the still greater and wholly personal error of believing that one could multiply paper-money (bank-bills) without having regard to the capital held for its redemption. The event favored his illusion longer than seemed possible; for we have seen that the advantages of paper were so well comprehended in France, that Law could risk, even at the commencement of his operations, what no bank of discount would dare attempt to-day, viz., an issue of notes ten times greater than the specie capital. Confidence was general; the error of Law lay in the abuse of it. The regent led him into this by degrees, in the intention of paying off the national debt; and he forced him, to use the expression of a contemporary,* "to raise seven stories on foundations that he had laid for only three." The true effects of the system are scarcely well known to us at present. The writers of the time all speak of it with that affectation of horror which too often pursues

---

* Dutot.

the greatest reputations, when the hand of misfortune is
laid upon them. "On giving up this game," says Le-
montey,* "the lucky players had too much interest in
concealing their gains, and the unfortunate ones in exaggerating their losses. Those who judged of this complicated crisis were liable to confound the violence of the
remedy with that of the evil, and *what had only been displaced with what was destroyed.* * * * Meanwhile the
central provinces, where civilization was the most backward, experienced a salutary disturbance. These poor
and sluggish districts, where trade and money were scarcely known, and the fruits of the earth were without value,
and the collection of the taxes as distressing as it was unproductive, became animated with new life. In respect
to wealth, the price of provisions, the amount of the
taxes, social life and political importance, the new birth
of this vast territory dates from the cataclysm of Law ;
and its progressive civilization, since 1720, is a better
monument of it than the bank-bills still kept in some cottages."

The principal cause of the fall of *the system* was, then,
the excessive issue of bank-bills and shares in the India
Company. *Fictitious* capital was powerless to supply *real*
interest ; the result was only an exaggerated rise of the
prices of all things and a general change of fortunes, so
much the more dangerous as it was rapid. Similar catastrophes have since marked the same abuses of credit in
the old and the new world   Our fathers saw the *assignats*, when multiplied beyond measure, fall with a crash,
in spite of the guaranty of the wealth called national ;
England, in her turn, experienced a great monetary
crisis, for having exceeded the natural limit of specie in
the loans of her bank to her government. At the time I
am writing, a crisis more serious still has just deranged
all the circulation in the United States,† and one can be-

Histoire de la Régence, vol. i, p. 356.
† The author alludes to the crisis of 1838-9.—*Fr. ed.*

lieve himself transported back to the time of Law, when he studies the causes of that disturbance, which are almost identical with those of the fall of the system. In vain the *Convention* punishes with death the refusal of the paper money ; in vain the parliament of England authorizes the failure of the bank, and the United States precipitate the bankruptcy of theirs ; these formidable attacks only strengthen the fundamental bases of the theory of credit.* Credit should represent only solid values, and solidity of values can be increased only by confidence, but can never be decreed by force. If Law had been free in his operations, he would have restricted his issues of bills and shares within the limits indicated by the wants of the circulation and the probable revenues of the India Company. His first successes were dazzling. He conceived that he could reduce all France to small money and make all the land circulate under the form of paper. However, the effect he obtained from that gigantic attempt, was not without fruit. The innumerable changes which were wrought under the influence of *the system*, began the dividing up of landed property, from which France has derived so great advantages. The spirit of enterprise seized all classes of society, and the power of association, hitherto unknown, revealed itself by new and bold combinations of which our present operations in credit are only imitations. Had it not been for the prodigalities of the court, the public debt would have been considerably reduced by the reimbursement of a part of the creditors of the state, and the lowering of the interest would have soon permitted the rest to be paid.

Landed property came forth for the first time from the state of torpor in which the feudal system had so long kept it. It was a real awakening to agriculture, and land ose from this time to the rank of a productive power.

---

* The reader who desires a philosophical exposition of the subject of credit, should consult H. D. Macleod's *Economic Philosophy*, vol. i. chaps. vii and viii, and vol. 2, chap. xii, pp. 62–64.— *Trans.*

It had just passed from the régime of mortmain to that of circulation. The new proprietors, almost all of whom had sprung from the ranks of the workers, cultivated the land with all their customary ardor and with the ease which abundance of capital gave them. The storm, too, which had just overwhelmed it, seemed only to have given it new vigor, and from that time a new era began for it. Everybody clung to it as the most stable of values; so that, despite the disappointments experienced by the other branches of industry during the breaking up of *the system*, a new system almost immediately succeeded that which had just become extinct, and cast also a brilliant light before passing away, like the other. It will be readily divined that we refer to the system of Quesnay or of the *Economists*.

CHAPTER XXXII.

The system of Quesnay and the *Economist* school.—Origin of its doctrines.—Services they rendered.—Various shades of the *Economist* school.—Gournay.—Mercier de la Rivière.—Turgot.—Admirable probity of these philosophers.—Details about Quesnay.

THE sad issue of Law's system left all France plunged in a veritable stupor. People no longer knew upon what principles to rely, after having seen so many fortunes rapidly come and go. Some deplored the ruin of the manufactures founded with so much effort by Colbert; others went back a hundred years and recalled the patriarchal maxim of Sully; " Tillage and pasturage are the breasts of the state; " and we must acknowledge that circumstances had become very favorable for a return to these ideas. Of all the industrial values produced under the hot atmosphere of *the system*, nothing remained but ruin, desolation and bankruptcy. Landed property alone had not perished in that tempest. It had even improved by change of hands, and by being subdivided on a vast scale, for the first time, perhaps, since the feudal system. The importance that it thus acquired all at once, increased its value considerably; and soon the activity of minds freed from speculative illusions, was directed toward the cultivation of the soil, to demand from it reparation for the misfortunes of *the system*. One might say that every man felt the need of rest in the shadow of his own vine and fig-tree from the shocks and agitations of the Bourse.

Never was transition more sudden. People went on,

351

however, through a mass of books. There was a shower of writings on the circulation, on credit, on industrial arts, on population, on luxury: every one seemed to wish to explain the crisis from which people were emerging, and thought he had found, for his consolation, the key of that enigma. People had for some time deemed money to be wealth in an especial sense, and thought that in multiplying the paper which represented it, they were multiplying wealth itself. But the general rise in prices and the fall of the paper had unsealed the blindest eyes, and as is usual in similar circumstances, they had passed from infatuation to aversion, from fanaticism to incredulity. There were henceforth no true riches but land, and no secure revenues but those which emanated from its bosom. It was from this reaction that the agricultural ·system arose, better known under the name of the *Economists*, or of Quesnay, who was its principal founder. It was also the first system which constituted a school, and it stated its formulas with a dogmatic precision quite rare in the annals of science. We will make a simple summary of it, as to persons and things. If it had been only an exposition of doctrines purely economic, it would not, perhaps, have obtained so high a degree of attention from statesmen; but it presented itself from the very first as the instrument of a political reform, which was to facilitate the collection of taxes and repair the evils with which France was afflicted. It came after the disasters of Law and the somewhat crude attempts of the abbé Terray * in matters of finance; it was received with favor as a novelty, while waiting to establish itself by right of conquest.

And truly its first manifestoes appeared like a revelation. Every nation had, in turn, extolled the power of manufactures and freedom of trade: none seemed to have thought of agriculture, except from an exclusively

---

* The abbé Terray was not as absurd and as pitiless as most of his contemporaries have pretended. He one day responded to some opera singers who were claiming their arrears, " It is just to pay those who weep before those who sing."

pastoral point of view.   Not one had had the idea that the government should occupy itself with the cultivation of the fields, and take any administrative measures rela- tive to such labors.   All that had been done until then of this kind consisted in bad regulations against the exporta- tion of grain, or to prevent its importation, like the corn- laws of England.   And nevertheless, agriculture was always considered, by a sort of poetic tradition, as the nursing mother of the people.   About the year 1750, two men of great grasp of mind, M. de Gournay an ! Quesnay, attempted the analysis of that fecund power; instead of extolling it, they explained it.   They ravished from the earth her mysterious processes, and if they did not give the best theory about them, they at least pre- pared its elements for posterity.

Their starting point was admirably chosen.   They attempted first to establish the true principles of the formation of wealth and of its natural distribution among the different classes of society.   It seemed to them that all wealth proceeded from a single source, which was the earth, since this it was which furnished the laborers their subsistence and the raw materials for all branches of industry.   Labor, applied to the cultivation of the earth, produced not only means of support during the progress of the work, but an excess of value which could be added to the mass of wealth already existing : they called this excess the *net product*.   The net product must necessarily belong to the proprietor of the land and con- stituted in his hands a revenue at his disposal.   What then was the net product of the other occupations ?   Here begin the errors of these ingenious men, for in their eyes the other branches of industry were unproductive, and could add nothing either to the mass of things upon which they worked, nor to the general revenue of society. Manufacturers, traders, workmen, were all paid clerks of agriculture, which was the sovereign creator and dis- penser of all wealth.   The products of their labor repre-

sented, in the system of the *Economists*, only the equivalent of their consumption during the work, so that after
the labor was finished, the sum total of wealth was absolutely the same as before, unless the workmen had put
in reserve, that is, *saved*, what they had a right to consume.   Thus, then, labor applied to land was the only
labor productive of wealth, and that of the other branches
of industry was considered as *sterile*, because no augmentation of the general capital resulted from it.

In virtue of this system, the *Economists* admired as a
necessity at the same time *social* and *natural*, the pre-
eminence of landed proprietors over all other classes of
citizens.   These proprietors reaped the total of the wealth
produced, of which they distributed a portion, under
the name of wages, to the non-proprietors; and the circulation of wealth took place, in society, only by the
continual exchange of the labor and services of some for
the disposable portion of the income of the others.   What
became, on that hypothesis, for it is to-day no longer anything but an hypothesis, the basis of taxation?   It was
evident that taxes could not be assessed on people reduced to wages, without attacking the source of their
existence: besides, the *Economists* declared that the tax
must be exclusively borne by the proprietors of lands,
and deducted from the *net product*.   It was consequently
the general interest of all classes to multiply agricultural
products, because the proprietors found thereby a larger
income to distribute to all the wage-paid occupations.   The
population was encouraged and increased by abundance
of means of subsistence, and thus was verified the maxim
borrowed by the new school from the holy books: " He
that tilleth his land, shall be satisfied with bread." *

We need not say wherein the *Economists* were mistaken.
Their principal error arose from their attributing to agriculture alone the power of creating products susceptible
of accumulation.   The fine analyses of Adam Smith have

---

* Prov. 12 : xi.

completed, since then, the catalogue of the sources of wealth, by demonstrating that the real social value is exchange value, and that there is profit to society, whenever that value is increased by labor. Grain would be of very little utility if some one did not make bread of it, and wood would not have great value if the joiner and the cabinet-maker did not transform it into furniture. Experience has proven, also, that manufactures and commerce are much more favorable than agriculture to the increase of exchange value, either from the division of labor being better adapted to that end, or on account of the perfection of the machines. How would cities have become the centres of wealth and civilization, if agriculture alone had the gift of creating values? and how could we explain the fortune of Venice and of Genoa, which had no territory? Is it not rather because, by means of commerce and manufactures, a country can import annually a quantity of means of subsistence much greater than its own lands could furnish it? The theory of openings for trade (*débouchés*), so well developed, since the *Economists*, by J. B. Say, has put that truth in a clear light and worthily completed what Adam Smith, the master of us all, so well begun. But what light did the brave theses of the *Economist* school throw upon this grave question! What immense consequences we have derived from that very simple proposition that the wealth of nations does not consist in wealth that cannot be consumed, such as gold and silver,* but in

---

* This proposition is clearly expressed in the following passage from Mercier de la Rivière :

"Let me be permitted to repeat here that money does not rain down into our hands, does not grow in our fields, in nature. To have money, we must buy it ; and, after that purchase, one is no richer than he was before : he only receives in money, a value equal to that he has given in merchandise. An agricultural nation is very rich, people tell us, when we see much money there ; people are doubtless right in saying so, but they are wrong not to see also that before acquiring that money, it was equally rich, since it possessed the values with which it paid for the money ; it cannot even enjoy that wealth in money without making it forever disappear, unless it maintains it by the reproduction of the values whose sale, or rather exchange, have procured for it money wealth : so this wealth in money is only a secondary wealth representative of a primary wealth for which it is substituted." (*Ordre Naturel et Essentiel des Societés Politiques.* Vol. ii, p. 338.)

consumable wealth produced by the incessant labor of society!

To complete their good fortune, the *Economists*, considering the subordinate condition and the inferiority of the non-property-holding classes, as they appeared to them in their system, thought nothing more just than to claim for them absolute freedom of manufactures and commerce. A good market for provisions and an abundance of raw products could be assured them only by the unlimited competition of the sellers. This competition was the sole means of stimulating industrial enterprises, and of favoring the cultivation of the earth by removing all restrictions; a doctrine which the new school summed up in these memorable words, so badly interpreted since: *Laissez faire, laissez passer.* It was from this time that most of the barriers which arrested the development of agriculture were broken down, and a general war commenced against corporations and customs, those two fortresses of privilege, which contain them all within their walls! The *Economist* school rendered other services equally important, by analyzing the principal phenomena of the distribution of wealth. For this end principally Dr. Quesnay, physician of Louis XIV, and chief of that school, published his famous *Tableau Economique*, so heavily commented upon in *L'Ami des Hommes* by the Marquis de Mirabeau, and reproduced in the *Physiocratie*[17] of Dupont of Nemours.

This Economic Table, of which the first proofs were printed at Versailles, from the very hand of the king, with this epigraph: *Poor peasants, poor kingdom; poor kingdom, poor king*, presented a series of formulas bristling with figures, in which the author indicated such a distribution of the territorial revenue, as seemed to him to result from the general laws of production. This was the part which, of all the system, was most talked of, and which is to-day the most forgotten, because founded on bases recognized as erroneous. Nothing can depict the enthusiasm which its publication aroused among all the adepts of the sect. Dupont of Nemours, called it " that astonishing formula which depicts the origin, the distribution and the reproduction of wealth, and which serves for calculating with so much certainty, promptitude and precision, the effect of all the operations relating to wealth." Mirabeau added : " There are three marvellous inventions in the world, *writing, money and the Tableau Economique.*" This *tableau* was commented on, amplified and developed by all the adepts, with the same assurance as the theorems of geometry in our colleges. It was learned by heart as a sort of catechism, in which every class of citizens should study the duties they had to fulfil in the social hierarchy Now that we no longer consider those occupations as unproductive of which the author spoke, their more or less ingenious classification has no farther interest to science.

The dominant thought of the *Economist* school is revealed more fully in the little work of Quesnay, republished under the title of *General Maxims for the Economic Government of an Agricultural Kingdom.* Here are expressed more clearly the political views of that school, which has been accused, with some ground, of a systematic tendency toward an absolute government. We will quote a few of these maxims, isolated, as they are in the original work, under the form of aphorisms.

" Let the sovereign authority be single, and superior to all the individuals of society and all the unjust enterprises of private interests ; for the object of domination and obedience is the security of all and the lawful interest of all. The system of counter-forces in government is a harmful one, which only produces discord among the great and the oppression of the weak."

" Let the sovereign and the nation never lose sight of the fact, that the earth is the only source of wealth, and that it is agriculture that multiplies it. For the increase of wealth insures that of population ; men and the rich make agriculture prosper, extend commerce, animate manufactures, and increase and perpetuate wealth."

" Let the tax not be destructive, nor disproportioned to the total revenue of the nation ; let its increase follow the increase of the revenue ; let it be assessed directly on the net product of the landed property, and not on the wages of men, nor on provisions, where it would multiply the expenses of collection, be prejudicial to commerce, and destroy annually a part of the wealth of the nation. Neither let it be taken from the wealth of the farmers of landed property, for the advances of the agriculture of a kingdom must be looked upon as fixed property, which must be carefully preserved for the production of the impost, the revenue, and the subsistence of all classes of citizens : otherwise the tax degenerates into spoliation, and causes a dwindling away which quickly ruins a state."

" Let the lands appropriated to the cultivation of grain be combined, as much as possible, into large farms worked by wealthy farmers ; for there is much less outlay for keeping and repairing buildings, and much less expense and much greater net profit proportionately in great agricultural enterprises than in small ones. A multiplicity of small farmers is prejudicial to the population. The population the most secure, the most disposable for the different labors which divide men into different classes, is that which is supported from the net product. Every saving made to increase this, by labors which can be executed by means of animals, machines, rivers, etc., reverts to the benefit of the population of the state, because more net product procures more gain to men for other services or other labors."

" Let openings for the sale and transportation of the products of manual labor be facilitated by the repair of the roads, and by navigation on the canals, rivers, and sea ; because the more that is saved in the expenses of commerce, the more the revenue of the territory is increased."

" Let not the comfort of the lower classes of the citizens be diminished, for they would not be able to contribute to the consumption of such provisions as can be consumed only within the country, which would diminish reproduction and the revenue of the nation."

" Let land-owners and those persons who have lucrative occupations not indulge in unprofitable hoarding, for this would take from the circulation and distribution a part of their income or gains."

" Let no one be deceived by an apparent advantage of reciprocal trade with foreign countries, by judging simply by the balance of the sums in money, without examining the more or less profit resulting from the merchandise that is sold and that which is purchased. For often the loss is to the nation which receives a surplus in money, and that loss occurs to the disadvantage of the distribution and reproduction of the revenues."

" Let entire freedom of trade be maintained ; for the regulation of the internal and the foreign trade, which is the most secure, the most exact, and the most profitable for a nation and a state, consists in full liberty of competition."

" Let the government be less occupied with the matter of saving than with the operations necessary to the prosperity of the kingdom ; for very great expenses may cease to be excessive by the increase of wealth. But we need not confound abuses with simple expenses, for abuses might swallow up all the wealth of the nation and of the sovereign."

" Let no one hope for resources of extraordinary advantage to a state, except from the prosperity of the nation, and not from the credit of financiers ; for pecuniary fortunes are clandestine riches which know neither king nor country."

" Let the state avoid loans which form government funds, for they load it with devouring debts, and occasion a commerce or traffic in money, through the intervention of negotiable paper, where discount increases more and more the unproductiveness of pecuniary fortunes. These fortunes separate finance from agriculture, and deprive the rural districts of the wealth necessary for the improvement of real estate and the cultivation of the land."

The above maxims belong especially, as one can see, to political order. The author seems to be concerned only with the payment of imposts, with population, loans, and public expenditures. In fact, the *Economists* looked at the science differently from us, and almost exclusively in its connection with administration and government. Their aim was to found a social theory and to subject all minds to the yoke of a tutelary authority, much like a despotism. They wished first of all to settle landed property, which seemed to them the most important of all, on an immutable basis; but they nevertheless respected personal property, and they admitted no duties without rights, nor services without compensation. The interest of the sovereign was naturally, in their view, the same as that of the people; a king was only a father of a family. They took pleasure in representing Louis XV as animating agriculture with his presence and diffusing abundance and peace along his pathway. Mercier de la Rivière even ventured to write : " It is physically impossible that any other government can last than that of a single person. Who does not see, who does not feel, that man is formed to be governed by despotic authority?" "—Because man is destined to live in society, he is destined to live under a despotism."—" This form of government is the only one which can procure for society its best possible condition." *

The abbé Baudeau, one of the most able interpreters of the new school, shared the opinions of Mercier de la Rivière. He thought, like him, that it was easier to persuade a prince than a nation, and that the triumph of *the true principles* would be sooner secured by the sovereign power of a single man, than by the conviction, difficult to obtain, of an entire people. As chance would have it, they found among their contemporaries more than one of these reform princes : the Empress Catherine of Russia, Emperor Joseph II, in Austria, the Grand-Duke of Tuscany, and the Grand-Duke of Baden. There was insensibly formed in France a nursery of statesmen imbued with their maxims : M. de Gournay, M. de

---

* *Ordre Naturel et Essentiel, etc.* Vol. I, pp. 199, 280, 281.

Trudaine, M. de Malesherbes, M. d'Argenson, and the illustrious Turgot who combined their virtues and their talents.   All these worthy men adopted unreservedly the patriarchal doctrines of Mercier de la Rivière ; but they gradually made the maxims of toleration of the *Economist* school penetrate the government, and, by brilliant attempts in some provinces, either as intendants or as ministers, they preluded the reforms achieved by the French revolution.   The abuses of corporations, custom-houses, corvées, and fiscal measures, were pointed out by them with indefatigable perseverance ; and in their ardor for scientific conquests, they raised, by the way, the most profound social questions.   Their errors even were useful, and their most vague presentiments seem always to contain something prophetic.   "Moderate your enthusiasm," exclaimed Mercier de la Rivière, "blind admirers of the false products of manufacture ! Before crying 'Miracle !' open your eyes and see how poor, or at least uncomfortable, these very workmen are who have the skill to change twenty sous into the value of a thousand crowns. Who profits by this enormous multiplication of values ? Why ! Those by whose hands it is brought about, do not know comfort ! Ah ! be distrustful of this contrast."* Mercier doubtless attributed the miseries of the manufacturing class solely to the distressed condition of agriculture and the insufficiency of the *net product* ; but although he was mistaken in the causes, he very well noted the effects ; and the contrast which he recommended them to regard with distrust, contained the problem which the present time has not yet succeeded in solving.

Adam Smith has written nothing clearer and more vigorous than the fine demonstrations of the *Economists* in favor of freedom of trade.   These ideas of general fraternity among nations, so popular in our day, were developed by Mercier de La Rivière with an irresistible enthusiasm and a power of reason which could not be

---

Ordre Naturel et Essentiel, Vol. ii, p. 407.

surpassed. There is even cause to think that this remarkable writer would have powerfully aided governments to find a better basis for the assessment of taxes, if he had not been swayed by the doctrine of the net product and of the classes reputed unproductive. The tax, he said, is a portion of the net revenue of the nation, applied to the necessities of its government. Now, that which is a portion of the net product alone, can be taken only from the net product; the tax can then be demanded only of those who possess the total net product of which the tax is a part. Consequently, the *Economists* considered as arbitrary and unjust any personal tax, and they included in a common reprobation all indirect taxes. What would they have said if they had seen, in our day, these taxes produce in England more than a milliard, and in France more than five hundred millions?

This fundamental error, which later became the basis of the financial doctrines of the Constituent Assembly, notwithstanding the efforts of Rœderer and some of his colleagues, was the result of a false idea of the principles of wealth. The theory of value, invented since, by Adam Smith, would have taught the *Economists* that labor as well as land is a source of wealth, and that they erred in not observing the similarity between the material multiplication resulting from a grain of wheat entrusted to the earth, and the multiplication of values produced by the processes of manufactures and commerce. That unfortunate doctrine of the net product, closed their eyes to an infinite number of truths which they would have deduced from the observation of facts, if they had followed the strict method of the writers who succeeded them. But, in their false route, they nevertheless made admirable discoveries, like those alchemists who found so many useful substances, while searching for the philosopher's stone. We are even indebted to them for the labors of the men who have surpassed them, and no one to-day doubts that Adam Smith himself, who resided some time in France and who lived on terms of intimacy with the *Economists,* derived from them his first acquaintance with the subject.   He always speaks of them in his writings with respect, and he intended to dedicate his great work on the *Wealth of Nations* to Quesnay, if that economist had been alive at the time of its publication.

The *Economists* have often been accused of a revolutionary tendency, because of the intimacy which prevailed between these savants and the Encyclopedic Philosophers.[18] We must not, however, forget that Voltaire had made cruel sport of their doctrines on taxation, in his *Homme aux Quarante Ecus,* and that Montesquieu had responded to their manifestoes in favor of free trade by a chapter entitled, *To what Nations it is Disadvantageous to carry on Commerce.*   It is certain that the Economist school contributed no less than the Philosophic school to the reform of European social order.   While the *Philosophers* earnestly attacked abuses of every kind, without regard to choice of weapons, the *Economists* contented themselves with showing, with magisterial calmness, the essential disadvantages of these abuses.   They kept a dignified and stern reserve in the midst of the running fire of epigrams or philippics with which the Encyclopedia pursued the past, and they lived at the same time on good terms with the court without being courtiers, and with the Philosophers without being railers.   Their impartial gravity caused them to be respected by both parties, and Louis XV, himself called Quesnay *his thinker* (*penseur*).*   The latter resided at Versailles in the palace of the king, which consequently became the rendezvous of the boldest reformers.   " While storms were gathering and scattering beneath the entresol of Quesnay," says Marmontel in his memoirs, "he was scribbling away at his axioms and his calculations in rural economy, as tranquil and as indifferent to these commotions of the court, as if he were a hundred leagues

---

* He had given him for arms three flowers of the pansy (*pensée*—a thought), with this device : *Propter excogitationem mentis.*

away." He never took part in any intrigue ; and he died at the age of eighty years, leaving a name revered throughout all Europe, which did not, however, comprehend the wide bearing of his doctrines. Quesnay wrote little, and in a manner nearly always sententious and obscure. He threw out his ideas to his followers like an oracle, without appearing to attach any importance to them, and as if to give something to think of. But his formulas were eagerly collected and developed by the numerous group that gathered about him. From their circle came forth the signal of all the social reforms carried out or attempted in Europe for the past eighty years ; and we might say that, with the exception of a few maxims, the French revolution was only their theory carried into action.

The *Economists* present themselves, in fact, with the advantage of a compact and serried column under the same colors. They have a common rallying cry, a common doctrine, and that dogmatic language which always exercises its accustomed influence over the vulgar. Their principles were everywhere proclaimed in the same terms, with the same mathematical precision, and Quesnay does not disdain to have recourse to specious combinations of figures, to justify his aphorisms. Three pages suffice to sum up the *new science*, as they call it, and yet Mirabeau the elder dilutes it to two enormous quarto volumes. It is essential that it penetrate everywhere. It is, in their opinion, as indispensable to the king as to the most humble citizen. It is promulgated under the form of tables, instructions, dialogues, treatises, letters, and journal articles. *Les Ephémérides du citoyen, Le Journal d'Agriculture* and *Le Journal Economique* propagate it without fear of censure, so well known are the *Economists* as friends of order, even to the point of sacrificing to it liberty.

The condition of the peasant, heretofore so humble and unjustly degraded, rises to the first rank among honorable occupations. People demand means of communication from all parts, and then begins that fever for roads and canals which is breaking out again in our day. Great roads are multiplied as if by enchantment. In many places, the corvée is abolished ; common pasturage is done away with ; free trade in grain is demanded. The rural districts have at length obtained a glance from the cities, and agriculture comes forth from the frightful condition in which it had languished for several centuries.

The *Economists* were not, however, all perfectly in accord in regard to the system of Quesnay. They agreed on doctrines ; they differed as to their application. M. de'Gournay, the son of a merchant and himself a merchant, was the real author of the famous adage ; *Laissez faire et laissez passer.** He it was who commenced the war on monopolies and demonstrated the imperative necessity of abolishing duties on raw materials. Quesnay, the son of a cultivator, had turned his attention more particularly to agriculture, and he was thus led to his ingenious hypotheses on the influence of agricultural production, with all their train of deductions, both in what concerns taxation and in connection with labor. M. de Malesherbes, the abbé Morellet, Trudaine, Doctor Price and Mr. Josiah Tucker belonged to the shade of Gournay ; La Trosne, Saint-Péravy, Mirabeau the elder, and Dupont de Nemours, preferred the absolute ideas of Quesnay. Mercier de La Rivière and the abbé Baudeau, more politic and less abstract, inclined towards supremacy of the civil power and wished to invest it almost exclusively with the direction of the social movement. Turgot proceeded by himself, being the issue of them all and destined to realize their ideas by prompt and decisive applications. He was eclectic and practical, like a philosopher and a statesman. But what especially distinguished that generous family of friends of the human race, was the admirable probity of each of

---

*i.e. " Let us alone, and keep the ways free."

its members and their sincere disinterestedness in every-thing. They sought neither splendor nor renown. They attacked none of the established powers, and they did not aspire to become popular, although they were anima-ted by a profound sympathy for the people. They were true philanthropists, in the noblest acceptation of this word. Their books are forgotten ; but their doctrines have germinated like a fruitful seed, and the precepts which they taught have made the circuit of the world, freed the industrial arts, restored agriculture, and pre-pared the way for commercial liberty. After Quesnay came Turgot; after Turgot, Adam Smith ; science hence-forth marches with giant steps.

CHAPTER XXXIII.

The ministry of Turgot.—Economic reforms he undertakes.—Opposition he encounters.—His influence on the course of political economy.

THE ministry of Turgot was only the doctrine of the *Economists* carried into action. It was the first time that the science had the good fortune to find a minister disposed to realize all its conceptions, and try thoroughly all its experiments. Turgot devoted himself to the task with the zeal of a neophyte and the conscientious persistency of a magistrate. The most illustrious of his predecessors, Colbert, had ventured to attempt much less, even with the support of a will like that of Louis XIV; it will be an interesting spectacle to view Turgot battling all the economic prejudices of the past ages, which he wished to root out at a single stroke. The consequences of that heroic attempt merit the consideration alike of peoples and of governments, for nothing less than a revolution was needed to assure its success.

Turgot was a pupil of the *Economists* and a supporter of their doctrines, principally in everything that concerned freedom of trade in grain, and the land-tax. His works contain a great number of articles in which he shows himself the defender of the fundamental maxims of the system of Quesnay. He was not so, however, unconditionally·; and his administrative experience had made him feel more than once, how much management was necessary in the execution of even the most indis-

pensable reforms. But the fierce opposition he encountered chafed his sense of probity, and prevented him from
always keeping a suitable moderation, in the midst of the
conflict of opinions. He had been early impressed by
the deplorable state of the people of the rural districts,
weighed down as they were by tithes, corvées, and exactions of every kind. In the cities, the wretchedness of the
working classes had no less pierced his soul, and the system of corporations, that system so contrary to respect
for personal property, had strongly excited his disapprobation. Accordingly, as soon as he had come into power,
he began his work with the precipitancy of a man who
fears he may not last long, and who wishes, at least, to
do all the good possible by the way. Reform edicts
succeed one another, stroke upon stroke, accompanied by
lengthy statements of the reasons for them, too lengthy,
perhaps, not to appear timid, and more like scientific
dissertations than publications from the highest authority.

Then, too, how much opposition he had to encounter,
how many prejudices to overcome, and coalitions to
break up! Turgot struck at everything ; nobles, financiers, bourgeois, priests, lawyers, monopolists ; he wished
everything to bend under the yoke of his reforms, and he
seemed to despair of nothing. " *I venture to assert*," said
he to the king, " *that in ten years the nation will not be
recognizable.*" * In conformity to the practice of the
Economists, he first turned his attention towards the rural
districts, and he considered it his duty to attack the absurd legislation which forbade the exportation of grain,
convinced that the best way to prevent scarcity was a
free circulation of the crops. It was, however, from this
quarter that came the most vigorous opposition and the
worst difficulties. Chance decreed that the emancipation
of the commerce in grain should be coincident with a
year of scarcity, and the people, accustomed to watch
over their supplies as a sacred trust, were irritated, in

---

* *Mémoire au roi*, in the collection of Dupont de Nemours, vol. vii.

many parts, at exportations which seemed to threaten them with famine. These exportations were in some sort only internal, since they only took place between provinces, and they could not deprive France of the possession of her grain; besides, Turgot had favored importations of grain from foreign countries: but what could these arguments effect against fear and calumny! and what could be expected of the multitude, when writers like the abbé Galiani and M. Necker himself descended into the arena to maintain the most foolish prejudices? Turgot, in desperation, decided to use force, and marched troops against the riotous bands who were covering the rural districts, stopping the arrivals and proceeding to the plunder of grain.

Such was the result of the first attempt at reform by this honest man and minister, of whom Louis XVI said, " Turgot and I are the only ones who love the people." He desired to put bread within reach of every mouth, and he was disgraced like a public enemy. People represented him as the protector of monopolists and the accomplice of the great land-holders. They quoted some unlucky passages * in the *Economist* writers, which had maintained the necessity of a high price for grain, in order to increase the *net product* of agriculture, and Turgot was accused of starving the people to make an absurd utopia succeed. He could triumph over the opposition of parliament only by means of *lits de justice*. At Rouen, the trade in grain was in the hands of one hundred and twelve merchants. They alone could buy and sell grain. A fraternity of ninety porters enjoyed the exclusive right of transporting the sacks under their orders; another association had the exclusive privilege of grinding for the consumption of the inhabitants. All was monopoly,

---

* Quesnay had said : " Let it not be supposed that a cheap provision market is advantageous to the humble class of people ; want and dearness is misery, abundance and dearness is opulence." (*General Maxims of Economical Government*, xix, xx.)
But how reconcile dearness and abundance !

abuse and tyranny. Turgot determined to apply here his hatchet; but every blow he struck rebounded upon himself. In reading the long preambles of all the edicts he caused to be issued, we know not whether to be more astonished at the patience of the men who suffered the exactions there pointed out, or the folly of those who endeavored to prevent this great minister from putting an end to them. He encountered the same opposition, when, after having secured free trade in grain, he attempted to repress the abuses which hampered that in wines. Accustomed as we are, since the Constituent Assembly, to the equality of citizens and of departments before the law, it is difficult for us to comprehend to-day the shouts of rage with which, especially in the south, the reform in local privileges, so numerous in the matter of wines, was received. What shall we say then, of the contest which ensued between Miromesnil, the keeper of the seals, and Turgot?

We can but observe in the collection of the works of the latter, in what an animated, and at the same time logical style, he shows the severity of a system which imposed on the poorest and most unfortunate class, the burden of the construction and maintenance of the roads.* And how much had he not already had to contend with in order to obtain the roads themselves! We overlook too much the fact, in France, that it is to the *Economist* system, the agricultural system, that we owe the idea of the first great lines of communication with which the country has been endowed,† and to Turgot their construction. When there was question as to the apportionment of the expense between the different classes of citizens, Turgot, faithful to his motto, took up the de-

---

* Vol. viii of the edition of Dupont de Nemours, pp. 178–262.

† " Let openings to markets, and the transportation of productions and of the results of manual labor, be facilitated *by the repair of the roads*, and by navigation on canals, rivers, and the sea ; for the more that is saved in the expenses of commerce, the more the revenue of the territory is increased." (*General Maxims of Economic Government*, xvii.)

fence of the poorer; M. de Miromesnil was moved by the fate of the richer. Here is a sample of their dialogue, written by the former under the form of observations, by the second under the title of responses. We regret that we can only quote this fragment; but this fragment belongs to the history of the science.

The Keeper of the Seals. " The land proprietors, who appear at the first glance to form the happiest and most opulent portion of the subjects of the king, are also those who bear the heaviest burdens, and who, on account of the necessity which they are under, of employing the men who have only their arms on which to rely for support, furnish the latter the means of subsistence."

Turgot. " Because the proprietor feels the blow of the ruin of his farmer, it does not follow that this farmer may not be still more unfortunate than his master. When a post-horse falls, overcome with weakness, the rider falls too, but the horse is still more to be pitied. The proprietors, by their disbursements, give support to the men who have only their arms; but the proprietors enjoy for their money all the comforts of life. The daily laborer works and earns by the sweat of his brow the scantiest subsistence. But when he is obliged to work for nothing, there is taken from him even the resource of subsisting from his labor by the expenditure of the rich."

Keeper of the Seals. " The land-owners are not the ones who profit by the public roads being well maintained. Travellers, wagoners, and peasants even, who go on foot, likewise profit by them : travellers get over more ground in less time and at less expense, and wagoners tire their horses and wear out their wagons less ; the simple peasant who goes on foot, walks more easily on a fine road than in a bad path. Hence the advantage of the highways extends proportionally to all the subjects of the king."

Turgot. " Travellers gain a more speedy passage from

the fine condition of the roads. Excellence of the roads attracts travellers, and multiplies their number; these travellers expend money, and consume the provisions of the country, all of which turns always to the advantage of the proprietors. As to the wagoners, their expenses in cartage are less in proportion as they are less time on the road and save their horses and carts more. From this diminution in the outlay for cartage, results a facility in transporting provisions further and selling them better. So all the advantage is for the landed proprietor who sells his produce better. In regard to the peasants who go on foot, the Keeper of the Seals will permit me to believe that the pleasure of walking on a road of well-broken stone does not compensate them for the trouble they have had in constructing it without pay."

In this rapid interchange of arguments, both Turgot and the Keeper of the Seals imperfectly apprehend the real effects of improvements in the highways. They both talk like men who are strangers to a sound theory of wealth, but what a difference in their language in what concerns the interests of the laboring classes! What lively sympathy in Turgot! what cold indifference in the other! But see by this what the lessons of the *Econo- mists* had already effected, and to what ground questions of political economy had been brought! Turgot kept them there during the whole of his ministry, and he invariably prosecuted, one by one, and so to speak, according to a programme determined in advance, the solution of every one of those which the school of Quesnay had raised. After the edict suppressing the corvées, came the famous edict of February, 1776, the chief work of Turgot, the charter of freedom for the working classes. The historian to-day has only to pay his respects to the memory of that brave act; which, however, was almost immediately followed by a return to monopoly and privileges,* though triumphant a few years later by the aid of

---

* The edict of 1776 was revoked three months after it was issued.

a revolution. The abolition of corporations was a great and fine measure, but how much was its merit enhanced by the terms of this memorable preamble, the noblest perhaps which administration has ever borrowed from science ! " God, by giving man wants," said the preamble, " by rendering the resource of labor necessary to him, has made of the right to work the property of every man ; and *that property is the first, the most sacred, the most imprescriptible of all.* We consequently desire to abrogate those arbitrary institutions, which do not permit the poor man to live by his labor, which extinguish emulation and industry and render useless the talents of those whom circumstances exclude from admission into a corporation ; which weigh down manufactures with an enormous tax, burdensome to the subjects and without any advantage to the state ; which, in short, by the facilities they afford members of corporations to league together and to force the poorest members to submit to the law of the richest, become an instrument of monopoly, and favor manœuvres the effect of which is to raise the provisions most necessary for the subsistence of a people, above their natural rate." All the rest is written in this stern and uncompromising style, which granted no favor to any abuse and which stigmatized them all before men who were astonished at the long oppression of their fathers and the absurdity of so many useless vexations. What we have already said * upon this subject, does not permit us to enter further into this question, henceforth solved, the solution of which has obtained the highest sanction of experience and time.

After having freed the laborer from the corvée and the mechanic from the power of the masters, Turgot determined to save the merchant from usury ; and he entered upon that reform with the lofty and adventurous views which distinguished his character. He had published, in 1769, an extremely remarkable memoir on *Money Loans,*

---

* See chap. xix of this work, devoted to the institutions of Saint Louis.

in which he pointed out the essential faults of restrictive legislation on rate of interest, a legislation so successfully confuted since by Jeremy Bentham: he wished to do more; and, to finish the work that he had so well begun, he promoted the establishment of a bank of discount, which would neutralize, by its low rate of interest, the excessive demands of loaners of capital. It even occurred to him to give publicity to mortgages, so that it should be impossible, he said, for owners of land not to pay their debts; and the security of the credit would lower the interest of money. Whether he was right or wrong in his hope, we cannot too much praise his solicitude in thinking of all reforms which might favor labor and production in our country.

There remained to Turgot one great experiment to try, that of reform in the taxes; and here the erroneous opinions of the *Economists* came near causing him disastrous miscalculations. The positive doctrine of the *net product* might, in fact, be very innocent, so long as it did not depart from the narrow circle of abstractions, but there was much danger in upturning, from bottom to top, the whole fiscal system of France for the triumph of a mere hypothesis. Turgot, prepossessed with the idea of a general removal of the burdens of the poor classes and the need of emancipating all branches of industry, was convinced that by reducing all taxes to one single land-tax he would reach simply the *net product*, that is to say, the annual creations of natural labor on the land. His plan was to devote one part of this product to taxes, and to leave the other in the hands of the proprietors, born-distributors of the wages, according to Quesnay. But the proprietors were justly alarmed by an experiment which attacked their revenue at its source and degraded their property, which thus became the objective point of all taxes. The project of Turgot was, besides, unjust in this respect, that the real wealth created by laborers other than agriculturers, was exempt from taxation as if it were not wealth, although it really was so. Thus the proprietors of lands were made to bear the fiscal consequences of an error of doctrine, and the government was ruining them in the best faith possible, while proclaiming them preëminently *the* producers. It was a great misfortune to science that Turgot was so precipitate in applying a theory so hazardous and so radically false, as if its correctness had been demonstrated with mathematical certainty. Moreover, in this case, the past commanded great consideration from a statesman. Whatever the intensity of his convictions, he should not have proceeded to such reforms with the eagerness of a partisan, but with the prudence of a legislator. His error, which was shared later by the Constituent Assembly, precipitated France into an abyss of evils, by depriving the government, for several years, of the immense revenues it would have found in indirect taxes, the principle of which rests on the production of immovable (*immobilière*) wealth, as the land-tax does on the production of agricultural wealth.

Turgot wished no more loans, and his bank of discount was not a measure preparatory to a reëstablishment of great public credit. The economist school denied the influence of public credit on public prosperity. They did not allow that the annual revenue of the state should be anticipated, even for useful purposes; and because they had dreamed of the age of gold, they seemed not to suppose that there could ever be hard times to be encountered. It was this confidence in his philosophy which animated Turgot when he had corporations abolished. He did not even suspect that this great act of emancipation, which cannot be too much praised, would be followed by formidable complications, whose solution would some day demand a genius more bold, if not more loyal than his. He was so happy to restore freedom of labor to that multitude of comrades bound down to the glebe of the workshop! He presaged such brilliant destinies for the French nation, reinstated in possession of so many living forces! Who could have told him that after a half century, competition among laborers would bring about a reduction of wages, pauperism, and all the miseries which dim the lustre of our civilization? He marched with as firm a step, in the pursuit of utopias, as in the reform of abuses, and the mind is overpowered at all which he undertook with his simple forces as minister, at a time when ministers did not have many of them at command. He had projected the suppression of monasteries, the just distribution of taxes, one single civil code for the whole kingdom, unity of weights and measures, a new system for public instruction, the establishment of a record of the survey of lands, not to mention a multitude of special measures which attest the solicitude of an administrator as well as the intelligence of a savant. "He acted," says Sénac de Meilhan, "like a surgeon who operates on dead bodies, and he did not dream that he was operating on sensible beings: he only saw things, and did not concern himself sufficiently with persons. This apparent harshness had its origin in the purity of his soul, which pictured men to him as animated with an equal desire for the public good, or as knaves who deserved no consideration."

Accordingly, from every direction, the projects of Turgot encountered obstinate resistance. Much of it came from the court; still more, from the city. Most of it was unjust and shameful, because dictated by private interest;* some, on the contrary, seems to have had good foundation, because the reforming minister had not

---

* Among the useful creations of Turgot which made great talk, we must mention the establishment of the first public stage-coaches, the competition of which injured the old monopolizers of transportation. It was an immense advantage for all classes of citizens : the minister, however, was satirized in ballads. One may judge of them by the following epigram published on that occasion :—

> " Ministre ivre d' orgueil, tranchant du souverain,
> Toi qui, sans t'emouvoir, fais tant de misérables,
> Puisse ta poste absurde aller un si grand train,
> Qu'elle te mène à tous les diables ! "

sufficiently taken into account the exigencies of the past. The first germ of opposition came from the parliaments, which too many people are accustomed to consider as the defenders of all progressive ideas, but which made the fiercest war on Turgot which he had to sustain. This truly virtuous minister cannot be too highly honored for the courage with which he persevered in the long struggle with which his whole administrative career was agitated. One of his friends reproached him with being in too much of a hurry about his reforms: " How can you reproach me for that ? " he replied : " You know that in my family we die of gout at fifty years." The whole explanation of his conduct is in these words. Turgot committed no other wrong than that of wishing too soon and at any cost, the success of that which appeared to him advantageous to his country. His love for improvements extended to everything, poetry, education, astronomy: " There you are," said the Abbé Morellet to him one day, " doing in physics as in administration, fighting against Nature, which is stronger than you and is not willing that man should have the precise measure of anything." Even to his last breath, in spite of the miscalculations and the hindrances of his administration, he held to the doctrines of the *Economists*, with all the strength of religious conviction. He carried philanthropy so far as to wish his servants to be as well lodged as he, and he went to considerable expense on this account in his mansion.

Turgot left a great number of writings which were carefully collated by Dupont de Nemours.* Administrators in all times and all countries will obtain from them useful

---

* This collection is composed of nine octavo volumes, which appeared from 1808 to 1811. Dupont had it preceded by a life of Turgot, which is not worth the notice published by Condorcet. (*Author's Note.*)

The works of Turgot have been reëdited by M. Eugène Daire, with the notes of Dupont de Nemours and unedited letters, questions on commerce, and observations and new notes by Messrs. Daire and Dussard. This important publication (1844, 2 vol., gr. in 8vo.) makes a part of the *Collection of the Principal Economists*, by Guillaumin.—*Fr. Ed.*

information, for never did this minister touch upon a single question before having investigated it thoroughly; and almost all the preambles of his edicts are complete treatises on their subject matter. But the most interesting of his works is his *Treatise on the Formation and Distribution of Wealth;* and although it bears the impress of the ideas of the *Economists,* we can see in it the dawning symptoms of a dissent which leads to the theory of Adam Smith. Division of labor, the true functions of money, and the operations of commerce are there set forth with remarkable clearness and precision. The most learned economists of the nineteenth century have not demonstrated better the influence of the rate of interest on all enterprises. " It may be regarded," says Turgot, " as a sort of level, below which all labor, all culture, all manufactures, all commerce, cease. It is like a sea spread over a vast country: the summits of the mountains rise above the waters and form fertile and cultivated isles. If that sea should flow back, as it descends, first the lands on mountain slopes and then the plains and the valleys appear and become covered with products of every kind. If the water rises or falls one foot, it is enough to inundate or to restore to cultivation immense areas. It is abundance of capital which animates all enterprises, and low interest for money is at the same time the effect and the indication of abundance of capital."

The treatise on the formation and distribution of wealth preceded by nine years the publication of Adam Smith's work, and was not without influence on the doctrines of the celebrated Scotch economist. Turgot thought as he did on interest-loans, free trade, free manufacture, the influence of lines of communication, the elements of price, and the formation of capital. It is a real glory to have thus preceded, in this work, the greatest writer who has honored science, and to be considered, in so many respects, as his precursor; but the most incontestable honor which belongs to Turgot will always be, to have opened the field of experiment to the first theories of political science which were boldly formulated; to have submitted them to the test of practice, and to have invited, not alone savants, but also the people, to judge them. All the literature of the last half of the eighteenth century bears the impress of this influence. Montesquieu, D'Alembert, Marmontel, Condorcet, Raynal, Condillac, J. J. Rousseau and Voltaire even, speak of political economy in their writings, the daily papers, the collections of writings of every kind, henceforth devote to it a place. People from this time begin to comprehend that there is a physiology of the social body as there is of the human body, and that there are laws according to which nations prosper or waste away, like individuals. Economic science is henceforth admitted to the councils of governments: it will go no more out from such councils, as soon as Adam Smith shall have impressed it with the seal of his genius.

CHAPTER XXXIV.

The labors of Adam Smith and their influence on the progress of political economy.—Difference between his doctrines and those of the *Economists.* Statement of the creations due to him.—His fine definitions of *value, labor, capital and money.*—Great results of his discoveries.

THE principal merit of the *Economists* consisted in rais-ing the profoundest questions of political economy, and that of Turgot, in attempting their practical solution, by means of the administrative power. We have seen with what talent and what meritorious perseverance these philosophers devoted themselves to the cultivation of a science which seemed to them to include *the destinies of the human race:* but not for them was reserved the honor of laying its foundations in a solid and enduring manner. They had only perceived, under a false light, its principal aspects; but their errors had served, at least, to awaken a profound examination of the questions which it had been impossible for them to resolve. Instead of proceeding by the experimental method and by the observation of facts, they had pro-claimed as infallible dogmas certain formulas, which seved to explain to them all the phenomena of social physiology. When an argument capable of modifying their belief in these dogmas came in their way, they strove to connect it with their system by ingenious or bold hypotheses; and they fell, without perceiving it, into the abyss of utopias. We have seen that their aphorism of the *net product* had prevented them from re-cognizing the immense part manufactures and commerce have in the production of wealth, and that their theory of property had led them to the suppression of all indirect taxes. They had touched upon all questions and they had resolved none; but they had called the attention of all Europe to the most difficult, and Europe responded to their appeal.

A Scotch philosopher, of that school from which so many thinkers have sprung, was teaching at Glasgow, at the same time as the *Economists* at Paris, the principles of the wealth of nations. It was about the year 1752, nearly at the time when Quesnay was publishing his *Tableau Economique*, and laying the foundations of his doctrine. But the Glasgow professor had early accustomed himself to study facts, compare them and deduce conclusions from them : consequently he was led to results very different from those obtained by the *Economists*. The two schools had in common only the same love of the well-being of society, the same directness and the same scrupulous fidelity to the interests of truth. As to everything that concerns science, the starting point being altogether different, the results could not be the same, and soon the widest difference of opinion became manifest. The Economists attributed productive power only to the earth; Adam Smith found that power in labor, and from that luminous idea he brought forth the most unforeseen and the most decisive conclusions. Here begins the history of the revolution produced by the publication of his *Inquiry into the Nature and Causes of the Wealth of Nations*, which appeared for the first time in 1776, that is to say, twenty-four years after the opening of his career. A day will soon come when that celebrated publication will bring forth all its fruit, and its memorable date will be engraven on all minds. Let us then attempt to imitate the logical and severe method of the great writer who was its author, and in a brief sketch ascertain the importance of this fine work to the future of civilization.

In investigating the causes of the wealth of nations, Adam Smith recognized that this wealth originated not only from the fertility of their soil, but also from the labor of their inhabitants.   It was labor which alone could render the earth largely and regularly productive, and it was moreover to labor that human society owed the products of its manufactures, and the profits of its commerce.   Adam Smith summed up the result of his thought by saying that the *annual labor* of a nation was the primitive source from which it derived its wealth, that is to say, the products necessary for its consumption, or those by means of which it produced for itself the products created by other nations.   Wealth consisted in the *exchangeable value* of things, and one was the more rich in proportion as he possessed or produced more things having that value.   Now, how did people give things an exchange value?   By developing by labor a utility which they would not have had without it.   Wealth could then be created, augmented, maintained, accumulated, destroyed.   This simple definition overthrew at one stroke the doctrine of the *Economists*, and restored to their position all the laborious and honorable occupations which Quesnay considered as tributary and subordinate to landed property.   No one was thrust back from the banquet of life; labor had access everywhere and ceased to be unproductive : feudal servitude, maintained by Quesnay under the name of reprisals of the land proprietor, had received its death blow.

Labor being once recognized as the source of all wealth, *economy* and *saving* became the only means of accumulating it, that is to say, of creating *capital*.   And here Adam Smith, with his rare intelligence, profited by the labors of his predecessors.   He did not limit capital, as did the supporters of the mercantile system, to gold and silver; but he included in it wealth of every kind amassed by the labor of man, especially the wealth employed to create new wealth by the aid of a new labor.   At the same time, he gave the finest analysis of labor which ever came from the pen of any writer.   This analysis serves in a certain way as a frontispiece to his immortal work, and the author has displayed in it a clearness of deductions and a nobility of language truly worthy of admiration.   Here are pointed out the marvellous effects of *division of labor*, often partially seen before Adam Smith, but nowhere demonstrated with that irresistible evidence and simple familiarity which leave no refuge for doubt and hesitation.   Others would have taken their examples from the great works of industrial art : Adam Smith takes a pin, describes the various operations in its manufacture, and makes us see how ten workmen can make 48,000 pins a day, instead of four or five hundred, which is a hundred times less than they would do without that division. After this modest and conclusive example, he passes in review the advantages of the principle of division of labor, and describes them in so animated and forcible a manner that no one, from that time, has dreamed of contesting them.   " Every workman has a great quantity of his own work to dispose of beyond what he himself has occasion for ; and every other workman being exactly in the same situation, he is enabled to exchange a great quantity of his own goods for a great quantity, or, what comes to the same thing, for the price of a great quantity of theirs.   He supplies them abundantly with what they have occasion for, and they accommodate him as amply with what he has occasion for, and a general plenty diffuses itself through all the different ranks of the society." *

Having analyzed division of labor, Adam Smith had to explain by what agencies the products of labor were exchanged by means of money.   What would regulate what is called the *price of things ?*   What are the elements of this price?   What are the functions of money?   These grave questions he resolved in an incomparably superior

---

* *Wealth of Nations*, Book i, chap. i.

and lucid manner. He, in fact, was the first to successfully establish the influence of *demand and supply* on the
rise and fall of prices, at the same time that he explained
the functions of money in the circulation of products.
The applications he made of his theory to bank-bills and
paper money are of the highest importance in practice,
and may be considered as one of the most useful conquests of science. It is henceforth impossible to write
on monetary science without adopting the bases which
he imperishably laid down for it. In his course, Adam
Smith unveiled the mysteries of the constitution of
banks, and deduced from the consequences of their
establishment, the principles on which they must rest
in order not to bring disaster. Every man desirous
of examining thoroughly the science of credit ought
to commence his studies by that of the analyses which
the illustrious Scotch economist has given of banks of
circulation and banks of deposit. These are complete
treatises which will never be surpassed, because they
contain not one gap, not one superfluity. But the
principal merit of Adam Smith lies in the perfect clearness of his definitions. They are generally based on a
rigorous observation of facts. Once stated, he deduces
conclusions from them by a method peculiar to himself
which would alone suffice to assure him a high rank
among the finest geniuses of modern times. The reader
will be able to judge of it from a rapid exposition of his
doctrines.

As we have seen, according to this author, the essential
quality which constitutes wealth, is *exchangeable value*,
Exchangeable value differs from value in use, or *utility*,
in this, that with the former, people can procure for them
selves many things; while the second, though useful,
cannot be the subject of an exchange. There is nothing
more useful than water; but it can buy scarcely anything. A diamond, on the contrary, though of little
utility, may serve to purchase a large number of commod-

ities.   The relation which exists between two exchangeable values, expressed in a value agreed upon, which is the
money, is called price.   The *nominal* price of things differs from the *real* price, which represents the quantity of
labor they have cost.   The price of exchangeable things
depends upon the accidental circumstances which make
the present or *current* price deviate from the natural
price.   Price is ordinarily composed of three distinct
elements ;   the *wages* of labor, the profits of stock
and the rent of the land which supplies the first material for labor.   After having established in a perfectly
methodical manner these introductory principles so simple and so ingenious, Adam Smith determines the laws
according to which the rate of wages is naturally established, and the accidental circumstances which make
them vary temporarily from this natural rate.   He then
examines the laws in virtue of which the rate of profits
is determined, and the exceptions to these laws ;   then
he defines the *rent* of land which we call *farm rent*
and which the Economists called *net product*.

Wealth once created, Adam Smith divides it into two
parts : that which is to be consumed immediately or in a
short time, and that which is employed as capital to furnish a revenue.   The capital is *fixed* when it is transformed into a workshop with all its instruments of production ;   it is *circulating* or *movable* when it is used to pay
the wages of the workmen and renew purchases of raw
materials.   Improvements made on land form part of
the fixed capital ; money and provisions belong to the
circulating capital.   The first is sometimes changed
into the second, and the second sometimes in its turn
takes a course which confounds it with the first.   Money
appears as the instrument of this double transformation ; but notes, promises to pay, often take its place
and even with advantage.   This advantage depends upon
the conditions on which one has borrowed and consequently on the rate of interest.   Adam Smith adopts in

this regard the liberal theories of Turgot, and he demonstrates by irresistible arguments their incontestible
equity.

Labor is now fully equipped : it is in possession of capital : we shall next see it at work. Nothing is more simple and admirable than the way in which Adam Smith
explains its marvels ; we have cited his example drawn
from the manufacture of pins. But what noble subjects
for reflection are his numerous reviews of the army of
laborers ! How naturally he has rendered an account of
the progress of nations, by the progress in *division of
labor !* How happily he has introduced, as a consequence of that division, the necessity of the exchanges !
How successfully he explains the increase of wealth, the
perfecting of products and how their prices become daily
more accessible ! It was he who revealed the secret of
machines, those powerful modifications of the arm of
man, those benefactors of the human race, which a distinguished philanthropist * has unfortunately made the
mistake of not appreciating. No one has more ably described their varied, infinite and lasting services, and
without concealing their temporary disadvantages. At
the same time, Adam Smith clearly laid down the limitations in their employment, and demonstrated that the
extent of the market must be the habitual regulator of
division of labor. On account of having neglected these
wise doctrines, more than one manufacturing nation has
seen formidable crises, resulting from obstructed circulation and restrictive measures. Thus Adam Smith arrived at free trade by a road quite different from that the
school of Quesnay had followed ; but he was led to it by
a much more just appreciation of the phenomena of production.

His doctrine on taxation differed also essentially from
that of the *Economists*. After having proved that all
production came from labor, aided by capital, it was not

---

* Sismondi.

difficult for him to demonstrate that every citizen being qualified to create values, and consequently to make profits, owed to the state his contributive part of defence and of taxes. Every one obtained freedom in his work in return for his coöperation in the public burdens; and there were no longer any *sterile* occupations, since everybody was capable of giving things an exchange value, by means of labor. What an encouragement to men ill-favored by fortune and to those who did not expect the boon of an inheritance! They learned thenceforth at what price one acquires his independence; economy was no longer an ascetic virtue, but the companion of labor and the source of capital. Instead of limits imposed on the products of agriculture, by the nature of the soil and the rotation of the seasons, one had before him the un-limited horizon of exchange values, that is to say, unlimited wealth. Adam Smith did not, doubtless, foresee all these results, and many writers before him had advanced principles as true; but he was the first one to show why they were true. He did more: he indicated the true method of pointing out errors. His work is composed of a succession of demonstrations which have raised several propositions to the rank of incontestible principles, and which have forever annihilated a multitude of errors until then considered as principles. It was he who completely crushed the prohibitory system and the doctrine of the *net product*, with his train of reflections on taxation and on imaginary classifications. Finally, and it was perhaps one of the greatest services he rendered to science, this immortal economist showed how private interest, when freed from restrictions, necessarily led the possessors of capital to prefer, all things being equal, the employment of it most favorable to national industry, because it was also the most profitable for them.

It is true that Adam Smith sometimes wandered off into many digressions which prevent one from easily following the thread of his ideas. As soon as he encounters an old abuse, a hurtful prejudice, or an erroneous system, he does not stop until he has done justice to it; and these side skirmishes often divert him from the plan of his operations. But never does he take final leave of a subject without having exhausted it; and he habitually presents the same idea under all its forms, until the reader has become familiarized with it. He had so much opposition to overcome and so many false doctrines to combat! The *Economists* themselves, whom he esteemed and who certainly contributed to the direction of his ideas, were not those who rendered his task the least difficult. He had to struggle against the innumerable works they had just published and which had been scattered throughout Europe, and more or less comprehended, with the authority of names most revered, like those of Gournay, Turgot, and Trudaine. He was obliged to destroy most of the theories which they had just established at the cost of so many efforts, and to combat them under unfavorable auspices. This was the first memorable lack of harmony that appeared among the founders of political economy; and it has not a little contributed to give rise to the general indecision of the public on economic matters. Which was one to believe, Quesnay or Smith, maintaining with equal assurance contrary doctrines, and both simultaneously invoking the authority of facts! But we must not forget that there is not a science which did not begin by quarrels between its illustrious chiefs, and that these severe trials contributed, almost as much as their discoveries, to the progress of which we are to-day so proud.

Adam Smith did not, however, have the honor of creating political economy at a single stroke; and our respect for his memory must not prevent our rendering justice to his predecessors and his successors. The demonstration of the whole theory of values, of the effects of division of labor, and of the true functions of money, was of itself such a great historic fact! Such anaiyses would suffice for the immortality of an author; and we may boldly criticise what was incomplete in his writings, after having described wherein they merited glory and consideration. The *Economists* were too much prepossessed with the importance of land; Adam Smith accorded to labor a too exclusive preponderance in the creation of products. He did not sufficiently note the effect of land and capital, and notwithstanding his magnificent expositions of the coöperation of machines, he does not present the theory about them best founded on the reality of things. In reserving exclusively the quality of riches for values embodied in material substances, he erased from the book of production that unlimited mass of immaterial values, offspring of the *moral capital* of civilized nations, and which form a part of their support and their glory. He struck out, at one stroke of the pen, lawyers, physicians, engineers, artists, public functionaries, producers all of real services exchangeable for material products since they live by them and live well, when they have sufficient merit to secure generous payment. He had not perceived that the talent of these men was an accumulated capital, quite capable of giving interest in gold and silver, and very useful to society, which profits in its turn by their services.*

The influence of trade and its effect on general production do not seem, either, to have been sufficiently appreciated by Adam Smith; and some of his finest demonstrations are set forth by way of digression, in a place where they do not belong. Such are the principles relating to the real and the nominal price of things, which are found in a dissertation on the value of the precious metals for the four last centuries; and the information on moneys, which the author has misplaced by putting it into the chapter on commercial treaties. It is the dis-

---

* Blanqui is in error here. Adam Smith expressly recognizes in *Wealth of Nations*, Book ii, chap. i, the talents of individuals as *fixed capital*. Smith's definition of wealth, was, however, too narrow.— *Trans*.

order which prevails around a productive mine, where
fragments of the purest metal sometimes lie in confusion
near the coarsest mineral. Besides, the *Inquiry into the
Nature and Causes of the Wealth of Nations* is not comprehended by every body, nor should we advise one to
commence the study of the science with this book. It
should be re-read several times for one to divine its fine
construction and rightly estimate the results it has produced. Then may one venture to contest a few of the
propositions which Adam Smith has expressed in the
most dogmatic form, such as that according to which
private interest, free from restraints, seemed to him
always sufficient to determine the employment of capital most favorable to the community, since it determined
that profitable to the managers of business. This doctrine, which prevailed in England, and gave an extraordinary impulse to the arts and manufactures, is nevertheless beginning to produce bitter fruits: it has created
immense wealth, side by side with frightful poverty; it
has enriched the nation, while often treating a part of
its citizens very cruelly. Is this the social end of the increase of wealth, or rather is it not an unhappy deviation
from the social way? Can this excess of profits, deducted, according to Sismondi, from the share of the poor,
and according to us, from labor, by capital, be truly
called riches?

Thus, universal competition originated from unlimited
freedom of labor; and from this competition, a torrent
of wealth has been poured out upon the world, which
indeed fertilizes many provinces, but which has left in
more than one country fatal traces of its passage, like a
brilliant and mysterious car, whose passengers cannot
even see and pity the passers-by whom it crushes. The
question has come to the point that the people are demanding whether they should congratulate themselves or
be disquieted at an advance in wealth which entails so
many miseries and which multiplies hospitals and prisons
as well as palaces. This is the great problem of the nine-

teenth century, the one which Adam Smith had not foreseen and could not foresee, at a time when the steam-engine and the spinning-machine, those two giants of English industry, were only just born, like his book! We are to-day obliged to seek a regulator and to put a curb on those gigantic instruments of production, which feed and which starve men, which clothe and which despoil them, which relieve and which crush them. The question is no longer, as in the time of Smith, exclusively that of accelerating production: the latter must henceforth be governed and restricted within wise limits. The question is no-longer of absolute wealth, but of relative wealth; humanity demands that masses of men who will not profit thereby, be no longer sacrificed to the progress of public opulence. Thus decree the eternal laws of justice and morality, too long disregarded in the social distribution of the profits and the labors; and we will no longer consent to give the name of wealth, save to the sum of the national product equitably distributed between all the producers. Such is the French school of political economy to which we profess to belong, and its ideas will make the circuit of the world.

Such as it appeared, nevertheless, the doctrine of Adam Smith wrought a complete revolution in the course of political economy. His opinions on the colonies acquired great weight from the events which were taking place in America, and his analysis of banks prepared the awakening of Europe in the matter of public credit. Manufactures owed to him the removal of almost all their restrictions, and commerce a beginning of the reduction of all tariffs. The questions of agriculture and population remained, which this great economist had only lightly touched upon and whose solution concerns our children; but the most dangerous prejudices had disappeared before his powerful argumentation, and their sway is forever ended. Balance of trade, restrictive system, agricultural system, have all been precipitated into the gulf of vagaries; Adam

Smith has demonetized them all by his severe logic and by his impartial observation of facts. One single uncertainty survived his doctrines ; what connection is there between population and means of subsistence ? Why does private want increase ·in our society, at the same time with public wealth ? Why does not the sun of industry shine for everybody ? Two English writers are going to give you, each in his manner, an explanation of this social anomaly : the reader will divine that we mean Godwin and Malthus. It is time to hear them ; for, after Adam Smith, they became chiefs of a school by the same right ; each of them had a grand thought, a clear and striking thought, which commands attention and for the moment inspires terror.

CHAPTER XXXV.

The system of Malthus *On Population.*—An exposition of its formulas.—
Exposition of its results.—Doctrine of Godwin.—It has the fault of being
as absolute as that of Malthus.—It is more humane.—Remarkable boldness of Godwin's book.—Various writings on the same question.—*New*
Ideas on Population, by Mr. Everett.—Book on *Charity,* by M. Duchâtel.
—*Christian Political Economy,* by M. de Villeneuve-Bargemont.—Protests
of M. de Sismondi and of Abbé de La Mennais.

A FEW years had elapsed since the publication of the
work of Adam Smith, and his doctrines were aiready
adopted by the economists of all countries. His clear
and cogent reasoning had dissipated most of the dreams
which many minds still took for realities. There was
at length an agreement on the fundamental bases of the
science. Labor was restored to honor; exchange value
was defined; the employment of capital was henceforth
subject to regular laws. It was known how riches were
produced and how consumed; but there remained, as we
have said, one problem to solve : Why are riches so unequally distributed in the social body! Why are there
always unfortunates? And this problem was thrown out
one day, by the redoubtable hand of the French people,
as a challenge to all the governments of Europe. Turgot, who had attempted to resolve it, died in the effort,
and the French revolution had shed torrents of blood to
find its solution, without being more fortunate than
Turgot.

Did the evil come from nature or from society? Was
it without remedy, or might one succeed in curing it,
with the aid of time? Impressed with what laws can do

for the morals and condition of people, some illustrious writers had thought that the miseries of man were his work, and that it only depended on him to put an end to them, much less by restraining his passions than by changing political institutions. It was 1798 : a memorable attempt had just been made in France, and people had seen, within a few years, the boldest reforms, supported in turn by reasoning and by force, leave the human race a prey to the same uncertainties and the same inequalities as in the past. The dividing up of landed property into small portions, had been substituted for the old system of concentration ; power had been bestowed upon the poorest masses, who had not opposed the *maximum,* nor the forced loans, nor bankruptcy, nor the suppression of indirect taxes ; and there were still poor people, men clothed in rags, old men without bread, helpless women, foundlings, malefactors, and prostitutes. What remained to do after what had been done ? What monarchy would attempt what the courage of 1793 had not been able to accomplish ? Philosophers and economists, struck with stupor, were experiencing that bitter disappointment which follows political revolutions, when suddenly there appeared, with a brief interval between them, two writings from two men celebrated in different ways, the book of Mr. Godwin on *Political Justice* and that of Malthus on *Population.*

Mr. Godwin, in his work, attributed all social evils to the imperfection of political institutions and the faults of governments. Malthus was more impressed by the obstacles which man imposes in the way of social progress, by the passions inherent in his nature and his little disposition to restrain them. The reading of an article by Mr. Godwin on *Prodigality and Avarice,** decided him to publish his ideas on this subject ; and after some retouches, easy to conceive in a labor of that importance, the essay on the *Principle of Population* appeared in England in the last

---

* Inserted into a number of *The Inquirer.*

year of the eighteenth century, as a sort of *résumé* of the universal disenchantment of minds. This book created a great sensation, because it was based on one simple idea, easy to comprehend and retain ; and it has been cruelly abused, because it seems to favor more than one bad inclination of man, egotism, harshness, and indifference to the suffering of his fellow creatures. The principles on which it rests have obtained, nevertheless, the sanction of several governments, and they tend so rapidly to penetrate into institutions, that there will soon be nothing more to do except to record their conquests, instead of discussing their value. We must, then, here set them forth undisguised before examining their consequences, a double task which calls for all the impartiality of the historian.

The doctrine is presented with the inflexible and absolute character of fatality. The author dispenses with oratorical precautions ; he establishes, without flinching, as an evident, constant and necessary fact, that the human race blindly obeys the law of indefinite multiplication, while means of subsistence do not multiply in the same proportion. This fact appears to him so well demonstrated, that he does not hesitate to formulate it as a mathematical axiom ; and he affirms that men increase in geometrical progression, and provisions in arithmetical progression. There would then come a time when provisions would be insufficient for the voyagers, if diseases, poverty and death, those sinister correctives, did not regularly intervene to re-establish the equilibrium. Malthus pronounced this sentence on the unfortunates, in cruel terms: "A man who is born into a world already full," he said,* "if his family have no means to support him, *or if society has no need of his labor*, has not the least right to claim any portion of food whatever, and he *is really redundant on the earth*. At

---

* This cruel passage was suppressed by Malthus in the later editions of his book ; but the spirit of his doctrine is nevertheless summed up in it with emphatic truthfulness, and it was the doctrine rather than the language that needed modification.

the great banquet of nature there is no plate for him. *Nature commands him to go away*, and she delays not to put that order into execution."· Here is the foundation of the doctrine of Malthus on population. Let us now look at the arguments by which he has attempted to establish it.

Instead of observing carefully what takes place in long-established civilized communities, the author transports himself to America, to the United States, a virgin country, fertile, immense, where the population doubles every twenty-five years. This is the country which he takes for a type of the rest of the world, and he unhesitatingly admits that the human race would increase with the same rapidity everywhere else, if the force of things did not restrain this development within certain limits. When once, in fact, the population has risen to the level of the means of subsistence, the latter beginning to fail, vices, diseases, and calamities of every kind begin to rain down *upon the men who are redundant*, according to Malthus, and the population diminishes until there is food for everybody. History in hand, he attempts to prove that the same consequences have always followed the same conditions, and that in a barbarous state as in a civilized, there has never been any compromise between famine and death. And if death only came alone! but it never appears, in these sad conjunctures, without being accompanied by a train of crimes and horrors of every kind—without raising its mournful standard over hospitals, in galleys, and over scaffolds. Thus Malthus depicts it, just as we have seen it many times without daring to think, as he does, that it comes under that form, by order of God and as a necessity even of our social order.

We begin by contesting the double progression established by Malthus: but before pointing out that fundamental error of his system, let us see what terrible conclusions he deduced from it. He proclaimed, to begin

with, the danger of alms, public or private aid, permanent or temporary; he prohibited marriage, except to
certain men, and he condemned to death thousands of
children at birth. Charities bestowed on the poor in a
religious spirit, or through love of beneficence, were in
his eyes only murderous favors whose principal result
was to encourage idleness and to multiply the number of
unfortunates. " For nothing multiplies like poverty,"
he said; "and people who have nothing to lose, care
very little what happens to their descendants." This is
what Montesquieu had already said in ironical terms :
" People who have absolutely nothing, like beggars, have
many children ; for it costs the father nothing to teach
his trade to his children, who are from their very birth
instruments of that trade."* But Montesquieu had
drawn no conclusions from that general disposition of
proletaries to unconcern : he contented himself with
pointing it out, without investigating its cause. Malthus
thought he had found that cause in the encouragement
afforded to idleness by beneficence ; and, directing his
attention to the alms-houses and foundling hospitals, he
pointed out all the miseries which the abuse of public
charity had engendered. He then addressed himself to
the noblest and most generous feelings of man, and
sought to demonstrate the superiority of prudence over
all other resources offered to old age and infirmities.

    Never, perhaps, up to that time, had any system been
formulated in terms so absolute. The *Economists* themselves admitted some modifications in their theory of the
net product ; but Malthus knew of no possible capitulation in the struggle of men against nature ; these lamentable contests must always end by decrees of death.
He consequently undertook to preach, under the term
moral restraint, a doctrine little favorable to marriage.
He attempted to demonstrate to the laboring classes, that
by multiplying the number of children, they were creat-

Spirit of the Laws, book xxiii, chap. xi.

ing competition which would bring about a fall in wages, and that the surest way of bringing capitalists to terms, was not to furnish them a permanent opportunity of choosing workmen at the lowest price. It was for the interest of society itself to interpose salutary obstacles to inconsiderate unions, since the inevitable consequence of these unions was the multiplication of crimes and miseries of every kind. Unfortunately, Malthus soon perceived that celibacy did not prevent births; it only rendered them illegitimate, and this was an additional misfortune. What, then must be done to put a limit to the increase of population, since the birth of children could not be prevented? Malthus saw that obstacle, but was not disconcerted by it. He armed himself with stoical courage, and he decided that children should be out of the protection of the law, even before they were born. He proposed* that a law should be passed declaring that "no child born from any marriage taking place after the expiration of a year from the date of the law, and no illegitimate child born two years after the same date, should ever be entitled to parish assistance." "This," he said, "would operate as a fair, distinct, and precise notice, which no man could well mistake." * * * "No one would be deceived or injured, and consequently no one would have a right to complain." So children in the cradle became responsible for the error which had brought them into the world. "Why do you shrink?" said Malthus, "your charity is more cruel than my severity, and your foundling asylums are only catacombs." He at the same time unrolled the mournful tables of the mortality of children in these asylums, and people were obliged to acknowledge that they almost all died in their first year.†

---

* *Principle of Population*, Book iv, chap. viii, 6th edition.

† According to the calculations of M. Benoiston de Châteauneuf, the mortality of foundlings was 67 per cent at Madrid, in 1817; 92 per cent at Vienna, in 1811; 79 per cent at Bruxelles, on the average, from 1802 to 1817; as we have already said, at the foundling asylum in Dublin, from 1791 to 1797, of 12,785 children, 12,561 died in six years. What a slaughter house!

These terrible presentations of facts produced a great sensation in Europe. Malthus continued them with inflexible persistency; he wished to alarm humanity at their own errors and to force all men of heart to consider well their course before marrying. By suppressing the inclination natural to all governments to multiply institutions of beneficence, he hoped to put a limit to the abuses of these institutions, which, he thought, only served to aggravate social maladies, instead of curing them. Celibacy, of late dishonored as a selfish condition, was restored to honor, and almost raised to the rank of a virtue. Hospitals and asylums were closed; people ceased to distribute alms; they no longer concerned themselves in matters of beneficence and public assistance. Harshness alone was henceforward in conformity to the true principles of science, to the laws of nature; insensibility was erected into a system. It must be confessed that such a system must have been deeply revolting to generous and tender souls to whom the pleasure of bestowing charities is a constant necessity. Consequently there arose on all sides a general cry of disapprobation at the doctrines of Malthus. The author came near being distinguished as a man without feeling, who would impudently hurl the horrible irony of his system at the human race. It was the first time, people said, that any one had dared thus to eulogize pestilence, war, famine, and all the scourges which afflict humanity, by presenting them as in accordance with natural laws, and destined to maintain the balance between population and means of subsistence. Priests, women, and philosophers, revolted at the audacity of such a supposition; and Malthus, notwithstanding his private qualities, was, in consequence, long exposed to the most calumnious imputations.

The storm has at length abated above the grave of this great writer, and posterity have begun to do him justice. He himself acknowledged, in his latter days, that he had overstated the consequences of his principle. "It is very probable," he said, "that having found the bow too much bent in one direction, I was led to bend it too much in the other, with the view of making it straight; but I shall always be disposed to eliminate from my work that which shall be considered, by competent judges, as having a tendency to prevent the bow from righting itself, and to put any obstacle in the way of the progress of truth." And, in fact, we have seen that he suppressed, in the later editions of his book, the harshest and most revolting passages. His principal error lay in attributing the evils of humanity almost exclusively to the too great multiplication of the race, and in having, so to speak, absolved in advance the governments of all countries, from reproach. Moral causes are ordinarily complex, and they cannot be known by looking at them from a single side. Neither did Malthus take sufficient account of the increase in the means of production, under the influence of labor and by the coöperation of machines. He pretended not to perceive that the population of our time, though infinitely more numerous than that of past times, enjoyed nevertheless many comforts, were better clothed, better lodged, better fed, and less exposed than ever before to the danger of devouring one another. Perhaps they experience more of moral suffering from the greater number of temptations which cannot always be gratified; but these very temptations are an energetic stimulant to which we must refer a good part of the progress that has been made in all branches of industry. Accepting the hypothesis of Malthus, yet as population approaches the level of means of subsistence, the demand for new products leads to useful discoveries by which all humanity profits; emigrations lead human races by degrees towards the unoccupied regions, which become fertile as they become populous, and civilization thus penetrates into unknown countries, which return a hundred fold the advances

necessitated in working them.   Thus North America
has seen its prairies and its woods tilled by European
colonists, and the valleys of its great rivers covered with
opulent cities, where lately wandered miserable hordes of
hunters and cannibals.*

When one examines with some attention the map of
the globe and considers the fertility of a great number of
regions scarcely explored, he ceases to fear for the human
race the evils with which it is threatened by the predictions of Malthus.   Emigration even appears only as a last
resource, in view of the improvements which the genius of
man never fails to lavish on the earth, because new profits
appear in proportion as it is called upon to satisfy new
demands.   Mr. Ricardo † has left the opponents of Malthus nothing to desire on this point, and we are persuaded that the author of the book on *Population* must
have been himself reassured against the consequences of
his own system, on appreciating at their just value the
fine analyses of agricultural progress presented by his
illustrious fellow-countryman.   Besides, a continual exchange of manufactured products for natural products
is going on among all nations, so that commerce remedies
the insufficiency of agriculture and never leaves any intelligent and industrious people without means of subsistence.   The daily increasing intimacy of the relations
between civilized nations, renders all useful discoveries at
once common to them ; for example, steam navigation,
gas illumination, and railroads, which we have seen almost
simultaneously adopted in Europe, Asia, America, and
even Africa.   So to-day steamboats plough the Red Sea
and the Adriatic, ascend the Nile, the Ganges and the
Mississippi, as well as the Seine and the Thames, and
bring to our populous cities, in case of dearth, wheat from
the Black Sea and from the United States.   Malthus was
not the first to utter a cry of alarm on the subject of the

---

* v. art. *anthropophagi*, Encyc. Brittanica.— *Trans.*
† In his work on the *Principles of Taxation*.

increase of population, and we might cite more than one writer of his country, who deplored, a hundred years ago, in the style of Jeremiah, the immediate dangers of that increase. What would those prophets of misfortune have said could they have beheld the England of our day, rich, powerful, and twice as populous as then!

The doctrine of Malthus will nevertheless have the merit of having called the attention of governments, as well as of citizens, to the danger of improvident unions and of aid bestowed without discretion. That doctrine has already kept France from imitating the vicious laws which have created in England the poor-tax, and which have made of beggary a remunerative occupation. Even in the country where these laws have so long had sway, they have just been modified; and public generosity, henceforward enlightened by the experience of the past, is learning to distinguish unmerited misfortune from voluntary poverty. Christianity, as we have said, discovered beneficence; political economy has systematized it. Prudent men have also learned to reflect on the consequences of marriage; and this solemn act of life has ceased to be considered as lightly as it was, before Malthus had caused an appreciation of the immense responsibility which it imposes. Society, in showing itself more strict in the distribution of public aid, has put upon every citizen the responsibility of providing for himself by saving up for the necessities of his old age or his days of suffering; and if it has not yet ventured to follow the advice of Malthus and close the asylums now open to deserted children, it has, at least, taken measures to recall a greater number of mothers to their natural duties, which they neglected less frequently from any fault of heart than from the influence of poverty. We must then pardon Malthus for having struck hard instead of striking justly, and for having bent the bow too much to one side, as he himself said, in order to make the other right. He yielded to the very natural impulse of generalizing a simple and striking idea and throwing it out like a spectre before a frightened world. His aim was to profit by the fear such an idea would inspire, to arouse in his contemporaries greater activity in all things, and to demonstrate to them the economic sense of the menacing cry of Bossuet : "Advance! Advance!"

We have seen that Malthus was drawn into the publication of his work by reading the political writings of Mr. Godwin, that energetic utopist who would make governments exclusively responsible for all the imperfections of humanity. This was also the teaching of J. J. Rousseau, and he expressed it in dogmatic terms when he said · "Everything is good when it comes from the hands of the Creator; everything degenerates in the hands of man." Condorcet had been still bolder, and had not hesitated to affirm that if man would follow nature, he would indefinitely extend the limits of his existence on the earth. Godwin imagined that he was only drawing the natural conclusions from their ideas by proposing the destruction of governments, religions, property, marriage, and institutions of less importance which are derived from these. We must recur to these exaggerations, in order to explain the exaggeration in the system of Malthus. "Though human institutions," says the latter, " appear to be and indeed often are, the obvious and obtrusive causes of much mischief to society, they are in reality light and superficial in comparison with those deeper-seated causes of evil, which result from the laws of nature and from the passions of mankind."* " Far from the evils of humanity being due to the incapacity of governments and their repugnance to reforms, it is rather to excess of population that we must attribute all the evils with which humanity is oppressed. The ambition of princes would lack for instruments of destruction, if poverty did not drive the lower classes of the

---

* *Principle of Population*, Book iii, chap. ii.

people to their standards." Malthus thought that the multitude, incessantly goaded on by distress, could be restrained only by the harshest despotism. In his opinion, the shouts of demagogues rallying to the aid of the established power the comfortable classes of the society whose existence they threatened, were the cause of all the bad laws and of the continuance of all abuses. He could not conceive that an enlightened nation could long endure bad institutions and the malversation of a corrupt government, if it did not think itself threatened with evils more serious by a blind and famished populace.*

It is easy to conceive with what favor this doctrine would be received in a country like England, whose aristocracy were maintaining, at the time when the book by Malthus appeared, a fierce contest against the principles of the French revolution. Babeuf had not yet written ; but people remembered the pamphlets of Marat, and the sanguinary attempts of our levelers. They had seen the reformers of that school at work, and the general sentiment of horror they had inspired contributed not a little to the success of the doctrine of Malthus. His theory of population was extolled with partisan enthusiasm, for it placed under the protection of Providence, as its work indeed, the greatest social inequalities and all the miseries which they entail. The popular writers ranged themselves on one side, the advocates of privileges on the other, the former to attack, the latter to defend, this new dogma of fatality. It was no longer a discussion, it was a fight, from which truth would have had much difficulty in coming forth safe and sound, if time, which puts everything in its proper place, had not forced the parties to acknowledge at last what was unreasonable in their respective pretensions. Godwin was already much more moderate in his *Inquiry concerning Population* than in his treatise on *Political Justice ;* and Malthus himself,

---

* Ch. Comte, " *Historic Notice on the Life and Labors of Malthus,*" read at the Institute, Dec. 28th, 1836.

as we have said, had amended his views, in consideration of *competent judges*, that is to say, of the events which had modified his ideas.

His doctrine, in fact, could not bear a serious examination in the absolute terms in which he had stated it. Those decrees of proscription issued against children, against the aged and infirm, did not merit the sanction of the public conscience. A voice within each man cried out that the most imperious and the most tender of all feelings, those of love and paternity, had not been given him by the Creator as a source of bitterness and of miseries. Vices and crimes could not have the same origin as virtues. The most simple analysis of human labor was sufficient to demonstrate, on the other hand, that if the increasing population demanded a greater quantity of means of subsistence, it possessed in itself the power of providing it. People saw every day a single man create by his labor enough products to support ten of his fellow creatures. New lands were brought under cultivation whenever the demand for food assured regular profits to agricultural capital. The laws in favor of the poor, which Malthus had pointed out as so pernicious,* were to be considered only as a compensation for the alms bestowed by the monasteries, whose revenues English Protestantism had confiscated, and not as an encouragement to vice and idleness. It was in vain for the author to say: "It is necessary to leave to nature the care of punishing the poor for the crime of poverty;" no one regarded poverty as a crime and wealth as a virtue.

Mr. Godwin refuted with great superiority of reason all that part of the doctrine of Malthus, which had been so well received by the English aristocracy, because it accorded perfectly with their natural sympathies. "Woe to the country," he says, "in which a man of this class" (*i.e.*, the people) "cannot marry, without the

---

* Malthus called these laws "an evil in comparison with which the national debt, with all the terror it inspires, is but of little importance."

prospect of forfeiting his erect and independent condition! Woe to the country, in which, when unforeseen adversity falls upon this man, he shall be told he has no claim of right to be supported and led in safety through his difficulties! We may be sure there is something diseased and perilous in the state of that community, where such a man shall not have a reasonable and just prospect of supporting a family by the labor of his hands and the exertions of his industry, though he begins the world with nothing."*

Experience has not ceased to justify this opinion. Public wealth continues to increase in almost all the countries of Europe at the same time with the population; and this phenomenon is reproduced in so general and decided a manner, that an American economist, Mr. Alexander Everett, has even gone so far as to consider the increase of population as the essential cause of every kind of progress. He judges that since the products of labor are always in the ratio of labor itself and consequently of population, the means of subsistence for individuals depend only on the more or less equitable division of the profits between those employed in the various branches of industry These industries themselves become daily more developed upon a limited territory, either by the perfecting of agriculture, or by the extension of commerce. The young branches, far from exhausting the trunk, give it a new vigor and become elements of prosperity, instead of being, as Malthus supposes, a cause of ruin and decay.

For the rest, the errors relating to the development of population date from a time much anterior to the publication of the celebrated work of Malthus. The old writings on political economy all bear the impress of the uneasiness of our fathers at the sight of the great family which they also contributed so valiantly to increase. Their cries of distress were heard principally in the chief

---

* *Inquiries into Population*, book vi, chap. vi.

cities ; and more than one king of France, in desperation, thought necessary to restrict the extent of the city of Paris, whose constantly retreating boundaries are still tending to enlarge. The same phenomenon has been observed in London, a city as populous as certain kingdoms, and in which more than a million consumers live at ease on a space which would not suffice for the support of five hundred persons, if it was destined to furnish it.* But these vain fears disappear before the absurdity of a pretended increase of population in geometrical progression. Malthus himself recognised that one could cite no nation whose population has not been maintained, by physical or moral influences, below the level fixed by the products of the soil ; without which we should have seen permanent dearth, or periodic epidemics, while these scourges have generally appeared only at times when the various nations were much less populous than at present. The choice that Malthus made of America, where the population doubles every twenty-five years, is not more conclusive than that of Sweden, where, according to Mr. Godwin, it doubles only in a hundred years. Communities do not proceed thus by regular periods, like the stars and seasons, as we have said ; and political institutions, as well as the habits of the people, exercise an influence which greatly modifies the natural tendency, arithmetical or geometrical, of man to multiply.

It was then in vain that Malthus declared war on the home affections, on public and private charity, on childhood and on old age, in the wrongly understood interest of humanity. Heaven did not decree that wealth should have the monopoly of all enjoyments, including those of love and marriage, nor that one part of the human race should be sacrificed as a holocaust to the other ; in a word, society should no more be a convent than a warren. However, by exaggerating the dangers of population,

---

* Written in 1836.   The population of London is now, 1880, over 4,000,000.

Malthus at least warned governments against the abuses of beneficent institutions, and made every man feel that the social law imposed upon him sacred duties of forethought in providing for himself and his children. England began, from this time, the reform of her poor-laws, and other countries have guarded against the danger of imitating these laws. Charity will not, hereafter, be less earnest, but it will be more enlightened. It will consider itself subject, like all other virtues, to rules ; and these rules have already been marked out for it, in France, in a work * which partakes at the same time *of the severe prudence of Malthus and the generous philanthrophy of Godwin.* We might add that that way appeared unsatisfactory to religious minds, to whom beneficence is the most holy of duties. One of our most honored magistrates * has published under the title of "Christian Political Economy," a manifesto often eloquent and always sincere, against the doctrines of Malthus. He attacks them doubtless much more as an apostle than as an economist and statesman ; but he has well shown their powerlessness to make the people moral and to prevent an invasion of the miseries with which humanity is afflicted. Several years before the appearance of his book, a protest which created some sensation in Europe, had pointed out for public animadversion the doctrine of the unlimited labor of workmen and the right of abandonment exercised in reference to them by masters. M. de Sismondi had not hesitated to propose a law in virtue of which employers should be held to provide *for all the needs of their workmen, in health, in sickness, at all ages of life*, on condition that the latter could marry only with the authorization of the former. He was thus going back to the wardenships and masterships, and demanding of the working classes *their liberty* in exchange for their bread ; so serious and difficult is the question, so

---

* *Charity*, by M. Duchâtel.

* M. de Villeneuve Bargemont, a former prefect.

alarming is it, when one recalls the attempts of 1793 and the sufferings of 1830; of the Luddists at Manchester and the insurrectionists at Lyons.

All the governments of Europe have not ceased to struggle, since that time, against the principle of disorder and perturbation which the unsettled condition of that question everywhere involves. In vain has production advanced with giant strides; markets do not always offer it a favorable outlet, and the distribution of profits is not made with that evident equity which rallies all convictions and all interests. The *moral restraint* of Malthus does not hinder one single imprudent marriage, nor prevent any illegitimate birth. The counsels of M. Duchâtel are addressed only to intelligent men, and the intervention of the law, as M. de Sismondi demands, is not less rejected by our institutions than by our customs. The discussion in regard to it is still at the point where Malthus left it; and although that author may have found, like Turgot, a government disposed to favor his experiments, these experiments are not yet sufficiently conclusive for us to hope from them a truly scientific and decisive solution. We shall soon see deliberative assemblies at the work, bold innovators who will attempt to untie the gordian knot and to establish a distribution of the profits of labor on better bases: the Constituent Assembly, the Convention, the Saint-Simonian school, the Socialist school, and many others. In what have their great attempts advanced us? We hear rumble, like a voice from the depths, the austere words of M. de La Mennais, the Father Bridaine[19] of political economy; but he complains of the workmen as much as of the masters; he contents himself with recommending charity to the latter and resignation to the others. His vehement parables sometimes recall the *Philosophic and Political History* of Abbé Raynal; but the disasters of Saint-Domingo are no longer forgotten. It was not the feverish eloquence of Raynal which emancipated the blacks; it was the reason of Wilberforce and the wisdom of the English Parliamer·'

CHAPTER XXXVI.

Influence of the writers of the eighteenth century on the progress of political economy in Europe.—*Spirit of the Laws.*—Economic works of J. J. Rousseau.—Economic opinions of Voltaire.—Abbé Raynal.

IT is just to give the philosophers of the eighteenth century a part of the honor which accrues to the Economists for all the reforms carried out or attempted in the latter part of this century. Their writings contained the germs of them, and although a vague uncertainty is manifest on most of the social questions so boldly approached by the schools of Quesnay, Adam Smith and Malthus himself, we can but acknowledge that Montesquieu, Rousseau, Voltaire, and the abbé Raynal were the precursors of these great masters in economic science. The great renown of the literary works of the Encyclopedists, seems to have exclusively absorbed the attention of posterity; but the part which escapes us to-day, that which is least read, is the true starting point of all the modern economic theories. There they are in an embryonic state, all ready to be born under the hot atmosphere of the French Revolution; and the least practiced eye is sufficient to recognize them and note their signs.

Montesquieu occupies the first rank among the publicists who have turned their attention to the most pro found questions of political economy; and although he often makes mistakes, although he has shared in many respects the prejudices of his contemporaries, we are indebted to him for the first truly new and bold views which have been published on the influence of commerce, and for some careful analyses of the theory of moneys. What more true, even to-day, than this fine appreciation of the character of imposts: "A poll-tax is natural to servitude; a tax on commodities is more natural to freedom, because it has a less direct connection with the person." It was Montesquieu who first dared to say that the freest governments were also the dearest;* and if that doctrine is true in our days, for other reasons than those of which this great man spoke, he nevertheless has the merit of having discovered it. He began by going forward; later, the movement was explained.

We vigorously attacked, thirty years ago, the colonial system and the trade in blacks; but, apart from the act of affranchisement passed by the English parliament, what is there anywhere more eloquent than the chapter of Montesquieu on negro slavery! "Those whom we are considering," he said,* "are black from head to foot, and the noses are so flattened that it is almost impossible to pity them. One cannot bring himself to believe that God, who is a very wise being, can have put a soul, especially a good soul, into a body wholly black . . . . It is impossible for us to suppose these people to be men, because if we suppose them men, people would begin to think that we ourselves are not Christians. Small minds exaggerate too much the injustice done to the Africans: for, if it were such as they say, would it not have entered the head of the princes of Europe, who make so many useless agreements among themselves, *to make a general one in favor of mercy and pity!*" This agreement has been made, thank God; but who would deny that it is mainly due to the sublime irony of the plea of Montesquieu? Political economy has proven the dearness of the labor of the negroes, and the superiority of

* *Spirit of the Laws*, Book xiii; chap., 12.
* *Spirit of the Laws*, book xv, chap. v.

cultivation by free hands. Montesquieu did better; he inspired a horror of slavery; he stigmatized it, he branded it on the forehead; legislators had only to record his decree. The *Spirit of the Laws* had already settled that grave question, much before the declamations of Raynal and the decrees of the Convention.

I hasten to pay Montesquieu the debt of science and of the present time. Listen to his definition of commerce, which one might think taken from some discourse from the throne, this year, in France or England: "The natural effect of commerce is to tend towards peace. Two nations which trade together render themselves reciprocally dependent; if the one has interest in buying, the other has interest in selling, and all unions are founded on mutual need." Is not this, in brief, the programme of modern policy? We are taking great steps towards the realization of this grand harmonic thought, that it was given to Montesquieu to enunciate, without being able to demonstrate its correctness. This task devolved on the economists, and never, perhaps, were their labors more clearly distinct from those of the philosophers of the eighteenth century, than in everything connected with this subject. In fact, Montesquieu has no sooner explained the true bases of the trade of nations, than the demonstration escapes him and he falls into the most serious contradictions.* "Freedom of trade is not," in his eyes, "an opportunity given merchants to do what they may wish; it is rather a servitude. What injures the merchant is not for that reason injurious to commerce." Further on, he adds: "The state must be neutral between its custom-house and its commerce, and must so act that these two do not conflict, and then *people there enjoy commercial freedom."* The generous and enlightened instinct of this illustrious writer

---

* The most complete refutation of the errors of Montesquieu in political economy is due to the Count Destutt de Tracy, whose excellent commentary on *The Spirit of the Laws*, is esteemed almost equal to the book.

made him divine the true principles, and the prejudices
of his time concealed them at times from his view, as
witness his opinion on importations and exportations,
marred by the oldest errors of the *balance of trade.* "A
country," he says, "which always sends less merchandise than it receives, brings about a balance by impov-
erishing itself; it will always receive less, until, in extreme
poverty, it no longer receives anything."

This strange assertion is found, it is true, in a chapter
entitled: "To what Nations it is Disadvantageous to
Carry on Trade;" and Montesquieu there designates
Japan as one of the countries with which there are the
fewest disadvantages in trading, "because the excessive
quantity of that which it can receive, produces the excessive quantity of that which it can send:" but we can
but regret that such errors mar a work whose publication
has rendered so many services to society. In another
place,* the author exclaims: "It is not for me to pronounce on the question whether, if Spain is not able to
trade with the Indies herself, it would not be better
for her to make the trade free to foreigners. I will
simply say that it will be well for her to put the fewest
obstacles that her policy can permit, in the way of this
trade." Thus it was, that, possessed in turn by contrary
ideas, Montesquieu defended freedom and prohibitions,
and that his works have served as an arsenal to all philosophical, economic and political parties, because arguments are found in them for all causes, as at the time of
fermentation, we see the lees bubble up with a mass of
impure products, mingled with the most generous liquor.
It was difficult not to confound many different things, in
stirring them up in so lively a manner as did the immortal author of the *Spirit of the Laws*, and this consideration well explains why it has not been given to the
same men to propose questions and to resolve them. The
Philosophers of the eighteenth century only obscurely

---

* *Esprit des Lois*, Book xxi, chap. 23.

saw the solution of the social problem through the prism of their imagination, and, as it were, like poets: the Economists alone applied to it the experimental method, and it was, in fact, only in their hands that political economy became an experimental science.

One finds in the economic works of J. J. Rousseau the same contradictions and the same uncertainties as in Montesquieu. Like him, he makes war on luxury, and he devotes himself chiefly to extolling the marvels of agriculture. Commerce and finance seem to him adapted only to enervate people and to corrupt them. " When one wishes only to win," he says, " he always wins more by being a knave than an honest man. Those who handle money soon learn to embezzle it, and what are all the inspectors appointed over them, but other knaves sent to divide with them?" To avoid this fatal management, J. J. Rousseau proposed to pay public functionaries in commodities, and to have public services performed by means of corvées. This, in his estimation, was the spirit which should prevail in a good economic system: "To think little about foreigners, to care little for commerce, to suppress stamped paper, to tax live stock, and especially to tax the land, as the Physiocrates proposed, because, in short, *it is that which produces which ought to pay.*" And yet the tax on lands was to be, in his view, only an excise-tax, (*mise en régie*), in order that the state should have money without the citizens being obliged to give it.

This economic policy was the natural consequence of the famous paradoxes of which Rousseau never ceased to be the eloquent propagator. It led straight to the régime of Sparta and the laws of Lykurgus. "Cultivate," he said, "the sciences, arts, commerce, and manufactures: have regular troops, fortified places, academies, above all a good system of finance which will make money circulate well, which will procure you much of it; in that way you will form a people who will be intriguing, ardent, covetous, ambitious, servile and knavish, like others; you

will enter into all the political systems, nations will seek
alliances with you, and will make treaties with you ; there
will not be a war in Europe into which you will not
have the honor of being thrust. But if, perchance, you
prefer to form a nation free, peaceable and wise, apply
your people to agriculture and the arts necessary to life ;
render money contemptible and if possible useless." It
did not occur to Rousseau, that, to make people cultivate the arts necessary to life, capital was needed, as it is
needed for agriculture itself, unless it be carried on by the
patriarchal system of the heroic times and of small countries. It is not sufficient to exclaim : " Cultivate well
your fields without concerning yourself about the rest ;
soon you will harvest gold, and more than you need to
procure what you want : " this result, in fact, can be
obtained only by commerce and by speculations which
call for large capital. The Genevan philosopher was also
led by his system to demand the suppression of cities,
that is to say, of civilization itself, against which he had
opened hostilities in that memorable discourse which was
crowned by the academy of Dijon.

Rousseau desired taxes on commodities, as we lately
had on gaming-houses ; then he bethought himself of the
smuggling it would occasion, and he proposed, in order
to avoid it, to .exempt from all duty laces and jewels,
which were too easily concealed. A sad means for preventing that inequality of conditions, whose phantom
terrified him, and which is inherent in civilization itself !
" If, for example," he said,* "government can interdict
the use of carriages, it can, with still more reason, impose
a tax on carriages ; a wise and proper way of *censuring
their use* without abolishing it. Then the tax may be regarded as a sort of fine whose amount compensates for
the abuse which it punishes." Who would suppose that
after that sally, worthy of an old Roman censor of the
sternest days of the republic, Rousseau would have taken

---

* On *Political Economy*, the latter part of the article.

up the defence of governments against certain economists who wished to exclude them from any participation in the industrial affairs of the state! "Such ideas must be rejected. If, in each nation, those to whom *the sovereign* commits the government of the people were their enemies on account of their position, there would not be the trouble of seeking what they should do to render them happy." * And he was right. What then must we conclude from that incoherent amalgamation of doctrines liberal almost to anarchy, and, as is said to-day, *governmental* even to arbitrariness? That the true principles of social physiology were still little known, because the decisive experiments were not yet made, and political economy was still to the finest geniuses a science of imagination.

The incursions of Voltaire into the domain of political economy, offer us new evidence of this truth. In attacking the theories of others, he had occasion to expose his own on these grave matters, and I regret to say that he has confined himself to laying the varnish of his elegant prose over the most superannuated commonplaces of his epoch. His *Homme aux quarante Ecus* † (*Man with forty crowns.—Trans.*), composed for the purpose of ridiculing the Physiocrates and especially their most able interpreter, Mercier de la Rivière, is only a spirited reproduction of all the prejudices in favor of the balance of trade and of prohibitions. In it, Voltaire maintains that the humble live only from the luxury of the great, and he thinks, like Louis XIV, that princes are giving alms in expending largely. "Everywhere," he says,* "the rich give support to the poor. That is the only source of manufactures and commerce. The more indus-

* This is the last sentence of his article *Economie Politique*, in the *Encyclopédie*.

† The economists had claimed that, in a state organized according to their doctrines, an average sum of 120 francs (forty crowns) would suffice for the subsistence of every citizen. Hence the title which Voltaire gave to his burlesque refutation of their system.

* See *L'Homme aux quarante Ecus*, vol. xiv, p. 12, edition of Dupont.

trious a nation is, the more it gains from foreigners. If we take from foreign countries ten millions a year for the balance of trade, in twenty years there would be two hundred millions more in the state. But it is not certain that the balance of our trade will always be favorable to us: there are times when we lose. I have heard much talk about population. If we should have double the number of children that we do; if we had forty millions of inhabitants instead of twenty, what would happen?— It would come to pass that each one would have only twenty crowns to expend, or it would be necessary for the earth to produce double what it does, or there would be double the number of poor, or there would have to be double the amount manufactured and double the amount obtained from foreigners, or half the nation would have to be sent to America, or one half the nation would eat the other."

Although these lines are very light, they nevertheless contain a summary of the economic doctrines in favor at the time when the first writings of the Physiocrates appeared. This was the sentiment of the time throughout almost all Europe, and Voltaire was only the echo of his contemporaries, when he wrote in his defence of the worldling:

> " Sachez surtout que le luxe enrichit
> Un grand Etat, s'il en perd un petit.
> Cette splendeur, cette pompe mondaine,
> D'un règne heureux est la marque certaine.
> Le riche est né pour beaucoup dépenser ;
> Le pauvre est fait pour beaucoup amasser." *

It is far from these elastic doctrines to the fine analyses of production by Adam Smith ; but it was much that people

---

* Literally translated :

> " Know above all that luxury enriches
> A great State, if it ruins a small.
> This splendor, this worldly pomp.
> Is the certain mark of a happy reign.
> The rich man is born to spend much ;
> The poor is made to amass much."

accorded them so much of a place in all works of any importance, and that the finest talents in our literature had become their organs. When the founders of the science put their hand to the scattered materials in the books of the Philosophers, they found public opinion prepared for discussions of social interest, and they had only to speak to find hearers. Mercier de La Rivière was certainly less eloquent than J. J. Rousseau, and certainly Adam Smith was not so great a writer as Montesquieu; but these Economists had the advantage over the Philosophers of a closer logic and of a method more certain and more solidly grounded on facts. This gave at once a peculiar character of gravity to their works, better received by governments than the works of the Encyclopedists, those bold railers, who seemed more occupied in destroying than in reforming. The triumph of the latter, too, preceded by some length of time that of the Economists, and the political revolution of which they were the first apostles, had time to make the circuit of the world, before the economic revolution had more than chosen its first battle fields. Civil and religious freedom is assured in almost all Europe; commercial freedom is yet to be born. There are laws to protect political rights; there are none for industrial rights. Nations respect an acre of snow on the boundary which separates them, and they steal without shame literary próperty, as filibusters might do. Here, enormous taxes weigh heavily upon commerce; elsewhere, commerce is less taxed. We have seen sovereigns pretend to exclusive domination over the mouth of a river; others decree to close the seas, interdict ports, debase coins: all is still anarchy in production, while order reigns in politics.

Raynal is the first economic writer of the eighteenth century whose works present a picture of that interior struggle of the two revolutions. We feel, in reading him, that he worked in preference for the political revolution. He declaims like a tribune of the people; he

apostrophizes, he inveighs, in the manner of demagogues;
but his vehement philippics against the trade in blacks
and his animated pictures of monopoly and its consequences in the two Indies, assign him a respectable place
among the founders of industrial and commercial emancipation.   Although his views are at times somewhat
vague and incomplete, Raynal foreshadowed the economic
revolution of the nineteenth century, of which the independence of the United States forms the first episode.
One sees that he has dreamed of happier days for the
laboring classes, whether he depicts them to us roving on
a vessel, or shut up in a workshop, or grows indignant at
the abuses of European power toward the weak races of
the American continent.   He is scarcely ever read to-
day ; his writings are treated as scaffoldings which the
architect takes down and removes as his edifice rises ;
but the *Philosophical History* will remain as a souvenir of
the first efforts consecrated to the defence of labor and
the regeneration of the laborers.   This book seems written in the breach ; there prevails throughout an impetu-
osity of style which announces the approach of revolutions ; it is a last challenge hurled before the combat.
It remains for us to see the combatants at the work ; a
sublime and convulsive work where everything becomes
an instrument of war and of destruction ; where philosophy itself finds it necessary to have recourse to the
axe to clear the land on which our children will be called
to build.

CHAPTER XXXVII.

The economic doctrines of the French Revolution.—They have all a social rather than an industrial character.—They are cosmopolitan in theory and restrictive in practice.—The Convention and the Empire make of them weapons of warfare.—General view of the consequences of the *continental blockade.*—It existed in fact before being decreed.—Injurious prejudices it spread in Europe.

THERE is a celebrated saying of the Abbé Siéyès which very well characterizes the tendency of political economy, at the beginning of the French Revolution : " What is the third estate?" he said. " Nothing." " What ought it to be?" " Everything." This profound expression summed up the judgment of the eighteenth century ; it restored to honor the forgotten programme of Turgot and announced the advent of the power capable of carrying it into effect. Hardly were these words pronounced, when the work was begun ; and in a session of a few months, the Constituent Assembly had done justice to privileges, destroyed internal customs duties, mitigated the system of frontier duties, suppressed corporations, subjected all citizens to the payment of a tax and prepared the way for the emancipation of labor. Never at any other epoch had people made such a harvest of inveterate abuses, and manifested so firm a disposition to march boldly on in the way of reforms. The social edifice was, so to speak begun again at the foundation, and there was not one single important institution which was not more or less profoundly modified.

The immortal night of the fourth of August, 1789, saw most of these memorable changes effected. A few hours sufficed for the abolition of the wardenships of trade corporations, of mortmain, feudal rights, privileges of birth, and fiscal inequalities. At the same time, the Constituent Assembly laid the foundations of a territorial division which destroyed the privileges of the provinces, while creating national unity. France could henceforth advance as a single man towards the new destinies which the revolution had just opened to her. Labor was free.; the citizens were so likewise ; no career was closed to their capacity, no hope interdicted to their ambition. The central government, vigorously organized, could have its orders executed from one extremity of the kingdom to the other. The experiments decreed at Paris encountered no serious opposition in the departments ; and thus began that series of more or less fortunate attempts which have furnished economists and statesmen with so many subjects of study and meditation.

There was everything to do in matters of industries commerce, and finance : the Constituent Assembly boldly put its hand to the work. The suppression of corporations was followed by the creation of patents : the abolition of internal customs duties was accompanied by a mitigation of the system of exterior customs ; the land-tax was based on the principle of the equality of all Frenchmen before the law. There were doubtless many errors committed in that period of bold attempts, too often effected in the midst of the greatest political excitement ; but those errors have become for us grave matters of instruction, and conscience profits by them to-day, as by a light-house destined to warn us against new shipwrecks. Still, however bold and original were the reformers of 1789, they were too much imbued with the principles which prevailed at that time in the philosophic and economic world, not to yield to their influence when an opportunity presented itself to make application of them. Thus, the ideas of the Physiocrates decided the Constituent Assembly, in spite of the wise remon-

strances of Rœderer and a few advanced spirits, to concentrate the whole burden of the taxes on landed property. It was with reluctance that they consented to add
to this the tax on personal property and the custom-
duties. France was deprived, at one stroke of the pen,
of the immense resources she could have derived from
contributions imposed on all producers who were not
living on their annuities, and she was soon obliged to seek
in the *assignats* a compensation for this voluntary deficit,
added to the deficit of the old monarchy.

The creation of the assignats was a fruitful source
of changes advantageous to our social order. It
favored the division of the soil and restored to cultivation a multitude of lands formerly consecrated to unproductive uses. It multiplied the number of producers by
procuring for them the first element of production, land,
and the most effective stimulant to labor, property. In
the reports of the principal members of our great deliberative assemblies, the serious men of our days will find
ample subject for study upon these important matters.
Mirabeau, Necker, Rœderer, Dallarde, and Cambon have
left us works to which posterity is beginning to render
justice, and which deserve to figure among the interesting
monuments of political economy. What more favorable
to manufactures than patents for inventions and the fine
discussions on this subject which took place in the Constituent Assembly? Later, the National Convention secured literary property by a decree ; it consolidated unity
of weights and measures throughout France by the
adoption of the decimal system, and by gigantic creations
which powerfully contributed to increase the fortune of
the state, nobly repaired the injuries which circumstances
forced it to inflict upon the fortunes of citizens. There
was a brief period when it dared to decree industrial conquests as well as military conquests ; the telegraph, chemistry, physics, were at the order of its committees, as victory at the orders of its generals.

We cannot pass over in silence the formidable expedients to which that assembly was obliged to have recourse in order to contend against the coalition of kings. The day of justice begins to dawn for it, and every one knows that in its view the *maximum*, the requisitions, the forced loans, were not regular resources, but measures of public safety demanded by the most unyielding necessity. In the extreme peril in which the country was, it was necessary for it to provide for its needs in the most urgent haste, and nevertheless its most violent resolutions were always distinguished by a breadth of view rarely found even among the most enlightened governments in the calmest times. We must go back to the starting point of these grand measures, to justly appreciate their rigorous and inevitable consequences. Let one then picture to himself the Convention reduced simply to the property of the clergy and of emigrants, to face the whole of Europe and civil war. In order to put into circulation the value of this property, it had devised the assignats which were the representation of it, and which, by means of purchases, were to return to the treasury and be burned ; but few people bought the property. In vain were assignats multiplied in anticipation of demand ; the more of them were created, the more their value depreciated. It was necessary to interdict the employment of specie, and to commence again the edicts of the regent against gold and silver, as was seen at the end of Law's system. Every day prices rose with the issues of paper money. Then it was determined to establish a *maximum ;* but commodities disappeared.

It is easy to be indignant to-day, in the name of science, at the infractions the latter suffered in those agitated times. We still speak of them under the influence of the terror of our fathers' day ; but when we see, after the bankruptcy, Cambon open with so firm and tranquil a hand the *great book of the public debt*, and make the creditors of all periods pass under the same level, by attaching their guaranty to the preservation of the new régime, we cannot help a feeling of admiration and respect. Interest was brought back to a single rate; all the debts were converted into a perpetual loan not payable unless the government should wish to purchase it when it was below par, which was virtually equivalent to an amortization. The science of public credit was born anew in the very assembly which seemed to have dug its grave. At the same time, the Convention attempted a great reform in pauperism by numerous decrees issued in favor of the indigent classes. It proclaimed education a national debt; and if, since, this grand principle has not received an entire application, it remains as a monument of the official solicitude of France for the amelioration of the fate of all her children. One might say that the Convention worked for the human race, so vast was its horizon and so high and generous its thoughts.

Among all the economic attempts made by our great assemblies, there is only one which has not been able to receive the sanction of an experiment, even for a very short time: that is, freedom of commerce. This alone remained unknown to the French, during the period when they tried them all. The Constituent Assembly adopted a system of very moderate duties; but it plainly inclined towards the restrictive system. The Convention made a weapon of warfare of the customs, directed principally against England; and its prejudices, carefully kept up by the Empire, contributed not a little to the triumph of the narrow ideas which still prevail in France on commercial questions. This is a misfortune that we cannot too deeply deplore. It was so important to science that this great trial, opened several centuries ago, should at least have been judged by one first court! Far from being so, liberty has only broken down internal barriers; it has freed labor from only a part of its fetters, and those which remain are sufficient to so complicate all questions of political economy, as to render them almost impossible to resolve. Thus, in England, the poor-tax is one of the principal causes of the maintenance of the corn-laws,* which are prohibitory ; and the increasing embarrassments of our commerce are the incontestable result of the artificial life which tariffs have given our manufactures. Napoleon, who started them decidedly in that direction, by the establishment of the Continental Blockade, did not conceal its serious consequences : " It has cost us dear," he said, " to return, after so many years of civilization, to the principles which characterize the barbarism of the earlier ages of nations ; but we have been constrained to oppose the common enemy with the same weapons which he used against us." †

The Continental Blockade may be considered as the last expression of the economic system adopted by France at the beginning of the Revolution. Although Napoleon only intended a legislative act of reprisal against the British Government, the Berlin Decree became the basis of the industrial and commercial system of France and of continental Europe during the whole of the Empire. This decree, which laid England under an interdict, caused the barriers to fall which separated the other nations. It established a sort of confederation between them against the common enemy, and it opened the entire continent, while shutting up one island. For the first time, liberty seemed to be born again from excess of prohibition. The various European states, subject by conquest or by treaties, to the same commercial laws, formed now only one single producing people , and never did the development of their manufactures take a wider extension than under the influence of that competition which animated them all. These were the finest days of French industries, and yet France then possessed Belgium, Italy, and Rhenish Prussia, whose manufac-

---

* These laws were repealed in 1846, as a result of the efforts of the Anti-Corn-Law League.

† Message of Napoleon to the senate on sending it the Berlin Decree, November 21, 1806.

tures of cloths, silks and linens, rivals of ours, far from injuring the prosperity of the latter, enhanced their reputation and their value. The continental blockade would have opened the era of free trade in Europe, if the latter could have originated from a feeling of hostility and of reprisals, like that which had inspired the emperor.

But the definitive result of this system was to accustom European industries to live by protection and tariffs. All our manufactures, encouraged by the exclusion of the products whose competition could be most dangerous, and by the sure markets which all Europe, almost wholly subject to our arms, offered us, became immensely extended. The iron and coal of Belgium, the linens of Holland, the silks of Italy, and the wools from Germany, being admitted into our markets the same as French goods, did not at that time hinder the development of our national manufactures ; how then could there have been necessary, in order to maintain them, after the peace of 1815, tariffs that were daily increasing and directed against these same people whose competition had caused no injury to France during their union to her territory ? Each of them has, since, shut itself up in a triple cordon of custom-houses, and we have seen the fiercest industrial war succeed the political wars, as if general peace was a chimera, a utopia incapable of ever being realized. In vain had the Revolution emancipated labor by the suppression of wardenships and masterships ; by allowing the prohibitory system to remain, it maintained a virtual commercial feudalism, which secured to certain classes of producers benefits obtained at the expense of the community ; it gave birth to the intestine wars with labor, in which so many laborers have succumbed as victims to laws which seem made for their protection. The great error of this system consists in having treated foreign producers, that is, the creators of exchangeable products, as adversaries rather than as customers. Old political grudges have been employed for keeping up the prejudices of manufacturers, by placing under the auspices of patriotism the interested calculations of privilege and of monopolies. The Convention and the Empire used protection as a weapon of warfare; our civilization continues to employ it after twenty-five years of peace.

We must not then seek in the great works of the French Revolution for the germs of the economic reform whose dawn seems to be appearing among us. All that the French Revolution did to this end, it did in an indirect manner: it embodied it in its codes, and for that reason they have ceased, in many respects, to be in harmony with our needs. The suppression of the law of primogeniture, the nearly absolute equality of inheritances in a direct line, the legislation for commercial companies, the unity of weights and measures, are incontestable benefits; but equality before the law ceases to be a truth, when we see laborers of every sort, who are already dependent on capital for wages, become so also for consumption. In the present state of legislation, no guaranty protects labor in its relations to the wealth which commands it and which pays it; no guaranty secures to the one who is paid the free disposal of his wages. The price of labor tends constantly to diminish and that of articles of consumption to increase, because both are in reality fixed by one alone of the contracting parties. The French Revolution found itself, like us, confronted with this formidable problem, of which it determined to force the solution by penalties; but penalties were as powerless as laws to accomplish that end. The *maximum* produced famine; the arbitrary determining of wages suppressed labor. Bounties to the poor created mendicancy; the exclusion of foreign products opened the way to monopolies.

The bold attempts of that period are not without resemblance to those Turgot had made, under the monarchy, in the interest of the laboring classes. The only thing which distinguishes them is that the reformers of the Convention, more powerful than the minister of Louis

XVI, took no account of the facts and opposing forces before which Turgot had been obliged to recoil. One would say that in their view the human race was inert matter capable of enduring all experiences, so many systems did they propose that were absurd, anarchical, and destructive to all society. Marat, Saint-Just, and Babeuf have left us curious memorials of that monomania which disturbed minds eager for novelties and disposed to put in practice the most extravagant social dreams, as one tries chemical processes and combinations in a laboratory. Soon there was but one single phrase in the economic vocabulary of French language : this was the celebrated saying of Danton : " Audacity, more audacity, and audacity always ! " When the Paris Commune came to solicit the National Convention to establish a *maximum*, its president said : " This concerns the indigent class, for which the legislator has done nothing, when he has not done everything. Let no one bring up in opposition the rights of property : the right to property cannot be the right to starve one's fellow-citizens. The fruits of the earth, like the air, belong to all men." * Marat had gone much further, and we could quote similar extravagances from that energumen, if posterity, who have begun to take note of him, had not already classed him with madmen.

Saint-Just was the boldest and most lofty expression of that school of tribunes, revived from the Gracchi, in comparison with which those illustrious factionists were moderate men. The writings he left contain his economic views entire, energetically summed up by the orator of the Paris Commune, and clearly formulated in the decrees issued by the National Convention during the rule of the Mountain Party. It was reserved for Babeuf to go beyond these doctrines and to preach openly the agrarian law, the abolition of property and the permanent rebellion of the poor against the rich. But these rash

---

* *Parliamentary History of the Revolution*, vol. xxvi, p. 52.

speeches had no other result than to alienate for a long
time the best minds from all social speculations, so much
did they dread to see themselves confounded with the
mad demagogues of the anarchical school. A serious
lesson, too, came from all the hazardous attempts of the
French Revolution : namely, that habits are not so easily
reformed as institutions, and that the finest laws are not
sufficient to secure to each citizen a prosperous condition,
if he does not coöperate with them by his labor and his
morality. Those seductive dreams have henceforth vanished. All the wealth and felicity which the philanthropy of legislators could decree was decreed; and
people learned that public wealth followed other laws
than those of force and tyranny. Had only this step
been taken, it was an immense advance, for it forced
governments and individuals to seek the elements of
future greatness elsewhere than in legislative programmes.

What then remains of all those brilliant and generous
dreams which have agitated the world from Turgot down
to our time, and what social conquests has political economy made, which have in the end redounded to its glory?
We can mention two memorable ones, the emancipation
of the English and the Spanish colonies of America, and
the abolition of negro slavery ; to which should perhaps
be added the suppression of corporation privileges, that
is to say, the affranchisement of labor. We have still
two other victories to gain : the affranchisement of the
workers and that of commerce, a difficult and complicated
task in times like ours, when governments themselves
share the common prejudices against commercial freedom
and consider it hostile to national labor. Of all the
economic errors of the revolution, that alone has survived, more deeply-rooted than ever, and it has risen triumphant over the ruins of the others. People no longer
defend slavery, corporations, or privileged companies;
national hatreds have nearly disappeared to give place to
industrial rivalries and jealousies. The battle-field is no

longer on the plains, it is in the workshops. There the war is going on, intelligent, unrelenting, indefatigable; and it takes victims from all parties occupied with injuring each other instead of rendering mutual aid; a veritable war, in which the combatants make use of ingenious and powerful machines, which, pitying neither infancy nor old age, leave on the ground of poverty millions of panting laborers, men and women.

This war is to-day the last expression of the old political economy of Europe, and the last reverberation of the great social contest raised by the French Revolution. It is not merely an international struggle; it is a serious contest between the various classes of workers. France has doubtless the appearance of competing with England; but capital is carrying on a much deeper struggle with the workman. Under pretext of making the country triumph in the first of these combats, an organization is maintained in regard to labor, which has ceased to be in harmony with its needs and the progress of civilization. So there is nothing new in the science from 1789 to 1814, except the experience of actual facts and a facility in deducing conclusions from them in order to go forward and complete the work of our fathers. However, there will soon come forth from the midst of industrial labor, an irresistible power, destined to cure, like the spear of Achilles, the wounds it makes: a power born of our commercial discords, and which will end by extinguishing them all: it is *association*, imported from England, where the excessive taxes made necessary by the war, furnished it the means of supplying that need by force of prodigies: but it is well to trace this new element of social progress to its principal causes, and to study the facts which prepared the way for it.

CHAPTER XXXVIII.

The economic revolution effected in England by the discoveries of Watt and Arkwright.—Economic results of the independence of the United States.—Reaction from the French Revolution on the financial system of England.—Increase of taxes.—Suspension of payments by the bank.—Development and abuses of credit.—Enormity of the public debt.—Consequences of the general peace.

WHILE the French Revolution was making its great social experiments over a volcano, England was beginning hers on the solid ground of the industries. The end of the eighteenth century was distinguished there by wonderful discoveries, destined to change the face of the world and to increase in an unexpected manner the power of their inventors. The conditions of labor underwent the greatest modification they have experienced since the origin of society. Two machines, henceforth immortal, the steam-engine and the spinning-machine, overturned the old commercial system and gave birth almost simultaneously to material products and social questions unknown to our fathers. The small workers were about to become tributary to the great capitalists; the spinning-frame replaced the wheel, and the steam-cylinder succeeded the horse-power. At the same time, the fine attempts of the Duke of Bridgewater at canalization were beginning to produce results, and the perfecting of transportation coincided with the increase of merchandise. The production of iron and that of the other metals improved with that of coal, to which activity had been given by the employment of steam in the work of drainage. One would have thought that England had discovered

430

new mines and had suddenly become enriched by unexpected treasures.

The contemporary generation, more occupied with reaping the advantages of these conquests than with investigating their causes, appear not to have estimated at their just value the embarrassments which ensued from them. That transformation from patriarchal labor into industrial feudalism, in which the workman, the new serf of the workshop, seems bound to the glebe of wages, did not alarm the English producers, although it had a character of *suddenness* quite adapted to disturb their habits. They were far from foreseeing that machines would bring them so much power and so many anxious cares. Pauperism had not yet appeared among them under the threatening forms it has since assumed, and the mechanical trades had not developed that power of labor which was to be for a time so fatal to many workers. However, hardly was the industrial revolution born from the brain of those two men of genius, Watt and Arkwright, when it took possession of England. At the end of the eighteenth century, there was not a single piece of cloth consumed in Europe which did not come to us from India, and twenty-five years after, England sent cloth to that very country, from which she had hitherto obtained all like products. "The river," says J. B. Say, "had gone back to its source." * Thus, two little cylinders turning opposite ways, had sufficed to wholly

---

* Before the invention of spinning–machines, there was estimated to be in Great Britain only five thousand spinners at spinning wheels, and three thousand weavers of cotton goods, in all about eight thousand workers; while to-day this number amounts, in England alone, to more than eight hundred thousand. The total value of cotton cloths, in that country, was estimated, in 1836, at the enormous sum of *eight hundred and fifty* millions of francs. One can consult in reference to it the statistics of Mr. Mc Culloch and Mr. Porter, and the documents published by order of parliament. (Note of author.)

In 1876, the total value of the cotton manufactures of Great Britain (see Ency. Brit.) was estimated at £89,856,000 ; the number of spindles, (including doubling) 41,881,789, number of persons employed 479,515 ; estimated capital invested £90,000,000 ; number of yards of cotton goods exported, 3,668,582,100 ; number of persons directly or indirectly dependent on the cotton trade probably not far from 2,000,000.— *Trans.*

change the relations of Europe with Asia, and the venerable traditions of labor. At the same time, the independence of the United States carried with it a decisive blow to the colonial system, and gave the signal of retreat to all domination of parent countries. The city of Bristol, which had addressed to parliament such spirited petitions against peace with the rebellious Americans, besought, a few years after the signing of the treaty of peace, authority to dig new harbors made necessary by the extension of commerce with the emancipated colonies. Thus was prepared a general independence of the new continent whose last * colony subject to European laws is now struggling to complete the work of Franklin and Washington. It was then proven that colonies were more injurious than useful to their parent countries, and that there were greater profits to be made from a free and industrious people, than from enslaved and oppressed vassals. The United States have given Europe this lesson in political economy, which will make the circuit of the world and will avenge the descendants of the colonists for the state of oppression in which their fathers lived. The prophecies of Raynal have become fulfilled. Rich and powerful nations have succeeded the weak and precarious settlements of the Europeans in one of the two Indies, and one would say, to see the state of torpor of some old parent countries, that the purest of their blood had passed forever into the veins of their colonies.

This is, indeed—however the pride of the old continent may suffer from it,—an immense revolution, the consequences of which we are beginning to experience. We are tributary to our former vassals for a great number of raw materials and special products, without which the work of our manufactures would cease to exist. America sends us the heaps of cotton by which our innumerable manufactures of cloth are supplied, and the dye woods

---

* Canada (written in 1836).

which are used in printing them. Coffee, cocoa, Peruvian bark, which cures fever, the drugs which give it, all come from abroad. Our wants make us daily more dependent on people beyond the sea. The city of Lyons trembles to its foundations at the shocks which agitate New-York or Philadelphia. A failure at New-Orleans may ruin ten merchants at Liverpool. The extraordinary development which the invention of machines has given to production, demands continually increasing markets, which must be sought at a distance and competed for by a lowering of prices among the most advanced nations. Markets have-become battle-fields. Diplomacy no longer bargains for provinces, but for tariffs; and armies, when they move, are like bands of messengers going to make way for commerce. This is what has been produced by the emancipation of the New World, to which our great European manufactures will soon be no more than colonies.

No age has seen such economic revolutions accomplished in so little time, and it is not surprising that such unusual changes should have disconcerted all systems. That sudden prosperity of the United States was such a solemn contradiction to all the old school of Charles V! What became, in the face of that great event, of the theories about balance of trade, and the administrative habits of the colonial régime? So many odious wars and so many maxims still more odious, had then been kept up, only to be reduced at last to a most humiliating recantation. Those laws for the protection of commerce were then only a dreadful abuse of power! Never, it must be confessed, had human vanity received a more cruel blow, and yet, in spite of this striking lesson, the pretensions of parent countries have scarcely moderated. They must all drink the chalice of bitterness before they will relinquish their despotic habits; being in this respect, like monarchies by divine right, which believe that all rights rest on one sword, until the very moment when that sword breaks in their hands.

The American Revolution was not the only decisive economic fact of the latter part of the eighteenth century. We have seen that the discovery of the two machines of Watt and Arkwright had completely changed the conditions of labor, by substituting machinery for the arms of men, and great associations for petty industries. This single fact was to give a death blow to all corporations, and reduce to dust their old and barbarous codes; but it could not fail to react at the same time on the financial system of Europe. The natural end of taxes being to reach incomes wherever they may be, one readily divines that the science of finance hastened to work the new field which offered its harvests. The extreme increase of industrial products called the attention of legislators and statesmen to this young branch of public wealth, and, consequently, in England the increase of indirect taxes went side by side with the development of manufactured products. Efforts to diminish the burdens of the people suddenly ceased; it appeared more advantageous to give the latter strength to bear them. "*Since it is not possible to diminish the burden, let us strengthen the beast,*" said an English minister, and this saying well characterizes the financial tactics of modern governments. Nations as well as individuals have ceased to shut themselves up in the narrow circle of privations; they have more wants because they have more means of gratifying them: they only need to increase the quantity of labor.

England had reached that point in her economic experience, when it was necessary for her to suffer her part in the reaction from the ideas disseminated by the French Revolution. A singular contrast, indeed, was that of two nations, one of which was rushing into indirect taxes, while they were being abolished by the other! And these opposite courses are easily explained. The aristocracy, all powerful in England, found it a simple matter to throw upon labor all the weight of the imposts; the democracy, victorious in France, committed the same injustice towards property. Here, the property of emigrants was sold, and landed property was tithed; there, the smallest articles for consumption were taxed, even to the air necessary for the lungs. It is not surprising that an implacable war broke out between the two principles so opposed; and this war only ceased to prevail when political economy effected a compromise, founded on a true analysis of the elements of wealth. When Adam Smith had demonstrated that manufacturers and traders were producers by the same right as cultivators were, the necessity had to be recognized of taxing manufacturing and commercial products as well as agricultural products, and each of them proportionately to its income. What remains to-day to be decided, is, at what point equity and analysis permit taxation of the classes who live by their wages and not by profits; and this is why the question, first propounded between the aristocracy and the bourgeoisie, has come down into the arena of popular passions.

The long wars of the revolution, between France and England, by laying the two countries under the necessity of extreme measures and hazardous attempts, contributed no less than the Economist writers to the solution of several important problems. We are far from admitting, with Ricardo, for example, that the increase of taxes was the principal cause[20] of the development of manufactured products in England. No one works simply to pay taxes, and there is no production possible on that condition; but it cannot be denied that a desire to procure many indispensable objects of consumption, which are taxed, will incite, in most men, a very strong disposition to labor. Unfortunately, the English government, induced by the exigencies of war, took unfair advantage of this disposition, which soon became insufficient, and the mania for expedients seemed to revive in the latter part of the century, as it had prevailed at its commencement. The most extravagant theories of finance were proclaimed as positive maxims of the government. The imposts ceased to respond to the distress of the treasury: it was necessary to have recourse to loans, to multiply them, to combine them in a thousand ingenious ways, in order to make good the constantly increasing deficits; and hence arose the theory of *amortization*," that chimera of which England was to be, within a few years, the cradle and the tomb.*

The English have nevertheless had the honor of founding modern public credit in Europe, by proving that it could very well survive the most critical circumstances, and even aid a great people to emerge from them with honor. Indeed, notwithstanding the perpetual growth of taxes and loans, the population of England had not ceased to increase, its agriculture to become enriched, and its manufactures to daily become more productive. New canals had been opened, docks hollowed out, colossal enterprises executed with admirable rapidity; the national capital had increased with production itself: so that today the English nation is perhaps that which disposes of the largest revenue, although it pays enormous taxes. That which was to lead it to bankruptcy led it to fortune, and its very bankruptcy,(for, like France, it passed through that trial,)was to it another opportunity for progress and a source of improvements. We might say that to it was given to overthrow the received systems, in everything, and to astonish the world by its operations in finance, as much as by the processes of its manufactures. Pitt ventured to maintain that the fictitious capital created by the loans had been transformed into fixed capital, and had become as advantageous to the public

---

* M. Pebrer (*Histoire financière de l'empire Britannique*), estimates at nearly *fifty milliards* of francs the sum of the revenues collected and loans consumed by the English government, from the beginning of the French Revolution to the treaty of 1815. This is a sum five times greater than the whole mass of money existing in Europe at that time, during which the precious metals were the most abundant. *Fr. Ed.*

as if an equivalent real treasure had been added to the
wealth of the kingdom. What more absurd than such
an assertion, and what more surprising, too, than the
marvellously fecund results of those multiplied loans,
under the weight of which England was expected to
succumb!

Thus it was that the English, not satisfied with their
funded debt, invented the *floating debt*, by means of those
enormous issues of treasury notes, the employment of
which, wisely regulated in times of peace, has become
one of the most convenient and safe resources of modern
states. Administrators have made economists comprehend that there was often much economy in being able
to employ by anticipation in January the revenue of
December; and the boldness of an attempt justified by
the critical condition in which England found herself, has
permitted a useful financial institution to be substituted
for the onerous expedients of past times. The floating
debt has become the refuge of all inactive capital and
the reserve of constitutional governments. It is no longer
necessary to hoard capital beforehand to the deprivation of
labor, in order to provide for unforeseen wants. Who could
have persuaded the school of the Physiocrates, or even that
of Adam Smith, of such things, before the truly gigantic
experiments of Great Britain had permitted a belief in
them and a recognition of their strong and their weak
points!

The same astonishment struck the economic world at
the news of the suspension of payments by the Bank of
England in 1797. Surely, if any doctrine was ever judicious and sound, it was that of Adam Smith on the constitution of banks, and the necessity of their limiting
their issues of bills, under penalty of being obliged to
purchase specie at great expense after having seen their
notes depreciate: one day, however, the Bank of England,²² exhausted by discounting treasury notes, found
itself forced to suspend specie payments. It was a vir-

tual bankruptcy, since the notes were payable to the bearer in gold ; and such a bankruptcy under the circumstances then existing in England, seemed as if it must bring about the most fearful catastrophes. It did not so eventuate, however, because the government had the good sense to stop on that declivity, and not to multiply beyond measure the bank-bills, which had become paper-money. The slight difference between the rate of gold and that of paper was scarcely perceptible, and the export of specie seemed to have no other result than to make monetary wealth more productive. When, later, the issues exceeded the limits within which the making of paper-money had been restricted, there only resulted a general rise of wages and prices. The nation seemed to have become richer, because the nominal amount of wages was higher, and this increase produced a general feverish condition of national labor.

On the other hand, while these curious phenomena were manifest in England, contrary experiments were having a distressing termination in France. The *assignats* and the *mandats*, although secured by national property, suffered a depreciation unheard of in financial history since the failure of Law's system. They fell to the last degree of demonetization, while the bank of England notes maintained their value in spite of the bankruptcy. The former, exchangeable for land, were no longer worth anything; the others, deprived of specie security, preserved their nominal value. France, with all the elements of prosperity, was plunged in anarchy ; England, with all the elements of anarchy, was prosperous. Production seemed to double in the latter country in proportion as specie was withdrawn from it : it was paralyzed in France, notwithstanding the sale of the property which created millions of landholders and consequently the most energetic stimulus of production, as we have said, viz., land-ownership. No period has ever been more fertile in grave economic instruction, unless we except that which

followed the return[23] to specie payments, when the peace
of 1815 permitted England to resume them, in pursuance of
the famous act of Mr. Peel.   The consequences of that resumption came near being more disastrous to Great Britain
than suspension had been, or rather, than it had seemed that
it must be.   The English people had become accustomed
to the small bank notes, and had adopted them for money.
The landowners, the government employés, the fund-holders, those of every rank who received pay, had cradled themselves in the illusion of an increase in their fortune, because
they received higher farm-rents, emoluments or incomes.
Suddenly the arrival of specie, flooding the national
market, found numerous transactions made under the
rule of paper-money and high prices.   Many a man who
had made a bargain under those conditions, was obliged
to pay in specie.   One can readily divine what a disturbance must have accompanied that financial revolution,
which particularly affected agricultural leases, and which
resembled, in an opposite way, the final crisis of our
paper-money.   It was necessary to prevent the ruin of
farmers by heroic remedies, and workmen living on salaries
or wages were condemned, by the corn-laws, to pay the
debt of the agriculturists to the land-proprietors.

This crisis was not the only one which affected the British people, and Europe was going to be witness of more
than one revolution, when the treaty was signed, which
seemed as if it would conclude them all.   We have seen
that the continental blockade gave an extraordinary impulse to French manufacture, henceforth almost alone
invested with the markets of the continent.   England,
under the influence of this same blockade, had taken possession of the seas and of all the colonial markets, which
secured to her her maritime preponderance.   The result
to her had been also a great activity in manufactures, to
which besides smuggling lent its support.   Suddenly
peace *breaks out*, as a complete and sudden war might
have done ; and the treaties which restore repose to the

world prepare new struggles for commerce, a thousand times more serious and more inextricable than the struggle of arms. France, reduced to her former limits, is surrounded by a triple cordon of custom-houses, almost to the gates of her capital, and England, which furnished supplies to the colonies, is forced to yield their markets to their mother-countries, now at peace with her. Spain attempts to take back South America; the Dutch regain Java; each desires to recover possession of her prey ; and the bayonet-war changes into an ignoble war of *fathom-lines* and of custom-officers. The conditions of labor were then once more modified throughout all Europe by the overthrow of French domination and by the opening of the seas, so long English, to the trade of all nations.

European administration presented at that time a spectacle well adapted to arouse people to the study of political economy. States which but a short time before were prosperous notwithstanding the rivalry of neighbors subject to them, solicited against these very neighbors, which had become free, restrictions each day more severe, and closed their boundaries against themselves by interdicting to them theirs. England seemed more repelled from the continent by the tariffs of her allies than she had been by the arms of her enemies, and poverty invaded her deserted workshops, while her victorious policy was seeming to secure for her the monopoly of the world. All that remained to her from so many efforts was the alarming figure of her public debt and of the population enfeebled by the taxes which an inexorable aristocracy had imposed upon them. What a magnificent subject of study for economists ! How many facts were presented for their observation by that long series of events new in the history of the science, the division of property, the abolition of wardenships, indirect taxes, public loans, *amortization*, paper money, the suspension and resumption of payments by the bank of England, and above all, that astonishing contrast of opposite results from similar causes, and like results from opposite causes! From that time, people comprehended that there was nothing absolute in social physiology; it passed naturally into the rank of experimental sciences, and its judgments were to be founded on experience and the comparison of actual facts rather than upon original theories. I do not hesitate to affirm that it is from that vast encyclopædia, which dates from 1789 and ends in 1830, that political economy has drawn its most valuable materials and the most solid bases of its doctrines. Economists, from that time, approach positive questions and mingle seriously in human things; they depart from the arid ground of abstractions to rise to practice, that is to say, to become useful and truly popular; a signal honor, and one which belongs especially to one of our fellow coun-trymen, J. B. Say.

CHAPTER XXXIX.

J. B. Say and his doctrines.—Important consequences of his theory of openings for marketable produce.—The services that writer has rendered to science.—Character of his school.—It has popularized political economy in Europe.

IT could not be otherwise than that the great experiments made in France and England, during the long struggle these nations maintained against each other, should furnish political economy with new elements of observation and contribute to its advancement. Adam Smith had unquestionably laid the essential bases of that science with a firm and positive hand ; but we have seen that he had left to his successors deep questions to resolve. What principally remained to be done, was to fix the limits of the science and to properly determine the field which its researches should cover. Adam Smith had thrown much light on the theory of banks, division of labor, and the foundation of the value of things ; he had made virtual discoveries : but he had not lived long enough to observe their applications. It was only after his death that people could judge of the effects of unlimited competition, of which he was one of the first apostles : and the complicated pauperism of our days had not yet disturbed the serenity of those in which he lived. Political economy was only the science of the production of wealth. It was reserved for a Frenchman to complete the work and to initiate us into the mysteries of the distribution of the profits of labor, at the same time that he

442

made known to us the so varied phenomena of the consumption of products.

The situation of France was very favorable for that study, after the storms of our revolution. Had not the people tried all systems and carried to their last results the most hazardous principles? Had they not had a near view of bankruptcy, the wasting of capital by war, the momentary destruction of commerce by the *maximum*, the blockade of the seas and that crowd of industrial and financial catastrophes with which the history of the time is wholly filled? The time had come to draw conclusions, and to sum up in one body of doctrine the theories which naturally arose from that mass of new and unheard-of facts. It was necessary to explain this economic cataclysm unparalleled in the world, which appeared nevertheless as the precursor of a general renovation. This is what J. B. Say did, in publishing, under the consulate of Bonaparte, the first edition of his *Treatise on Political Economy*. From this book dates, in fact, in Europe, the creat on of a simple, strict and intelligent method of studying political economy, and the time has come for us to judge of it.

The principal merit of this work consisted in having clearly defined the bases of the science. J. B. Say separated it from politics, with which the Economists of the eighteenth century had constantly confounded it, and administration, which the Germans thought inseparable from it. Thus reduced to more precise limits, political economy ran no further risk of being lost in the abstractions of metaphysics and the details of bureaucracy. J. B. Say rendered it independent by isolating it ; and he proved that its study was as suitable for monarchies as for republics. Everywhere there was need of knowing its laws, because, under all forms of government, the production of wealth was the most prolific source of the prosperity of states. At the same time, he explained its principles in the clearest and most methodical manner, and he created the nomenclature henceforth adopted by all the economists of Europe. His theory of value founded on utility completed that of Adam Smith, and although it left, like all theories, some gaps to be filled, it nevertheless served to resolve the most difficult questions, with all the certainty of which they are susceptible.

Whatever controversies may have arisen since then on several points in his doctrines, every one to-day recognizes the superiority of his method over all those of his contemporaries. Political economy is, in his view, only a science which treats of the production, distribution, and consumption of wealth. Wealth is produced by means of three great branches which sum up all human labor, viz., agriculture, manufactures, and commerce. Capital and land are the principal instruments of production : by saving and accumulation, people obtain the former ; ownership guarantees the free action of the latter. The labor of man, combined with that of nature and of machines, give life to all that combination of resources from which the riches emanate which are the common fund of associations. Smith had admirably demonstrated the advantages of division of labor ; J. B. Say perfected his work and showed some of the abuses of that division, which were later overstated by M. de Sismondi.*

But what assures immortal renown to the French writer is his *théorie des débouchés*, (literally, *theory of outlets, i.e.,* openings for sale of products ; generally translated, *theory of markets.—Trans.*),which gave the last blow to the exclusive system and hastened the fall of the colonial régime. This fine theory, wholly founded on most careful observation of facts, has proved that nations pay for products only with products, and that all the laws which forbid them to buy, prevent them from selling. No misfortune in the world is henceforth without its counterstroke ; when the harvest fails at one point, manu-

---

* *Nouveaux Principes d'Economie Politique.*

factures suffer at another; and when prosperity reigns in a country, all its neighbors share in it, either because of the demands which come from it, or because of the good market which results from an abundance of products. Nations are then conjoined in good as in evil fortune: wars are follies which ruin even the conquerer, and the general interest of men is to render mutual aid, instead of injuring each other as a blind policy has too long impelled them to do. We are beginning to comprehend the consequences of this truly rational and elevated doctrine, and one can readily judge from the solicitude of governments to avoid war, that the principles of J. B. Say have penetrated the councils of kings. His most glorious title to honor is to have demonstrated as a positive truth and one of material interest, what appeared only a philosophic utopia; and this merit is so much the greater because Montesquieu, Voltaire,* and La Fontaine, our finest geniuses, professed the contrary error.

The restrictive system could no longer be maintained before the overpowering arguments by which J. B. Say provoked its destruction. " People buy more," he said, " whenever they receive more. One prosperous branch of commerce furnishes means with which to buy, and consequently procures sales for all other branches of commerce; and, on the contrary, when one branch of manufactures and certain kinds of commerce languish, most of the others suffer in consequence. A nation, in its relation to another nation, is in the same condition as a province in its relation to another province, or a city in its relation to the country; it is interested in seeing them prosper, and sure of profiting by their opulence.† The

---

* We read in the *Dictionnaire Philosophique*, article PATRIE : " Such is the condition of human beings, that to wish the greatness of one's country, is to wish evil to its neighbors. *It is clear that one country cannot gain unless another loses.*"

Happily, that is not so clear to-day.

† " It would be as absurd to attempt to impoverish a people with whom we trade, as it would be in a tradesman to wish for the insolvency of a rich and frequent customer."—*Buckle, Hist. of Civ.*, vol. i, p. 157.—*Trans.*

United States have then acted in accordance with reason; in seeking to give industrial arts to the savage tribes by which they are surrounded; they wish them to have something to give in exchange, for one gains nothing in dealing with people who have nothing to give." How many experiments were we not obliged to make before arriving at these generous conclusions! J. B. Say also wrote towards the end of his career: " Forty years have elapsed while I have been studying political economy, and what years! They are worth four centuries for the reflections to which they have given birth."

This writer had the inestimable advantage over all his predecessors and most of his contemporaries, of having followed the march of events as a judicious observer and having profited by the numerous experiences which these events offered. Besides, he did not confine himself to the study of the phenomena of wealth in a purely theoretical and abstract manner: we recognize at every step the practical man, accustomed to follow out the consequences of his doctrines and to subordinate the latter to the greater or less utility of their applications. The distinctive characteristic of his writings, perspicuity, is especially manifest on the questions which had been obscured by economists of all times and countries, and chiefly in that of moneys. He explains their elements with admirable clearness, and he reduces to nothing that innumerable mass of writings which sprang up in Italy, Spain, France, and England, at the period when the governments were, in turn, playing the part of making debased coin. If he speaks of the various classes of workers who coöperate in production, we feel that he has lived with them, and that he knows their needs and has an exact idea of their troubles. It is to him that savants

---

" The feelings of rival tradesmen, prevailing among nations, overruled for centuries all sense of the general community of advantage which commercial countries derive from the prosperity of one another ; and that commercial spirit, which is now one of the strongest obstacles to wars, was, during a certain period of European history, their principal cause."—*J. S. Mill,* Polit. Econ., 1849. vol. ii. p. 221.—*Trans.*

owe their restitution to the industrial hierarchy; and although *immaterial* products are not susceptible of accumulation, J. B. Say has demonstrated their salutary influence on the prosperity of states. Public functionaries alone and the services they render to society, have found less favor with this illustrious economist: the indignation he experienced at seeing England overburdened with taxes, and his hatred of the despotism of the empire, did not permit him to be just toward the emperor, nor to measure with a correct eye the distance between use and abuse. J. B. Say, notwithstanding the superiority of his mind, was not inaccessible to political passions, and although his writings present few traces of the prepossessions to which he was exposed during our long political reactions, one cannot help recognizing that he yielded more than once to feelings very excusable in those agitated times.

But these generous resentments are much more manifest in his writings by a few epigrammatic sallies, than by passionate theories. The subjects which affect us most keenly to-day, those indeed which have at all times been privileged to move minds most sensibly, the questions of wages and population, seem hardly to move him; he proceeds to the critical examination of them with his natural rigidity, and he adopts entirely the views of Malthus in regard to them. It is here that his writings are henceforth vulnerable, and they cannot fail to be surpassed by the school of M. de Sismondi, notwithstanding the errors it has committed and its powerlessness, up to this time, to find a remedy for the evils of which it has given so spirited a picture. J. B. Say considered production too independently of the producers. He was captivated by the prodigies of English industries, the great manufacturing industries, and he had not time to take into account all the evils they entail. He conformed to contemporary prejudice, which considered wages as sufficient, not when they produced life, but

when they prevented death.   His studies on the distribution of the profits of labor are dominated by the influence of capital, and his considerations on the effects
of public consumption bear too visible indications of his
bitterness against the abuses of tyranny.   There were
two powers which this great writer treated unjustly,
though with equal injustice: capital, by giving it too
prominent a part, and governments, by denying them
any efficient action on the happiness of citizens.*

   But no one has popularized economic science to the
the same degree as J. B. Say.   It is in vain to reproach
him with having reduced it to the narrow proportions of
chrematistics or the science of wealth: he has very well
proven that political economy only began to be a science
when its limits were exactly marked out, and he protested in his later writings against the purpose that had
been attributed to him of wishing to restrict it to an abstract analysis of the laws of production.†   He especially
detested hypotheses and systems, as the source of almost
all the evils which have weighed heavily on society; and
political economy seemed to him truly useful, only because it was called upon to refute successfully the disastrous prejudices with which the human race is afflicted.
He leaves, too, not a single objection unanswered; and
the usefulness of his works consists much more in the

----

* " The insignificant administration of Cardinal Fleury," he said, " proved
at least that at the head of a government to do no evil is of itself doing
much good." *Discours préliminaire*, p. 48.

† " The object of political economy," he said, "seems to have been
hitherto restricted to an acquaintance with the laws which control the formation, the distribution and the consumption of wealth.   It was thus that I
myself considered it in my *Treatise on Political Economy*, published for the
first time in 1803.   One can see, however, that this science has connection
with everything in society.   Since it has been proven that immaterial property, such as talents and acquired personal abilities, form an integral part of
social wealth, and the services rendered in the highest positions have their
analogy with the most humble labors ; since the relations of the individual
with the social body and of the social body with the individuals, and their
reciprocal interests, have been clearly established, political economy, which
seemed to have for its object only material wealth, has found that it embraced the entire social system."—*Complete Course of Practical Political
Economy*, vol. i, p. 7.

errors he has dissipated than in the truths he has discovered. J. B. Say marked out the first complete programme of political economy, and even the writers who do not share his opinions, agree in recognizing the excellence of his method and the rigorous accuracy of his deductions. Thanks to that method, the commercial crises which have afflicted France and England at various times may be easily explained, and their recurrence may be prevented or their effects diminished by efficacious measures.

The influence of J. B. Say contributed more than that of any contemporary writer, to extend in Europe a taste for political economy. His theories, so naturally applicable to political questions, were studied with ardor during the Restoration as a weapon of opposition and of war ; and perhaps they owe a part of their success to the services they rendered in the parliamentary discussions of the period. Publicists sought in them decisive argu· ments against the enormity of the burdens imposed upon the nation, and they accustomed themselves to those minute analyses of the budget, which later degenerated into disputes about figures or quarrels over portfolios. J. B. Say did not approve of governments undertaking public works, and he severely censured their intervention in the industrial affairs of a country. Most of the taxes seemed to him as much scourges as hail, conflagrations and invasions, and although his philanthropy was sincere and profound, he showed himself more hostile to governmental power than favorable to the toiling masses. He perseveringly labored for the latter without seeking their favor or fearing their disfavor. He told people and kings stern truths, with the unconcerned and stoic impartiality of a philosopher occupied only with the interests of science and of humanity. The whole French press was penetrated with his doctrines, without knowing their author, who lived apart, surrounded by his family and a little circle of friends, while his works, translated into all

languages, obtained, in less than twenty years, five successive editions extended to a large number of copies.

It was, in fact, by the voice of J. B. Say that the first
attacks were directed in France against the economic
system of the Restoration. The reaction of 1815 wished
to restore the right of primogeniture, entail, corporations, and privileges; later, beaten on this ground, it
tried to make again a landed aristocracy, half feudal,
half industrial, by raising the duty on iron, which increased the price of wood and the income of the owners
of forests. Then came the grain laws, the tax on foreign
cattle, the emigrant loan, and differential duties on colonial
sugars; and each of these measures was blasted beforehand in the chapters of the *Treatise on Political Economy*,
impressed with the soundest judgment, and which had
neither been written to this end nor for this case. Entire
Europe profited by these hard lessons which seemed to be
destined for France, since they were published in a French
book; and more than once, the author found himself
engaged in a lively contest with the most learned economists of his time. Malthus, Ricardo, M. de Sismondi,
and M. Storch, maintained against J. B. Say memorable
theses on some points of doctrine; but all agreed in
recognizing in him the most indefatigable athlete of
the science, and next to Adam Smith its most illustrious
propagator.

J. B. Say sided with Malthus in his ideas on population. He adopted them fully, freely, without reserve,
and he caused them to prevail in France up to the time
when the Saint-Simonian doctrines gave them the first
blow. His attention was little given to the abuses of the
English manufacturing system, and he attributed the
evil of pauperism in that country, to causes purely
political. The glutting of the markets seemed to him
only the consequence of commercial restrictions. In his
view, the reason why there was not enough sold in any
one place, was because not enough was produced in some

other. Production and consumption were, in his opinion, correlative operations, and he sought for no other cause of the distress of certain countries than a lack of production in the countries with which they had relations. Experience has already taught us that it is not permitted to establish commercial relations on that basis alone, and that a people ought not to leave the fate of their manufactures exclusively to the chances of external commerce. Besides, J. B. Say persistently demonstrated that the best consumers of a nation's products were the national producers themselves, to whom the exchange secured regular and stable markets, when the incapacity of governments put no obstacle in the way. The analyses he gave of the mechanism of the exchanges have cast the brightest light on all questions connected with them, questions very important, since upon them depends the prosperity of nations. "Almost all the wars fought for the past hundred years, in the four quarters of the world, have been for a *balance of trade* which does not exist; and whence comes the importance attributed to that pretended balance of trade? From the exclusive application that has been made of the word *capital*, to gold and silver money." *

It was by such simple and striking statements of facts that J. B. Say succeeded in making war unpopular, and modifying those national prejudices which tend to perpetuate it. This immense work, the mere idea of which had caused the Abbé of Saint Pierre to be relegated to the rank of visionaries, is becoming accomplished under our eyes. Far from raising new barriers between nations, efforts are being made to break down those which exist: bridges are thrown across frontier rivers, railroads are built in common, most of the prohibitions are becoming suppressed. This fine part of the programme of J. B. Say was carried out before his death,†

---

* *Treatise on Political Economy*, vol. iii, p. 261.
† d. Nov., 1832.

and we daily behold the progress of public opinion favor the execution of the rest. The only thing in which this writer lacked was, not looking at questions of pauperism and wages from a more elevated and more social point of view. One feels, in reading him, something harsh and repulsive, which recalls the abstract formulas of Malthus and of Ricardo. His logic is merciless when he treats of the unfortunates who appear to him deservedly so; and one would say, to hear his severe warnings against beneficence,* that it has more encouragement for bad conduct than consolation for misfortune. But in everything that concerns the great principles of the science, in questions of custom-duties, moneys, public credit, and colonies, this author is the safest guide one can follow and the most classic writer in Europe.

The last of his works, which is also the most voluminous,† presents noteworthy modifications of the first opinions professed by the author. There is in it less sharpness against the governing powers, perhaps because M. Say had recognized the usefulness of their influence in certain cases, or because he thought he owed some sacrifices to the position he occupied. All those who knew his character will adopt in preference the first hypothesis, which besides is confirmed by remarkable passages, in which it is evident that this writer was acting in obedience to a new conviction. Thus, in one important case he had maintained that the labor of slaves was more economical than that of free men; and he had the good faith to publicly acknowledge that he had been mistaken. He had no charity for persistence in error, and he let pass no occasion of stigmatizing the bad books on political economy. Errors in that science appeared to him more disastrous than in any other, and he pursued them

---

* "Has the man, who, by his improvidence and idleness, has fallen into poverty after having exhausted his means, any claim to help, when his very faults deprive the men whose capital supports industry, of their resources?" *Treatise on Political Economy*, vol. iii, chap 7.

† Entitled : *Cours Complet d'Economie Politique Pratique.* 6 vols. in 8°.

wherever he thought he saw them, even in his most celebrated rivals, in the hope of establishing political economy on impregnable foundations. But it is time to notice the labors of those renowned economists.

CHAPTER XL.

Political economy in England from the beginning of the nineteenth century.—Pitt's system, supported by Thornton, attacked by Cobbett.—Doctrine of Ricardo.—Writings of James Mill.—Of Mr. Torrens.—Of Mr. McCulloch.—Of Mr. Tooke.—Labors of Mr. Huskisson.—Of Sir Henry Parnell.—Treatises of- Mr. Wade.—Of Mr. Poulett Scrope.—*Economy of Manufactures*, by Babbage.—*Philosophy of Manufactures*, by Dr. Ure. —Great popularity of political economy in England.

THE long list of English economists subsequent to the time of Adam Smith, and the harmony between their works, prove how vigorous and prolific had been the impulse given to political economy by its illustrious founder. The ideas which he had just popularized were already bearing their fruit. Economic questions had ceased to be left to chance, and government itself experienced the necessity of submitting its most important measures to the supervision of science. People had striking testimony of this at the period of the suspension of specie payments by the Bank of England, in 1797. This was the first case in which theories were invoked in support of a great financial measure, and from this time the discussion passed from the solitude of books into Parliament. The movement having once begun, was no more arrested: every one thought he must have recourse to the authority of principles to support his opinions, and the tribune became one of the most powerful auxiliaries of political economy. Consequently, *the Inquiry into the Causes of the Wealth of Nations* may be considered as the source of all the good writings published on this subject for the last fifty years.

Before the long struggle of France and England, under the influence of our revolution of 1789, the doctrines of Adam Smith had as yet received only one great and solemn application, viz., in the Independence of the United States. People were doubtless beginning to appreciate the advantages of division of labor and of the employment of machines; but no serious question had as yet put to test the theories of the celebrated Scotchman on the constitution of banks and the evils in the monetary system. It was necessary that the adventurous genius of a Pitt should risk bankruptcy, for people to recognize the accuracy of the analyses which Adam Smith had given of the phenomena of the circulation. Then appeared, at divers intervals, a multitude of works to attack or to defend the doctrines of Smith; and public opinion began to be formed in the din of these memorable quarrels. One of the most interesting works published at this period,* by Mr. Henry Thornton, had for its aim the justification of the suspension of specie payments; and although it abounds in errors, no other work has ever given a clearer comprehension of the advantages of the monetary circulation, whether in paper or specie. The author maintained that banks could indefinitely favor labor and multiply production without having need of specie, on the single condition of prudently regulating their issues. He proclaimed the benefits of credit, in full view of a measure which would seem to have annihilated it; and the future has justified his most reasonable predictions.

However, towards the end of the year 1810, England, exhausted by the efforts she had made to break down the power of Napoleon, saw all her gold exported to the continent to pay the coalitions, and the price of provisions rise to a point which rendered very difficult the continuation of the financial system devised by Pitt. Then

---

* *An Enquiry into the Nature and Effects of the Paper Credit of Great Britain*, London, 1802.

appeared the famous letters by Cobbett,* who attacked
with indomitable energy the abuses of paper-money and
the financial deceptions of the government.   We know
no study more interesting than this book for whoever
desires to estimate at their just value the advantages and
disadvantages of the system of credit.   Never had the
spirit of a writer to struggle with a subject so difficult,
and never since the *Provinciales* of Pascal and the *Mémoires* of Beaumarchais had more wit been placed
at the service of reason.   Political parties have attacked Cobbett as a pamphleteer without address
and without dignity: but posterity,²⁴ more just to him
than he was to his contemporaries, will assign him
a very distinguished rank among popular economists.
If all questions of political economy had been treated
with that vigorous and simple perspicuity, there would
not perhaps be to-day one single point of doctrine still
contested, and this science would have become accessible to all classes of the population.   Cobbett did
not seek his arguments in questionable hypotheses or
in the dogmatic treatises of the writers who had preceded him; he attacked with the simple resources of a
good judgment, and his inflexible logic threw the brightest light on the most profound discussions.   His economic pamphlets, almost all dated from the state-prison
at Newgate, are masterpieces of reason and of style, and
cannot be studied too carefully by men desirous of fath-
oming the mysteries of public credit.

Almost at the same time, England was enriched by the
first writings of Mr. Ricardo, which were to throw so
much light on political economy.   It was in 1809; the
rise of the price of gold and the fall in the exchanges
which took place that year, had taken strong hold of
public attention.   Ricardo published a pamphlet entitled: *The high price of bullion a proof of the depre-*

---

* *Paper against Gold, or the History and Mystery of the Bank of England.*
This enormous pamphlet had more than seven editions.   See Appendix.

*tiation of Bank-notes.** In it he demonstrated scientifically the proposition maintained by Cobbett, namely, the disadvantages of too great an issue of paper-money. He showed that rise and fall of the course of exchange are only relative terms, and that, so long as the circulation of a country is composed only of gold and silver money or of paper convertible into these forms of money, it is impossible that the course should rise above or fall below the course of other countries, by a sum greater than the cost of importing specie or bullion in case of scarcity, or the cost of exporting a part of the excess, in case of superabundance. But when a country issues an inconvertible paper money, as was then the case in England, this paper cannot be exported when it is too abundant in the country; and consequently whenever exchange with foreign countries falls, or the price of bullion rises above its price in coin, to the amount of the cost for exporting the coin, it is evident that too much paper has been issued, and that its value has fallen by reason of the excess of the issues. Ricardo contributed much to the nomination of a committee charged with examining this question, and the measures he proposed to remedy the evil, though postponed at first through ignorance or malevolence, were subsequently adopted, mid the plaudits of his country and of all enlightened friends of truth.

It was at this time that the author conceived a banking system in which the notes should be exchangeable, not for coin, but for bullion. The security of the holders of the bills was thus reconciled with that of the banks. The latter were obliged to restrict their issues, so as not to have to increase their security in bullion : and as the bullion was not current like money, the banks were less

---

* This writing, to-day quite rare, is one of the most remarkable documents of political economy, in point of simplicity and clear and practical precision. —*Author's note.*

Since Blanqui wrote the above, this writing has been published in a collection of Ricardo's works edited by J. R. McCulloch (John Murray, London). — *Trans.*

exposed to demands for payment. Nothing was more ingenious than this system, since it presented all the advantages of credit without having its dangers, and all the
security of gold money without incurring its expense; it
is therefore probable that the attempt will some day be
successfully made in more than one country.*

The principal work of Ricardo, *The Principles of Political Economy and Taxation*, published in 1817, created profound but diverse sensations in the economic world.
Some writers have considered it the most remarkable
work which has appeared since Adam Smith; others have
reproached him for having thrown political economy into
abstractions and filled it with algebraic formulas. As a
simple historian little disposed to enter again into controversies now exhausted, I will confine myself to pointing out the distinctive characteristics of that work. Ricardo there maintains that the revenue is entirely foreign
to the cost of production; that a rise of wages brings
about a fall in profits and not in the price of commodities, and that a fall in wages brings a rise in profits and
not a fall in prices. After having proved that the varia-
tion of profits is in inverse ratio to that of wages, he
sought to discover the circumstances which determine
the rate of wages and consequently that of profits. He
thought he had found them in the expense of producing
the articles necessary for the consumption of the laborer.
However high may be the price of these articles, it is
clear that the laborer must always receive a sufficient
quantity of them for his subsistence and for that of his
family. However, as raw products must always form the
principal part of the subsistence of the worker, and as
their price has a constant tendency to rise, by reason of
the constantly increasing sterility of the lands to which it
is necessary to have recourse in advanced conditions of
society, it follows that wages must have also a constant

---

* This project is set forth in a writing by Ricardo, entitled : *Proposals
for an Economical and Secure Currency.* (London, 1816).—*Fr. ed.*
This is to be found in McCulloch's edition of Ricardo's works.—*Trans.*

tendency to rise and profits to fall with the increase of wealth and population. In short, the fundamental doctrine of Ricardo on agricultural rents lay in maintaining that the profit which a land-owner makes on his land, that is to say, what his farmer pays him, represents only the excess, for a like expenditure, of the product of his land, over the product of the worst lands cultivated in the same country.

This opinion, supported by a remarkable exposition, was vigorously attacked by Malthus and by J. B. Say; and yet these authors arrived by different paths at the same conclusions: only, the opposers of Ricardo maintained that if the bad lands were cultivated, it was the extent of the wants of society and the price it was in a condition to pay for grain, which permitted a land-profit on the best lands or the best situated. To say that it is the bad lands which are the cause of the profit made on the good ones, was to admit in other terms a principle already known, that the cost of production is not the cause of the price of things, but that that cause lies in the wants the products can satisfy.* The controversy raised on this point was then no more than a quarrel of words: nevertheless, Ricardo put into his book such high considerations on the influence of taxes in the matter of incomes, profits, wages, and raw products, that even while contesting the theory of the author, we cannot help recognizing the light he shed on that difficult department of the science. It is a pity that this writer should have too often made chance suppositions, to deduce from them abstract and inapplicable conclusions, like a mechanician who should estimate the action of machines, without taking into account the friction and the materials of which they were constructed. Ricardo liked too well to generalize; he often launched out into a sort of economic metaphysics, bristling with arguments and difficult formulas, for which people blame the science, although it has suf-

* J. B. Say, *Traité d'Economie Politique.* Vol. ii, p. 358.

fered much from them. Consequently, "under pretence of extending it," said J. B. Say, "they have made it void.* "

The greatest reproach that we think can be made against Ricardo, is that he considered wealth in an abstract and absolute manner, without regard to the fate of the workers which contribute to its production. Mr. Ricardo was much more preoccupied with the collective power of nations, than with the individual well-being of the citizens which compose them ; and his severe logic considered men too much as instruments, instead of treating them as sentient beings. His book attracts at the first glance, by its dogmatic and clearly outlined forms of expression. He there treats of human questions in the manner of the savants who have established the theory of chemical proportions, and who think themselves sure of finding in the analysis of certain salts the same quantities of acid and of base that they combined there. He supposed subsidies could be raised for a year of war by an equivalent increase of taxes ; and he thought it suitable and practicable to pay the public debt[25] by an assessment (*cotisation*) on capital. He was certainly the man who has had the most new ideas in political economy since Adam Smith ; but the only ones which will survive are those he owed to the observation of facts rather than to the boldness of his reasoning. The last writing he published on agriculture † contains very profound reflections on the influence of the price of grain on profits and wages, and the effects of taxation on agriculture and manufactures. This work alone would suffice to place its author in the foremost rank of economists.

With his qualities and even with his faults, Mr. Ricardo would naturally found a school: that school al-

---

* "The chief of the new school, Mr. Ricardo, it is said, himself declared that there were not more than twenty-five persons in England who had understood his book." Sismondi, *Nouveaux Principes*, vol. ii, p. 374.

† A pamphlet of about a hundred pages, entitled : *Protection to Agriculture*.

ready counts several celebrated disciples, among whom may be mentioned Mr. Mill, Mr. Torrens, and Mr. McCulloch. James Mill, whom science has just lost,* is principally known by his excellent history of British India ; he has left an elementary treatise on political economy which manifests a little of the obscurity of the master,† and which sums up his doctrines as the writings of Justin sum up the lost fragments of Titus and Livy. Mr. Torrens departs further from the fundamental doctrines of that school, in his *Essay on the Production of Wealth,* and he accepts the doctrines of his illustrious fellow citizen only with considerable reservations. This writer generally shows himself eclectic ; he does not attach an exaggerated importance to the verbal disputes which too long divided economists, and he explains very well how most of the latter are in accord on the essential bases of the science. The book that he published in 1834 on *Wages and Combinations,* quite full of generous sympathy for the working classes, will be profitably consulted on the question of machines and on the circumstances which produce a rise and fall of wages in manufacturing countries. The author there attacks the corn-laws, as Ricardo had done, with an independence very honorable in a great landed proprietor.

For Mr. McCulloch was reserved the honor of presenting in a popular form the ideas of Ricardo, modifying them in the superior manner possible to his eminently positive and practical mind. The author had already published an excellent edition of Adam Smith with notes ; it then belonged to him more than to any other to make known to us the principles of Ricardo, and complete by less abstract analyses the labors of that celebrated economist. Unfortunately, Mr. McCulloch seems to us to have adopted the inflexible absolutism of the manufac-

---

* d. 1836.

† It would, in our opinion, be difficult to find a work of more marked perspicuity than that of Mr. James Mill.— *Trans.*

turing system which consists in making production advance without consideration for the producer, if not
through indifference to humanity, at least through abuse
of principles. Mr. Thomas Tooke has been more faithful to the experimental method of Adam Smith,* but he
has not kept as closely as several of his predecessors to
those careful definitions of the words *value, utility, and
wealth*, the precise meaning and application of which
have been long fixed. Being a practical man and versed
in the science of affairs, he seizes the most legitimately
recognized doctrines and applies them immediately to
industrial questions, as Mr. McCulloch made the most
happy applications of statistics to political economy.†
By thus neglecting no occasion to utilize the science, the
English economists have rendered it popular and raised
it from the list of utopias to the first rank among useful
branches of knowledge.

Two English ministers, Mr. Huskisson and Mr. Henry
Parnell have also contributed to this happy result. The
former of these statesmen, whose recent and premature
loss science still laments,‡ was not without resemblance
to Turgot. Impressed with the sad results of the prohibitory régime and the abuses of the system of protection, he had resolved to strike with a bold hand this old
institution, unworthy of our time and fatal to the progress
of civilization. But he knew how to ally the spirit of reform with the prudence of a legislator, and he never undertook any improvement without having first surround-

---

* His work, *Thoughts and Details on the high and low prices of the last
thirty years*, and that entitled, *Considerations on the State of the Currency*,
will be read with especial interest.—*Author's note*.

His famous *History of Prices, and of the State of the Paper Circulation
from* 1798 *to* 1857, is more valued for its statistics than for his reasoning
from those statistics. Some of his extraordinary fallacies and self-refuta-
tions are pointed out by Col. Torrens in his book on "Sir Robert Peel's
Bill of 1844."—*Trans*.

† See his *Dictionary of Commerce*, and his *Statistics of England*, where
grave economic questions are often treated with great ability, notwithstanding difficulties natural to the alphabetical order.

‡ Mr. Huskisson died of injuries received at the opening of the Liverpool and Manchester railway, September 15, 1830.

ed himself with the most conscientious documents and having proceeded to careful investigations. Political economy would have seen glorious and prosperous days, if this courageous and eloquent minister had lived long enough to bring to a good conclusion the reforms he had undertaken. "When I speak of improvements," he said in the House of Commons, " I mean that temperate and gradual melioration which, in every complicated and long settled state of society, is the best preservative and guarantee against rash and dangerous innovation. To improvement of that description it is the duty of each of us to contribute to the utmost in his power. It is by acting steadily upon this principle, that we shall maintain the lofty position which we now hold in the civilized world. That position, with all the fame and influence which justly belong to it, England has acquired by having hitherto taken the lead in this noble career of usefulness and distinction. In that career, we must go forward, impelled by the retrospect of past associations, by a just sense of our present greatness, and by a due regard to the obligations which both the past and the present impose upon us, toward those by whom we are to be succeeded." * * * " Our country cannot stand still, so long as there exists out of doors a free press to collect and embody, and a free discussion in Parliament, to guide and direct, the influence of public opinion."

The two circumstances in reference to which Mr. Huskisson was led to these solemn declarations of principles, are too well known for it to be necessary to explain them at length. Suffice it to say, that the question concerned in the one was the admission of foreign silks, and in the other, amendments to the laws relating to navigation, which had remained so exclusively restrictive since the famous act of Cromwell. Spirited opposition immediately arose from the manufacturers of silks and from the owners of vessels, both claiming that the ministry would leave the national manufactures defenceless against for-

eign competition. Mr. Huskisson was not moved one
moment from his position by this double storm of opposition ; and, refuting his adversaries by each other, opposing the recriminations of the latter to the studied
lamentations of the former, he obtained the finest triumph that a statesmen can desire, the adoption of his
measures without any restrictive amendment. A few
years later the doctrines of his opponents received a
striking disproof : not only manufactures of English silks
had not given way before foreign competition, but they
had increased and become perfected to such a degree as
to contest successfully with it ; and the sum total of navigation had surpassed the most exaggerated expectations.
A few petitioners, pretending to dread the Prussian marine on account of the tariff coalition of which this country had just become the centre, proposed to *employ cannon*
to compel it to recognize the long-established monopoly
of Great Britain. " I hope," replied Mr. Huskisson, " that
I shall never bear any share in the councils of England,
when the principle shall be set up that there is one rule
of independence and sovereignty for the strong and another for the weak, and when, abusing her naval superiority, England shall claim for herself, either in peace or
war, maritime rights which she refuses to acknowlege in
other states in the same circumstances. Such a pretention
would call for and warrant a combination of all the world
to defeat it."

Such were the economic and political doctrines of Mr.
Huskisson during his too short ministerial existence.
They have not ceased, since his death, to prevail in the
councils of the British government, and the slowness
with which we have seen them adopted by civilized
states, must be attributed to opposition from private interest, much more than to an unfavorable disposition on
the part of the administration. All good minds are to-
day in agreement as to the infallible results of lowering
the taxes, and enlightened governments hasten to antici-

pate in that regard the wishes of the people. Mr. Huskisson has found a worthy successor in Mr. Henry Parnell. This distinguished writer has reviewed the whole economic system of England, in a work entitled, *Financial Reform*, which contains the germ of all the improvements of which English legislation is susceptible, in matters of finance, custom duties and commercial interests. This work is a model for all governments desirous of reforming abuses in a prudent and progressive manner. The author sets forth in it all the facts relating to each question, and the disadvantages connected with the preservation of the present condition, whenever that condition seems contrary to the general interests. He shows himself more bold than Mr. Huskisson in everything that touches freedom of trade, and never have the principles on which the necessity of that freedom rests been supported by developments more conclusive and arguments more irresistible. Sir Henry Parnell has brought forward convincing proof of the advantages of reduction of the taxes, whether on raw materials or manufactured products: he has opened a new era in the science by following a system of a particular application of it to each economic question, so as to elicit a solution at some not distant future. Two English publicists, belonging to the same school, Mr. Wade and Mr. Poulett Scrope, have recently* published small popular treatises in which political economy is brought within reach of the laboring classes. That of Mr. Wade is preceded by a historical summary of the condition of laborers, and the author has there treated in a superior manner the questions of wages, pauperism, grain-laws and the influence of education on the masses.

Mr. Poulett Scrope has declared himself a decided antagonist of the doctrines of Malthus on population, and he has risen to high considerations on the phenomena of the distribution of wealth. His book is one of those in

* In 1833.

which the causes of public and private poverty, as well as the effect of restrictions on the exchanges, have been the best explained. "The happiness of the human race," exclaims the author at the close, "may easily, by means of foresight, equal and even exceed the increase of population." The doctrine of Mr. Wade and Mr. Scrope differs essentially from that set forth at about the same time in the works of Mr. Babbage and of Dr. Ure, on the economy of manufactures. The book of Mr. Babbage is nothing but a series of ingenious observations on division of labor and the employment of machines; that of Dr. Ure is a hymn of praise in honor of the manufacturing system, which the author proclaims the most favorable for the relief of the working classes. Babbage thought that much at least remained to be done by the manufacturers to profit by the industrial discoveries and to improve the moral status of the laborers. Dr. Ure, a most pronounced defender of manufacturing on a large scale, skilfully conceals its imperfections and considers it as the last term of civilization.

Such is the dominant character of the English economic school; and it is justly reproached with not taking sufficient account of the complications inherent in manufacturing labor, despite the stern warnings of the poor-tax and the periodical crises by which England has been afflicted for the last forty years. At the sight of those increasing thousands of ill-starred children and corrupted girls in the English manufactories, one is surprised to read in a work entitled *Philosophy of Manufactures*, such a passage as this: "Where children work at home, they are shut up all day long with their parents, and they have scarcely any acquaintance with others and with the feelings of their neighbors. The whole of the feelings which they thus imbibe may be selfish." * But

---

* *Philosophy of Manufactures*, by Dr. Ure, London, Book iii, chap. iii, pp. 419, 420. From testimony of John Redman before the Parliamentary Committee.

the English school has seen, in the production of wealth, only an element of national power, and the economists of that school are too much accustomed to consider workmen as simply instruments of production.   Scarcely a cry of pity escapes them at the sight of the crowded hospitals and prisons, filled with all the victims of our social inequalities.   They close their ears to the complaints and let themselves be dazzled by the prestige of civilization, without asking themselves if this splendid edifice is not cemented with tears, and if its foundation is so solid that there is nothing to dread from shocks.   Happily, France has claimed her accustomed privilege of defending the rights of humanity, and while Great Britain advances with giant steps in the industrial career, our writers are calling her back to the sacred principles of an equitable division of the profits of labor.

We enter now upon the social era of political economy.

CHAPTER XLI.

The social economists of the French School.—*New Principles of Political Economy*, by M. de Sismondi.—*New Treatise on Social Economy*, by M. Dunoyer.—*Christian Political Economy*, by M. de Villeneuve Bargemont.— *Treatise on Legislation*, by M. Ch. Comte.—*Political Economy*, by M. Droz.

FOR several years, the doctrines of Adam Smith, Malthus, and the industrial school, had been adopted without discussion throughout Europe, when M. de Sismondi brought out the first serious attack against the abuses of these doctrines, while accepting what was positive and incontestable in them.* Struck by the contrast between the great opulence and extreme poverty of which he had been witness in England, and surprised to see the improvements in the industries profit almost exclusively a few men, without sufficiently benefiting the community, he sought the causes of that anomaly, and he thought he had found them in the very constitution of manufactures, which was, in his opinion, badly adapted to the general necessities of the workers. " I have attempted to prove," he said, " that increase of production is a good only as it is followed by corresponding consumption ; that likewise economy in all the means of producing, is a social advantage only as each one of those who contribute to production, continues to receive from production an income equal to that he received from it before that economy had been introduced ; which he can only do by selling more of his products."

* See his first work entitled, *Commercial Wealth* ; published in 1803, the same year as the first edition of the *Treatise* by J. B. Say.

468

In examining from this new and bold point of view the industrial constitution of European society, M. de Sismondi encountered the great questions of competition, prohibitions, banks, and population. It seemed to him that competition between the workers would constantly tend to lower wages, while the machines furnished by the banks were gradually diminishing the demand for labor. There was doubtless a greater mass of wealth produced ; but the income of the laboring people was not increased by it, and consequently their means of subsistence were becoming insufficient : hence resulted all the evils with which humanity was afflicted in civilized countries ; and M. de Sismondi was led to adopt the theories of Malthus, if not as an inevitable fatality, at least as a result of the imperfect constitution of industry. Public happiness depending, in his view, on a just balance between population and income, and the income of the laborers being daily reduced by competition and the employment of machines, society could not fail to reach a series of catastrophes whose precursors were becoming manifest in every direction. Could one not see everywhere within the country competition with its ignominious train, the lowering of wages, commercial frauds, and a bad quality of products ; and abroad, tariff wars, contrabandage and all the crimes which it entails ?

The new tendency of manufactures, victory by great battalions, and the unavailing struggle of labor against capital, have inspired in M. de Sismondi eloquent pages. He utters a cry of alarm at the sight of the banks adding new weapons to the already well tempered arms of those who carry on manufactures. If only these ephemeral creations of productive instruments benefited the great family of workers ! But no ; banks but add to the existing means of making the condition of the laborer worse ; they multiply machines, reduce the price of a day's labor, and by giving an unlimited field to production, they facilitate those deplorable gluts of the market followed by crises in

trade and by ruin in manufactures. Henceforth all ability
consists in selling at the lowest possible price; it is re.
garded as patriotism to have ruined foreign manufactories;
but the national manufacturing establishments have been
treated no better. They have substituted more productive, but more expensive machines, for those which formerly existed; they have obtained a reduction in the rent
of buildings, in the interest of capital, and in the income
of landed proprietors. An annual manufacture of one
hundred thousand francs, when increased to a million,
puts an end to nine rival establishments; the new machines annihilate the capital represented by the old.
There is a loss of revenue to society by the diminution
of the interest of money, by the diminution of the profits
of manufacture, by the loss of rent on all the establishments, and by the reduction of the total number of workmen and of the wages of each. There is then a diminution in the consumption of all these classes; and while
the manufacturer works with all his might to increase the
quantity and improve the quality of the cloths he ex-
poses for sale, he works quite as effectively to diminish
the number of buyers of either, and to make all those
who are becoming impoverished make their clothes serve
them longer and be satisfied with still coarser qualities.*

It is not then true, according to M. de Sismondi, that
the struggle of individual interests, so much lauded by
the English school, is sufficient to produce the greatest
good of all; since, under the influence of that struggle,
we see every day the most serious complications arise
and the most crying acts of injustice consummated. So,
Malthus was right to counsel prudence to the predestined
victims of these industrial holocausts which are celebrated
on the altar of competition; and our fathers were not so
much out of the way when they kept in the bonds of
wardenships and masterships that fatal exuberance of pro-

* Sismondi on the *Revenu Social*, in the *Revue de l' Economie Politique*, vol. iv, p. 220.

duction which has transformed the world into a battle field where the great business managers devour the small ones. There was at least, under the old régime, a natural curb to marriage; the same restrictions were laid on the multiplication of men and of products; the competition of workers and that of merchandise were maintained within wise limits. The greatest evil of the present social organization is that the poor man can never know upon what demand for labor he can count, and that the power of working is never an exact and sure income to him. Such is, in substance, the doctrine maintained by M. de Sismondi in his *New Principles of Political Economy*, and developed by him with superior talent, which has, nevertheless, not succeeded in concealing the paradoxical side of his system.

We readily grant that a family which has only a thousand francs of income, will spend only a thousand francs, whatever be the price of most of the provisions which it must buy. But, if it procures with these thousand francs more articles than it obtained before the diminution of the expense of producing them, it will in reality enjoy a greater degree of comfort ; it will buy more products and will cause greater demands for labor. Let sugar diminish, for example, either by a progress in art or by a discovery in nature, and a portion of the income formerly devoted to the purchase of sugar can be employed in other purchases and favor new industries or the development of those which exist. If the progress in manufactures, the perfecting of machines, or the multiplication of the means of labor by the banks, were real evils, how could we then explain the progressive development of public prosperity and that increase of well-being which has penetrated the ranks of even the humblest laborers ? Is it not rather true that every saving in the expense of production is a conquest by which the entire community gains, too unequally, doubtless, but nevertheless incontestably ? M. de Sismondi has allowed himself to be led astray by the se-

duction of a simple and striking idea, like that of Malthus,
when he proclaimed his famous principle of population ;
and he thought he had found the true principle of public
felicity in his theory of the social revenue. But, in truth,
the illustrious economist only discovered one of the
pests of industrialism carried to its extreme limits. Distressed at the sight of the abuses, he has attacked the
practice itself, which he has endeavored to render responsible for all the evils of modern society ; and after having
described in pathetic terms the sufferings of the laboring
classes, he has been obliged to confess his inability to
remedy them.

His admirable book ends with a cry of despair. " I
confess," he says, " after having indicated what, in my
view, the principle is, I feel powerless to indicate the
means of carrying it out. The distribution of the profits
of labor between those who coöperate in producing them,
appears to me vicious ; *but it seems to me almost beyond
human power to conceive of a state of ownership absolutely
different from that which experience makes known to us.*"
And in fact, M. de Sismondi has well demonstrated that
the cultivation of the tropical regions by slaves was odious
and ruinous ; but he has proposed nothing to resolve the
great question of the emancipation of the blacks without
injuring their very subsistence and security. He has
pointed out, with a rare perfection and a perfect acquaintance with the subject, the abuses of paper money and the
dangers of money-paper ; but his work offers no compromise which can be applied in their use. We only know that
there is a powerful steam-engine which may explode and
cause victims ; but the author does not speak of a safety-
valve, and the conclusion would consequently be to renounce the employment of the machine to escape its
dangers. The improvements in mechanics have awakened
his anxiety and at times his wrath ; but he has offered us
no practical and serious plan to mitigate the rigors of
those transition periods and long cessations from labor

which keep whole populations in hard circumstances. There are social plague-spots, originating in the times and customs, slow in forming, slower in healing, over which it is not enough to lament in eloquent jeremiads, to make them disappear. Surely not all capitalists are merciless, nor all workmen without foresight ; but how many premature marriages ! how many children who ought not to have been born ! How many harvests destroyed by storms ! How many unforeseen wars ! How many commercial crises difficult to foresee ! Here is what daily baffles the theories of the economist and the calculations of the statesman. These are maladies which accompany growth, but they do not arrest it.

M. de Sismondi has been the historian of that transitory and distressing part of the developments of modern industry. No writer had hitherto shown a more noble and touching sympathy for the laboring classes; none has more energetically stigmatized the selfishness of the rich and the heedlessness of the men charged with watching over the interests of the greater number. His book is the best critical work in existence in political economy ; but a better book will be that which shall refute it. The slightest observation of facts suffices to demonstrate that the condition of the laboring classes is to-day much superior to what it was before the discovery of the great machines of modern industry. The workmen, even the worst paid of them, participate indirectly in the benefits of civilization; they go about the streets cleaner and better informed ; they receive the gratuitous advantages of an elementary education; they travel more comfortably and more economically than their fathers, and every day sees wealth or at least a competency reach numerous classes to whose lot it would never have fallen but for the improvements in machines. The principal defect in the method of M. de Sismondi lies in generalizing too much, like Ricardo himself, his most illustrious opponent. He is not at all cautious ; he goes straight to his end, and he sometimes deduces exaggerated conclusions from a reasonable principle. The abuse of banks in England and the United States, where they only serve to enrich those who are rich and to multiply machines without knowing how their products will be disposed of, has appeared to him a sufficient reason for the maledictions with which he pursues these valuable instruments of public fortune. " Capital so easily obtained," he says, " incites to hazardous enterprises, which the authors would have hesitated to undertake, if they had been obliged to risk their own funds." This is true, doubtless; but is the necessity of suppressing banks a legitimate conclusion from it ? M. de Sismondi has not recoiled, as to machines, from the rigorous conclusions from his system. He does not hesitate to declare that a new industrial improvement would be a national misfortune; for the number of consumers can hardly be increased, according to his ideas, and the number of producers would diminish by the employment of the new machines. He asks what would become of England if governed by a king who. by means of an immense crank, should perform all the tasks of his subjects, who were dying of hunger because his powerful machine had taken away from them all their work. And we answer at once that England would be a very fortunate country to be able to rely for its subsistence on the care of a ruler capable of executing by himself alone such immense labors.

Notwithstanding the paradoxical character which distinguishes them, the opinions of M. de Sismondi have exercised great influence in Europe. It was he who first revealed the secret of those social troubles principally occurring in manufacturing countries, and who gave warning of the danger of banks, much before the recent catastrophes which have so sadly justified his predictions. Thanks to him, the condition of the workman has become a precious and sacred thing; he has his place at the banquet of life, from which the theories of Malthus would have excluded him; and henceforth progress in wealth will be considered truly an advantage, only as its benefits extend to those who have coöperated in it. The principle is established: it belongs to legislators to deduce the conclusions. Already, profound industrial and commercial questions have fallen within the domain of parliamentary discussion; it will not be long before they will be resolved, under the auspices of the new economic school,* with the generosity of sentiment and the lofty views which should characterize a special jury of savants.

M. de Sismondi has given proof of true courage in being the first to point out, with a firm hand, the dangers of the artificially and *blindly* productive system lauded by England and adopted by most of the economists of Europe. Surely if a courageous man had been needed to call public sympathy to the lot of the working men, victims of a selfish and one-sided organization, that man would not have been lacking in France; but it was necessary to explain the hidden faults of that system; it was necessary to show how private poverty increased at the same time as public wealth, and by what afflicting contrast the profits of labor are more frequently concentrated in unoccupied hands than at the fireside of the laborer. M. de Sismondi has not solved this problem, but he has shed much light upon it and has boldly stated it to economists and statesmen. Since then, prohibitions have begun to take on a different aspect from that of former times; the fictitious impulse they give to production has been found to have a compensation in the restraint they put on consumption. We have seen that the mechanic lost, in his character of consumer, all which the heads of protected industries gained in their position of manufacturers. The coöperation of machines, so energetic and so useful, when its aim is to economize the

---

* Witness the question of prisons, that of slavery, that of the labor of children in manufactories, the great enterprises of public charity, etc.

time and the toil of men, appeared murderous as soon as
it had been proven to result too frequently in crushing
humanity in its gearing. Perhaps M. de Sismondi, deeply
moved in view of the sufferings so common in manufacturing countries, has exaggerated evils which did not all
depend on the same cause ; but it will be to the eternal
honor of his name to have sounded the alarm in Europe*
and put himself at the head of the most unjustly disfa-
vored classes of our social order.   We shall soon hear his
cry of alarm, repeated with a solemn voice by the Saint-
Simonians, resound in the midst of our cities and in the
tumult of insurrections—a mournful warning which politics cannot disregard nor science leave longer unavailing!

Numerous writers have hastened to respond to the
generous appeal of M. de Sismondi.   Among the most
intelligent advocates of his doctrines, France counts the
author of *Christian Political Economy*, the Viscount Al-
ban de Villeneuve-Bargemont, whose investigations in
regard to pauperism have obtained less success than so
commendable a work merited, because of the evident insufficiency of the *therapeutic* part.   M. de Villeneuve surpasses even the mournful complaints of M. de Sismondi
in regard to the manufacturing system : he depicts in
most vivid colors the evils of every kind by which the
laboring classes are overwhelmed ; but the remedies he
proposes are those of an apostle rather than of an economist or an experienced administrator.†   However great,

---

* See especially chapters xii, viii and ix of the seventh book of his *New
Principles of Political Economy.*

† " What appears certain," he says, " is that the times of monopoly and
oppression are forever ended, and that a great transition is approaching.
Now, this can take place only in two ways ; either by a violent irruption of
the proletary and suffering classes upon the property-holders and manufacturers, that is to say, by a return to a state of barbarism ; or by a practical and general application of the principles of justice, of morality, of humanity and of charity.   All the genius of politics, all the efforts of men of
property, must then tend to prepare that transition by ways of persuasion
and wisdom.   Evidently the world calls for a new phase of Christianity.‡
Christian charity, finally put into action in politics, laws, institutions, and

---

‡ The Saint-Simonians called their doctrine at one time by the name of *New Christianity.*   This is the title of one of the writings of Saint-Simon.

in fact, may be the resources of the religious mind, they cannot remedy all social diseases. Christian charity alone cannot provide for the material wants of humanity. It is desirable, without doubt, that it should penetrate politics and morals; but even supposing it to penetrate them deeply, it would still have to be ascertained if its intervention would be sufficiently efficacious to cure an evil as inveterate and as inherent in civilized society as the poverty generalized under the name of pauperism. At a period now remote, the religious spirit had sovereign sway, without being able to remedy human miseries, and if there were then fewer poor in Europe than in our day, it was because there were fewer inhabitants.

We cannot doubt, however, that public poverty is a great social fact, peculiar to modern states, and manifesting itself more and more as civilization advances. Must it be admitted that such a fact is inevitable or fated, or that it depends on human institutions to modify it in a favorable way? If politics can do nothing for it, will religion be able to do more? The author of *Christian Political Economy* has sincerely entertained this latter hope; and I regret to say that the reading of his book does not permit me to share it. His conclusions are nearly the same as those of M. de Sismondi; everything is committed to the hands of God, and the author would freely take refuge in prayer, so great is his fervor and so sincere his piety; but what can prayers effect in the face of the terrible and keen reality? in vain does M. de Villeneuve recall regretfully the old system of corporations and the monastic life which wisely limited the increase of population: of what use is it to regret what has ceased to be in harmony with present customs, in a word, what is no longer possible? It is doubtless easy to bring forward in evidence the embarrassments which savants and

---

customs, *can alone preserve* the social order from the frightful dangers which menace it : outside of that, we venture to say, there is naught but illusion or falsehood."

statesmen experience in solving this formidable problem ;
but the hand of the priests in our days * is far more
powerless to give us an equitable solution of it. M. de
Villeneuve was not able to obtain any results from his
ideas, although he preached to hungry people moral †
restraint, frugality, temperance and other like virtues,
with Malthus and the apostle Paul. He is reduced
to regretting the loss of the religious celibate while attacking the doctrines of Malthus, which counsel abstinence for other reasons, and to deploring the services of
machines, notwithstanding the relief they have brought in
the hardest kinds of labor to the working classes. Political
economy has then received no new light from that eloquent lamentation, in which M. de Villeneuve has deplored all the sufferings of human society without proposing any efficacious remedy to cure them. His conclusion is this : 1st. Moral, religious and *industrial* instruction given gratuitously and with obligation to profit by
it, by means of charitable schools at the expense of the
communes. 2nd. Banks to encourage economy and forethought, established at the expense of manufacturing
towns- and communes, or of charitable associations,
with obligation on the part of the workmen to put in
them a portion of their wages, when the rate of the latter will permit without inconvenience. 3rd. The institution of corporations of workmen, which, without embarrassing industry and having the fatal results of the
old masterships and wardenships, would favor the spirit
of association and mutual helpfulness, give certificates

---

* M. Guizot has well expressed that powerlessness in a fragment published
by the *Revue Française.* "In our days," he says, "by the course of events
and by reciprocal errors, religion and society have ceased to understand each
other and to walk side by side. The ideas, the feelings, the interests which
now prevail in temporal life, have been, and daily are, reproved in the name
of the ideas, feelings and interests of the life eternal. Religion pronounces
anathema on this new world and holds itself separate from it ; the world is
ready to accept the anathema and the separation."

† " Abstinence from marriage could never be more efficaciously inspired
in the poor than by the religious sentiment." *Econ. Polit. Chrétienne,* vol.
i, p. 235.

of instruction and of good conduct and take the place of the deplorable institution of trade-unions.* But it is evident that these palliatives, otherwise salutary, could have no important influence on universal competition, the abuse of political privileges, the struggle of great amounts of capital with small fortunes, and the unfair distribution of taxes.

M. Droz seems to us to have more justly estimated the true character of political economy. "Let us not take," he says, "riches for an end; *they are only the means*. Their importance results from the power of mitigating suffering, and the most valuable wealth is that which serves for the well-being of the greatest number of men. The happiness of states depends less on the quantity of products than on the manner of their distribution. No country is so remarkable as England in respect to the formation of wealth; in France, its distribution is better; hence I conclude there is more happiness in France than in England. In reading certain economists, one would think that products were not made for man, but that man was made for products."

Such is the direction given to the science by the economists of the new French school, which I call the social school, because it refers all progress to the general improvement of society, without regard to race or caste, pursuing with the same anathemas the trade in blacks and the exploitation of the whites. M. Droz is the one of all the writers of that school who has most clearly stated its programme, without hostility to the present or illusions in regard to the future. M. de Sismondi, of a mind eminently critical, had to uproot widely-spread prejudices in favor of names most respected in science; and he could not help, in his generous ardor, being more than once almost led into a paradox. He, too, according to the expression of Malthus, having found the bow bent too much to one side, believed in the necessity of *forcing*

---

* *Economie Politique Chrétienne*, vol. iii, p. 156.

it to the other, and for this reason his doctrines have not produced all the fruit humanity might expect from them. He expected too much from governments, as M. de Villeneuve expected too much from Providence ; but Providence and governments have made severe conditions for man !

Two works remarkable in different ways, the *Treatise on Legislation*, by M. Charles Comte, and the *New Treatise on Social Economy*, by M. Dunoyer, have recalled economists to more just if not as attractive ideas of the true difficulty of economic questions. M. Comte, faithful to the experimental method followed by J. B. Say, has demonstrated by historic facts, selected with much judgment and most ingeniously compared, that most of the obstacles to social improvements come from those who would derive most profit from them, and who are perpetually conspiring to hinder their accomplishment. He has shown how the fatal habits of servitude corrupted the masters while brutalizing the slaves, and how much opposition has awaited, at every conquest of civilization, the devoted men placed in the vanguard. " For," he says,* " the nature of things or of men is not modified according to our desires. The founders of slavery never succeeded in exempting the masters from all evils, nor in securing for them the monopoly of enjoyments ; the men who have attempted to distribute pleasures and pains equitably among all the members of society, have succeeded no better. The first failed, because they had to contend with human nature ; the second failed, because they had to contend with the same obstacle." It seems to me that such a confession from the lips of a writer whose entire life has been devoted to labors for civilization, merits the consideration of generous minds who might be disposed to adopt with enthusiasm the doctrines of M. de Sismondi or of the *Christian Political Economy.*

---

* *Treatise on Legislation*, vol. iv, p. 503.

M. Dunoyer has censured still more severely the dreamers of indefinite perfectibility in political economy. In his opinion, the initiative in improvements of every kind belongs to nations. " It is the agriculturists who perfect agriculture ; the arts are advanced by artists, the sciences by savants, politics and morals by moralists and politicians. Only there is this difference between things which are the private affairs of each and those which are the affairs of everybody, :hat, in the former, the improvements are applicable immediately for the one who discovers them, while in the second, *i.e.*, in politics, the applications can be made only when the thought of the publicist has become the common thought of the public, or at least of a very considerable portion of the public. Until then, attempts to realize them will only be ineffectual. A civil power, amicably disposed towards such reforms, may possibly undertake to establish them ; but it will not accomplish a lasting work. The object may possibly be attempted in defiance of the civil power, by a party overthrowing the latter and taking its place : but the most fortunate insurrections will have no more effect than the most benevolent concessions. The change aimed at will only become established after a long time, and in proportion as it passes into the ideas and habits of the greater number.† * * * Thus, in the social state most exempt from violence, it would be almost impossible that inequalities in conditions should not be established ; and when these inequalities are once established, it is still more difficult for them to be effaced. People never, except with extreme difficulty, rise from an inferior condition to a higher state, and families in a certain degree of abasement are liable to remain so, simply because they are there."

Such is the severe character of the doctrines of M. Dunoyer that we can do no better than to contrast them with the adventurous philanthropy of M. de Sismondi

† *New Treatise on Social Economy*, vol. i, p. 9.

and the religious preaching of M. de Villeneuve and M. de La Mennais. M. Dunoyer is, no less than these generous writers, pervaded with a lively sympathy for the suffering classes, of which the greater part of the human race is composed; he, too, would wish for them days more prosperous and destinies more pleasant; but his cool judgment obliges him to repress the glow of unreflecting emotion and not to admit blindly the possibility of an equal state of happiness for all, as if all men had the same intellectual and moral value and the same rights to an assured tranquillity; which would destroy every principle of activity, honesty and virtue. M. Dunoyer has had the courage to tell the people stern truths which others address to kings. He has well demonstrated that it is imprudent and rash to promise all men an ocean of felicity of which it is given only to a very few to get a glimpse even of the shores. Civilization, which is nothing else than progress towards the general welfare, is itself subject to rigorous, slow and gradual conditions, which suppose above all the coöperation of those whom it is attempted to render more happy. It is consequently to these that this economist has addressed himself, to show them the inevitable laws of industrial and social progress. This progress seems to him impossible without the inequalities of which it is erroneously supposed that he would bring about the entire abolition. It is by these inequalities that division of labor exists, without which there would not be sufficient production to meet the wants of society. Where would the workmen be, if all wished to carry on business for themselves? What would become of an army all of whose soldiers claimed to be generals?

M. Dunoyer has developed this proposition, a bold one in these times, with a rigor of logic and a clearness of language not common. He has not been at all moved by the clamors which it might raise, sure of his intentions and of the assent of enlightened friends of economic progress.

His somewhat rigid morality is not hostile to improvements compatible with our complicated social state, and he
frankly acknowledges that, if it is not possible to secure to
all men an equal sum of material advantages, it is a thing
practicable and at times easy, to ameliorate relatively
the particular condition of any single one.   But every
one must help himself by the practice of social virtues,
such as labor, economy, and forethought, which are conditions of success, as temperance is a condition of health.
Society can no more secure advantages to all its members than physicians can a cure to all their maladies.   To
maintain the contrary, would be to flatter all human passions and to prepare the way for their outbreak under
favor of impunity.   M. Dunoyer nevertheless recognizes
that the principal causes of poverty proceed from the unequal division made at first of wealth by the original dis-
possession of the most numerous classes of society, from
the state of servitude in which they were kept for centuries, from the taxes by which they are crushed, from
the laws which prevent them from getting the best possible advantage from their labor, and from all the vicious
institutions which attack them in their subsistence or
their morality.   " However," adds the author, " the condition of the lower classes does not alone proceed from
the wrongs the higher part of society may have been
guilty of toward them; it has also its root in their
especial vices, their apathy, their heedlessness, and their
ignorance of the causes which make the price of labor
rise or fall.   Their distress is at least as much their own
fault as that of the classes that may be accused of having
oppressed them; and, if society should be reëstablished
on more equitable bases, if the strong should abstain
from every sort of domination over the weak, I do not
doubt that there would still be developed a more or less
numerous class of miserable beings at the bottom of
society."

Surely, these are severe warnings and well suited to
calm the exaltation of those philosophers who think they

can attribute exclusively to the fault of institutions the moral and physical sufferings of several millions of men. M. Droz, whose noble sentiments as an economist and moralist no one will contest, had already made it clear that science and administration could not alone provide for all the wants of humanity. While proclaiming clearly that the aim of political economy was to *render comfort as general as possible*, he had allowed himself no illusion as to the limits of its influence, which is like that of law in constitutional countries, that is to say, subject to the essential condition of a perfect harmony between all the powers.   Differing from the principal found-ers of the social economic school, who denied that gov-ernments and institutions had any responsibility for public miseries, M. Dunoyer and M. Droz thought that responsibility should be shared by the people governed, who too often are a dead weight upon the most useful reforms.   They desired the coöperation of the laborers in the distribution of the profits of labor, and the con-currence of all forces in the work for the amelioration of the condition of all.   Here, if we mistake not, we have a new phase in the history of the science, and we know not to which of the economists who have brought it about is due the most gratitude, to those who, with M. Sismondi and M. Villeneuve, have revealed the grievances of the poorer classes, or to those who have recalled these classes to a true sense of their dignity and their duties, like M. Droz and M. Dunoyer.   The two former authors have taken wealth to task, and have reproached it for its selfishness; the two others have chided poverty and blamed its heedlessness: a double task, difficult to ac-complish, and one which will some day bear its fruits, when the time has come for a compromise between the present and the past, between the capitalist and the laborer!   That compromise has been unsuccessfully at-tempted by the economists of the school which I shall call *eclectic;* we will take a cursory view of its most dis-tinguished representatives.

CHAPTER XLII.

Eclectic political economy and its principal representatives.—M. Storch. —-M. Ganilh.—M. De Laborde.—M. Florez Estrada.

THE great economists of the latter part of the eighteenth century, authors of the celebrated treatises in which science came forth for the first time in a methodic form, had almost all adopted absolute theories which experience and facts would necessarily modify. Thus the *Physiocrates* had considered land as the only source of value : Adam Smith had accorded this honor only to labor; Ricardo subordinated all the phenomena of the circulation to his theory of *rent ;* M. de Sismondi to that of revenue ; J. B. Say to the extent of access to markets, that is to say, to freedom of trade ; Malthus attributed most social maladies to excess of population; Godwin censured the indifference of governments. It was evident, however, that if these causes combined had some influence on social development, none of them could be regarded as the exclusive cause, that is to say, the doctrines of the economists were applicable only to certain cases and certain conditions. While they were making war to maintain their systems against one another, there became established among their pupils intermediary shades, a virtual emanation from those bright and decided colors which particularly distinguish the founders. The writers whose works best represent these shades of transition, are very numerous in Europe. They have not a stamp of their own ; they have invented nothing, dis-

485

covered nothing ; but they have admirably perfected the work of their predecessors and softened the asperities of the absolute theories from which the reason or the preju- dice of contemporaries recoiled.

M. Henri Storch is in the foremost rank of these eclec- tic economists, seeking the truth in good faith, in the agricultural system as well as in the industrial régime, and disposed to make concessions to both.   A judicious observer, and conveniently situated * for judging well a multitude of special facts, M. Storch knew how to borrow from his predecessors, like a man already rich in his own funds, and he cast much light on the question of slavery, in the country where it seemed most difficult to speak freely upon it.   He does not belong exactly to any school, and he would have deserved to found one, on ac- count of the importance of the documents which he has contributed to science, if the boldness of his mind had corresponded with the extent of his knowledge.   In his view, political economy had no other aim than to procure for men the means of satisfying their moral and physical needs, and to teach them to produce well in order to place them in a condition to consume with profit.   This is attained by labor, as every one knows ; but, hitherto, only the action of free trade had been studied : M. Storch has explained the phenomena of forced labor, that is to say, that of slaves, so common still in Russia,† that it powerfully contributes to the national wealth of that em- pire.   In the same way, the author makes the sledge, which is unknown among most of the people of Europe, figure among the means of transport.   Nothing could be more ingenious than his theory of the relative wealth of the nations, which he classes as *loaning, borrowing* and *in- dependent*, as also his fine analyses of the *income of talents*

---

* M. Storch was instructor to the grand-duke Nicholas, late emperor of Russia.   He spoke, with an independence which honors alike his country and his character, of the fatal effects of slavery in all countries.

† Serfdom in Russia has since been abolished by Alexander II, and all peasants have been entirely free as to their persons since 1863.— *Trans.*

and qualities ; analyses so much the more worthy of attention as they demonstrate the superiority of that element of wealth, too long neglected, which I first proposed to call *moral capital.** Moral capital is nothing else than the sum of the capacities of every kind by which nations become enriched while becoming civilized, and which permits them to daily increase their wealth and their civilization.

At the time when M. Storch published his lessons to the Grand-dukes of Russia, the doctrine of Ricardo on farm rent, which he calls rent of land, had not yet appeared ; and I confess that the theory of the Russian economist seems to me much more simple and more natural than that of the celebrated British writer. M. Storch calls *ground-rent* the price paid for the use of land ; *primitive-rent*, the rent of uncultivated land, founded on the exclusive right the proprietor has to dispose of his land ; and *rent of improved land*, the rent of the improvements at the current rate, combined with the primitive rent. " The rent of fertile lands," he says, " determines the rate of all other lands which compete with them. Accordingly, so long as the product of the most fertile suffices for the demand, the less fertile lands cannot be worked, or at least pay no rent. But, as soon as the demand surpasses the quantity of products that fertile lands can supply, the price of the product rises, and it becomes possible to cultivate the less fertile lands and to derive a rent † from them." It is remarkable that this doctrine is exactly the same as that which Ricardo developed at almost the same time in England, drawing the conclusion that it is the *least fertile lands* which determine the rate of the rent of all the others. It would be too tedious to enter here into the reasons which make me adopt in preference the theory of M. Storch ; but I

---

* See Blanqui's lessons at the *Conservatory of Arts and Trades*, published in 1837.

† *Course of Political Economy*, book iii, chap. xii.

consider the developments by which he has accompanied
it one of the most remarkable labors which has honored
political economy.

Storch was less original, but more profound, in his explanation of the theory of money, where he tried to keep
the balance between the extreme partisans of banks and
the exclusive defenders of coin. He had had a near view
of the abuses of issues of paper and of debased coin;
and his long experience permitted him no illusion as to
the disadvantages of *assignats*, by whatever name it
should please the government to baptize them. However, his account of the functions of banks cannot be
compared with the immortal effort of Adam Smith on
the same subject. M. Storch has completed the demonstrations of the great Scotchman ; he has enriched them
with a multitude of examples drawn from the financial
history of all nations, and he has been the first to make
known the organization of almost all the banks of Europe. By his work, one can become acquainted with
them and learn how to distinguish clearly the dangers
against which they have to guard. The latter part of this
important book is devoted to consumption. The author
has well explained in it the reasons why commerce and
manufactures cause a more rapid increase in wealth than
agriculture. What he says of the effects of slavery, principally in Russia, the only country perhaps where slavery
still exists as a social institution, merits the consideration
of economists and does the greatest honor to the independence of the writer. It was not without cause that
we ranked him among *eclectics :* his sound sense, the
moderation of his character, his great erudition, which
seems unacquainted with no previous work, give him a
title to that appellation, nobly justified by an impartiality so much the more worthy of eulogy, as the author
was, as is generally known, imperial preceptor at the
court of St. Petersburg.

We should also count among the eclectics the indefatigable Ganilh, the author of *Systems in Political Economy*, who died * recently at a very advanced age, without having left any truly original creation. Ganilh was more of a financier than economist, and his labors contributed more to the progress of financial science than to the advancement of political economy. Besides, most of his works have not survived the circumstances which gave rise to them. He wrote under the régime of censorship, and he sought to reconcile the circumspection demanded by imperial susceptibility, with the interests of truth which sincerely occupied his mind. Nothing at that time seemed to indicate the gravity of the questions which our day would have to resolve; M. Ganilh followed quietly the usual beaten track of discussion about net product and raw product, the restrictive system and freedom of trade; but France, distracted by the tumult of battles, gave little heed to his numerous writings. His merit consists in not having despaired of the future of the science and in having connected for it the links in time, broken by the clash of arms. Ganilh did in political economy as recluses do who have withdrawn from the world, who write for themselves without concern as to the effect their books will produce, and moreover, without adapting them to the wants of their time. These works are to science what summaries are to history. He was the sole economist of the Empire.

The *Essay on the Spirit of Association*, by Count De Laborde, published in 1818, obtained much greater success. This book is especially remarkable for the accuracy of its previsions and for its excellent appreciation of the institutions most favorable to the development of public prosperity. All forces were divided in France as well as all opinions, when M. De Laborde published this exposition of the advantages of the spirit of association, rich in facts and full of luminous ideas on the true sources of the industrial and political power of states. In this book

---

* Died in 1836, aged 78.

we find well expressed the sufferings manufactures and
commerce had to undergo under military rule,* the new
formalities to which they had to submit, and the delays
of the bureaucracy unfortunately introduced by the administration into the legislation concerning labor. M.
De Laborde nevertheless recognized the utility of the intervention of the government in questions of public
wealth and material production ; but he wished it to
be according to the principles of a division of labor, without despotism, and without encroachment on the rights
exclusively vested in manufactures.   This was the way
he understood associations for public credit, associations
for labor, associations for the protection of labor.   The
army had its *rôle* here, as commerce had its own, and as
the government employés had theirs.   The author would
have a working country moderately governed ; and without adopting the absolute doctrine of free trade, he
thought it advantageous to rely on individual intelligence
and the competition of interests.

These judicious doctrines have by degrees penetrated
people's minds ; and since then we have seen savings
banks, insurance companies, joint-stock companies (*sociétés en commandite*),[16] at once the effect and the cause
of the increasing prosperity of the nation.   M. De Laborde has very happily demonstrated the influence that
foreigners, attracted to our associations by the hope of
increasing their capital, would have on that prosperity.
This idea, a bold one at the time when proposed, is beginning to become so popular in France, that a proposition
was even made, for a moment, to establish between the
Bank of France and the Bank of England relations quite

---

* " The greatest defect of the imperial government," said M. De Laborde,
" was that constant jealousy of manufactures and commerce.   It extended
its spirit of domination to the smallest matters, and it would have liked to
carry on all branches of manufacture for its profit, as it directed all affairs.
It was a trader in sugar, coffee, printed calicoes, proprietor of all woods,
seller of sheep, administrator of canals, undertaker of public works, man-
ager of the property of the communes, of the hospitals, farmer of th:
games," etc. (*Spirit of Association*, p. 44.)

like those which exist between many merchants by the intervention of *accounts current*. This was a prelude to the reforms from which some day the new doctrines of manufactures and commerce will arise, when universal competition, crowding back on each nation the products of its manufactures, will force them all to sign a compact finally divested of the spirit of monopoly and prohibition. And what to-day are these enterprises of steamboats, railroads, and canals, which tend to unite all states by mutually dependent lines of communication, but the commencement of the great fusion of European interests?

Never, perhaps, has any economic doctrine received the sanction of experience to such a degree as that of association. Its very eclecticism, that is to say, the compromise it effected between facts and principles, could but contribute to favor its success. Hence it has constantly advanced from victory to victory, and we have seen within a few years all Europe asking from the spirit of association the realization of a great number of enterprises which seemed not only beyond the power of individuals, but even beyond that of governments. There is no longer anything impossible for these armies of workers who are marching on to the conquest of wealth with the accumulated forces of an entire people, and who know how, in their way, to conquer rivers, level mountains or tunnel them, at the will of industry. Before that time, people had only attempted to associate *things ;* since they have undertaken to associate *men*, everything around us has changed in appearance. There are countries which this powerful lever has almost suddenly rendered unrecognizable : witness North America, whose virgin forests are traversed by railroads, and whose rivers, lately solitary, are covered with flotillas of steam-boats. There are now two portions of the public wealth, one of which goes to the treasury, the other reverts to labor ; a profound revolution, which brings manufactures

and government, production and consumption, constantly
face to face, on the footing of equality! Beneficence
even has borrowed new resources from the spirit of association, and our modern civilization has no finer gem in
its crown, than those numerous philanthropic societies of
which Christianity is the principle, and association the
means.

Economic eclecticism has even penetrated into Spain,
that old land of absolute doctrines : and one of her most
honorable exiles, M. Florez Estrada, has given us, under
the title of *Eclectic Course of Political Economy*, one of
the most remarkable treatises that have been published
since that of J. B. Say.   The method of M. Florez Estrada resembles somewhat that of the celebrated Russian
economist, Henri Storch.   He begins by conscientiously
examining the opinions of his predecessors, which he
adopts or refutes according to the degree of value which
that examination has made him recognize.   In this way, he
has added really new considerations to those of Malthus
on population.   His fine exposition of the doctrines of
Ricardo on rent, is accompanied by a series of subtile and
ingenious analyses, which raise this piece of criticism to
the rank of original creations.   No writer before M.
Florez Estrada, had approached the questions of taxation with that deep insight which characterizes him ; and
although the author has given particular attention to the
taxes levied in his own country, statesmen of all other
countries will find in this work useful suggestions and
valuable information.   M. Florez Estrada has incontestably demonstrated the inequality and injustice of the
fiscal system which weighs to-day upon all the nations of
Europe, and the necessity of introducing into it important modifications at some not distant day.   By some
wholly new ideas, he has completed all the discussions
relative to banks, paper-money and circulation, taking up
these questions at the point where Adam Smith, Ricardo,
J. B. Say and M. de Sismondi had left them.   The *Eclec-*

tic Political Economy would be an excellent book for students if some ambiguities of expression did not detract from its simple and regular arrangement. Such as it is, however, this book may be considered as the necessary complement of all those which have preceded it: methodical with Say, social with Sismondi, algebraic with Ricardo, experimental with Adam Smith, it differs in many respects from these grand masters, and it shares in their good qualities without falling into all their errors.

Being a Spanish citizen, M. Florez Estrada would naturally have in view the interests of his country, and he has pointed out with rare plainness the evil results of the economic system which has ruled Spain since Charles V. The questions relating to tithes, entailment, primogeniture, and *majorats*, have nowhere been treated better than in his book. Here one can study, even better than in the work of Jovellanos, the real causes of the decline of Spain and of the harm which the bad economic laws which have afflicted this fine country for more than three hundred years, have caused her. M. Florez Estrada has criticised them with a breadth of view which extends even to the fiscal organization of the principal powers of Europe; and his fine analyses of the influence of taxes on the various industries, remain the necessary starting point of all the reforms of which these taxes are susceptible. Such are the essential claims of the author to the gratitude of economists; and we regret that he did not touch upon social questions, upon which no one was more capable than he of throwing a strong light. M. Florez Estrada, in doctrine, belongs to the English school: he is an advocate of the system of Malthus, and his theory of the rent of land is no other than that of Ricardo, perfected and *illustrated* by comparisons and examples alike ingenious. M. Florez Estrada has, moreover, shown himself more eclectic in regard to persons than in regard to things. Production seemed to have attracted his attention much more than consumption, and although he pro-

posed to add to the ordinary programme of political
economy a division relating to the *exchanges*, his piece of
criticism was arrested by the complications to which the
industrial system exaggerated by England and already
naturalized in France, daily gives rise. Most of the eclectic economists, except M. De Laborde, have shared this
reserve, which we should call timidity, had it not been
demonstrated to us that in the opinion of these writers,
freedom of labor and freedom of trade would suffice to
bring to a good end all the difficult social evils of our
time.   But each country has its problem to solve, and
when the final moment has come, it is not by hesitating
between doctrines equally powerless that we can hope for
a serious and permanent solution.   In the present state
of things, eclectic political economy is no longer anything
but an experimental science, while the progress of events
demands a political economy of action.   When governments, overcome by the wave of conflicting interests,
demand of science categorical answers, the latter cannot
remain vague and take refuge in dissertations: the reforms which have become necessary must be executed
with that impartial and prudent zeal which distinguished
Mr. Huskisson.   Such was the bold attempt of a school
henceforth celebrated, in spite of its errors, and whose
efforts have failed for having lacked moderation, but
have left a luminous track behind.   This school is that of
Saint-Simon, and it aimed to be to the old political economy what the Constituent Assembly was to the old régime, and, like that Assembly, it passed away in a
tempestuous storm.

CHAPTER XLIII.

Saint-Simonian political economy.—First writings of Saint-Simon.—Boldness of his attacks.—Theory of his disciples.—The *Producteur.*—What they meant by *Industrialism.*—They found a church.—Their attacks against inheritance.—General view and estimate of their labors.

WHEN the first writings of the Saint-Simonians saw the light, all the great questions propounded by the economists were awaiting a solution. Europe had never taken a more active part in that controversy, notwithstanding the uncertainties which it involved, and which were daily increased by the debates kept up by the chiefs of the various schools. At the same time, the immense development of manufactures, promoted by the general peace, had given rise to new complications, which it was necessary to remedy by measures that would be efficacious and adapted to the circumstances. The time had come to act, as we have said : numerous diseases afflicted the social body : pauperism was invading manufacturing countries more and more ; people had witnessed distressing and unforeseen commercial crises, without a hope that they would disappear for a long time. On all sides discussions were raised relative to wages, to foundlings, to openings for trade, without governments daring to take the initiative in those decided measures which either destroy the evil or aggravate it, according to the skill with which they are applied. It was in this state that Saint-Simonism found France and Europe, when its first publications began to awaken public attention. The doctrines of that school have exercised too much influence on the course of political economy to permit us to pass them over in silence, even in presence of the stormy con-tests they have raised.

A man, eccentric and misunderstood during his whole life, became, probably without his knowledge, whatever his disciples may say in that regard, the founder of the sect of Saint-Simonians. He was the Count of Saint-Si-mon, a descendant of the celebrated family of this name, and had been in his youth on the American expedition, and was reduced, during the rest of his career, either by the misfortune of the times, or by personal excesses, to a precarious and miserable existence. It appears that in the midst of these vicissitudes, Saint-Simon, already oc-cupied with projects of reform, had formed the plan of a reorganization of society on bases which seemed to him preferable to all those which the economists of his time proposed. He operated by means of a series of short and substantial publications which summed up his ideas under incisive and picturesque forms of expression. In one of these regenerating pamphlets,* he proposed to put the spiritual power into the hands of the savants, the tem-poral power into the hands of the property-holders, and to pay governments for their services. But his counsels had little success at that period. It was towards the end of Napoleon's reign, and circumstances were scarcely fa-vorable for utopias of this kind. Saint-Simon found the field more free at the beginning of the Restoration; and in 1819, he brought out the first clear and bold expression of his industrial theories. The little writing that he pub-lished, under the title of *Parabole* (parable), was extreme-ly remarkable, coming from a man of such high extrac-tion, however modest might be his present fortune. In it Saint-Simon developed, under the form of a jesting hypothesis, his favorite doctrine of the supremacy of the industrial occupations over all the other occupations in society. He feigned not to conceive how it was that

---

* *Letters of an inhabitant of Geneva to his contemporaries.*

the men most competent in arts and manufactures did not occupy the highest positions in the state, in virtue of their quality of creators of all products and consequently of all wealth ; and the inferior situation in which he saw them seemed to him the *world turned upside down*. See how he expresses himself in his *parable*, from which we quote literally an extract to give at the same time an idea of his style and of his practical views:

"I will suppose," he says, "that France suddenly loses her fifty first physicians, her fifty first chemists, her fifty first printers, architects, physicians, in a word her three thousand first artists, savants, and artisans.

"As these men are the Frenchmen most essentially producers, those who give the most imposing products, those who direct the labors most useful to the nation, and who render it productive in the fine arts and in the arts and trades, they are really the flower of French society : they are of all Frenchmen the most useful to their country, those who bring it the most glory, who advance the most its civilization and its prosperity. France would need at least one entire generation to repair this misfortune, for the men who distinguish themselves in labors of public utility, are virtual anomalies, and nature is not prodigal of anomalies, especially of this kind.

"Let us pass on to another supposition : let us admit that France keep all the men of genius she possesses in the fine arts and in the arts and trades : but that she has the misfortune to lose on the same day Monsieur, brother of the king, Monsigneur the duke of Angoulême, Mgr. the duke of Berry, Mgr. the duke of Orléans, Madame the duchess of Angoulême, Madame the duchess of Orléans, Madame the duchess of Bourbon, and Mademoiselle de Condé.

"That she lose at the same time all the great officers of the crown, all the ministers of State, all the *Maîtres des requêtes*, all the marshals, all the cardinals, archbishops, bishops, grand-vicars and canons, all the prefects and sub-prefects, all the employés in the minister's office, all the judges, and more than that, the ten thousand richest proprietors among those who live like nobles.

"This accident would certainly grieve the French, because they are good, and could not behold with indifference the sudden disappearance of so great a number of their fellow countrymen : but that loss of thirty thousand individuals reputed the most important in the state, would cause them sorrow only in a purely sentimental way, because no harm would result to the State.

"First, for the reason that it would be very easy to fill the places which had become vacant. There are a great number of Frenchmen living who could exercise the functions of brother of the king as well as *Monsieur ;* many are capable of occupying the positions of the princes, just as well as Mgr. the Duke of Angoulême, Mgr. the Duke of Orléans, etc.

"The antechambers of the castle are full of courtiers ready to occupy the place of grand officers of the crown ; the army possesses a great quantity of military men, who are as good captains as our present marshals. How many clerks are worth our ministers of state ? how many administrators more fitted to carry on the affairs of the departments than the prefects or sub-prefects now in active service ; how many lawyers as good jurisconsults as our judges ? How many curates as capable as our cardinals, as

our archbishops, as our bishops, as our grand-vicars and our canons ! As to
the ten thousand land-proprietors, their heirs will need no apprenticeship to
do the honors of their drawing rooms as well as they."

This audacious pamphlet produced sufficient sensation
to excite the anxiety of the magistrates and to obtain an
acquittal notwithstanding their prosecutions.   It was the
programme of the industrial power which Saint-Simon
proposed to establish, and it was soon followed by a multitude of other publications which have been carefully
collated, since, by M. Olinde Rodrigues, one of his disciples.   The most curious of these writings bore the title
of *The Organizer, the Catechism of the Industrial Interest,*
the Industrial System.   "We invite," it said, " all persons engaged in the arts and manufactures who are zeal-
ous for the public welfare, no longer to suffer themselves
to be designated by the name of *liberals;* we invite them
to set up a new standard and to inscribe on their banners
the device; *industrialism.*   The designation of liberalism
having been chosen, adopted and proclaimed by the rem-
nant of the patriot and of the Bonapartist party, that
designation has very great disadvantages for men whose
essential tendency is to constitute a solid order of things
by pacific means.   We do not pretend to say that the
patriots and Bonapartists did not render service to society.
Their energy was useful, because it was necessary to de-
molish before being able to construct.   But to-day the
revolutionary spirit which animated them is directly contrary to the public good ; to-day a designation which does
not indicate a spirit directly contrary to the revolutionary spirit, cannot be suitable for enlightened and well in-
tentioned men."   We have quoted these various passages
in order to call attention to the strange amalgamation of
contrary sentiments which distinguished the Saint-
Simonian doctrine at that first period of its development.
Since then, that school has constantly professed a sort of
blind respect for the precepts of authority, even to the
point of investing it with the chief surveillance over all

the processes of labor and of thus creating a universal intervention of the administration in the affairs of all private individuals   One readily conceives that Saint-Simon might have had so much the more inclination for this despotism of authority, because, according to his ideas, it was into the hands of the workers that it would naturally fall.

It is not for us to examine here the purely religious portion of the doctrines of Saint-Simon, as it appears in his *New Christianity*, a very remarkable work in which the author has proclaimed the urgent necessity of ameliorating the fate of the poorest and most numerous classes. Still less shall we criticise the metamorphosis of all that industrial school into a metropolitan church having its doctrines and its casuists. This part of the history of the Saint-Simonians belongs to the history of religious errors, as well as the attempts at the emancipation of woman and the succession of audacious acts by which these attempts were accompanied. Our aim is only to point out the economic labors of the sect and the results accruing from these labors. Immediately after the death of Saint-Simon, his disciples published, under the name of the *Producteur*, a periodic journal which aimed to propagate the doctrines of the master, adapting them to the necessities of the times, and with reservations from which they judged proper to free themselves after the revolution of 1830. However it came about, the authors of this journal had certainly succeeded in spreading among the most advanced men of the press, ideas favorable to the development of industrial power, and in weakening the importance which was then attached exclusively to political means. They attacked by simple and vigorous arguments the old prohibitory system which had been aggravated by the Restoration: they pointed out with calm and dignified pride the importance of the *rôle* of the savants, manufacturers and artists, the new trinity of the religion of love and labor which they proposed to establish. From this period, a real change becomes effected in the absolute ideas of the press militant, the guide of popular opinion in France : military tendencies lose much of their sway ; war is obliged to render up its accounts, and for the first time in a long while, people begin to perceive that there exists, outside of the classes privileged by fortune and politics, an immense mass of workers whose turn has come to figure on the world's stage and to have their legitimate representatives.

The Saint-Simonians had reached this point when the revolution of July occurred.   I think I do not exaggerate the importance of their writings in affirming that it was under their inspiration that the troubles of the period took that social character which excited so deep an interest throughout Europe.   The *Producteur* had ceased to appear, but only to be surpassed.   A new *Exposition* of the Saint-Simonian doctrine, maturely discussed in council by the pontiffs of the great college, boldly proclaimed the abolition of inheritance and the classification of positions according to capacities.   We perceive how much this dogma would please human vanity, always disposed to judge itself with benevolence, and what flattering results the men who had nothing to lose might derive from the abolition of inheritance.   The Saint-Simonians shrewdly profited by the circumstances which had given to the insurgent masses a victory illustrious for the most admirable disinterestedness of which history makes mention.   They commented like practical men on the famous *mot* of Siéyès : " The Third Estate is everything," and they determined that the Third Estate of 1830 should not be reduced to the slender proportions of a bourgeoisie.   But while in their language, they chose the most pacific forms, the masses, little enlightened, were marching straight to their end, and endeavoring to obtain, by means of insurrections, the realization of that deceptive promise : " To every one his capacity, to every capacity according to its works."   Bold commentators were not lacking, to show

the painful contrast of the poverty of some and the opulence of others. More than one orator of the street cor-
ners readily demonstrated the great advantages which
humanity would derive from the abolition of these odious
inequalities, which were represented as veritable spoliations. Such was not, however, the idea of the Saint-
Simonians in publishing their celebrated creed. They
had not heard community of goods preached, nor that
with which they were later reproached, community of
wives ; and the manifesto they addressed on this subject
to the house of deputies leaves no doubt as to their real
intentions. Here is the most remarkable passage in that
document :

" The system of community of goods is universally understood to mean
an equal division among all the members of the society, either of the producing capital, or of the results of the labor of all.

" The Saint-Simonians reject this equal division of property, which
in their view would constitute a violence greater, an injustice more revolting, than the unequal division primitively effected by force of arms, by conquest.

" For they believe in the natural inequality of men, and regard that inequality as an indispensable condition of the social order.

" They reject the system of community of goods, for such a community
would be a manifest violation of the first of the moral laws which they have
received a commission to teach, and which requires that in future every one
shall be situated according to his capacity and rewarded according to his
works.

" But, in virtue of that law, they demand the abolition of all privileges of birth, without exception, and consequently the *destruction of inheritance*, the greatest of these privileges, the one which to-day embraces them
all, and whose effect is to leave to chance the distribution of social privileges
among the small number of those who wish to lay claim to them, and to condemn the most numerous class to depravity, ignorance and poverty.

" They demand that all the instruments of labor, the land and capital
which to-day constitute the divided up lands of private proprietors, be
worked by association, under the direction of hierarchs, so that the task
of each one may be the expression of his capacity, and his wealth the measure of his works.

" The Saint-Simonians propose to interfere with the constitution of
property only in so far as it sanctions for some the impious privilege of idleness, that is to say, of living on the labor of others ; only in so far as it leaves
the social classification of individuals to the chance of birth."

Notwithstanding this protest of the Saint-Simonians,
it was easy to see that their attacks upon the transmission of property would end in an actual spoliation of
families. They thus threatened citizens in the enjoy-

ment of the one of their rights considered as the most sacred : they struck a blow at the dearest hopes of fathers,
and they struck the fortune of society itself by stifling in
man the most energetic stimulant to labor and economy.
Who, pray, should exercise in each country the functions
of distributor of enjoyments and of duties? What intellect would be found sufficiently high, and what spirit sufficiently impartial to be secure from error and injustice?
It could not be less than a high priest, as infallible as the
pope, and besides a sovereign dispenser of the products
of labor. The adepts of the doctrine did not shrink from
even this difficulty, and they gave themselves this sovereign disposer of pleasures and punishments, under
the name of *father-supreme*. From this time, Saint-Simonism degenerates into a sort of mundane theocracy
and ceases to stop at the limits of economic utopias. It
is no longer considered as a school, but as a church, and
it is already pursued by the ridicule which mercilessly attaches in France to all founders of churches. At the
same time, the crazy attempts at the emancipation of
woman result in discrediting what might be good and
useful in the other Saint-Simonian propositions. People
include them all in a common reprobation. They laugh
and they grow indignant at that contest between two
eminent personages of the sect, one of whom, a married
man, claims that in a family every child should be able
to know its father, while the other, a celibate, maintains
that the woman alone should be called upon for a solution of that grave question. Serious men no longer see
anything but a mental debauch in this outbreak of licen-
tious propositions which lead to subversion of the family
and of property. The magistrates become alarmed, society is aroused. In vain the Saint-Simonians organize
churches, and give the key to their enigma in eloquent
sermons to which their words attract rich and poor with a
sort of irresistible fascination ; in vain even that they have
the art to gather in adherents and multiply proselytes :

their decline is approaching, and their most rational theories are confounded with the wanderings of their imagination. The insurrections which are breaking out on every side pass for the fruit of their excitation; and in the presence of flowing blood, laughter gives place to wrath. The authorities cause their halls of conference to be closed, and the courts prosecute them as disturbers of the public peace.

What a sad end for beginnings which appeared so favorable! Who would have believed that the learned analyses of the processes of manufacture, published by the *Producteur*, would have for a conclusion community of wives and the creation of a *father-supreme*! But in spite of these extravagances, one profound thought had survived the dispersion of the Saint Simonians, a thought separated from the impure alloy of the sensualities of the *Rue Monsigny*.* This thought had been formulated by one of the principal representatives of the sect: "Society, according to them, is composed only of idlers and workers. Politics should aim at the moral, physical, and intellectual improvement of the fate of the workers, and the progressive forfeiture of the idle. The means are, as to the idle, a destruction of all privileges of birth, and to the workers, a classing according to capacities and remuneration according to the work. The Saint-Simonians very well understood that it would be impossible for them, in the present state of society, to attain their end at once; so they themselves proclaimed the necessity of a gradual transition, and they rejected the idea of an immediate suppression of the privilege of inheritance. Their project was to first promote the abolition of inheritance in a collateral line to remote degrees, in order to insensibly accustom minds to more decided reforms. They wished

---

* In this street, the Saint-Simonians had established the head-quarters of their worship, when they made priests. They gave soirées there which were quite popular, and conferences which were not less so. It may be that the intoxication of these parlor successes contributed not a little to the tendency towards epicureanism which led these remarkable men astray.

to make the value obtained by the state from the property which would be added to to its domain, and the
product from the right of succession in direct line, which
would have been considerably augmented, serve for the
reduction of taxes. By means of this newly created budget, they would give an active impulse to all branches of
industry, dig canals, lay out roads, raise public monuments and found the institutions for instruction demanded
by the wants of the country.

One cannot to-day read without a lively interest the
views they each day presented in the journal *Le Globe*,
which had become their property. Singularly enough,
this journal had previously belonged to an association of
distinguished men, whom the tide of 1830 carried into
power. What the former *Globe* had attempted to accomplish for thought, for the middle classes, the Saint-
Simonians claimed for labor, for the inferior classes.
They took an active part in all the reform projects
favored by the renovating movement of July. Their
sheet, distributed gratuitously to the number of several
thousand copies, treated with incontestable superiority
the questions of finance, public works, banks, associations
and pauperism, and we must allow that never did any
company of savants put in circulation a like fund of
ideas. These ideas were certainly not always just, nor
always practicable ; some of them were often strange and
their expression was marked by an affected use of new
phrases ; but as minds have become calmed, the posterity
which is beginning for the Saint-Simonians have got rid
of the alloy, and much pure material has remained at the
bottom of their crucible. To them it is that we owe the
industrial tendency of the present period, and the direction, perhaps too exclusive to-day, of all activities towards
this end. By restoring the worship of labor, whether by
their preaching or by their analyses, they attracted the
attention of the civil power and of the higher classes to
the laboring classes, to whom they had been too long

indifferent. Their learned expositions of the theory of banks, their original views on the system of mortgages, on the insufficiency of the public instruction, and on foundlings, have familiarized men wholly unacquainted with economic science, with the fundamental principles of that science. While the economists were discus-sing theories, the Saint-Simonians were trying coura-geously the hazards of practice, and were making, at their risk and peril, experiments preparatory to the future. Their personal disinterestedness equalled their religious enthusiasm for the cause they had embraced; and not-withstanding the contrary accusations which have been brought against them, it is an averred fact that they all went forth from their temples or their workshops poor or ruined.

I will say nothing of the attempt, unfortunate to them-selves, they made in withdrawing to the heights of the village of Menilmontant, with the intention of glorifying labor there. It was a deplorable spectacle to see skilful chemists, distinguished engineers, original and profound thinkers, abased to the lowest rank of laborers, and re-duced by an aberration of their own will to the most vulgar labors of domestic life. In acting thus, they de-graded intelligence, and failed to comprehend the first rules of division of labor. What would they have said, they so seriously hierarchical, if the laboring classes, leav-ing the plowshare or the hammer of industry, had seized the domain of intellect while the chiefs of the industrial religion were humbly devoting themselves to manual la-bors? What a contradiction between the actions and the words! And this was not the only one: we are sur-prised, in studying their doctrines, at the independence of the principles and the absoluteness of the prescrip-tions: we find it difficult to associate these projects for the emancipation of the laborers with the severe rules which were imposed upon them. The Saint-Simonians have one point of resemblance with the Physiocrates, from whom they seem to have borrowed the dogma of passive obedience and of an idolatrous respect for authority. That error, however, was less injurious than useful. People in France had, under the Restoration, become too much accustomed, and, unfortunately, with some reason, to find fault with the civil power: they observed it with mistrust, they obeyed it with ill humor. A systematic hostility received most of its measures and paralysed their effects; so that public authority became daily weakened, to the great detriment of the prosperity and dignity of the country. The Saint-Simonians, toward whom the civil power showed itself very ungrateful, taught the French people that a government is good for something: this was indeed something new in the times then passing, and especially at a time when every one considered it to his credit to have contributed to the overthrow of the dynasty which had just fallen. Saint-Simonism attempted to arrest all the hands armed with destructive weapons, that a first fire of enthusiasm, suddenly suppressed, had not yet disaccustomed to demolition: it wished also to arouse in the heart of the higher classes sympathies for the more humble, which they had rarely experienced. One may fail in that noble task, by committing errors; and who does not commit them, even while doing good? But there always remains a luminous trace from these bold attempts, which succeeding generations never fail to take up again on another plan. To-day the Saint-Simonians, scattered among the people, have resumed the exercise of the professions to which they were severally destined by their former studies. They construct railroads, they make journeys useful to their country; they are managers of manufacturing establishments, and everywhere we see them at the head of projects for improvement. They honor their past by the dignity even of their silence, satisfied with having propounded the most grave questions of the present time, and having prepared the principal elements of their solu-

tion. Europe, which scoffed at them, follows their counsels, and the government which persecuted them employs
them. Is it thus that people treat the vanquished?

CHAPTER XLIV.

The utopian economists.—The *societary* system of Fourier.—Review of his principal works.—Fundamental idea of his doctrine.—Developments of which it appears susceptible.—The *social* system of Mr. Owen.—Ineffectual attempts made by him at New-Lanark and at New-Harmony.—Sketches of the peculiar views of that economist.

IN chronological order, the Saint-Simonians were not the first reformatory economists of the nineteenth century. A few years before the publication of their writings, two men remarkable in different ways, Mr. Fourier and Mr. Owen, had laid the foundation of a reform called *societary* by the former, and *social* by the second; the latter founded on the community, the other on association. Both started at the same point, without tending to the same end : both were impressed by the uncomfortable condition of contemporary society, the vices of our morals, the sufferings of the greater number of our fellow creatures, and the necessity of terminating them ; but they differed essentially as to the means. The Saint-Simonians created more of a sensation and thrived better, because the chief of their school, being taken away the first from his disciples, left ardent and resolute followers, to whom nothing would have been wanting to secure the triumph of his doctrines, if any great renovation could have resulted from them.

The ideas of Fourier and Owen have obtained only very lately the favor of that noisy publicity which commands attention and sometimes success. Fourier died a little more than a year ago, and Mr. Owen is still living.* These two circumstances explain the different interest felt in the preaching of the Saint-Simonians and the writings of Owen and Fourier. However, the attempts of these two philosophers preceded by several years the labors of Saint-Simon, and they present themselves under an organization more complete and more vast than that of the Saint-Simonian school. Fourier, whom his disciples wish to-day to have considered a great man, evidently has an advantage over his two rivals in the boldness of his views and the admirable stability of his character ; more than they, he claimed to have solved the social problem, and he accused all contemporary economic doctrines of barrenness, without perceiving that he only brought, as they did, his share of uncertainties and vagaries to the universal centre of all the doubts and utopias of civilization. A rapid survey will enable us to judge of his doctrines.

Fourier had been early impressed by the conventional falsehoods with which the social order is infested. He had seen childhood struggling with imperious passions and exacting masters ; later, in society, his honesty had revolted at the tricks of trade, family discords and political corruption. He had been shocked at the contrast of honest poverty and opulent vice. Before his reason had demonstrated to him that Providence must have had higher views, his heart had bewailed the contradictions and bitter disappointments of our society. What then ? In the presence of this magnificent spectacle of nature, of this sun which shines for all, of these fruits so abundant and so savory, of these fountains so limpid, there are men who live in darkness, who languish in hospitals, in prisons, who die of hunger and thirst ! There are men a thousand times more unhappy than the beasts, since they have to submit to moral torture, beside physical suffer-

* Fourier died October 10, 1837, aged 65, and Owen, December, 1858, at the age of 87 years.— *Trans.*

ing! Everything would advance with a regular step in this world, except humanity itself! Was the house so beautiful and the light of the stars so brilliant, only to illumine the unutterable griefs of the master! What blasphemy and what absurdity!

Struck by this contrast as by a revelation, Fourier sought for its causes with the persevering and profound sagacity which distinguished him. It seemed to him that the passions, burdened with all the weight of our iniquities, could be made to serve for our good, and that it was easy to utilize them, like any living force, by assigning to them an intelligent and reasonable employment: thus he laid the foundations of his system in the first of his works, the *Theory of the Four Movements*. These four movements took the names of *social* movement, *animal* movement, *organic* movement and *material* movement. The theory of the first was to explain the laws according to which God regulated the arrangement and succession of the various social mechanisms in all inhabited globes. The theory of the second would explain the laws according to which Providence distributes passions and instincts to all created beings in the various globes. The theory of the third would give an account of the laws according to which the Author of things distributes to substances property, forms, colors, and savors: Finally, the theory of the material movement, a veritable new cosmogony, was to make known the laws of gravitation according to the ideas of the author. It is not easy to divine at the first glance in what applications that pretentious display of theories might end. This was the first error of Fourier, and he committed the still greater one of persisting in it. He transformed the flights of his imagination into geometrical theorems, of which he alone could give the demonstration, and upon which he admitted no controversy. One must believe or be excommunicated. Fourier recoiled before no celebrity, before no name. Philosophers were the shame of the world.

The world had been going astray for five thousand years. The science, morals, politics of all the ages were only a tissue of extravagances and absurdities.

Fourier lived thus several years, a prey to that devouring fever of hatred and disparagement of the past, which he retained to his last moments. His style, more strange than that of the Saint-Simonians, seemed a defiance of the French language: it was full of odd locutions and terms truly cabalistic. However, his dominant thought succeeded in finding its way through these obscurities. Fourier wished to make association prevail instead of separate interests, and to organize the isolated forces by means of what he called the *impassioned attraction*. His aim was to associate men, as he himself said, as *capital, labor and talent*. To attain it, he combined the efforts of agriculturists, shortened the hours of labor, distributed the ages and functions by series, and transformed the toil of the various occupations into a perpetual recreation, seasoned with agreeable pleasures and sensations. It is not easy, even since his disciples have divested his theories of the critical digressions under which they were smothered, to clearly distinguish what the author meant: it is much more easy to comprehend what he did not mean. He hoped, however, to find an opportunity to carry into execution some of his ideas, when he issued his *Treatise on Agricultural Domestic Association*, where are developed on an immense scale the *unitary impassioned series* which he had substituted for the present isolation of workers. In the place of our sad villages so scattered about, so squalid, so badly built, Fourier imagined in each locality a vast construction called a *phalanstery*, inhabited by the associated phalanxes of workers of every kind. An *impassioned attraction*, a desire for well-being, could not fail to make these associations (which he would have consist of eighteen hundred persons) comprehend the advantages of the new life upon which they were entering. No more huts, no more sheds; but a simple and commodious edi-

fice, surmounted by a tower provided with its telegraph
and ornamented with a clock. All the communications
were to be made under shelter, in street galleries venti-
lated in summer and warmed in winter. Every family
could be lodged according to its fortune and live accordingly. It was not the régime of a convent, nor the discipline of barracks; but an association in which each
member would have his share in the advantage of one
cellar substituted for three hundred cellars, one garret
for three hundred garrets, and one kitchen for three or
four hundred kitchens.

Thus far the conception of Fourier much resembles
what we see in colleges, manufactories, places where
many combine together, and where the common life produces incontestable economies and advantages of various
kinds. But on what would the inhabitants of a phalanstery, rich or poor, live? Fourier was not arrested by
that difficulty. Each land-owner was to receive in exchange for his land, transferable shares, which represented its value; and then down fell walls, living hedges,
and fences, which separated their inheritances. The separate possession of property disappeared before that syn-
thesis. Five hundred portions were transformed into
one single domain ; there was no more labor on a small
scale, no more Irish agriculture. In the interior, vast
workshops succeeded the cold and dusty barns of our
hamlets. The task of each was simplified by a division
of labor, no longer absolute and permanent like that of
the economists, but light, agreeable and varied like the
relaxations of the great lords or like an exercise benefi-
cial to the health. In agriculture and in manufactures,
each followed his inclination, and, as the workers constantly lived in each other's presence, rivals in perfection,
quickness and devotion, the results of their work would
naturally and necessarily surpass all the products of continual and forced labor. The phalansterian association
thus gave advantages much greater than all the superan-

nuated modes of selfish working; the only question was that of making an equitable distribution of them. Here the author seems to us to have carried the spirit of association too far. He supposes that the capitalists of the *phalanstery*, whose interest it is to consider their workmen, without whom capital would be unproductive, would give them a reasonable portion, and that the workmen, convinced of the impossibility of working without capital, would in their turn consider the capitalists in the distribution of profits. There will then be one portion for capital, one for labor, and one for talent. But how estimate labor and talent? According to their utility; for Fourier gives useful arts the preference over the agreeable arts. He recognizes labors of necessity, of simple utility, and of pleasure. The first will be recompensed most highly, as being generally the hardest; the agreeable labors will find a part of their recompense in their very agreeableness. Common workmen will be better paid than artists. Fourier thought thus to raise the poor classes from the wretched state into which they had fallen, and he imagined that thus he would make the causes of hatred or envy which, from the foundation of the world, have separated them from the rich classes, disappear. There would no longer be any poor. The least portion of *repulsive* work would lead to high wages, and universal harmony would not be long in becoming established between classes which have too long been hostile. The great man, in the fine arts, in science, in manufactures, would be the elect of all the phalanxes, the one pensioned by all the workers. No more law-suits, no more hospitals, no more prisons, no more ingratitude or social rigors!

I forgot to say, also, no more armies! No more wars! or rather what armies! what wars! Armies of elect workers, advancing to the execution of the most gigantic labors on the face of the globe, some cutting the isthmus of Suez, others the isthmus of Panama; these deepening the bed of rivers, those connecting lakes, drying up marshes, or exhausting mines.   We have seen what the villages would be : judge what must be the cities.   The sympathies which unite the phalanxes, will direct the re-lations of a higher order which will be established be-tween the cities, and when their industrial forces are not sufficient, the armies will commence their march, no longer then to destroy and plunder as to-day, but to build up and to embellish.   In the political order, univer-sal election, absolute liberty, complete equality, in a word, absence of government.   Of what use to think of tempests, when all the winds are suppressed, except the zephyrs ! The author might from the same point of view proclaim perpetual spring.

One cannot, however, speak with irony of the dreams of Fourier.   A man who devotes his entire life to the worship of such an idea, who aims to make the passions coöperate for the good of humanity, who undertakes to associate families and interests, and who works with such energy for the abolition of social miseries, is not a vulgar utopist, though all his projects are of a utopian nature. An utopia is often only an advanced opinion proclaimed in the presence of a generation who do not yet compre-hend it, and destined to become a commonplace for the generation which follows.   Fourier has laid the founda-tion of a theory which is beginning to bear its fruit ; for the very men even who have not studied it, regard it by a sort of instinct, in associating themselves in material and moral interests under all sorts of forms.   The socie-tary school would have made many more proselytes still, if Fourier had not affected such a profound disdain for all the writers in the world, by failing in the first duty of every man of sense, respect for ancestors.   One has an-cestors in science as in nature, and it is an evidence of bad taste or of bad principles to manifest contempt for them.   The work of these ancestors, however defective it may have been, cannot be undone in a day, and it was the error of Fourier to imagine that he could succeed in doing it, all at once, in spite of institutions, habits, and prejudices. However, he turned, especially in the latter part of his career, toward childhood, as more fitted to receive the impress of his doctrines. What he says on the subject of children is of admirable correctness, freshness and delicacy. He rightly attaches an infinite value to their education, and although the system he proposes does not seem to us conformable with nature, since its first result would be to take away sons from their fathers to bring them *all* up in common, we nevertheless acknowledge that it contains the most ingenious views ever published on this difficult subject.

It would be rash to predict the near results of the societary theory of Fourier. We have not yet seen this system in operation; no *phalansterian* establishment has been permitted to carry out any decisive experiment on this subject. Nothing would have a better claim to our interest than an exact analysis of the social revenue of one of these model establishments, whose foundation we regret the government itself has not encouraged. What a check to innovaters, if, under such patronage, a serious experiment should fail; **but** also what a shaft of light, if it should succeed! Fourier died, heart-broken at not having been able to attain that favor from his contemporaries: and, in his despair, he accused the economists of having prevented, as far as lay in their power, the carrying out of his idea. What could they gain by preventing an attempt of such importance? The accusation then falls of itself, and the cause of the evil is attributable to the author of the system, to whom it was not given to make a capital attempt, because the circumstances or his powers never permitted him to decide upon it. His book will remain as the boldest critical work which has ever been published against modern political economy: but it has been no more fortunate than the latter in the discovery of solutions to social questions. This is because such solutions are daughters of time, and appear only at long intervals, adapted for a moment, perhaps, to the essentially transitory wants of humanity, and changing like them.

Mr. Owen, in England, set about the investigation of the same problem as Fourier, without being more fortunate. Their doctrines, which have often been confounded, resemble each other in only a few points. The coöperative societies of the English *socialist* had scarcely anything in common with the *phalanxes* of the French *associationist*. It was not by economic reforms that Mr. Owen attempted to ameliorate the condition of the workingmen, but rather by good administration and moralization employed with intelligence and firmness. The establishment of New Lanark, improperly considered as a social attempt, was only a great manufactory invaded by drunkenness, debauchery, and lack of discipline, when Mr. Owen applied to it his· principle of regeneration and of a somewhat puritan rigidity. He made strict rules, inflicted fines, settled little difficulties amicably, and attained satisfactory results both as to products and order, as an active and judicious manufacturer might have obtained them. At the same time, the dwellings of the workmen became cleaner; stores were opened for the sale of articles of consumption at the lowest possible prices and of the best quality. The system of Mr. Owen, applied for sixteen years to the population of New Lanark, composed of more than two thousand souls, obtained a brilliant reputation for this philanthropist, and numerous visitors to his manufactory: but he ventured no absolute idea, for fear of wounding the umbrageous susceptibilities of his fellow citizens, and it was in France alone that I heard him speak stern truths of the English aristocracy.

Mr. Owen nevertheless rashly admitted the abolition of property. He wished to suppress all social inequalities, and he demanded at the same time the closing of dramshops, reform in instruction, *reform of the church*, and of all abuses. His teaching therefore was somewhat declamatory and vague, and his prescriptions resemble too much the commands of a preacher. So long as he was present at New-Lanark, in the manufactory where his experiments were made, order reigned there, labor was productive and discipline was maintained; but after his departure, every one took up again his accustomed way and the system disappeared. Mr. Owen having hoped that attempts would succeed better on virgin soil, went to America and founded his famous establishment of New Harmony. He took with him many proselytes of both sexes, and the location of his domain seemed happily chosen. However, in a short time, human passions had resumed their sway; he found in that regenerated society, as in ours, cowards, the jealous, the idle, and the intemperate, and the serenity of the founder was once more disturbed. A journey which he was obliged to make to Scotland, completed the ruin of his establishment, in which anarchy reigned, and which was sold to a German illuminate, named Rapp. Miss Martineau, who visited that society in 1835, reports that the remains of the Owenist colony resembled a community of Moravian brothers, and that the new chief had succeeded in keeping them together only by isolating them from all foreign contact, in the manner of the dictator Francia, in Paraguay.

Notwithstanding these serious checks, the popularity of Mr. Owen had only increased. Several editions of his theories, more fortunate than his practice, had been quickly exhausted, and people talked everywhere only of the great things promised by the new English reformer. It was at the period of the philosophic reaction, excited in France by the attempts of the Jesuits, and in England by the discussion of the bill for Catholic Emancipation. Mr. Owen issued a violent manifesto *against all religions*, accusing them of all the evils of the human race; and, strange to say, this bold publication, extended to thirty thousand copies and circulated through all the journals, caused him to lose none of the good will of several sovereigns who had become interested in his experiments. The Duke of Kent, brother of the king of England, one of his warmest admirers, consented even to preside over a public assembly where the latter were to be explained. Mr. Owen was a firm supporter of order ; it was in vain for him to point out social imperfections, and the disquieting contrast of great riches and poverty : every one knew that he wished to arrive at his ends by a strict discipline to which he would have wealth itself subjected ; and this sort of reform could not be looked upon unfavorably by absolute governments.

The economic views of Mr. Owen were summed up in a most complete manner in a memorial which he addressed to the representatives of the allied powers, assembled at the congress of Aix-la-Chapelle. He there concisely set forth the immense increase in the mechanical powers of production, and he declared that these powers were more than sufficient to satisfy very liberally all the wants of the population of the globe. He forcibly described the disastrous consequences of the absence of all order in the production and distribution of wealth, and the necessity of substituting for competition unity of interest : he demonstrated, in fine, how a superabundance of products, by depriving the working classes of labor, plunged them into frightful poverty in the midst of abundance ; and how urgent it had become to remedy these evils, by organizing things so as to aid manual labor by mechanical labor, instead of substituting the latter for the former and leaving the laboring classes without any security for their subsistence.* Mr. Owen had proposed, at various times, subscriptions for the purpose of founding agricultural and manufacturing settlements, based on unity of production and consumption ; but parliament, when consulted, gave

---

* See a series of remarkable articles on Owen, in the *Journal de la Science Sociale*, by M. B. Dulary.

no furtherance to these projects.   It is supposed that such was the origin of the agricultural colonies established at Frederick's Oord in Holland, which did not, however, produce results as satisfactory as had been hoped.   Nevertheless, the indefatigable reformer was not discouraged ; and after a series of vicissitudes which prove, at least, the extreme difficulty of these social improvisations, after having traveled over Europe to set forth his plans, Mr. Owen lately returned to France, a little discouraged with men and resolved, like the dying Fourier, to devote himself to children.

It is through childhood especially that it is possible to arrive at a serious reform of the present economic order. So long as the children of an industrial community shall be brought up at hazard, almost all for liberal professions whose number is restricted, there will be an insufficiency of capable persons in many occupations and a redundancy in many others.   After having tried all systems, after having criticised governments, institutions, methods, people and kings, one is evidently brought to a recognition that it is intelligence which is lacking to resources, and not resources to intelligence.   Three-fourths of the living forces of society are languishing in a deplo rable atony, and there are still more unproductive men than sterile lands.   Governments cannot, doubtless, secure to all citizens an agreeable and gentle life ; but it would be less difficult than is supposed to facilitate the means of their procuring it for themselves.   The personal value of men, *in all occupations,* seems to us capable of indefinite increase, by an education which will allow childhood to lose nothing in the development of its faculties.   Fourier and Owen are in accord on this point, and one may consider as a discovery even the exaggerations of their confidence in that regard.   The great association must begin at school and be followed up outside. Is it not, in fact, at school that the real superiority of intelligence and labor dominate, notwithstanding the absolute equality which governs all relations. If people should bestow on the education of children the solicitude that is expended on the government of men, it would suffice in a few years to change the face of economic questions. By increasing the *moral capital* of nations, their resources would be increased, and the catastrophes by which they are afflicted would be prevented. There are many sanitary regulations to prevent physical contagion : why should there be none to prevent the moral contagion of ignorance, idleness, and incapacity? You complain of the encroachments of the poverty which knocks at your doors and encumbers your hospitals and your prisons; but what are you doing with your children? What wealth, pray, do you expect to see created by those myriads of neglected creatures swarming in the mud of your cities and your villages, or ruined in the impure atmosphere of your manufactories? Respect the utopists who blame your heedlessness, and regret their errors, for they are consuming their lives in thinking for millions of ingrates !

CHAPTER XLV.

WE are approaching the termination of our course. We have rapidly gone over the history of the experiments which have been made among civilized people to ameliorate the physical and moral condition of man. Greece, Rome, the middle ages and modern times, have in succession passed before us, and everywhere the same problem has been presented ; everywhere the struggle between the slave and the master, the rich and the poor, the employer and the workman. This struggle, which still lasts under new forms, has given birth to all the systems of political economy which have succeeded each other, from the *Economics* of Xenophon, who proposed to brand slaves on the forehead to prevent them from escaping, to the societary theory of Fourier and the co-operative companies of Owen. The mind is confounded at the similarity of tone in these social experiments, which always meet with obstacles and yet constantly recur, to die and to be born again from generation to generation. At both extremities of the Christian era, and at the ends of the earth, in old Rome and in the United States, we always find slavery such as it was when continued by the Barbarians and kept up by the feudal system ; and we might think that humanity had remained stationary, to see the extreme slowness of its conquests and its heedlessness in preserving them.   However, social progress has never been arrested since ancient times, although it may appear to us confused and irregular at certain epochs. The advent of Christianity, the invasion of the Barba-rians, the crusades, persecutions of the Jews even, the es-tablishment of the Hanse towns, the affranchisement of the communes, the organization of corporations by Saint Louis, the industrial and commercial movement of the Italian republics, protestantism, and the discovery of America, have brought gradual changes in the course of political economy.   Experiments have not discontinued theories, but have always preceded them.   We have seen these laborious developments of science in facts ; it is time to sum them up in systems.

These various systems have always borrowed some-thing from the character of the nations among which they have taken rise.   Italy, which had the honor of lighting the torch of all the sciences, was the first to de-vote herself to the study of political economy.   While most of the great states of Europe were a prey to finan-cial expedients and to poverty, banks were established at Venice, Milan and Genoa ; the first budgets of public expenses and receipts were being prepared at Florence ; a silk and wool nobility was being substituted for the nobility of the sword.   Excellent writings on money re-vealed the secrets of credit and created the science of finance.   There was nothing, even in the misfortunes of the Peninsula, which did not favor the progress of politi-cal economy, by making the Italians experience, under Charles V, the disastrous influence of monopolies, high taxes and prohibitions.   In 1582, Gaspard Scaruffi pub-lished his work *On Moneys and the True Proportion between Gold and Silver*.   He proposed the creation of a *universal medium* of circulation and the mark of all goldsmiths' work.   The Neapolitan Serra, who wrote in 1613 his *Treatise on the Causes which make Gold and Silver abound in Kingdoms*, comprehended the productive power of manufactures. Bandini, the precursor of Quesnay and of the Physiocrates, pointed out the advantages of one single tax, as more easy and more economical; Broggia published the first methodical writing on the theory of taxation. But the most celebrated of the Italian economists is unquestionably the professor Genovesi, who may be justly considered the rival of Adam Smith, if not in correctness of doctrine, at least in the impulse he gave to the teaching of the science in all Italy.

No writer, in fact, represents more exactly the character of the Italian economic school. That school has been at all times philosophic and reformatory; it takes pleasure in the chances of politics and its counsels are less frequently addressed to the people than to kings. Genovesi had the courage to keep it in that perilous and honorable line. He contended for free trade in grain, for the abolition of laws on the interest of money and for the reduction of the number of religious communities. He proclaimed the superiority of labor over the productiveness of mines, to enrich nations. He clearly foresaw, in 1764, the independence of the United States of America and the ruin of the colonial system. His high morality, his eloquence, and his vast erudition constantly attracted to him a multitude of disciples, and although his doctrines favored the mercantile system, he may be considered the founder of political economy in Italy. Algarotti, one of his most celebrated successors, has given us the first analysis of the phenomena of the division of labor, of which the Marquis of Beccaria was to complete the theory almost at the very time when it received, in England, the fine demonstrations of Adam Smith. Beccaria, in his picturesque language, called iron the *father-metal*. He was a follower of the French Economists of the school of Quesnay.

The *Meditations on Political Economy*, by Count Verri, contributed not less to the success of the Italian school. Verri was the precursor of Adam Smith. His concise

and energetic style, and his ingenious and striking comparisons have given much popularity to his works, despite the important deficiencies one finds in them. Vasco
and Ricci, who wrote on poverty and on benevolent institutions, represent in Italy the theories of Godwin and
of Malthus. The former maintained that governments
should help the poor; the latter established the inutility and danger of all systematic and compulsory aid.
We find in Vasco the Saint-Simonian idea of the abolition of inheritance. Ortès, his contemporary, has been
too much lauded; but this author has the merit of being
the first one in Italy to point out the encroachments of
pauperism and the means of remedying it. He has well
shown the contrast between wretchedness and opulence
in the large cities. According to him, " Population is
maintained, increases or diminishes always in proportion
to the wealth; but it never precedes wealth. The generations of brutes are limited by the action of man; the
generations of men are limited by reason. Population
diminishes from excessive taxation and slavery. Celibacy
is as necessary as marriage to preserve the population.
To reproach a celibate for celibacy would be the same
thing as to reproach a married man for marriage. Work-
houses provide for a few and fail to provide for a greater
number."

Filangieri was one of the most able defenders in Italy
of freedom of trade, and the constant enemy of the numerous standing armies. "So long as the evils of humanity
are not cured," he exclaimed, " so long as the errors and
prejudices which perpetuate these evils find advocates;
so long as truth, known only to a few privileged men,
remains hidden from the greater part of the human race;
so long as it manifests itself far from thrones, the duty of
the economic philosopher is to preach it, to maintain it,
to promote it, and to illustrate it. If the information he
gives is not useful to his age, to his country, it will
certainly be to some other age, to some other state. A

citizen of all countries, a contemporary of all ages, the universe is his country the earth is his pulpit, his contemporaries and his descendants are his disciples." Never, perhaps, was the cosmopolitan expression of the Italian school more manifest than in this author, unless it were in the numerous writings of Melchiorre Gioja, the Atlas of the science in Italy. His famous *Prospectus of the Economic Sciences* had for its aim to reduce to a system all that writers have thought, governments sanctioned and people practiced, in public and private economy. In it, the opinions of all Italian and all foreign writers are examined. It is a real encyclopædia of the sciences; but it is not always impartial, especially in regard to the French.

The distinctive characteristic of the economic school of the Italians consists principally in their broad and complex manner of looking at questions. They do not concern themselves with wealth from an abstract and positive point of view, but in its relation to the general welfare. For an economic measure to appear important to them, there must be connected with it not only some money question, but some moral or political interest. Business partnerships are not in their eyes banking-houses and the workmen machines. They consider man as the perpetual object of their solicitude and study. They are publicists as much as economists. Montesquieu best represents in our language the true type of the economist in theirs. The questions in which they have excelled are those of moneys, free ports, agriculture, loan-banks, and benevolent institutions. If their numerous works have not obtained a great reputation, it must be attributed to the umbrageous precautions of almost all governments and the personal position of the authors, some of whom were ministers, others counsellors, and some few ecclesiastics; but political economy owes to them its propagation in Europe and excellent treatises on a great number of important subjects. Most of these economists had to brave the inquisition of Rome, that of Venice, con-

temporary prejudices and the despotism of their governments. They wrote against existing abuses, and, as it
were, in the breach. Their life was a combat, and political economy meant with them social science, the universal science ; everywhere else it was only the science of
wealth.

In Spain, it was always considered an ally of the
treasury. All the economic legislation of that country is
stamped with an exclusive character which traces back to
the expulsion of the Moors, and the discovery of the
New World. Industrial freedom early succumbed there
before the establishment of manufactures by seignorial
or royal monopoly ; and the supposed necessity of securing to Spain the American market, gave rise there to the
prohibitory system which has since infected all Europe.
All the economic pests proceed from that source. By
pursuing with the utmost hostility the Moors and the
Jews, the Spanish destroyed the spirit of enterprise and
speculation in the Peninsula ; by multiplying convents
and monks, they gave a premium to indolence and raised
beggary to the rank of a trade. The majorats, mortmain, and hatred to foreigners were equally prejudicial
to agriculture, manufactures and commerce. There is
perhaps no country in the world where the economic
administration has caused more evils, and one might say
that Spain had tried on herself all bad systems, as certain
experimenters try poisons. What useful thing could be
attempted under threat of the tortures of the inquisition,
and in view of the American mines, whose inexhaustible
products seemed suddenly produced expressly to repair
all errors, to produce an illusion as to all dangers?
That prosperity was as fatal to Spain as the greatest misfortunes. It lulled her into a disastrous sense of security,
it made her believe that the power of states resided
in the precious metals and not in labor ; it engendered
the absurd prejudices of the balance of trade and the draconic laws against the exportation of money ; it covered

with flowers the edge of the precipice over which that monarchy was one day to be plunged.

It is in the writings published under the influence of these deplorable prejudices that we must seek the explanation of the decline of Spain and of the progress of bad economic doctrines in that country. Almost all these treatises having been prepared by priests or by those in the employ of the treasury, are virtual manifestoes against the fundamental principles of the wealth of nations. Oppression within, exclusion without, such is their motto. One would suppose, on reading them, that the human race had been created for the good pleasure of a few families and a few corporations. However, towards the end of the eighteenth century, the philosophical movement, originating in France, penetrated into Spain, and produced there, in the reign of Charles III, a reaction favorable to political economy. Commissioners were appointed to explore the American possessions; canals were made and roads opened in the mother country, and the bank of Saint Charles seemed to desire to initiate the Spaniards into the advantages of credit. At the same time, Cabarrus, Jovellanos, Danvila, Martinez de la Mata, Semparé y Guarinos, and, in our time, Valle Santoro, Florez Estrada, and several distinguished members of the Cortès, attempted to call back the nation to the too long uncomprehended principles of political economy.

But all these efforts were futile against the stubbornness of national prejudice and the misfortunes with which Spain had been overwhelmed since the beginning of the nineteenth century. The system of prohibition made her lose her finest colonies; industrial monopolies destroyed all her manufactures; the tithe and the majorats struck her agriculture with sterility; war scattered what capital she had left, and anarchy still paralyzes the efforts she makes to resume her rank among nations. Never did a people present a more striking example of the

chastisements which follow errors in political economy,
and never did the citizens of any country expiate in a
more cruel manner the faults of their government. There
is not one single social pest of that monarchy which is
not the result of a bad doctrine, and one may say that
she has served as an example to all others by teaching
them to profit by her mistakes. The Spanish economic
school is in fact the one which has spread abroad in the
world the most commercial prejudices, and Spain is the
country which has suffered the most from them. Her
political economy is still the same as that of Charles V,
and the eloquent protests of Jovellanos and Florez
Estrada have not succeeded in making any impression
upon it.

Political economy had in France a happier fate. Not
a century has passed without generous voices being
raised for the triumph of the eternal principles of justice
in the distribution of the profits of labor. In the reign
of Saint Louis the corporations secured to each trade-
body, if not to each worker, a certain independence; the
workman was subjected to a severe discipline, but the
corporation, at least, was free. Under Henry IV, agriculture had its turn, and the peasants, freed from a multitude of vexations, came forth for the first time from
the state of torpor in which the feudal system had
plunged them. We see, in reading the writings of Sully,
that this great minister worked in a systematic manner
to emancipate agriculture, and that this important branch
of production occupied in his mind the rank which is its
due. Colbert organized the industries on new bases; * he
gave them encouragement and laws; and we have shown
that he was less hostile than is generally supposed to the
agricultural interests. Then came the period of Law,
the foundation of credit and its stormy times, those distressing experiences which had at least the advantage
of making France acquainted with one of the prin-

---

* See chap. xxvii of this history.

cipal elements of her future wealth. The Economists of the eighteenth century completed the work of the preceding centuries, by propounding the first economic theory which served as an introduction to the science. This was as a signal given to Europe; and from that moment, human thought seemed to take no respite. Everyone comprehended that social science concerned the most humble citizens as much as the most august heads. Society wished to become acquainted with itself; it studied the phenomena of its own functions, and thus it was that from experiment to experiment, even at the cost of misfortunes, France has attained the point of stating the problem of the future, with her accustomed clearness, to all peoples and to all governments. Political economy was philosophic in Italy and fiscal in Spain; in France alone has it assumed an organizing and social character.

England has given it a physiognomy and a tendency exclusively industrial. Political economy is considered in that country only as the science of wealth. English writers have studied wealth in an abstract manner and independently of the evils which too often accompany its production. They have been justly reproached with having considered questions of manufactures and machines as too separate from the welfare of the laborers, and of having manifested an insensibility to the sufferings of the working classes. Most of the modern writers of that school, renouncing the attractions of style so potent for the triumph of even their doctrines, have treated political economy like algebra, and have ventured to maintain that all the propositions of the science could be demonstrated with mathematical certainty. This tendency has not led them to the most philanthropic solutions, but it has permitted them to follow out the consequences of their principles with inflexible logic. They have thus succeeded in giving to economic language a precision which has contributed much to the progress of

ideas.   It is the English who have best defined the words
production, capital, competition, credit, and a host of others
not less important.   They have created a nomenclature,
which has finally been adopted by all the economists of
Europe, and which will serve as a starting point for their
future labors.

We have shown the radical fault of this severe and
positive school and the danger of the complications to
which its doctrines have given rise.   By sacrificing all
social considerations to the desire of creating wealth, the
English have developed beyond measure the productive
power of the nation, but they have not added proportionately to the well-being of the workers : happy the
latter, when commercial crises have not made them victims of competition or of a fall in wages !   The time
has not yet come to affirm how far this system of in-
citing to consumption has been able to contribute to the
development of production, by multiplying with wants
an ardor in working which will permit their satisfaction.   The continual increase in taxes, principally on
objects of consumption, has condemned the inhabitants
of that country to a perpetual fever of improvements.
England has become an immense manufacturing establishment, a universal counting-house.   Seated on a double
couch of coal and iron, open to foreign commerce by
more than a hundred excellent ports, she has found in
her midst men of genius who have furrowed her soil
with canals and roads ; who were the first to make common, if not to invent, the steam-engine ; who have endowed their country with the spinning-frame and with
railroads.   She has founded her credit on a basis so broad
that the national fortune is increased by it as by a metallic conquest ; she has scattered instruction with so liberal
a hand, that no aptitude would run the risk of remaining
sterile there.   To complete her good fortune, this empire
has found in most of her ministers superior intelligence,
which has been put to the service of science and has

executed with rare ability its most difficult prescriptions. Besides, England has become the classic land of economic experiments, and it is from this great laboratory that they to-day come forth to the world.

The German economists have considered the science from a philosophic and political point of view which distinguishes them wholly from other European writers. In their view, political economy comes near being the science of administration, the science of the state, the union of the *cameral* sciences, as they call it. They almost always include in it diplomacy, constitutional law, statistics, and even the regulation of the state, a strange combination in which the best minds could not have helped being lost, if the very difficulty of the subject had not imposed upon them a salutary restriction. Among them may be counted many believers in the system of Quesnay, particularly Mr. Schmalz, who has published in these latter years a treatise that one might suppose destined to revive the doctrines of the *Physiocrates.* The professors Rau, of Heidelberg, and Poelitz, of Leipzig, have set forth in a most complete manner the principles of political economy as they are understood in Germany; not that Germany has claimed to have its particular science and more perfect processes in the production and distribution of wealth, but that in this country political economy has always been considered in its relations to public law and administration. Several writers have even had an idea of giving it a theological basis; and it nowhere presents itself with a more numerous train of developments and applications. The Count of Soden, who calls it the science of the economy of the state (*Staats-Haushaltungs Kunde*) divides it into *theory, legislation, and administration.* Finance, public order, and education occupy in it an extended place.

The tendency of German political economy to encroach upon the domain of the publicist, has become almost general in Europe. J. B. Say, in his *Complete Course,*

had already allowed himself a great number of digressions on public consumption, works carried on by the
state, the instruction of youth and the expenses of a fleet
and army. The progress of general wealth had demonstrated to him the utility and even the necessity of the
intervention of the government in great enterprises of
public utility. He relaxed by degrees the rigor of the
exclusive principles which had so long made him reject
that powerful intervention. England, on her side, entering for the first time the career of parliamentary investigations, brought new light to political economy, and
proved in the most incontestable manner how many services can be expected from the influence of governments
on production. Germany, however, has remained faithful to her metaphysical habits ; and we know nothing
more opposed than the writings of her greatest economists to the perspicuity of the French writers, and the
severe and didactic forms of the English economists.

The development of the industrial arts and of commerce in Germany has however begun, within a few
years, to modify the too speculative tendency of economic science in that country. Mr. Krause, to whom
his fellow countrymen owe a remarkable work on Prussian custom-duties, has come down from the regions of
metaphysics to the solid land of applications, and he has
presented views of great interest to agriculture, notably
a matured plan of a territorial bank, which seems to us
worthy of consideration. Mr. Zachariæ, Professor Her-
man, Mr. Malchus, Mr. de Nébénius and Mr. Buchholz,
have entered more and more into the way of practical reforms, and we cannot help recognizing that Germany
continues to make decided and intelligent progress in
them. The tariff association, organized by Prussia, is
the most vast and bold economic reform which has been
carried into execution for a century. The eminently
electic spirit of the Germans early shielded them from
any infatuation for systems, and they had the good for-

tune to profit by the experiences of their neighbors, without adopting their prejudices.   As they had always kept equally removed from the exclusive régime of the Spanish, the manufacturing system of the English, and the anti-commercial violence of the French revolution, a reform could be wrought among them without overthrowing the factitious capital which to-day throws so many obstacles in the way of improvements in other countries. Less absolute, the Germans are less embarrassed in their movements: they have no victims to make, no interests to sacrifice; reform has had full scope as on a virgin soil; and perhaps, while discussion continues in the states renowned for their practical habits, it is in the country of metaphysics that the most decisive attempts will be made.

Whatever may be the characteristic differences which to-day distinguish the systems of political economy in Europe, they all are coming gradually to coincide in one common opinion, the necessity of a more equitable distribution of the profits of labor.   Even in the country where the press and the tribune are mute, a prophetic instinct warns the governing powers of the true needs of the people, and imposes on them the obligation of satisfying them.   The energy formerly expended in works of war, is now directed to industrial enterprises; the condition of the workman is honored, and we are rapidly advancing towards the achievement of a new compact, either between the workmen, or between nations.   The individual aspires to his share of the collective power of the masses, and we no longer conceive of any other social state than that which secures to each a lot proportioned to his personal talents and his daily labor.   Governments even are obliged to earn their living by the sweat of their brow, and to resolve difficulties that they could with impunity elude a few years ago.   A salutary emulation has become established between them in measures favorable to increase of the general welfare, and one would find

it difficult to cite a single important administrative act
which does not aim at progress in public wealth and the
amelioration of the fate of the humblest citizens. How
many results of this kind has not political economy promoted since the beginning of the nineteenth century!
Order has become reëstablished in the finances and faith
in public engagements has become a sacred thing; savings banks have offered protection to the savings of the
poor; benevolent associations and mutual aid societies
have multiplied in all enlightened countries; commerce
has brought people together whom war had too often
long separated. No economic school dares openly to ad
vocate the exclusive system, and no one longer believes
that any country can grow rich by the ruin of its neighbors. The respective beliefs of the old sects will soon
be combined in a universal religion, in an industrial and
pacific catholicism which will sum up the great labors of
the past to the advantage and satisfaction of the wants
of the future. When a line of railroads shall unite Marseilles and Moscow, there will no longer be either German
or French political economy, and the Prussian custom-
duties will have ceased to exist. People will no longer
discuss the matters which occupy so much of our thought
to-day, except to regret that they should have deliberated
so long instead of acting!

CHAPTER XLVI.

Economic complications resulting from industrial affranchisement since 1789.—Disadvantages of competition.—Contradiction between facts and laws.—Necessity of harmonizing them.—Revolutions which have taken place in commercial relations since the nineteenth century.—Modifications of political economy resulting from them.

THE time has indeed come for action, for everything advances with rapid pace, and the movement which is bearing us on scarcely leaves us time to look about us. Nothing more remains of the ancient social state on which the institutions of our fathers were based; a half century has sufficed to renew the face of the earth and the field of experiment. The restless condition of present society is especially due to the incompatibility between the old systems and the new interests. The economic principles which govern us date back more than two hundred years, and our industrial constitution has no longer anything in common with that of the period when they originated. In whatever direction we turn our eyes, this contrast strikes us and presages a renovation. The examination that we are about to make of it will be the conclusion of this history, and will sum up its moral reflections.

The first blow was struck by the French Revolution. This abolished in a single night the right of primogeniture, entail, majorats, tithes, and privileges of every kind. For the old system of concentration of landed property, it substituted its extreme division, the excess of which brings again in question to-day its first benefits. It freed labor by abolishing corporations, and gave new life to commerce by suppressing interior custom-duties. But we have since beheld growing up an unlimited competition, a multiplication of rural enterprises, with insufficient capital, and agriculture after the Irish mode. One single class was, before 1789, subject to the impost tax; equality before the law has subjected all the others to it. The distribution is doubtless more equitable; but the burden has singularly increased. The destruction of wardenships accorded freedom to the workmen, but it took away the responsibility of the masters. The Revolution gave much; it demanded more. Thus, at the first steps, all the old social organization was profoundly modified, and the new institutions remained subject to the old customs or left to chance. In emancipating the men, the fetters had been left on their feet; liberty was going to become more disastrous to them than servitude. Instead of making war on their masters, they made it on each other.

Every one knows the unforeseen complications which have arisen from this state of things. It was a fine spectacle, certainly, to see the lists open to all capacities; but how many mistakes! How many disappointed hopes! How many unfortunate enterprises! Some, rushing into marriage as the promised land, engendered only pauperism and reaped only misery; others, venturing without experience into the chances of business, encountered only bankruptcy and thought to escape through prohibition. A strange blindness that, which made them invoke, as a remedy for their evils, the very scourge which had caused the evils of their fathers, and which was, after all, only the revival of a privilege! Such was the starting-point of the first and most fatal contradiction in our industrial legislation: while restoring freedom to manufactures, they did not restore it to commerce, and consumption was attacked by the false measures taken to increase the elements of production. Far from departing from that false course, France has every day gone forward in it, so that for the old feudal aristocracy has been substituted a tariff aristocracy, who profit by monopolies, to the detriment of the mass of workers. The result of this system has been to bring about a permanent hostility between the heads of the manufacturing establishments, and to compel workmen to compete continually at the lowest price, that is to say, to increase their chances of wretchedness and privation. The tithe of our day is levied in the workshops; our forges and our spinning-mills have become castles where sit, clothed in their armor of gold, the high and powerful lords of modern industry.

The present colonial government is not less incompatible with the true situation of the colonies. There are no longer any colonies in the acceptation of the word; traffic in negroes has been interdicted by solemn treaties; slavery has been abolished by the English parliament; and, in the New World, a black republic has just made a treaty with its mother country, on terms of equality. The English and the Spanish have lost their finest possessions in both Americas. And yet the colonial régime still exists: for want of a body, people attach themselves to its shadow: there is a pretence of keeping up towards free nations the despotic and exclusive practices that had been adopted towards subject colonies. In vain have experience and political economy demonstrated that more would be gained by treating on a liberal basis; habit gains the victory, and the inconsistency survives. The commerce of a great people continues to be subordinated to the badly-comprehended interests of some little isles, like a vessel lashed to those bollards which float at the entrance to our roadsteads. Meanwhile, interests become complicated and suffer; slavery is in a ferment and nations do not perceive that their colonies are going off.

There is nothing, even to the great highways of commerce, which has not experienced a revolution since the beginning of this century. The Mediterranean has re-

gained its sceptre; and the city of Alexander is becoming again the entrepôt of trade with the Indies. A flash
from the genius of Napoleon has lighted again in Egypt
the torch of industry, which had been extinguished for
more than a thousand years. Algiers has yielded to our
arms; and Greece has come forth from her ruins. Piracy
has ceased its ravages; and into Constantinople even, the
spirit of reform is daily penetrating, in favor of our influence and our ideas. Our steamboats freely coast along the
extensive shores of the Mediterranean, and unforeseen relations are established between nations long unknown to
each other. Are not all these events destined to produce
profound changes in European political economy? And
is it not to be feared that by persisting in a legislation
made for other times, we may be surprised by some fatal
catastrophe?   Did not Venice begin to decline the day
when the Portuguese doubled the Cape of Good Hope?

The changes which we have just indicated are not the
only ones which have taken place for the last fifty years,
and which merit the attention of economists. Without
going beyond the domain of material facts, we have only
to cast our glance over the advance in the physical sciences, chemistry and mechanics. An entire new world
has been discovered here, and we to-day consume several
hundred million francs worth of products which were
hardly known to our fathers. The general production of
cotton cloths amounts to nearly two milliards; that of
sugar to more than five hundred millions. By calculating
the increase in the manufacture of woolen goods, linens,
glass, the working of iron and coal, and the enormous development of the thousands of domestic manufactures
established in the heart of our great cities, one cannot be
slow to recognize that all the elements of production
have changed, and that this world needs new laws. Every
day brings us its discovery, and while the ships of commerce are multiplying the cargoes of raw materials which
arrive, the genius of mechanics is teaching more eco-

nomical processes of working them. The more numerous exchanges have in their turn led to modifications in the system of public and private credit. Necessity is by degrees familiarizing minds with the organization of banks and with public loans; and confidence, formerly so slow in coming, sometimes exceeds the limits of the possible in the great speculations of our time. The power of association no longer knows any bounds. As soon as an obstacle presents itself, an army of besiegers hasten to remove it and seem to make sport of even the opposition of nature. Here a suspension bridge unites two mountains; further on, a marvellous tunnel attempts to pass under the bed of a great river; elsewhere some canal * flies from reach to reach, like an imaginary line through space.

Governments have earnestly taken hold of these bold works, and, to speak of only one country, we have seen France within a few years, though scarcely recovered from the troubles of her late revolution, resume and complete her public edifices, multiply her canals, open her railroads, clear out her rivers, and vote immense sums for the enlargement of her ports. Virtual discoveries are thus being made in every country, which are equivalent to an increase of territory and which increase the private fortune of the inhabitants at the same time as the public wealth. No one can henceforth deny the importance of official intervention of the government in the great enterprises of general utility. If the civil power went a step farther and took the initiative in a great reform in such of our laws as have ceased to be in harmony with the present tendency of civilization, political economy would have gained one of its greatest victories. Our civil laws still bear the marks of the times when they were passed and of the principle which inspired them. Napoleon, who gave his name to this Code, succeeded a régime of contests and spoliation; he worked to reëstab-

---

* Erie canal, U. S.

lish an aristocracy, and he was returning to feudalism, without reflecting that a new power had arisen on its ruins and henceforth ruled the world : this was industrialism. Its wings were yet folded under the protection of England ; but it was beginning to take its flight from the height of those great manufactories, which the genius of labor has multiplied since in all Europe. In vain the privileges of landed proprietorship, carefully maintained, seemed destined to perpetuate the old distinctions of caste and the superiority of the lord over the slave : commerce escaped by the bill of exchange from the restrictions of the mortgage system, and prospered from the severity of the law at the same time that land-proprietorship seemed dying of its favors. This immense question will some day be discussed. In face of the mortgage of more than eleven milliards which weighs upon the land of France and paralyzes her, the more independent attractions of manufactures and of commerce, still much restricted, must be a serious subject of reflection for economists and statesmen. There is an age of gold to be anticipated for agriculture, from an improvement in legislation in its regard.

But the present solicitude of nations is especially directed toward the great works of intercommunication. The isolation which had kept them so long immersed in barbarism, gives place to relations daily more intimate, and the fall in the price of transportation adds an immense value to products hitherto despised. It must not, however, be expected that the great difficulties of political economy will be solved at a near future. Those which remain to be conquered belong henceforth to practice, and there the smallest mistakes may result in deplorable consequences. After having discussed for more than a century the greater or less importance of the intervention of governments, we must put them to the work wherever the isolated resources of private individuals have become insufficient. In matters of finance, practice has given more than one solemn contradiction to theories. Who could have told, for example, when Dr. Price unfolded his ingenious theory of amortization, that that expedient, reputed so efficacious, would some day be ranked among the most sterile financial contrivances? When France, drawn into the fiscal system of the Restoration, thought to protect the colonial monopoly by loading foreign sugars with duties, who could have believed that that favor so eagerly demanded, would be the principal cause of the decline of the colonies? England thought for more than two hundred years, that the surest way of diminishing the number of the poor was to have a poor-tax, and the poor-tax has given rise to pauperism. It has been found that after having expended more than four milliards of francs to relieve the indigent,* Great Britain is obliged to reconsider her steps, to strictly revise her laws in that respect, and to combat, not without peril, the scourge to which an error in her political economy gave rise.

A profound study of facts has permitted a just estimate to be made of the value of the conclusions of economic theories. Most of these theories being only inductions derived from anterior facts, careless observation in obtaining those facts necessarily influenced the correctness of the conclusions deduced from them. Since the attention of governments has taken this direction, science has been able to advance with a safer step and administration to proceed with more certainty. How could taxes be levied on an equitable basis when there were no data, even approximate, of the profits of the various branches of industry, of the distribution of the profits among them, and of the number of workmen of whom their *personnel* was composed? Is it long since we have known of the number of foundlings, the population of our hospitals and that of our prisons? And yet these bases of every reform and even of every good adminis-

---

* See the *Statistics of England*, by Mr. Porter.

tration are the most easy to collect, and the importance of the others has been appreciated for so long that the great Colbert had planned the execution of a work of this kind.*   No one henceforth approaches any question of political economy without having given himself to serious investigations into all the facts connected with it. When the English government wished to reduce the enormous duties which bore heavily upon the silks of France, a solemn investigation permitted all interests to be heard ; and that investigation became a complete treatise on the subject.   The discussion on renewing the charter of the bank gave rise to a similar work, the most thorough perhaps which has been made on a question of finance.   The project of establishing a system of communication with India by the Red Sea was likewise preceded by the most thorough investigation.   Finally, the investigation made on the occasion of the revision of the poor-laws, was the signal for an analogous work in all the countries of Europe : every nation has desired to learn the gravity of its wound and to seek the means of healing it.

Political economy, being appealed to for a solution of all these problems of social interest, gains new light every day, even in countries subject to an absolute government. The budget of expenses, that of ways and means, and the law concerning the accounts, permit an estimate of the true condition of the public fortune; by the account rendered annually of civil and criminal justice, one can obtain an exact idea of the movement of affairs and the state of morals: the results of primary instruction, the budget of the communes and the local statistics, prepared with extreme care in some departments,† leave no refuge for the arguments in favor of the old routine and

---

* This grand thought of Colbert was carried into execution.   There exists in the department of manuscripts in the Royal Library a series of nearly one hundred volumes of statistics, written out by the superintendents of the provinces, under the orders of the minister, which might still serve as models to our prefects.

† That of the Upper Rhine, for instance, which leaves little to be desired.

prejudices. Industrial documents are more rare. The government, penetrated with the idea that all questions relative to production should be left to the vigilance of private interest, published only very late and very incompletely at first the facts of which it was the depository, such as tables of the imports and exports of merchandise, the product of the mines, and the number of industrial establishments of every kind. People knew nothing, a short time ago, of the situation of the entrepôts, of the importance of transit, of the extent of our coasting trade. By degrees, however, as facts are obtained more accurately, questions grow clearer and advance toward a solution that could never have been hoped for from the influence of principles alone. Thorough discussions in the Chambers have come, to complete, in these latter times, the instruction which had already resulted from the progress of statistics, and political economy has entered upon a new era, entirely of experiments and applications.

On whatever side one turns his attention, it is impossible not to be impressed by all the progress which has been realized since peace has permitted governments and peoples to concentrate their attention on reforms favorable to the general prosperity. In all directions, people have comprehended that material power is only an auxiliary to moral improvement, and that the production of wealth should be considered as truly useful only as there results from it a greater sum of well-being and of morality to the workers. Consequently, in England even, the hours of labor for children have already been reduced, and the physical sciences have been appealed to for new means of rendering the workshops healthful. The prisons are no longer abandoned to the good pleasure of the jailers; they have become vast industrial establishments, where every day are made, with a solicitude that cannot be too much praised, attempts at improvement which will soon bear their fruit. Official travelers, volunteers in that fine cause of humanity, have been over both worlds to study in them the methods that have been tried with the object of reforming criminals hitherto neglected. Beneficence itself takes counsel with science: it has become less prodigal of aid. The foundling asylums no longer keep the gates of their cemeteries wide open : a few ingeniously devised formalities have sufficed to recall mothers to a sense of their duties and to save the contributors considerable sums. Lotteries have been suppressed ; the public disapproval has caused gambling houses to be closed.

In purely material matters, political economy has promoted no fewer surprising changes and unexpected improvements. An entirely new population of possessors of personal property has arisen in the presence of landed property, and daily increases with unexampled rapidity. The wealth created by their industry makes numerous markets for agricultural products and immense resources for the public treasury. This explains the progressive increase of indirect taxes, designed to reach the industrial fortune of nations, and to increase with it. Each year, the figure which represents the results of these taxes rises: letter-postage, stamps, tobacco, custom-duties, octrois, beverages, give revenues which are continually increasing, because they are in proportion to the increase of public wealth. The same phenomenon is reproduced in all civilized countries, and the creations of manufacturing and commercial industries have taken such a development in certain countries, like England and the United States, that the indirect tax has become almost the sole basis of the budget of the receipts of these states. At the same time, the savings in them favor the multiplication of capital and permit labors to be undertaken under the auspices of association, which are productive of new savings and of indefinite wealth. All boundaries seem to have enlarged before these armies of workers ; unknown mines are discovered ; virgin forests are worked; products which seem fabulous are created. In France, the beet and the mulberry have doubled the consumption of sugar and of silk; in England, flax threatens to supplant our linens; in Belgium, the construction of machines is already increasing on an immense scale, and seems yet scarcely begun. Who would dare maintain, in the face of these results, the possibility of keeping up an economic régime originating in other necessities and in circumstances so different?

Scarcely twenty years ago, Europe was thrown into extreme confusion by a general war, unprecedented in the annals of history. Maritime commerce was annihilated, manufactures suffering, capital dissipated; credit seemed forever lost. Suddenly, France proclaims the principle of fidelity to engagements: she borrows enormous sums to pay her debts, and scarcely ten years have elapsed ere she has regained her strength, restored her manufactures and carried her commerce to the ends of the earth. At the very time when I am terminating this work, the capital in our country invested in industrial enterprises amounts to more than two milliards of francs: it has reached twice that sum in England; and the amount of capital invested in the public loans of all nations * cannot be estimated at less than five times that sum. The opening of canals † and the improvement of roads have tripled the value of an immense amount of landed property, and in a few great cities land has been known to rise to the exorbitant price of a thousand francs the square metre. The national capital has everywhere increased with such

---

* R. Dudley Baxter, in his work on :" National Debts," (London, 1871), p. 79, gives the total public indebtedness of the world in 1869–1870 in pounds sterling at £3,911,000,000. That of the various states of Europe is stated as then amounting to £2,165,430,000. *Trans.*

† " It is established, from reliable data. that the canal of the South (of France) has increased the annual revenue of the countries it crosses more than twenty millions and the treasury receipts more than four millions. It has likewise been ascertained that the canal of the Centre has increased the territorial revenue of France from five to six millions."

(M. Pillet Will : *On the expense and result of the canals*, p. 61). *Author's Note.*

rapidity and in proportions so extraordinary, that one can boldly affirm that before twenty-five years real estate in France will have tripled in value. The same rising tendency is observable in all Europe ; and peace, without the violent aid of any internal revolution, is sufficient to relieve those in the humblest condition, by favoring the emancipation of the laborers while increasing the profits of their labor. One cannot estimate exactly the changes which are everywhere taking place in that manner; but their number increases so regularly, that the constitution of society will finally be entirely renewed. Thus the most shocking social inequalities will disappear, and perhaps also some day the last traces of the proletariat.

The science of political economy has a right to claim a good part of this progress and of the pacific disposition of Europe at the present time. The spirit of conquest and invasion has had its day. The most warlike nations have turned their activity toward more lasting works, and true patriotism henceforth consists in enriching one's country rather than in ravaging neighboring countries. Power has passed from the side of wealth ; barbarism has become unable to disturb the repose of civilized countries. Now, it is a fine thing to make conquests over nature ; it is by mastering rivers, exploiting mines, opening canals and roads, that a people proves its superiority and triumphs over its rivals. Men will soon be valued only in proportion to the services they can render and not to the ambition which they may please to manifest. Everything that can facilitate the increase of advantages in the various classes of society, has more claim to public attention than the promises, too rarely realized, of the most ardent innovators. The people do not live on ambrosia, and although political economy has been reproached with bowing their faces to the earth, by concerning itself too exclusively with material products, every one knows to-day that the surest way to raise the dignity of man, is to protect him from want. Riches alone, or at least comfort, procures the leisure by favor of which the citizen breathes freely, and properly enjoys the fruit of his labor. Whatever great and useful thing has thus far been accomplished in political economy, has had for its aim to procure men a little more leisure with less fatigue, and consequently to favor the development of intelligence among the more degraded classes. Besides, is not the greatest sum of personal independence among citizens, the surest guaranty of liberty? Does despotism reign among rich people or among poor people?

There is no longer to-day a single village which does not participate directly or indirectly in the benefits of industrial civilization. As soon as a useful discovery is employed to advantage at one point, it gives rise to consumption at another; and commerce transports into the most remote cantons of our provinces, the most ingenious and most recent products of our cities. Political economy has convincingly demonstrated the happy effects of that reaction which has given us the lines of communication, so varied and so numerous, with which the territory of Europe is furrowed. Geography plays an important part in the economic mechanism of modern times. Every one knows the value of the mouth of the Scheldt, that of the Rhine, and that of the Danube. The Rhine is no longer crossed by armies; no more bridges are thrown over the Danube for great battles; steamboats are established on these rivers. All these military rivers have become commercial lines. The contest now is between these rivers and the railways, the latest expression of industrial progress. Who could have told, in 1804, when, in an obscure corner of the country of Wales, a steam-engine was first put in motion over bars of iron to draw a train of cars, that this was the commencement of a revolution destined to change the face of the world! Hundreds of millions have been put, since then, at the service of that marvellous machine, which is still perhaps to the perfected locomotives of the future only as the match-lock muskets were to the fire arms of our day.

But to how many questions do the changes wrought as a result of these admirable machines, give rise! At one point, the value of property is increased ten-fold; at another, reduced perhaps to a tenth: here, new markets, in another place, the loss of all markets. Five hundred thousand travelers circulate where there were scarcely a few thousand, and the bringing together of distant places effects revolutions like those which displacement of territory might produce. Such are the new phases under which political economy must henceforth study the industrial and social movement of which humanity will demand of it an account. It must keep its eyes always fixed upon that great law of the most equitable distribution of the profits of labor; so long as there are thousands of men deprived of the very necessaries of life, in the midst of a society so rich in capital and machines, there will remain something to be done and the task of the economist will not be ended. Civilization is called upon to provide a common protection, as does the sun, for rich and poor, strong and weak, the inhabitants of the city and those of the country. Political economy must indicate to civilization the measures to be taken in order to extend each day the benefit of that protection.

I will cite, in conclusion, a striking example of what remains to be done in that noble career. It is to-day incontestable that public wealth has increased in Europe and principally in France, rapidly and brilliantly. In what proportion to the former fortune of the different countries, no one knows; neither is it known in what proportion the profits are distributed among the different classes of workers. One thing is certain, the population of the great cities, and especially of the manufacturing and commercial cities, have profited much more than that of the rural districts by the general progress in wealth. Our cities are every day embellished with new constructions; the citizens who inhabit them enjoy more of the amenities of life than formerly; the middle class are better lodged, better clothed, better fed. Elderly people who were able to observe the general aspect of city populations a half century ago, are struck by the contrast between their present appearance and that in the past. The suburbs of every great industrial and commercial centre, like Havre, Rouen, Lille, Mulhouse, Saint-Quentin, Lyons and Marseilles, are covered with opulent faubourgs and delightful country-houses. The villages alone remain unchanged, and preserve, from generation to generation, their aspect of poverty and of monotony. One sees in them only dirt and squalor; everywhere are walls in ruins, huts covered with thatch, children badly clothed and worse educated. Now, if we consider that the inhabitants of these dreary lodgings compose two-thirds of the French population and consume scarcely a fourth of the product of our manufactures, we shall recognize that there remains much to be done to ameliorate their condition and to secure markets for our manufactured products. Is it not a subject for reflection, this system of production which obliges us to seek consumers at the ends of the earth, when at our own gates, in the heart of our own country, we have workers who lack for everything! We cannot sell our cloths, and yet more than ten thousand of our fellow-citizens have no under-clothing! We ask for bounties on the export of sugars, and there are old men and children who have never known and perhaps never will know, that article! A hundred acres of land are sold for less in Sologne and in the Landes, than a ditch in Paris to be buried in! These are strange contrasts: political economy is full of them, and yet a new history full of contrasts more strange is beginning for her at the moment when this ends.

APPENDIX.

1. "Bottomry loans," p. 6.—These are loans where money is lent upon the ship's bottom, as it is termed : *i.e.*, the ship is pledged as security and the lender takes the risks of the voyage.

2. "theorikon," p. 12, 14. "theorika," p. 16.—Originally, money given to citizens from the public treasury to pay for seats at the theatre : later, given also for other purposes *Theorika*, the plural, is used both for the moneys paid, and for the theoric fund, from which the distributions were made.

3. "*jeton de présence,*" p. 12.—A counter given to a person present :—also contemptuously used for small coin.

4. "quarry," p. 16, *i.e.*, game, prey, booty : a hunter's term.

5. "*Sectionists,*" p. 16.—*i. e.*, such of the citizens of the sections as could bear arms and attend the meetings of the sections. Paris was at that time divided into 48 sections (electoral divisions), thirty-three of which had declared their votes for insurrection. The commissioners of the sections, ' vested with the full powers of all the sections," had annulled the constituted authorities, (as a majority of the sections could lawfully do), and reorganized the government as seemed to them desirable. Among the new measures adopted, was that in reference to the "forty sous," of which Thiers (Hist. Fr. Rev., Vol. ii.—Shoberl's translation) speaks thus :

"In order to insure the aid of the people and to keep them under arms in these moments of agitation, it was next resolved that forty sous per day should be paid to all the citizens on duty who were in narrow circumstances, and that these forty sous should be taken from the product of the forced loan extorted from the rich. This was a sure way of calling to the aid of the commune and against the bourgeois of the sections, all the working people, who would rather earn forty sous assisting in revolutionary measures, than thirty sous by pursuing their ordinary avocations."

Thomas Carlyle, in his *French Revolution* (Book iv, Chap. 6), says : " Danton, through the organ of Barère and *Sault Public* gets decreed, that there be in Paris by law, two meetings of Section, weekly ; also that the poorer citizen be paid for attending, and have his days wages of forty sous. This is the celebrated ' Law of forty sous,' fiercely stimulant to Sansculottism, to the life circulation of Jacobinism," etc., etc.

" Forty sous *per diem* were promised to the Sans-Culottes as long as they should be under arms." (Hist. of France, by Emile de Bonnechose, p. 537.) " Every indigent person received forty sous *per diem* for assisting at the assembly of his section." (p. 540.)

" Immediately the Commune (*i.e.*, the municipality of Paris) appoints Henriot, a coarse and brutal drunkard, chief of the sections ; it decrees to pay forty sous to every poor citizen who takes up arms ; " etc. (*French Revolutionary Epoch*, by Henri Van Laun, Vol. i, p. 276, Amer. edition.) " The section shall sit twice a week, and in order to insure the attendance of its members, all those present at its sittings shall receive forty sous for their loss of time." (*The same*, p. 284.)

6. " Octroi," pp. 20, 68, etc.—An impost levied by towns upon merchandise brought within their limits. The octroi was paid at the gates of the city or town.

7. " Proletary workmen," p. 56.—These were the lowest class of laborers, except slaves. They were valued by the State principally for their progeny, who were needed for war. Hence their name. Latin, *proletarii*, from *proles*, progeny.

8. " Corvée," pp. 67, 68, 122, etc.—Compulsory labor, either statute or feudal.

9. " frameas," p. 88.—A kind of javelin. (v. Gasc's Fr. Dic.)

10. " Harpagon," p. 111.—The miser in " L' Avare," a comedy by Molière.

11. " Assizes of Jerusalem," p. 131.—The code of feudal law framed for the kingdom of Jerusalem.

12. "sbires," p. 194.—A particular class of archers.

13. "*donzels*," p. 194.—The *donzels* were pages in attendance on the magistrates.—*v. Vocabulario degli Academia della Crusca.* Also, *Alberti, Dic. Ital. Français.*

14. "natives," p. 200.—The French word "*nationaux*" applies as well to those bred in a country as to those born there. The equivalent noun in English would be "nationals."

15. "Universal" suffrage of gold and silver, p. 245.—The Indians who used wampumpeag for money, (v. Prof. Sumner's Hist. of Amer. Currency), do not seem to have had any acquaintance with the precious metals. Travellers tell us of many peoples who do not use gold and silver for money ; among others, the Abysinnians, who use salt for money ; the people of Bornu, a powerful state of Central Africa, who employ cowrie shells for the same purpose ; and many others. In the Society Islands, gold and silver are very rare. Prof. Jevons tells us (*Money*, p. 1,) that when Mlle. Zélie, of the *Théâtre Lyrique* of Paris, sang an air from Norma and a few other songs at a concert in one of these islands, her share of the receipts was 3 pigs, 23 turkeys, 44 chickens, 5,000 cocoa-nuts, besides considerable quantities of bananas, lemons, and oranges. From the same source we learn that Mr. Wallace, a traveller in the Malay Archipelago, says that in some of the islands there was no proper currency, and he could not procure supplies for dinner without a special bargain and much chaffering on each occasion.· He was therefore obliged to keep on hand quite a variety of articles, to multiply the chance that one of them would suit the itinerant merchant.

16. "As a loan," p. 338. The French reads, "*en commandite.*" Companies "*en commandite*" are those where all but the managing partners are only responsible to the amount they have subscribed. In Law's system the owners of public stock were *commanditaires, i.e.,* silent partners with limited liability. The New York law for limited partnerships seems to be the exact equivalent of the French law for *sociétés en commandite.*

17. "*Physiocratie*," p. 356. "A few generous and righteous philosophers struck out the idea that there must be some great natural science, some principles of eternal truth, founded on nature itself, with regard to the social relations of mankind,

the violations of which were the causes of that hideous misery they saw in their native land. The name they gave this science was *Natural Right*, and their object was to discover and lay down an abstract science of the natural rights of men in all their social relations. And this science comprehended their relations towards the government, towards each other, and towards *property*. The term *politique* in French might in a certain way have expressed this science, but that word was so exclusively appropriated to the art of government that they adopted the name of Political Economy for it, and hence were commonly called the ECONOMISTS. One of their number proposed the name of PHYSIOCRATIE. or the government of the nature of things, and hence they were often called PHYSIO-CRATES ; but the word having been appropriated to certain doctrines of the sect, which are now shown to be erroneous, has fallen into disuse, and the term Political Economy, or Economics, has survived."—Macleod, *Econ. Phil.* Vol. i, p. 58.

18. "Encyclopedic Philosophers," p. 362. This term is applied to the various authors of high literary and philosophical attainments, who wrote for the famous *Encyclopédie* published 1751–1772, in 28 vols., edited by D'Alembert and Diderot. These writers were (besides the editors) Rousseau, Grimm, Dumarsais, Voltaire, Baron d'Holbach, and Jaucourt. Nearly all of them entertained ideas more or less revolutionary, and their articles were written with a boldness which brought the *Encyclopédie* under the ban of the government. Its contests with the latter form an interesting episode in the history of the times.—*v*. art. *Encyclopædia*, in *Ency. Brit.*

19. "Father Bridaine," 408. A preacher, b. 1701, d. 1767. Demogeot, in his *Littérature Française* (p. 547) calls Delille "the Bridaine of tragedy."

20. "increase of taxes the cause," etc., 435. We are unable to find this opinion in Ricardo's works. On the contrary, Ricardo says (p. 109, McCulloch's edition) : "Everything which raises the exchangeable value of commodities of any kind, which are in very general demand, tends to discourage both cultivation and production ; but this is an evil inseparable from all taxation, and is not confined to the particular taxes of which we are now speaking."

21. "Amortization," p. 436, *i.e.*, extinction of the public debt, particularly by funding. Dr. Price's theory of amortization, here referred to, was a plan for the extinction of the public debt of Great Britain, by a sinking fund. Blanqui, in his Bibliography, in noticing a work by Dr. Price, entitled, *Political Arithmetic*, says of him : " He was the first to propose a sinking-fund by means of compound interest." The work in which Dr. Price expounds his theory, is entitled : *An Appeal to the Public on the Subject of National Debt*, by Richard Price, D.D., F.R.S. (London, 1774). J. R. McCulloch, in his *Literature of Political Economy*, gives an account of Dr. Price's work.

Inasmuch as the sinking-fund delusion, so far from being dead, is now a part of the Law of the United States (by Sinking-Fund Act of Feb. 25, 1862), it may not be amiss to quote Mr. McCulloch's article. He says :

" This work contains a pretty full development of what its author believed to be the peculiar and distinctive properties of a sinking-fund, and is important from its being the foundation of Mr. Pitt's famous project.

"After the termination of the American war, and the consolidation of his ministry, the devising of means for the reduction of the public debt became an object of Mr. Pitt's special attention. To accomplish this he adopted one of the three projects furnished him by Dr. Price for establishing a sinking-fund.

"This fund was managed by Commissioners appointed for the purpose, and consisted of £1,000,000 a year set apart for that peculiar service, with what were called its accumulations at compound interest. These were formed as follows : at the outset of the scheme, the commissioners would purchase with the million assigned to them (which, be it observed, was wholly derived from taxation) a million's worth of stock, on which they receive a dividend of say four per cent : consequently at the end of the first year they would have their annual million plus the dividend accruing on the stock previously bought by them, or £1,040,000 to lay out in the purchase of fresh stock ; at the end of the second year they would have £1,081,600 ; at the end of the third year £1,124,864, and so on. Now this is what Sir Nathaniel Gould, Dr. Price and Mr. Pitt call paying off the public debt by a sinking-fund increasing at compound interest; but it is obvious that whatever diminution is effected in the amount of the public debt in the way now stated, is brought about by devoting a portion of the *produce of taxation to its extinction.*

" It is true that by applying any given sum to the purchase of stock, and then constantly applying the dividends upon the stock so purchased to the extinction of the debt, its reduction is effected in the same way as if the original sum had really been increasing by an inherent energy of its own, at compound interest; but it is essential to know, that though the results be the same, the means are totally different. The debt is reduced because the taxes required to pay the dividends or interest on the stock purchased by the Sinking Fund Commissioners, instead of being remitted to the contributors, continue to be taken from them, and applied to the purchase of stock. It is the merest delusion to suppose that the debt either has been or ever can be reduced by the agency of any independent fund increasing at compound interest. To make capital increase in this way, it must be employed in some productive industry; and the profits, instead of being consumed as income, must be regularly added to the principal, to form new capital. It is unnecessary to say that no such fund ever existed. Those that have been set on foot in this and other countries have all been supported either by loans or by the produce of taxes, and have never paid off, and never by any possibility could pay off, a single shilling of debt by their own agency.

" In 1792, some further additions were made to Mr. Pitt's sinking-fund; and it was then also enacted, that besides providing for the interest of any loan that might henceforth be contracted, additional taxes should be imposed to form a sinking-fund of one per cent. on the capital stock created by such a loan. As there was considerable excess of revenue, in the period between 1786 and 1793, the debt was reduced by about ten and a-half millions, and this reduction was ascribed to the effect of the sinking-fund increasing at compound interest, though, it is plain, it entirely resulted from the application of surplus revenue to the purchase of stock. Subsequently to the commencement of the revolutionary war, the income of the country uniformly fell greatly short of the expenditure, and the debt rap-idly increased.

"But though there was no *annual million* in the Treasury to transfer to the commissioners, the juggle of the sinking-fund was kept up. Dr. Price had been sanguine, or rather we may say absurd enough to allege that 'any suspension of the sink-ing-fund during war would be the madness of giving it a mor-tal stab *at the very time it was making the quickest progress to-ward the accomplishment of its end.*' (Appeal, etc., p. 17.) And even this was believed! In consequence, the loans for the service of the year were uniformly increased, by the whole amount of the sums placed at the disposal of the Sinking-Fund Commissioners, so that, for every shilling's worth of stock transferred to them by this futile proceeding, an equal or greater amount of new debt had to be contracted, exclusive of the loss incurred on account of management!

"Such was the sinking-fund, the object of laudation of all parties. It was universally considered as the great bulwark of the country, as a means by which 'a vast treasure was to be ac-cumulated out of nothing!' And so lasting and powerful was the infatuation, that after fourteen years' experience of its nullity, when a new financial project was introduced in 1807, it contained a system of checks to prevent the evils likely to re-sult from allowing the sinking-fund to accumulate without any limit, and deluging the country with a flood of wealth, by 'a too prompt discharge of the public debt!'

"The history of the world does not furnish another instance of so extraordinary a delusion. Had the sinking-fund involved any unintelligible dogmas, had it addressed itself to popular feelings or passions, or had the notion of its efficacy originated with the mob, the prevalence of the delusion would have been less unaccountable. But it was from the first a matter of mere calculation; it was projected by some of the best-informed per-sons in the country, who continued for upward of twenty years to believe that they were rapidly diminishing the public debt by the agency of a fund, which was all the while kept on foot by borrowed money! Dr. Hamilton of Aberdeen has the merit of having dissipated the illusion—the greatest, certainly, by which any civilized people was ever blinded and deceived.

He showed that the sinking-fund, instead of reducing the debt, had increased it: and he proved to demonstration that the excess of revenue above expenditure is the only real sinking-fund by which any part of the public debt can be discharged. 'The increase of revenue,' he observes, 'or the diminution of expense, are the only means by which this sinking-fund can be enlarged, and its operation rendered more effectual ; and all schemes for discharging the national debt, by sinking-funds operating at *compound* interest, or in any other manner, unless in so far as they are founded on this principle, are completely illusory.'

" The act of 10 Geo. IV. consecrated this sound principle ; and terminated the Sinking-Fund."

History repeats itself. We copied all the errors of England and profited not at all by her example.

(See Ricardo's essay on the Funding System, found in McCulloch's edition of his works.)

22. "Bank of England," etc., p. 437–8. (1.) "exhausted," etc. (2.) " Notes payable in gold." (3.) " virtual bankruptcy." (4.) " government had the good sense," etc. (5.) " rise of prices."

(1.) From the commencement of the war in 1793, to 1797, the Bank of England had made excessive loans to the Government, and its ability to grant even its usual discounts to customers had become impaired. Early in 1797, England was overtaken by a commercial panic, which was intensified by a reported invasion by the armies of France, and a consequent hoarding of money. On the 26th of February of that year, the Bank's stock of coin was so reduced that it is quite probable that the Bank would have been compelled to suspend cash payments (*i.e.*, payments in coin) if the Government had not intervened. The Government did intervene, and by an Order in Council forbade the Bank to pay out cash (*i.e.*, coin) until the sense of Parliament could be taken.

Parliament confirmed the restriction, and continued it by successive acts until 1821.

(2.) The notes of the Bank were on their face payable on demand in lawful money, which was gold or silver coin, silver being then a legal tender up to £25. (*v.* Lord Liverpool's *Letter to the King, on the Coins of the Realm*, 1805, p. 129.)

(3) This suspension, or restriction, as it was called, was ordered by the government, and was in no proper sense "a virtual bankruptcy." The Bank was entirely solvent, as an examination of its affairs by a Parliamentary Committee then showed, and as subsequent events fully confirmed.

The *assignats* and *mandats* of France, "though secured by national property, fell to the last degree of demonetization," because of the excessive amount of them put into circulation (many having been forged in England and smuggled into the country), while inconvertible notes of the Bank of England depreciated little, because the Bank increased its issues but slightly beyond the amount of coin displaced by its notes.

Confidence that others will willingly receive it, is necessary to give currency to inconvertible paper money ; but, while in general circulation as money, its value, *other things remaining the same*, depends upon the quantity. Tender-laws may aid, but they are not indispensable to give currency to such money.

Bank of England notes were not a legal-tender for debts. The merchants of London, immediately on the restriction being proclaimed, met and unanimously agreed to take Bank of England notes in all their transactions. Public opinion—not statute law—continued Bank notes, without any payment by the Bank, as the money of the country for twenty-four years, or during the whole period of the restriction.

(Consult McCulloch's *Dictionary of Commerce*, art. *Bank of England ; History of British Commerce*, by Leone Levi, p. 132 ; Macleod's *Dictionary of Political Economy*, under *Banking in England*, Vol. I, p. 94 ; *History of the Currency*, by James MacLaren, (1st edition,) p. 77 ; *A System of Political Economy*, by John L. Shadwell, p. 347 ; Doubleday's *Financial History of England*, p. 187 ; the opinions of all the judges of the Court of Common Pleas, in the case of Grigby *vs.* Oakes & Co., given *in extenso* on pp. 291–7 of Cobbett's *History and Mystery of the Bank of England ;* and Prof. Sunner's *History of the American Currency*, p. 235, in the chapt , on the bank restriction in England.)

It is true that Parliament passed two acts to add to the currency of Bank notes, viz.: (1) That any one tendering Bank

of England notes should not thereafter be subject to arrest for
that debt, and (2) the property of a tenant making such
tender, could not be distrained for rent; but all other remedies,
notwithstanding such tender, were open to creditors then as
now.

It is doubtless true that for the Bank of England notes to
have been discredited would have been a "most fearful catastrophe." No such catastrophe occurred, because the people
had full faith in the solvency of the Bank, and their faith was
well-founded.

(4) The government did *not* intervene, in the matter of issuing bank-notes, as Blanqui both here and elsewhere implies.
The Bank was subject to no restriction as to the amount of its
issues at any time during the suspension of its cash payments.
On the contrary, it was in this matter governed only by its own
discretion. By what rule the Bank ought to govern itself in the
issue of its notes, was a most fruitful source of discussion during the whole period of the Bank's restriction, 1797 to 1821.

(5) The issues of the Bank of England continued to increase steadily, though irregularly, from 1797 to 1817. That there
was no material depreciation of Bank notes compared with coin
from 1797 to 1808, is sometimes thought paradoxical. There
was, however, nothing mysterious about it. No material depreciation of Bank notes could take place until *after* the increase
had displaced all the coin; at least, all the coin of full weight
and full tender. In the case of England, the coin was *very
slowly* displaced, on account of the law against its exportation,
and because of its worn and degraded state.

It is true that the continually increasing issues of paper money
"seemed to make monetary wealth more productive;" but it
was in fact rising prices due to the over-issue of inconvertible
paper money which stimulated the production of commodities
of all kinds and the accumulation of wealth. It is not unlikely
that had it not been for the rising prices due to such issues, it
would have been impossible for England to carry on that great
war and bring it to a successful conclusion.

(For full elucidation of the principles involved in the phenomena here noted, see Francis A. Walker's late work, (1879),
Money in its Relations to Trade and Industry; also R. H.

Patterson's work on *Economy of Capital*, Edinburgh and London, 1865.)

(The dates and limitations of the thirteen successive acts of Parliament, proclaiming and continuing the Bank restriction, may be found in *Lawson's History of Banking*, as also a copy of the original order suspending or restricting cash payments.)

23. "return to specie payments." p. 439. Several years elapsed after the close of the war, before resumption of specie payments was finally effected. The act under the operation of which they took place (according to general opinion) is known as Peel's Act of 1819. This act did not compel payments in coin until May 1, 1823. Until that time and dating from February 1, 1820, the Bank was directed to pay its notes in ingots of gold bullion, if they were presented for sums of not less than 60 oz. at a time. "The accumulation of treasure in in the Bank became so rapid in 1820, that early in 1821, the Directors felt themselves in a position to resume payments in coin: and they obtained an Act, permitting them to do so on May 1, 1821, instead of 1823, as limited by Peel's Act." H. D. Macleod, Econ. Phil. vol. ii, chap. xviii, § 14. Macleod's account of the Bank will be read with interest. He, however, denies all efficiency to Peel's Act, (p. 460, Econ. Phil. vol., ii), and quotes one of the Bank Directors in support of his opinion. He says the Act enacting that the Bank might resume payments in gold coin May 1, 1821, was the real Act under which cash payments were resumed.

24. "Posterity," p. 456, 12th line. Posterity does not seem to have confirmed the judgment of Blanqui in regard to Cobbett.

Cobbett's strength lay in his use of language. He was direct, terse and forcible, and was a master of sarcasm and invective. It has been said that the popularity of his pamphlet, "Paper against Gold, etc.," was due "more to manner than to matter; that, with more of fancy than of fact, he was pungent, not personal; caustic, not critical; with more philippics than philosophy, more rhetoric than reason, more sarcasm than sense." We cannot, however, wholly agree with this judgment. The information he gave the people in regard to the origin and history of their funded debt and the Bank of England, as well as in regard to the Sinking-Fund, (anticipating on this latter subject, though crudely, the work of Dr. Hamilton in 1813), seems to us, when taken in connection with his vigorous manner of presenting subjects, to sufficiently account for the popularity of his writings. Cobbett opposed every species of paper money.

25. "pay the public debt," etc., p. 460. Ricardo's plan may be found on p. 149 of McCulloch's edition of his works. Ricardo himself says of it : " This scheme has been often recommended, but we have, I fear, neither wisdom enough, nor virtue enough to adopt it."

E. J. L.

INDEX.

Carthage. Its marine, 49. Contests with Rome, 50. Its superior civilization and economic effects of its fall, 51.

Cattle and farming implements protected by Sully, 267. Cattle as money, 250.

Cayenne, colonized, 297.

Celibacy, at Rome, 56. Required of clerks in Hanse trading-houses, 152. Among workmen in trade corporations, 187, 188. Its economic value, 188. Discouraged by Colbert, 289. Ideas of Malthus on c., 396–7. Of Ortès, 524.

Cellini (Benvenuto), a goldsmith, 250.

Cemeteries, restored to Jews, 137.

Charlemagne. His economy, 6, 110, 107–116. His capitularies, 109 et seq. Power of Church under C., 117. Solicitude for slaves, 115. Attempts at a *maximum*, 114. Provision for commerce, 114. His revenues, 113, 114. Hereditary transmission of benefices, 116.

Charles V., Economic results of his reign, 209–218, monopolies, 210–211, restrictions and prohibitions, debased coin, slave trade, convents, inquisition, etc., 212, et seq. 526–7.

Child (Sir Joshua), ideas on commerce, 300.

Children at Athens, 12, 15. C. of soldiers at Athens, 15. C. in Sparta, 26, 27. At Rome, 63. Acquire legal right to their own lives, 104–5. Abandonment of, punished, 104. Division of property among, 89. Right of inheritance, 104, 501, 503. Schools for c., 192. Considered a possession, 32, 300. C. of Spanish colonists in America, 215. In manufactories, 466, 475, foot-note. Their education, 423, 519–20. Malthus on c., 396–7, 401. Foundlings, 294, 397, 545. Views of some St. Simonians, 502. Fourier on, 509, 515. Owen on, 519. Hours of labor for, 544.

Christianity, First appearance, 72. Became State religion, 73. Its services to Polit. Econ., 77–86. Decline of, 84. Present standard bearers inadequate to their task, 85, 478, and foot-note. See *Priests*,

Convents, Church, Religion, Reformation.

Christian Polit. Econ., by Villeneuve-Bargemont, 407.

Church. Its services to Polit. Econ., 78–83, 215. Its relation to politics, 78. To slavery, 250. Its property in time of Charlemagne, 114, 115. Its power under C., 117. Opposed by barons, 130. By bourgeois, 158. Unites with sovereigns and lords against bourgeois, 158. Sale of ch. property, and economic results, 221, et seq. Property seized by Henry VIII, 265. Natural protector of ecclesiastical demands, 157. Struggles to maintain its privileges, 212. Reform of, demanded by Owen, 517. v. *Priests*.

Cicero. Interest of money in his time, 50. Exactions of proconsuls, 66.

Circulation of money. At Rome, 62. Jews make first attempts at, 145. Its simplest laws not understood, 174. Amount of, difficult to estimate, 246. Writings on, 352. C. of U. S., 348. C. at Bruges, 154. A. Smith's analysis of, confirmed by experience, 455. Advantages of monetary circulation, 455. A universal medium of c. proposed by Scaruffi, 522. v. *Money*.

Citizenship, jealously guarded by the Athenians, 10.

Claudian Law (ordered gratuitous distribution of grain), 63.

Clearing House (London). An economy in use of money, 249, foot-note. A universal C. H. anticipated, 259.

Clergy, power of, 78–82. Power given them by Ripuary Law, 96. Influence over lords, 96. To-day unequal to their task, 84, 478. Reminded of their duty, 85. Censured by Charlemagne for vices, 112, 113. Administer justice, protect widows, orphans, etc., 130. League against, by barons, 130. Their real-estate in time of Henry VIII, 221. Seized, 265. Condemn loans at interest, 105. Forbidden to take usury, 113.

Cleruchiæ (v. Kleruchiæ).

Clothing. Of Romans, 5, 56. In Ger-

nity, 163. Its importance in Italian republics, 190–208. Tax on personal p., 421. Division of landed p., 349, 351, 420. Rights of p., 427. P. in inventions secured by patents, 420, 421. French democracy unjust to landed p., 435. Immaterial p., 447. P. under Fourier's system, 512. Abolition of, advocated by Owen, *516. Effect of French Revolution on landed property, 535. Personal p., 545. Increased value of landed property, 546.

Prostitutes, 393.

Protection, Colbert aimed to make customs a means of, 283–4.

Publicity of accounts. At Athens, 12. Of mortgages, 373.

Public works. Of Athens, 11, 18, foot-note. Roman Roads, 58–62 et seq., and aqueducts, 58. Roads of France, 296, 369. J. B. Say's opinion about government intervention in industrial enterprises, 448, 449, 452. Changed views, 532, 539, 541.

Public debt, 342. Of Eng., 436 and foot-note, 437, 440. Debt of France in time of Sully, 266–7, 277. Of France, funded, 423.

Quebec—colonized, 297.

Quesnay. Chief of the Economist school, 352. Analyzed agriculture, 353. Doctrines of, foot-note 356–360, 357–360. Tableau Economique, 356–7. Other works, 357. Marmontel on Q., 362–3. Character and style of, 363. Disciples, 364.

Rate of interest. v. Interest.

Rationarium Imperii, 68.

Rau (Prof.), 531.

Raynal, 408. Precursor of the grand masters, 409. Denounced trade in blacks, 411, 418. Worked for the political revolution, 417. His Histoire Philosophique, 418. Characteristics of, 417–18. Speaks of Polit. Econ., 378. Prophecies of, fulfilled, 432.

Recoinage, 119, note ; 174, 250, 341.

Reform. Edicts of Charlemagne, 109. R. in church property, 221 et seq., 265. Of Protestantism. 296–298. In taxation, 421. Reforms of 1789, 420 et seq. Of criminals, 545.

Reformation (Prot.), 9, 219–228, 296 et seq.

Religion. Its power and economic effects, 79–86. A universal religion anticipated, 534. Owen's manifesto against religions, 517. v. Clergy, Priests, Convents, Church, Christianity, Reformation.

Republic. Plato's work on an ideal Republic, 29–34.

Republics (Italian). Their marvelous growth, and commercial, industrial and economic importance, 190–208.

Restriction (or suspension) of Bank of Eng., 330, 331, 437–439.

Restrictive system. 114, 134, 166, 174, 176, 200, 202, 213–14, 300, 305–15, 319, 373, 390, 415, 423, 425, 426. v. Protection, Prohibition, Exclusive System. Also Free Trade.

Resumption of specie payments (by Bk. of Eng.), 331, 438–9, n. 23, Appendix.

Revenue. Of Athens, 19. Of Rome, 246. Of Attika, (Treatise by Aristotle), quoted, 10. Of Florence, 192–3. Of Venice, 204–5. Of France under Charlemagne, 113, 114. Under Sully, 267. Under Colbert, 283–4, 286–9, 293, 302–3. Bank of Law collected revenues of the State, 338–9. Under Turgot, 373, 374. Indirect taxes the principal source of, in Eng. and U. S., 545.

Revocation. v. Edict of Nantes.

Revolution. v. French Rev.

Ricardo, 456–460. Economic value of his contributions to finance, especially of his work, " The high price of bullion a proof of the depreciation of bank-notes," 456–7. His " Proposals for an economical and secure currency," 457–8. His opinion of the perfect condition of money, 259, 332. On the effect of taxes on industries, 435, and n. 20, Appendix. His doctrine of agricultural rents, 458–9. On method of pay-

DISCARD

COLLEGE
LIBRARY